The Soviet Defence Enigma

sipri

Stockholm International Peace Research Institute

SIPRI is an independent institute for research into problems of peace and conflict, especially those of arms control and disarmament. It was established in 1966 to commemorate Sweden's 150 years of unbroken peace.

The Institute is financed mainly by the Swedish Parliament. The staff, the Governing Board and the Scientific Council are international.

The Governing Board and Scientific Council are not responsible for the views expressed in the publications of the Institute.

Governing Board

Ambassador Ernst Michanek, Chairperson (Sweden)
Egon Bahr (Federal Republic of Germany)
Professor Francesco Calogero (Italy)
Dr Max Jakobson (Finland)
Professor Dr Karlheinz Lohs (German Democratic Republic)
Professor Emma Rothschild (United Kingdom)
Sir Brian Urquhart (United Kingdom)
The Director

Director

Dr Walther Stützle (Federal Republic of Germany)

sipri

Stockholm International Peace Research Institute
Pipers Väg 28, S-171 73 Solna, Sweden
Cable: PEACERESEARCH STOCKHOLM
Telephone: 46 8/55 97 00

The Soviet Defence Enigma

Estimating Costs and Burden

Edited by
Carl G. Jacobsen

sipri

Stockholm International Peace Research Institute

OXFORD UNIVERSITY PRESS
1987

Oxford University Press, Walton Street, Oxford OX2 6DP

Oxford New York Toronto
Delhi Bombay Calcutta Madras Karachi
Petaling Jaya Singapore Hong Kong Tokyo
Nairobi Dar es Salaam Cape Town
Melbourne Auckland

and associated companies in
Beirut Berlin Ibadan Nicosia

Oxford is a trade mark of Oxford University Press

Published in the United States
by Oxford University Press, New York

British Library Cataloguing in Publication Data
The Soviet defence enigma: estimating costs and
  burden.
  1. Soviet Union—Military policy
  I. Jacobsen, Carl G. II. Stockholm International
  Peace Research
  355'.0332'47 UA770
  ISBN 0–19–829118–3

Library of Congress Cataloging in Publication Data
The Soviet defence enigma.
Papers presented at meetings held in Gleneagles,
Scotland, 1985, and in Stockholm, Sept. 1986.
  Bibliography: p.
  Includes index
  1. Soviet Union—Armed Forces—Appropriations and
expenditures—Congresses, 2. Budget—Soviet Union—
Congresses. I. Jacobsen, C. G. (Carl G.) II. Stockholm
International Peace Research Institute. III. Title:
Soviet defense enigma.
UA770.S659 1987 355.6'22'0947 87–15385
ISBN 0–19–829118–3

Set by Wyvern Typesetting, Bristol
Printed and bound in
Great Britain by Biddles Ltd.,
Guildford and King's Lynn

Contents

Part 2.   New approaches

Part 3. Historical context—future prospects

Preface

Realistic appraisals of the level and sustainability of Soviet defence efforts and burden are crucial to Western (and indeed Soviet) security debates, and defence and foreign policy considerations. Yet official figures are notoriously inadequate. SIPRI has long been acutely conscious of this and concerned about the methodological uncertainties that bedevil attempts to arrive at independent estimates. In 1985 Alec Nove brought together academic specialists whose recent original work in the field sought to address some of the problems at hand, for discussion and debate in Gleneagles, Scotland. SIPRI then decided to hold a follow-up workshop in Stockholm, in September 1986, for the Gleneagles discussants and a select group of Western academic and government specialists with the experience and background necessary for substantive comment, critique and elaboration. This book is the result. Only primary workshop papers are included. But the input of all participants (including those few invitees who could not be present) is reflected in the papers presented here.

The book leaves many questions unanswered. It presents the state of current knowledge and the gaps in knowledge that still persist. It explains the sometimes debatable premises and methodological uncertainties and approaches that lead different analysts to different conclusions. By rescuing the debate from the domain of little-known specialist journals it hopes to engage the attention and energies of a wider audience with other but complementary skills and knowledge. By providing a comprehensive review of the specialist debate, written so as to be accessible to those of more general expertise, it seeks to clarify outstanding issues and thus help chart the course of future research. Rather than provide answers that cannot yet be definitively provided, it seeks to isolate the questions that need to be asked.

Our appreciation goes to Connie Wall and Jetta Gilligan Borg for editorial assistance, to Anna Helleday and Åsa Pihlstrand, for organizing and administering the workshop, and, again, to Åsa Pihlstrand for typing assistance. Thank you also to Rita Tullberg, whose constructive comments on many of the papers were highly appreciated.

SIPRI, May 1987   CARL G. JACOBSEN

List of workshop participants and contributors* to this book

Ms Mary Acland-Hood*
Senior Research Officer
The Uranium Institute
Twelfth floor, Bowater House
68 Knightsbridge
London SW1X 7LT
UK

Professor Gérard Duchêne*
8, rue Georges Braque
75014 Paris
France

Professor Murray Feshbach
Office of the Secretary General
NATO
1110 Brussels
Belgium

Mr Brian A. Field
Assistant Director of the Economic
   Directorate
NATO
1110 Brussels
Belgium

Professor Carl G. Jacobsen*
Stockholm International Peace
   Research Institute
Pipers väg 28
S-171 73 Solna
Sweden

Professor Carl G. Jacobsen (cont'd.)
After 1 September 1987:
Canadian Institute for
   International Peace and Security
P.O. Box 3425, Station D
Ottawa, Ont.
Canada

Dr David R. Jones*
Russian Micro-project
Killam Library
Dalhousie University
Halifax, N.S.
Canada

Professor Kiichi Mochizuki*
Hokkaido University
Slavic Research Center
Kita-9, Nishi-7, Kita-ku
Sapporo 060
Japan

Professor Alec Nove*
University of Glasgow
Center for Development Studies
Adam Smith Building
Glasgow G12 8RT
Scotland

Dr Georges Sokoloff
Centre d'Etudes Prospectives et
   d'Information Internationales
75015 Paris
France

Professor Dmitri Steinberg*
1449 Cedar Street
Berkeley, CA 94702
USA

Professor Peter Wiles*
Department of Economics
London School of Economics and
    Political Science
University of London
Houghton Street
London WC2A 2AE
UK

Representatives of:
Swedish National Defence Research
    Institute (FOA)
Box 27322
S-102 54 Stockholm
Sweden

List of abbreviations, acronyms and definitions

Amortization	sums paid by *khozraschetni* enterprises to the central payments authorities (not the treasury), nominally in respect of the *iznos* of their own basic funds, q.v.; they may be reallocated by their own ministry, and even between ministries; product prices include allowances to cover these payments
Basic funds	fixed capital
BDA	budgetary defence allocation (the 'true' one)
Budgetary statistics	publication of budgetary statistics by USSR Ministry of Finance
$\triangle R$	the movement in OE as a whole
$\triangle R_w$	the movement in weapon stocks and the stocks related to military MOI, q.v.
CIA	US Central Intelligence Agency
CMEA	Council for Mutual Economic Assistance
CSA	Central Statistical Administration
Demographic statistics	Soviet census and other demographic data published in official handbooks
DIA	US Defense Intelligence Agency
Final product	the gross material product in the 'uses' wing of an I/O table. Consists of the 'NMP used' plus (exports minus imports) plus (amortization payments plus budgetary *iznos*) or rather plus (replacement and repair)
FNE	financing of the national economy: the first (and most mysteriously capacious) great division of budgetary expenditures
FYP	five-year plan
GDP	gross domestic product
GMP	gross material product
GNP	gross national product
Gosplan	Soviet State Planning Commission (Committee), attached to government
GSP	gross social product
GVO	global (*valovoi*) value of output
I/O	input/output
Iznos	the depreciation of any basic funds, but especially of those of budgetary enterprises; the corresponding replacement and repair is normally borne by the treasury, since the product is not priced and so cannot cover any cost at all

KGB	USSR Committee for State Security
Khozraschyot	economic or commercial accounting
Kolkhoz	collective farm (*kollektivnoe khozyaistvo*)
KV	*kapital'noye vlozheniye* or capital investment, the creation of 'basic funds' (minus certain items); equals net investment plus replacement but not repair
MBMW	machine-building and metal-working
M&E	machines and equipment
M&E commissions	M&E purchased by functioning budgetary organizations
MoD	Ministry of Defence
MOI	the current material operating inputs of any economic activity (e.g. fuel in the case of the MoD)
MPA	material product accountancy
MVD	Ministry of Internal Affairs (deals with normal police, civil registration, etc.)
Narkhoz	*Narodnoye Khozyaistvo*, here used as title of annual statistical yearbook (literally 'People's (or national) economy')
NATO	North Atlantic Treaty Organization
NEB	national economic balance (planner's system of Soviet national accounts)
NEC	not elsewhere classified
NFI	net fixed investment
NMP	net material product
NNP	net national product (or value added of a branch of the economy)
OBDA	overt BDA, q.v.
OE	other expenditures: the official name of the mainly military column in final product, q.v.
PIEBO	procurement of inventory and equipment by budgetary organizations (not KV but does go into basic funds)
Planners	Officials working in Soviet central planning agencies who are responsible for compiling Soviet national accounts
PMC	personal material consumption, e.g. of food
PuC	public consumption: the services rendered to the population by the government, whether freely (education, medicine, administration, etc.) or for money (passenger transport, theatres, etc.); only the MOI and *iznos* (q.v.) of such activities is counted into NMP
R&D	research and development
RDT&E	research, development, testing and evaluation
R&R	replacement and repair
SCF	social consumption funds
SCM	social and cultural measures: the budgetary expenditure division between FNE and defence

SNA	system of (UN) national accounts
SPM	servicemen's pay and maintenance
T&C	transportation and communication
T&D	trade and distribution
TSU	Soviet agency responsible for compiling the official statistics (*Tsentral'noe Statisticheskoe Upravlenie*)
UNI	usable national income
Vneshtorg	Soviet foreign trade handbook (*Vneshnyaya Torgovlya SSSR*)
W_w	the weapons write-off, whether the loss of value (by depreciation and retirement) or the activities making it good (replacement and repair)

Part 1. Introduction

Paper 1.1. Soviet defence costs—the unquantifiable burden?

CARL G. JACOBSEN

I. Introduction

Soviet defence expenditures, and the burden that these impose on the economy, defy easy calculation. The Soviet leadership acknowledges that the burden is substantive and that it can force painful economic choice.[1] But their official data is blatantly exclusive. And official and unofficial Western calculations rest on so many methodological uncertainties, assumptions and dubious extrapolations that their proffered numbers must also be treated with extreme caution. Yet some appreciation of the economic parameters that guide Soviet military planning is crucial to Western (as well as Soviet) security debates, and to decision making in both defence and foreign policy arenas. The discussion below presents a critical review of official data and discusses alternative sources of evidence and other methodological approaches, the strategic and socio-political context, and finally the political-military cultural prism that ultimately defines the burden and its sustainability.

II. Official figures

The Soviet defence budget is said to cover 'the cost of weapons, ammunition, technical equipment, fuel, food and other equipment supplied to the armed forces', military schools, hospitals, sanatoria, sports, pay of those employed, and 'the financing of capital construction',[2] but the descriptions are vague, and the official Ministry of Defence estimate (or *smeta*) is clearly not sufficient.

Most Western specialists assume that the official figure covers operational expenses such as pay, subsistence, administration and material utilization (fuel, heating, the use of practice ammunition, and so on), but that weapon production and stocks are separately financed, as is investment and research and development. Alternatively, the figure may cover the 'personal material' (i.e., non-service) consumption of troops plus net accumulation of weaponry[3] (see below).

The exact definition of what the Soviet figure contains remains elusive. There is also some controversy as to whether it even accounts for items within its domain. Some observers believe that the pace of Soviet military buildup and modernization programmes of the 1970s belie the actual slight decline of the official budget during these years. On the other hand, Soviet programmes then were not demonstrably more precipitate than those of the 1960s; operational expenses (and even net weapon accumulation) may have been containable within established parameters. Alternatively the gap between a lower budget and likely higher cost may have reflected increased military revenue from civilian efforts, personnel service, and operating, maintenance and construction activities financed from civilian accounts—self-generated revenues, rather than hidden subsidies.

With regard to the larger non-official budget, however, it is the latter that constitutes the main problem. The practice of assigning military expenditures to civilian accounts is of course not unknown elsewhere. The 1987 US Department of Energy budget request allocates about two-thirds of its funding to military programmes.[4] The pervasiveness of Soviet secrecy, however, means that the problem here is of quite a different order of magnitude.

The US Central Intelligence Agency (CIA) rouble figure for Soviet defence spending is inclusive, but it is also open to question. Their main approach proceeds from a calculation of the total physical product of Soviet military procurement which is generally regarded as reliable. The costing of this physical product, or output, is more uncertain. The other approach rests on a reconstructed GNP in which the residual between public sector income and outlays is presumed to constitute defence not elsewhere identified. But the reconstructed GNP accounts contain gaps in both incomes and outlays that make it difficult to establish Soviet weapon production with any certainty. The budget data is crude, including 'miscellaneous' charges that in 1970 amounted to 24.386 billion roubles. Consideration of bank loan income derived from population savings alone would reduce 'unidentified outlays' by 50 per cent.[5]

The CIA's rouble costing and defence burden calculations have undergone some marked shifts. In 1976 the CIA adopted the conclusion of a politically appointed 'B-team' which doubled the rouble cost and hence also the burden assumption. The revision suggested a far grander Soviet military effort and, ultimately, eased passage of the Reagan Administration's unprecedented defence buildup. The underlying message, that Soviet defence industry efficiency was only half of what had been assumed, and in fact not superior to civilian standards, also encouraged those who believed that stepped-up competition would exhaust Soviet resources and compel concessions. Assumed high rates of Soviet defence cost growth during subsequent years brought apparent Soviet defence spending well past US rates, and a defence burden estimate of 12 to 14 per cent. CIA re-evaluation of physical data, in 1983, led to the discordant conclusion that Soviet military procurement rates had remained constant since 1976 (the no-growth pattern has since been traced back further, to 1970), that the percentage allotment to strategic nuclear weapon systems had shrunk (this accords with Soviet doctrine's increased, contrary stress on non-nuclear alternative conventional and exotic options), that over-all defence costs had increased by only just over 2 per cent per year, and that even this might be an exaggeration, since it rested on a research and development growth postulate that the Agency described as 'the least reliable' of its findings.

Finally, in 1986, after pressure to arrive at a consensus estimate with the more alarmist US Defense Intelligence Agency (DIA), the CIA agreed to a 15–17 per cent defence burden figure. It did not agree to an upward revision of the procurement rate. Instead, it justified its new burden figure as a consequence of asserted high 'hidden inflation' in defence industries, with a rate twice that calculated by Soviet and Western economists, and in stark contrast to the DIA's insistence that no inflation had occurred.[6]

In late 1986 a report from the North Atlantic Treaty Organization (NATO) Economic Committee (to which the CIA contributed) stated that Soviet military expenditures rose by 50 per cent between 1970 and 1985, or 2.7 per cent a year. Actual spending was 'six to seven times' the Soviet figure (which 'just barely exceeded . . . 2% of GDP'). It was thus pegged at 12–14 per cent of GDP, a figure consonant with older CIA estimates, though when the report itself specifies a percentage range, it is 13–16 per cent—somewhat contrary to its analysis, but closer to the CIA–DIA 'consensus' of 1986.[7]

Rouble price and burden definitions are the most vexatious. Rouble pricing theoretically avoids the ludicrous exaggerations of dollar costing, that is, calculating what the equivalent cost would be to the systemically different US economy. The latter costs a Soviet conscript as receiving less than $100 a year at the US rate of $20 000 a year. The same procedure applied to China concludes that its military forces cost as much as those of the United States. Sturdy but simple weaponry, spawned by doctrinal bias and technological inadequacy, are costed as if produced by industry geared to far dearer, more exclusive standards (not to mention the all-too-prevalent phenomenon of 'gold plating'). But CIA rouble costing incorporates much of this upward bias. The CIA admits to having few precise rouble prices, even fewer up-to-date ones. Most of its rouble prices are therefore dollar cost exercises translated back into roubles.

Physical counts can also be subject to dispute. The DIA, which surveys year-to-year changes in about 350 Soviet weapon programmes (whereas the CIA covers total procurement), identifies significant hidden missile reserves. Their figures appear to take inadequate account of the Soviet Union's high rate of military tests and satellite launches, which may eat up the excess. Nevertheless, hidden military reserves conform to Russian tradition. And Soviet flaunting of 'pop up' techniques and 'hard pad' launch systems that require minimum preparation appear confirmatory. On the other hand, US investigation of Egyptian SAM sites, after that country switched allegiance, showed that 50 per cent of the missiles previously identified by surveillance and intelligence were in fact dummies.[8] The same may apply to other systems, within the Soviet Union. The Russian traditions of secrecy and deception (*maskirovka*) have always masked both strength and weakness. The Soviet–US agreement at Reykjavik in 1986 to aim for a 50 per cent reduction in strategic arsenals may indeed have different implications for the USSR than for the USA. Still, in-built redundancies are such that it scarcely matters; a 50 per cent reduction would not, in and of itself, affect either the risk or the horror of war.

III.   Other calculations

Two alternative high estimates of the Soviet defence effort received much attention during the late 1970s and early 1980s. One, prepared by Bill Lee, assumed that all unspecified or unaccounted-for production of the machine-building industries went to the military. This appears to have been wrong. Using the same data, but with updated input-output tables, the CIA arrived at a residual figure that was only half that claimed by Lee.[9] The residual also presumably covers space hardware, arms exports and other categories also absent from US definitions of military spending. The main problem, however, is that there is no real evidence concerning the machine-building industries' own use of machine-building output. This renders calculation by residual subject to serious error. The other estimate, by Steven Rosefielde, assumes very rapid Soviet introduction of disproportionately expensive sophisticated technologies in the military sphere, and no inflation. But the first assumption is contradicted by the CIA, by the testimony of the US Undersecretary of Defense for Research and Engineering, and by the historical Soviet pattern of sometimes rapid introduction of evolutionary and derivative technologies, but cautious and only gradual adoption of more novel concepts; and the no-inflation postulate that underpins his calculation is clearly wrong.[10]

Other approaches have recently attracted interest. They also look for residuals, items whose end-use is military, but which do not appear as such. One tries to identify military components in the input-output tables published for the years 1967 and 1972. Another tries to analyse all Soviet national income accounts—and other tabulations.

Peter Wiles defines the defence allocation as that which is legitimate to enter into national accounts; that is, current consumption plus net addition to weapons (net of retirements, amortization). He tries to combine this interpretation of the budget vote with defence elements hidden in and deduced from the input-output tables. The main problem with the analysis, at this stage, is that civilian amortization tables are fully accounted for, and there is no other account that might naturally harbour military write-off funds. Wiles also assumes that military costs are calculated in constant, perhaps 1965 prices, yet this appears inconsistent with Soviet practice. (See the following chapters for an in-depth discussion.)

Another high and intellectually challenging estimate is provided by Dmitri Steinberg. He acknowledges that his figures, like Rosefielde's and the CIA–DIA data, cannot be accommodated within published Soviet totals (in earlier years the CIA took care to emphasize that their numbers could be accommodated). Steinberg in fact stresses this point. He believes defence production and other defence sectors are in part funded from outside national accounts, in the form of grants that are never repaid (and which therefore are peculiarly inflationary). He tries to demonstrate that the value-added of defence production is excluded from national income accounts, but that it can be traced through gaps in other statistical tables, including financial, capital and labour statistics. His figures appear more precise than those of the CIA, which contain a 10–15 per cent margin of error. Steinberg's work is exceptionally thorough. Yet his precision also rests on inferences that in some cases can and should be challenged.[11]

Steinberg's methodological challenge compels attention, though, clearly, work remains to be done. His postulate of extra-budgetary credits (for which there is no precedent in Soviet accounting) also posits another difficulty: total GDP is understated. This in turn deflates the burden implications of any calculated defence expenditure level. This Steinberg postulate is uncompromisingly deviant from the assumptions of nearly all the leading academics in the field, and it is vigorously challenged; yet his detractors concede that there are areas where his postulate appears to be supported by hard evidence.[12]

A more traditional approach was encapsulated by Alec Nove in 1959:[13] material consumption of the Defence Ministry is seen as part of 'material consumption in institutions and enterprises in the non-productive sphere'; consumption by military personnel is personal consumption; accumulation (weapon increase) is 'investment in state reserves'; some military construction (such as new barracks) is considered 'investment in the national economy'; while other military hardware can be found in 'allocations to the national economy' (under heavy industries, and 'state reserves'). Research and development is taken from Science, that is, social-cultural expenditures, while paramilitary police comes under the Ministry of the Interior. One must caution that national income accounts and budgetary expenditures are quite different. Accumulation is a net figure, net of depreciation and reserves, and therefore smaller than gross expenditures on capital investments, or weapon acquisition. Soviet national income tables distinguish between 'consumption' and 'accumulation *and other expenditures*'—hence attempts to compute the accumulation residual, a likely locale for non-consumption military expenditures.

Gérard Duchêne and others have pursued this approach.[14] Their lower defence burden figures are particularly interesting in that they do fit into national income residuals, and thus dispense with the need to assume that Soviet official statistics understate national income (net material product), industrial production and budgetary expenditures.

Duchêne's computations place the defence burden at about 9.5 per cent of GNP (reconstituted, to conform with CIA practice), some 5 points below Steinberg's calculation and the CIA estimate. The contrast with the former represents a sharp methodological divide. The contrast with the latter, however, is less absolute. Duchêne's and other, similar, more traditional academic computations are, in fact, fully compatible with CIA findings when acknowledged inflators are discounted.

Three primary inflators affect CIA findings. One concerns the CIA's suggestion that military R&D constitutes 95 per cent of the Science budget; the suggestion is untenable. The second is the dollar-costing component that distorts rouble-costing. And, finally, there is the legacy of 1976, when presumed Soviet military industrial productivity was halved. This change in parameters now appears to have been too drastic. The military economy is not as distinct, privileged and efficient as once thought. But defence industries still 'recruit a high proportion of the best scientists, technologists, engineers and skilled technicians' and 'enjoy priority access to many material inputs'.[15] The implications of Secretary General Brezhnev's 1971 statement that '42 per cent of its [the defence industry's] output is used for civilian purposes' still hold true; the many transfers of military industry managers to civilian industrial positions during the early years of General Secretary Gorbachev's tenure presumably reflect achievement and efficiency records.[16]

IV.   The burden

The assigning of a higher relative efficiency rating to Soviet defence industries and discounting for other CIA inflators may argue for a 'real' burden estimate in the neighbourhood of 10 per cent. But this, of course, refers only to Soviet analogues to items incorporated in NATO definitions of defence. These are not inclusive; the USA, for example, includes narrowly defined military aid, but excludes the larger category of security assistance. A broader definition would include the cost of preserving excess war production facilities, protecting civilian infrastructure against wartime contingencies, space activities, foreign military aid (perhaps offset by arms sales) and other defence-related activities.[17]

The burden is clearly consequential. In the Soviet Union, quantity and, where relevant, technical quality have been bought at the expense of personnel quality and instant response efficiency; all Soviet forces suffer lower readiness standards than their US counterparts. Non-military priorities compel some military sacrifice.[18]

The transfer of military industrial resources to the civilian economy may be seen to serve the long-term interests of the military. Writing in support of civilian economic reform priorities, Major General Vasykov declared: 'fundamentally new instruments, computer-controlled machine tools, robot equipment, and the latest generation computers' are 'the leading indicators of scientific-technical progress and *simultaneously the best catalyst of military-technical progress*'.[19] Nevertheless, the recognition of the military's own need for a more dynamic civilian counterpart undermines the military's role as supplier of civilian high technology and consumer appliances, threatens military revenue expectations, and increases the cost of maintaining wartime production facilities in peacetime.

The transfer of military-industrial production managers and administrators to force through, implement and oversee civilian economic priorities may also be viewed as a drain on military resources. Yet, at the same time, this phenomenon (and the concomitant transfer also of military industrial quality-control procedures) effectively extends military influence on the civilian economy; whether by coincidence or by design, and whether ultimately ephemeral or substantive, this does *inter alia* entail a measure of compensation for constraints on traditional military resources.

All-encompassing burden calculations can reach very high levels. But one must also be cognizant of the military's societal role and contribution, and the differences occasioned by very different politico-military cultures. Military production for civilian ends, construction of roads, bridges and buildings, help in harvest gathering and the laying of sewage pipes may be less important, though indicative. More importantly, the military performs a crucial socializing role, as the one universal agency through which to attempt to inculcate the language and behavioural norms of the nation-state.

Soviet politico-military culture differs markedly from Anglo-Saxon tradition. The latter views the military as a distinct service-adjunct to the state. The Russian view was quite different; Muscovy always viewed its military as an integral and vital component of the state. The tradition was reinforced by Lenin's Clausewitzian predilections, and by the *realpolitik* implications of the Bolsheviks' early struggle against what appeared to be an immensely more powerful coalition of enemies: Bolsheviks were, *ipso facto*, soldiers; Red Army men were, *ipso facto*, Bolsheviks. And political leaders still serve on local defence councils, while military officers, as a matter of course, sit on legislative and executive bodies. The composite is deeply ingrained and fundamental.

The military is an integral part of the national elite. It is not outside the establishment; it is of the establishment. There are clearly factional differences, but they do not take the form of functional military–Party (or other) confrontations. They are, instead, played out within the confines of a larger, more inter-woven political-military-economic-cultural composite. Military and other factions achieve policy influence as component parts of larger amalgams, not as functional separatists.

Notes and references

[1] Jacobsen, C. G., 'Soviet military expenditures and the Soviet defence burden', in SIPRI, *World Armaments and Disarmament: SIPRI Yearbook 1986* (Oxford University Press: Oxford, 1986), pp. 263 and 272.

[2] Nove, A., 'The defence burden—some general observations' (paper 3.2); and *Gosudarstvenny Byudzhet SSSR* (Moscow, 1975).

[3] Nove (note 2). A variant view is provided by Kaser, M., in eds A. Brown and M. Kaser, *Soviet Policy for the 1980s* (Macmillan: London, 1982), pp. 202–7: he believes that the defence estimate covers only non-capital procurement, while pay and subsistence come from undesignated parts of the state budget.

[4] *International Herald Tribune*, 14 Jan. 1987.

[5] Duchêne, G., 'How much do the Soviets use for defence?' (paper 2.3).

[6] Zhuravlev, S., states, in *Ekonomicheskaya Gazeta*, no. 24 (1986), p. 4, that 'the rising cost of investment activity' (inflation) plus 'qualitative improvements' add 5–7 per cent annually to costs; *Voprosy Ekonomiki*, no. 3 (1985), gives a 5 per cent figure for the economy as a whole; for machine-building (and hence defence) Soviet sources

talk of $3\frac{1}{2}$ to $4\frac{1}{2}$ per cent inflation: see Hanson, P., 'The CIA, the TsSU and real growth in Soviet investment', *Soviet Studies* (Oct. 1984), p. 577; also Nove (note 1).

[7] NATO report excerpted in *Atlantic News*, no. 1882 (16 Jan. 1987).

[8] *Aviation Week & Space Technology* (11 Jan. 1982), p. 63; also Jacobsen (note 1).

[9] Burton, D. F., 'Estimating Soviet defense spending', *Problems of Communism*, no. 3–4 (1983), pp. 85–93. Lee also relied on what proves to have been an inaccurate reproduction of a Soviet chart prepared by V. A. Evdokimov; see Hutchings, R., 'Soviet defence spending', *Jahrbuch des Wirtschaft Osteuropas* (1981).

[10] Burton (note 9); US Department of Defense, *The FY 1985 Department of Defense Program for Research, Development and Acquisition*; Duchêne (note 5); and see ed. C. G. Jacobsen, *The Uncertain Course: New Weapons, Strategies and Mind-sets* (Oxford University Press: Oxford, 1987), papers 2.3, 2.4 and 2.6 on Soviet weapons and systems developments.

[11] For a full discussion, see Duchêne (note 5) and Steinberg, D., (paper 2.1). Steinberg's concept of extra-budgetary funding is not unprecedented in terms of Western speculation; see Bergson, A., *Review of Economic Statistics*, (Nov. 1947), p. 240. (Bergson noted, as does Steinberg, the gap between the total population reported as employed, and their total disposable income, which is greater than the number employed multiplied by their average wage.)

[12] The official number of defence-related enterprises appears clearly inadequate, as noted by Dr Julian Cooper (SIPRI round table discussion, Stockholm, 6 Mar. 1987).

[13] Nove, A. and Zauberman, A., 'A Soviet disclosure of ruble national income', *Soviet Studies* (Oct. 1959).

[14] Duchêne, G., Mochizuki, K. and Nove, A. (papers 2.3, 2.4 and 3.2).

[15] NATO (note 7).

[16] Jacobsen (note 1). See also Cooper, J., contribution to forthcoming United States Congressional volume on Soviet and Chinese defence appropriations.

[17] NATO definitions incorporate restrictive, though not exhaustive, consideration of some of these items.

[18] Jacobsen (note 1), pp. 263–74; *Pravda*, 3 Mar. 1984. For Chinese analogue, see Jacobsen, C. G., 'Far East survey', in ed. D. R. Jones, *Soviet Armed Forces Review Annual (SAFRA)*, no. 10 (Academic International: Gulf Breeze, FL, 1987).

[19] *Kommunist Vooruzhiennikh Sil*, Oct. 1985; see also writings by Marshal Ogarkov, N.V., and Colonel General Gareev, M.A.

Paper 1.2. Soviet national accounts

GÉRARD DUCHÊNE AND DMITRI STEINBERG

I. Introduction

This paper presents the framework of Soviet national accounts (material product accountancy or MPA) and their relation to standard national accounts, in order to facilitate understanding of the role and significance of military expenditure in the Soviet economy. As shown in the following papers, research on the evaluation of the Soviet military burden makes extensive use of published statistical material—mainly but not exclusively from the official statistical yearbooks of the Soviet national economy. The significance of this material is generally ignored by non-specialists. A number of technical terms (some of which bear the name of Western accounting concepts with different meanings) give rise to misinterpretations; they need to be explained.

The bulk of the methodological information given in this paper comes from a series of handbooks called *Methodical Instructions*, issued approximately every five years, since 1969, by the Soviet State Planning Agency or *Gosplan*. Although the 1986 issue had not been released by mid-1987, there is reason to believe that the general principles of accounting remain unchanged; previous editions of the handbook are consistent.

One may ask why principles of accounting are to be found in documents concerning planning. The reason is that the Central Statistical Administration (CSA) itself releases little information about procedure; differences between the methodologies of *Gosplan* and the CSA are established in the *Methodical Instructions*. Some standard textbooks in statistical courses also provide extensive information on the most usual indicators and their interconnections. A second basic question concerns the degree of reliability and the precision of the figures obtained through a refinement of the national account series. As concerns reliability, one should note that all Western works on Soviet military expenditure rely necessarily on some kind of official Soviet information, even if it is extended or modified by other sources; with a large and complex economic system such as the Soviet Union, it is not possible to reconstruct product aggregates from external data alone (as can be done for small developing economies). With regard to precision, it is clear that military expenditure estimates derived from examinations of global account figures preclude the detail that would be available if standard budget data were released. But the problem with Soviet military expenditure is more one of overall burden than one of detailed determination, at least as a first step of research. Since the Soviet budget data are misleading and incomplete, Western specialists are forced to engage in extensive analyses of the national accounts as a first step to illuminating the military burden.

II.   Productive and non-productive sectors

The first concept of any system of national accounts is the definition of productive activities. In the MPA, only those activities pertaining to productive sectors are considered productive. These are: industry, agriculture, construction, transport of goods, communication between productive units, trade, distribution, conditioning, forestry and 'other branches of material production' (such as destruction and disposal of industrial waste, berry and mushroom gathering and the like). The list of the sub-activities contained in these sectors is defined in *Gosplan* handbooks. The accounting sectors do not coincide with administrative divisions of the Soviet economy (ministries and so on).

Not all 'productive sectors' actually produce 'output': only industry, agriculture, forestry, construction and 'other branches' do; the other cited sectors are considered 'circulation sectors', which add value (by distributing or transporting) to the products of the output-producing sectors. At the level of production use (for instance, productive consumption), the value of distribution or transport services will not appear as such, but it is included in the value of the industrial or agricultural products used. This inconsistency, arising from a built-in disequilibrium between sector resources and end-use, is resolved in Soviet statisticians' input-output methodology, which otherwise follows MPA production concepts precisely and consistently. Unfortunately, input-output tables have been (partially) released only for 1959, 1966 and 1972. MPA is the only global framework that gives data for other years.

III.   Types of economic unit

Economic units can be productive or non-productive, according to the sector to which they belong, but they are also defined by their mode of operation and their legal status. Soviet statisticians refer to the concept of 'social sector'. Social sectors are: state co-operatives, collectives (*kolkhoz*) and the population. The first sector is subdivided according to mode of operation: enterprises, defined as profit-seeking (*khozraschyot*) units; co-operative organizations, present mainly in distribution sectors; and budgetary organizations, financed mainly through the state budget. There are thus five social sectors or sectors of property-operation, each of which may be either productive or non-productive. For instance, profit enterprises may be located in industry (productive) or in passenger transport (non-productive); the population has a productive activity in agriculture (individual plots) as well as—to a lesser extent—in industry and construction; budgetary organizations are mainly located in non-productive sectors (education, health and so on). An economic unit may be attached—from the statistical point of view—to several sectors, the basic unit being the 'factory' (*zavod*), or the establishment.

IV. Production concepts

There are several concepts of total production. The gross (*valovaia*) production at plant level is the total valuation of finished products, released works, inventory changes of semi-finished products and unfinished production. The market production (*tovarnaia*) is equal to gross production minus inventory change. Both concepts relate to the main (sector) activity of an establishment, and can be computed in various prices (see section V below). The MPA presents as one of its most important indicators the concept of gross social product (GSP), which corresponds approximately to gross production as defined above. The definition is clear-cut for industry, but needs clarification for other productive sectors.

In agriculture, gross product would include a market part, valued at different prices depending on the type of realized or projected sales (to the state at an administered price, to the market at a market price, in-village at a price 'not higher than the state price' and so on), and a non-market part. The latter includes self-consumption by the population (valued at an average market price), and inventory and capital changes of cattle growth (young are inventories; adults are capital), of orchards and vineyards, and of the next year's harvest, all valued at full cost.

In construction, GSP includes the value of building and assembly works, of drilling financed through investment funds, of project works, of gross repair of buildings and structures and other expenses (various compensations). Construction production includes two kinds of work in progress: those that are finished from the point of view of the builder but not yet available for use due to lack of other parts (so-called 'unfinished constructions'), and those that are not finished from the builder's viewpoint (the 'unfinished production of the construction sector').

In transport and communications (the productive part), GSP is simply the total revenue of the concerned units, be it service sales (transport, handling and the like) or local dues. In trade and distribution, gross production is the margin obtained by commercial units. Trade GSP includes also foreign trade revenues, a procedure which is explained in more detail below (see section VI).

V. Prices and subsidies

Output levels can be measured in several types of price, depending on the stage at which products are traded. In industrial sectors, factories fix their output in so-called 'enterprise wholesale prices' according to administered price-lists. These prices are supposed to cover the 'full expenses of production'—namely, the cost of material inputs, wages, social security deductions, amortization and other expenses (taxes and fines, rents, travel expenses, and so on)—and to leave a gross profit. In fact, this is not always so, because there may be deficit sectors and sectors (especially in the food industry) which do not pay the full cost of their agricultural inputs. There are two types of subsidies, corresponding to each of these cases. The gross profits of enterprises go primarily to the budget, in various forms, but some are retained and spent on investments or bonuses, and another part is redistributed through higher levels of control (ministries).

Statistics on profits and wages published by the Soviets are often incorrectly interpreted by Western scholars: published profits are a consolidated value of (positive) profits and (negative) losses for every sector; the distribution of profits, however, is published only for enterprises making a (positive) profit. Published profit figures are gross of bonuses paid to personnel. Wage data include the same bonuses. Soviet statisticians furthermore regularly provide the cost structure of industrial sectors. It is possible to reconcile disparate data on the composition of gross industrial production.

There is another type of price which is used to compute output aggregates: the 'industry wholesale price'. This is another administered price, which includes a tax component called 'turnover tax' added to enterprise wholesale price, and which excludes agricultural subsidies. Lastly, retail prices—also administered, with the exception of urban market prices—are supposed to cover industrial wholesale prices plus transport and trade costs.

The turnover tax concerns mainly industrial consumer goods—especially alcoholic beverages, durables and clothes—and is not defined as a regular percentage but simply as a difference between two types of price (industry and enterprise prices). Agricultural subsidies reflect the fact that agricultural prices have been raised several times during the last 25 years, while retail prices of important food industry products (such as meat and milk) have remained stable throughout this period. Special procurement agencies (financed through the budget) buy high-priced farm products, and sell them to the food industry at a low price. So when a balance of resources and uses is sought on a sectoral basis, agricultural output must be reduced by the amount of the subsidies, while, conversely, industrial output (in industry prices) must be raised by the same amount.

VI.   Accounting for foreign trade

Foreign trade is accounted for in Soviet published statistics in a specific category of prices called 'foreign trade prices'. These are an approximate conversion of world prices using a specific exchange rate for various products. But before being so valued, Soviet exports are produced and accounted for in internal wholesale prices, and included as such in the gross production of economic units. In an analogous fashion, imports are paid for by users at an internal price that corresponds (more or less) to the price of equivalent domestic products. Although Soviet statisticians have never released detailed data on exports and imports valued in domestic prices, some information can be extracted from input-output tables, and Western scholars now have a fairly good idea of the methodology used to account for Soviet foreign trade. The structure of domestic prices bears no relation to external (foreign trade) prices, and the conversion coefficients from the latter to the former vary across products (and differ for imports and exports of the same kind of product).

There are in fact two foreign trade balances: one in domestic and another in external prices. The balance in external prices—usually positive—represents the foreign currency earnings of the Soviet Union. It is converted into domestic prices using the mean conversion coefficient for exports (or for imports if the balance is negative). The foreign trade balance in domestic prices—largely negative—represents the profits of the foreign trade organizations in their relations with Soviet producers of exports and users of imports.

In the macro-economic balance of resources and uses, the trade balance in domestic prices is on the resource side and the one in external prices on both sides. The macro-economic balance then looks as follows:

$$YD + MD - XD + (XF - MF)c = A + D + (XF - MF)c$$

where YD is the gross domestic production, MD and XD imports and exports in domestic prices, A the value of intermediate consumption, D the value of final domestic demand, XF and MF exports and imports in foreign trade prices, and c the mean conversion coefficient for exports ($c = XD/XF$ in the case when XF>MF). The published aggregates of GSP include the whole left-hand side of the equation, non-YD elements being a part of the trade and distribution sector GSP. These elements are sometimes called 'foreign trade earnings'.

VII. Gross social product and net material product (national income)

Reducing the sectors' GSP by the amount of productive consumption (the 'material expenditure of productive sectors') leads to another important aggregate, equivalent to value added, called produced national income or net material product (NMP). This is a concept of net output because material expenditure includes amortization of productive capital, in accordance with the Marxian theory of value creation (the NMP is intended to correspond to 'newly created value').

NMP includes wages—including bonuses paid from profits—and other productive labour income (mainly in agriculture: earnings from *kolkhoz* and sales, and self-consumption from private plots); these constitute the labour part of the NMP. The other component of the NMP includes net consolidated profits, social security deductions, turnover and other taxes, and foreign trade earnings, but excludes agricultural subsidies.

The sectoral structure of the NMP is presented annually by Soviet statistics in the same manner as the GSP. This means that circulation sectors (transport and trade) are accounted for separately from production sectors (although both are 'productive'). But when the NMP is presented from the uses side, these circulation sectors do not appear: there is no such thing as final consumption or investment of trade or transport products; their NMP must thus be redispatched to production sectors if a sectoral equilibrium of resources and uses is sought.

VIII.   Amortization deductions and unamortized values

All productive units must include in their costs an amortization of the capital they use. Non-productive sectors do the same, but the accounting status of non-productive amortization is quite different.

Total amortization includes two elements: regular deductions as a percentage of the balance-sheet value of equipment or buildings—a series which is published every year—and the unamortized value of scrapped capital, about which there is scattered information (although as a rule fixed capital in fact is used longer than is implied by amortization rates, leading to over-amortization deductions; in certain cases it may scrap before the end of the period implied by the amortization rate).

Total amortization represents in Soviet statistics a material cost of production for productive units (or sectors) and a consumption of material goods for non-productive sectors. The former is then not included in the NMP, whereas the latter appears as one of the uses of this same NMP, in the consumption component. Another consequence is that the 'accumulation' component of NMP uses is a net investment concept.

Both productive and non-productive amortization are used for two purposes: replacement of capital, and the capital repair of buildings and equipment. Replacement of capital is a part of financing gross investment (regularly published data, though in constant prices). Capital repair—on which information is not very detailed—appears as another type of investment, not included in the gross investment series. One difficulty with capital repair is that the funds allocated to this purpose apparently are not all spent, according to Soviet specialist testimony.

IX.   Testing the consistency of net material product

One way to test the consistency (and completeness) of the NMP would be to calculate independently all the income components of the aggregate. Such a test, however, is problematic.

The determination of the total wages of 'workers and employees' would be feasible by multiplying the mean individual wage by the number of people employed in productive activities. Both data are released, but with some imprecision: employment in some mixed sectors is not recorded separately for productive and non-productive parts; the published mean wage excludes certain marginal components such as special bonuses or travel expenses. The resulting calculation can therefore only be an approximation. The uncertainty is still higher for the self-consumption part of 'other labour incomes'. One must thus refer to specific Soviet works on these topics if one seeks precision in the reconstitution of various elements.

On the public sector income side, the most problematic element is foreign trade earnings (this is one area that may benefit particularly if *glasnost*— 'transparency'—is extended to statistics).

These uncertainties impede a rigorous test of consistency. Nevertheless, they do allow figures compatible with the published NMP.

X.   Comparison between Soviet and Western aggregates

The main aggregate of Western national accounts is gross domestic product (GDP). The difference between NMP and GDP lies mainly in three areas: foreign trade, amortization (depreciation) and sector coverage. The foreign trade deficit is added to the domestic NMP of the trade-distribution sector, whereas it would not be included in the GDP. Capital depreciation is a part of GDP which is excluded from NMP. GDP includes incomes in profit sectors considered non-productive in the NMP approach, such as transport and communications (the non-productive part), 'everyday' services, housing, banking, insurance, and various tourism, health, education and science services.

Another difficulty arises from the fact that Soviet prices cannot be considered either market prices or factor-cost prices, due to discrepancies between profit (and tax) rates across sectors, and to the pervasiveness of shortages at official prices.

XI.   CIA methodology of calculating Soviet GNP

The Central Intelligence Agency (CIA) conceives the Soviet economy as comprising two sectors (households and the public sector) and establishes equilibrated accounts for each of these. The calculated expenditure of the household sector exceeds its income, and the calculated income of the public sector exceeds its expenditure. Gross national product (GNP) is determined as the sum of household expenditure and public sector income (both net of transfers). A further presentation of GNP is by type of income and by branches of the economy.

Sector coverage of the CIA's GNP is approximately as defined by the United Nations standard accounts. The CIA relies exclusively on piecemeal determination of each element which may be a part of income or expenditure of both sectors, and avoids the use of Soviet-type aggregates such as GSP or NMP. A comparison of the CIA's GNP with published Soviet aggregates is difficult because the CIA corrects its results by a factor-cost adjustment and computes GNP in constant prices (1970 prices until 1986, then 1982 prices) without giving details on the corrections. The last detailed explanation of CIA methodology dates from 1975; changes in GNP and military expenditure estimations since that date have not yet been exposed to necessary scrutiny and comment.

It should be noted that, although it has a Western format, the CIA GNP is based entirely on Soviet official data. The most serious weakness associated with CIA methodology is that it is not tested for consistency against Soviet aggregates (such as NMP).

XII.   Usable national income

The produced NMP (national income) reflects the resource side of a balance, the uses of which appear in the presentation of the usable national income (UNI). Soviet statisticians annually release figures of this aggregate in current and constant ('comparable') prices, with a division into two main components: the consumption fund and the accumulation fund. Returning to the GSP, one can say that it can be allocated to three 'funds'—reproduction, consumption and accumulation—that approximately correspond to the well-known Marxian 'formula' of value: $C + V + M$.

Until 1975, Soviet statistical yearbooks gave more detailed disaggregates of consumption and accumulation funds. The consumption fund was subdivided into three parts: individual consumption, material expenditure of non-productive sectors aimed at satisfying population needs and material expenditure of the science and administration sectors. The accumulation fund was also subdivided into three parts: the increment of fixed productive capital, the increment of fixed non-productive capital and (in one figure) the increment of circulating material capital, of reserves, and other expenditures. These details are no longer released.

XIII.   The gap between produced and usable national income

The global figure for UNI differs slightly from the one published for produced NMP. Soviet statisticians explain that the difference is due to 'the magnitude of losses and the foreign trade balance'. It is rather obvious that losses reduce the produced value by an amount which can neither be consumed nor accumulated, but they could be counted as a disaccumulation and some losses in fact are just that; 'eliminated' losses are only so-called planned losses, which are incurred in agriculture and construction.

The foreign trade balance that is lost between production and use of the national income is the factor $(XF - MF)c$, of the equation in section VI. This factor, contrary to the foreign trade balance in domestic prices, has no material counterpart, since it represents a claim on foreign resources, valued in prices comparable to those of other NMP components using coefficient c.

Taking account of the fact that the commercial balance in foreign trade prices has generally been positive, UNI tends to be smaller than NMP. This situation may change.

XIV.   Sectoral equilibrium of resources and uses

As concerns national income, it is possible to define (for the GSP) the concepts of produced and usable GSP. If there is no particular reason to a seek a sectoral equilibrium of national income, this can be extracted from the GSP output-input tables. If we seek sectoral equilibrium for each productive sector, however, we must verify the following equation of resources and uses:

Material expenditure (including amortization) + produced national income − commercial balance in foreign trade prices = material deliveries to productive sectors + amortization + consumption and accumulation of products + losses.

Several adjustments should nevertheless be made in order to construct such a sectoral equilibrium, in view of the fact that MPA has specificities that differ from the input-output structure. First, it must be recalled that sectoral structures differ between produced and usable GSPs. Circulation sectors appear only on the production side and are matched with production sectors on the uses side; the gross production of the transport-communication and trade-distribution sectors should therefore be reallocated to other sectors. Second, the foreign trade deficit is a part of trade-distribution (produced) GSP and must also be reallocated to production sectors benefiting from it. Third, agricultural subsidies should be substracted from agricultural GSP (because final users do not in fact pay for it) and added to industry GSP. With these adjustments, it would be possible to build the equivalent of an input-output framework. Such an exercise could provide good insight into the product-mix of final demand components. But, as yet, available data do not appear to permit a reliable solution to all the problems involved unless 1972 input-output coefficients are extrapolated for succeeding years. Construction appears as the only workable sector in this perspective, since it has no intermediate deliveries.

XV.   The place of defence in the national income

In his presentation (paper 3.2) Alec Nove recalls that early Soviet statisticians—and particularly Strumilin—pleaded for a partition of usable national income into three end-uses instead of two: consumption, accumulation and destruction; the last element would have corresponded to defence-related uses of resources.

All of the contributors to this book have differing ideas on the way this last concept has been circumvented or avoided. Dmitri Steinberg (paper 2.1) considers that a large part of the destruction end-uses is simply eliminated from the accounts, and that corresponding production of 'means of destruction' is also eliminated. Peter Wiles (paper 2.2) defends the idea that, as the national income is a net concept, destruction end-uses should also be net, which means that a share of amortization (included in the GSP but not in the NMP) consists of depreciation of 'weapons'. Gérard Duchêne (paper 2.3) states that destruction end-uses are incorporated into other end-uses, and that weaponry is incorporated in accumulation under the heading 'other expenditure', without any reduction for depreciation.

In contrast, these authors appear to agree—with some nuances—on the fact that the non-weaponry part of the military uses of resources is included in consumption, or in 'normal' accumulation funds: for instance, food consumption by permanent military staff or conscripts would be a part of individual consumption (here, everyone accepts Nove's and Zauberman's 1959 contribution).

XVI.   National income and state budget data

Budgetary data are presented in far more detail than material product accountancy, but they nevertheless leave many questions unsolved; published totals cannot be reconciled with the sum of published elements—there are very sizeable discrepancies. Moreover, the stability during more than 20 years of announced defence expenditures implies that the announced sum has a non-stable composition, and that other expenditure lines have been symmetrically altered.

Nevertheless, some budget data contribute to the determination of the NMP: various public sector incomes entering the produced national income come from budget income data, mainly turnover and other taxes. It is difficult to reconcile components of usable national income with state budget expenditures because budget data generally combine in one line material expenditure (included in UNI) and wages or financial payments (excluded as such from UNI); moreover, state budget expenditures cover only a part of total public sector expenditure in a given area: for instance 'science' (R&D) is financed partially by budget funds, and partially by enterprise funds.

XVII.   Individual consumption

Individual or population consumption forms the bulk of the national income consumption fund, or at least did, until these data ceased to be released. The components of this aggregate are well defined in *Gosplan* handbooks: retail trade sales of new consumption goods to the population valued at purchasers' prices, plus consumption in kind by the population, plus various housing elements.

Retail trade sales may be related to trade turnover—on which data are regularly reported in statistical yearbooks and yearly plans—with the following adjustments: sales to administrations ('small scale wholesale trade'), sales of second-hand goods and sales of producer goods must be excluded, while private sales in urban markets or of small-scale handicraft and gathering-type activities must be added to state and co-operative sales.

Consumption in kind by the population includes privately produced (mainly on personal plots) goods for own consumption, and the natural product non-monetary share of *kolkhoz* and *sovkhoz* wages.

Housing-related elements include payment for material utilities (electricity, gas, water and so on) and the depreciation of housing stock; this last element is an artificial device designed to replace the low rents of state urban flats and the free occupation of privately owned rural houses by a more realistic estimation ('real rent').

Reconstitution of these elements is necessary, first, to check the consistency of pre-1975 published figures and second, to allow post-1975 estimates of the aggregate. Tangential information can be gathered from specialized Soviet literature, but there are still uncertainties concerning many of the listed elements; there is still scope for extensive research on this topic, as on other elements of the UNI reviewed below.

XVIII.   Collective consumption

The non-productive sectors consume a part of produced NMP in the form of material expenditures (the products they buy or receive for their current functioning) and in depreciation of their fixed capital. Depreciation is reviewed in section XIX.

The direct material expenditure of the non-productive sectors could be checked by reconstitution of the equilibrated accounts of these sectors, taking into account all sources of financing and all kinds of expenditures. The financing of most non-productive activities comes from the public sector (the state budget, enterprises and associations, contributions to Soviet consumption funds) and from payments by the population (first published in the 1985 statistical yearbook). Expenditures in the non-productive sectors consist of wages, social security deductions, direct material expenditure, amortization deductions (only for profit-seeking units) and profits.

It is difficult to determine all these elements with certainty for each sector; hence the controversy concerning the inclusion of military items in this part of UNI.

XIX.   Depreciation of non-productive fixed capital

It has been noted that this element is part of the material expenditure of the non-productive sectors, and is included in the consumption fund of national income. The non-productive sectors comprise profit and non-profit units. The former have amortization deductions that cover replacement and repair of fixed capital, and that are determined by the rates applicable to various types of buildings and equipment. Non-profit units do not employ these deductions, but MPA incorporates in the cost of functioning of these services an implicit depreciation called *iznos*, or 'wear and tear' of fixed capital. This sum is determined by applying the same rates as for real amortization. The principle applied is the same as that applied to depreciation of the housing stock included in individual consumption.

The question is: what part of produced national income corresponds to these implicit depreciations? The answer is that the production of construction and of end-use machinery contributes to gross investment, whose replacement and repair parts are separated from the net fixed investment part; the *iznos* of non-productive fixed capital is the replacement and repair part of the corresponding gross investments.

XX. The accumulation fund: increment of fixed capital

Soviet statistics regularly report figures for total fixed capital, with rather detailed sectoral distribution. The increment of fixed capital which is referred to here does not correspond to this data: first, the published series are in constant prices, whereas most MPA data are in current prices; second, and not least, the fixed capital referred to in the accumulation fund is a depreciated capital, that is the residual value of buildings and equipment after deduction of their already amortized component, whereas the published series of fixed capital refers to balance sheet values.

This means that the increment of fixed capital measured in the accumulation fund is equal to net fixed investment. Again, this is a concept which is quite different from the regularly published series of gross investments (*kapital'nye vlozhenija*) and of installation of capital (*vvod v dejstvie osnovnykh fondov*), for several reasons.

First, gross investment includes only a part of the depreciation of capital, namely its replacement part; the capital repair part (approximately 40 per cent) of depreciation is not included in the gross investment. Second, gross investment does not cover all sources of capital growth including budget financed purchases of equipment (equipment given to non-profit service sectors, a rather small and stable sum), net growth of adult cattle and private investments in orchards and vineyards. Although all these components appear quite small, they must be taken into account when determining total investment. Third, gross investment includes the increment of unfinished constructions (works in process), including the part of these constructions which is definitely abandoned, the 'planned losses in construction'. This element must be excluded in the adjustment from gross investment to increment of fixed capital (one can here use the series on installation of capital). Fourth, gross investment series are given in constant prices whereas the MPA framework requires current prices, a difference that is difficult to bridge and that represents a real puzzle of statistical 'non-transparency'. Why is there no published figure of investment in current prices when (as Alec Nove has repeatedly documented) investment prices represent one of the most disputed problem areas of Soviet economics?

Reconstruction of the indicator of the increment of fixed capital is crucial because it conditions the determination of the residual part of the accumulation fund, which most probably is military. To accomplish this reconstruction is rather complex; it involves the determination of the sectoral structure of gross and net fixed investment, which contains the 'products' of the machinery, construction and agricultural sectors. The machinery part of investment is rendered still more complex by the problem of the valuation of imported equipment. This explains the divergence of the estimates that are presented in this book.

XXI. The accumulation fund: increment of material circulating capital

Material circulating capital consists mainly of inventory stocks of goods (with a larger share of inputs than in Western economies) and of unfinished construction stock. Though it has been reduced recently, information on these indicators is relatively detailed in Soviet statistical yearbooks. Two problems nevertheless arise in relation to the determination of inventory change. The first one is that, although it is well known that there are large fluctuations of cereal harvests and that these most probably imply large inventory changes, the series of inventory stocks in agriculture are quite regular (and the same is true for the trade and distribution sector). This suggests that agricultural stocks are part of the so-called 'reserves' and are not included in material circulating capital. The second problem is linked with quite important modifications of the published series of inventory stocks for the years 1981–83; these modifications, which have not been explained officially, appear to indicate a revaluation of inventories (but other explanations have also been suggested; see paper 2.1, Dmitri Steinberg's contribution).

XXII. Reserves and 'other expenditure'

This is the last—and the most mysterious—part of the accumulation fund of national income. As has been noted above, there is certainly a civilian component in this 'accumulation residual', at least in the form of grain reserves—even if these may have a strategic purpose. But there certainly is also a military component in it, first, because of the size of the residual, and second, because produced military goods (particularly weapons but also eventually 'material expenditure', such as fuels) must be located somewhére in the UNI if they are a part of the NMP. The contributors of the following papers propose various partitions of the civilian and military components of the accumulation residual, and it is left to the reader to evaluate their arguments.

Part 2.   New approaches

Paper 2.1. Estimating total Soviet military expenditures: an alternative approach based on reconstructed Soviet national accounts

DMITRI STEINBERG

I. Introduction

The method used by Soviet planners to conceal military expenditures in the published statistics has puzzled economists for many decades. While economists have proposed several conflicting hypotheses about the planners' concealment method, none have proven to be successful largely because economists have taken a piecemeal approach to studying the official statistics. It will be demonstrated below that the logic underlying the planners' method emerges only after comparing the structure of all planners' national economic balance (NEB) tables with the published statistics. After making this comparison it is possible to determine where and how military expenditures are hidden in each NEB table and then to estimate each component of these expenditures.

The NEB tables contain five integrated systems of national accounts: production, national income, financial and capital resources and labour statistics. Whereas the proposed estimates are based on the integration of all NEB tables, previous estimates that proceeded beyond the official defence budgetary figures focused exclusively on either production or national income statistics. This narrow focus has prevented economists from determining the precise contents of residuals found in the official statistics.

The major findings indicate that so-called 'other expenditures' of national income contain current material expenditures of the defence industry rather than the total cost of weapons.* These expenditures comprise only 50 per cent of the total weapon production cost. Capital expenditures of the defence industry comprise 10 per cent of the total and are hidden in capital outlays on other non-production service sectors. Labour outlays comprise 40 per cent of the total and are excluded together with defence industrial labour from the published production and national income statistics. Defence labour outlays, however, still can be estimated using the published portions of the financial statistics. All estimates based on production or national income statistics thus

---

* These exclude exports of weapons which are hidden in Soviet national accounts together with exports of civilian goods. The discussion of weapon production will be limited to supplies intended for domestic use.

make it possible to determine only current material expenditures of weapon producers. The entire value added in the weapon production sector consisting of labour and capital outlays has thus remained outside the scope of previous estimates.

As will be demonstrated below, the proposed alternative approach to estimating Soviet weapon production leads to estimates that approximate CIA estimates based on pricing individual weapon systems. In comparison, the traditional approach, according to which 'other expenditures' of national income contain the entire weapon production cost, leads to estimates that constitute around 50 per cent of recent CIA estimates. Economists deal with this 50 per cent discrepancy in three ways. The most popular way is unjustifiably to assume that the published statistics are so unreliable that any estimate derived from these statistics contains a huge margin of error.[1] Some economists expand the traditional approach in ways that contradict Soviet concepts of total and net fixed investment.[2] Other economists, primarily from outside the United States, remain faithful to the traditional interpretation of Soviet concepts and thus believe that the CIA overestimates prices on Soviet weapons.[3]

If Soviet planners exclude weapon production from published statistics, then they must account for defence industrial activities (excluding exports of armaments which generate foreign currency earnings) in the same way as those of budget-supported sectors. This means that defence industries do not earn profit and that science organizations serving defence industries are also budget-supported. These two conclusions permit far more precise estimates of total military expenditures derived from the official statistics. The total price of Soviet weapons produced for domestic use can be estimated as the sum of material, capital and labour inputs. Outlays on defence science in turn can be estimated precisely using published budgetary data on research expenditures. The published statistics are also useful for obtaining quite accurate estimates of military consumption and construction. Overall, the proposed estimates of total military expenditures appear to be more precise than CIA estimates, which contain a 10–15 per cent margin of error.[4]

II. Published views of Soviet economists

In the West, advocates of the traditional view that the total value of weapons is hidden in national income cite no supporting evidence, except for several brief quotes found in Soviet literature. Besides independently checking the validity of these quotes by statistical means, one must also be cautious in evaluating their import.

Soviet authors who mention defence production may have been exposed to past rather than current national accounting practices. None of these authors made independent estimates; they relied on second-hand evidence. They may unwittingly have taken part in disinformation campaigns aimed at preventing not only Western but also Soviet economists from learning about planning and accounting practices in the defence area. This line of reasoning is supported by the inherent contradiction that is apparent in Soviet authors' manner of addressing the issue of defence production in the published statistics.

On the one hand, Soviet authors profess adherence to a Marxist humanist principle according to which production of material wealth—the aggregate of producer and consumer goods—excludes weapons because they destroy rather than enhance social progress. Since the published total for produced material wealth, which planners call 'gross social product' (GSP), consists of producer and consumer goods, it follows from this principle that the GSP and hence national income exclude weapons.

On the other hand, these Soviet authors also argue that planners are compelled to treat weapons as producer goods for 'reasons of convenience', a euphemism for concealing the size of military buildup.[5] This type of convenience clearly makes little sense from the planners' point of view. It would be much easier for planners to conceal the total size of weapon production by excluding it from the GSP and national income altogether, rather than by trying to camouflage it among investment in producer goods. Soviet authors who write about 'reasons of convenience' must appreciate this contradiction. The history of debates among Soviet economists on the subject of defence production suggests that they may have been subjected to disinformation.

Soviet authors inform us that *Gosplan* officials treated weapons as Department III during the Fourth Five-Year Plan of 1946–1950.[6] Department I stands for producer goods, including those used in weapon production, while Department II stands for consumer goods and reserves. In 1951, *Gosplan* officials apparently decided to treat weapons as part of Department I for 'reasons of convenience'.

Soviet academic economists write as if the issue of how to treat weapon production was settled forever. However, it is far from certain that 'reasons of convenience' did not prompt planners to change their concealment practice on the eve of their publication of the first post-war annual statistical manual in 1957 (possible *Gosplan* policy changes after 1951 have not been released). The integration of Departments I and III made it impossible to analyse production of weapons, but did not thwart estimates of final demand by the armed forces. Planners still had to treat weapons as a separate component of national income available for end-use. The acceleration of the arms race certainly made it more and more difficult to conceal weapons in published national income accounts. A presumed additional concern to planners was the compilation of the input-output table for 1959, which threatened to expose military secrets.

The year 1957 was eventful in the history of Soviet statistics for several reasons. In addition to publishing the statistical manual, planners presented a revised version of the NEB to leading Soviet economists at the All-Union conference of statisticians. For the first time, planners revealed the estimation method for dividing the annual production output into Departments I and II.[7] It appears probable that planners devised a method for concealing military expenditures before presenting their new version of the NEB.

Sceptics may regard it as a coincidence, but at the turn of the year 1956/57 the sum of civilian and military working capital included in the investment component of national income declined without any apparent reason from 13.6 to 9.2 billion roubles, that is, by 30 per cent.[8] If one assumes that planners began to exclude weapons from national income, then the observed decline can be explained by the fact that the value of weapons exceeds current material purchases in the defence industry by the sum of wages, social security deductions and depreciation.

The 1957 conference generated lively debates among Soviet economists. Such prominent planners as Sobol, Strumilin, Turetskiy and Bor commented extensively not only on civilian but also on military economic issues.[9] The famous debate between Academicians Strumilin and Trakhtenberg on the GSP division into Departments I, II and III has been publicized in both Soviet and Western literature.[10] This debate is noteworthy because it pitted new planning ideas defended by Strumilin against those of the early 1950s, defended by traditional Soviet academic thought. The implications of Strumilin's arguments were clear: since the total GSP production consists of Departments I and II and since weapons are in Department III, planners must exclude weapons from the GSP altogether to preserve the logic of Soviet national accounts. Trakhtenberg's position, though poorly defended on Marxist theoretical grounds, indirectly echoed the arguments about practical considerations that prompted planners to conceal weapons in Department I in the early 1950s.

It is clear that Trakhtenberg's position cannot be defended theoretically because weapons are neither producer nor consumer goods. But what really undermines his position is that it is much less practical than Strumilin's and less 'convenient'. By removing Department III from the GSP, planners could halve the apparent gap in national accounts. This would greatly facilitate the goal of concealing Soviet military preparations, without distorting the ratio between Departments I and II.

Planners never revealed how they resolved the outcome of the Strumilin-Trakhtenberg debate. During the 1960s the military issue began to disappear from openly published literature; academic economists were no longer encouraged to explore it. The conclusion to be drawn from open publications released during the 1960s and 1970s is that academic economists were led to believe that planners made no significant changes in their accounting practices in the military area.[11] Michael Checinski, a former Polish planner, informed Professor Wiles differently: it was 'at the turn of the year 1958/9 [when] a friend, who was a high Polish officer, went to Moscow to be told about a great revision of military accountancy'.[12]

III.   Military expenditures hidden in national income

The Soviet national income equals the value of produced goods that are available for end-use—current consumption, investment and other expenditures that are always hidden as part of total investment. Other expenditures are referred to in Soviet literature as additions to state and strategic reserves.[13] The traditional view is that strategic reserves contain primarily additions to weapon stocks and agricultural strategic reserves.

In the published national income statistics, total consumption includes not only current consumption of goods by the population and non-production service sectors but also depreciation of these sectors' capital stock. Depreciation of the residential housing stock is added to the population's current consumption. Investment consists of net fixed investment (NFI), additions to unfinished construction works and inventories.

There are four residuals in published national income statistics: (a) in the total investment component of national income; (b) in current consumption by the population; (c) in state expenditures on education, health, housing, pensions and other social services, all of which are referred to as 'social consumption funds' (SCF); and (d) in capital outlays on other non-production service sectors. These residuals are estimated in tables 2.1.2 through 2.1.5 below, which serve as source tables for estimating total military expenditures in table 2.1.1.

It is hoped to demonstrate that the first residual contains additions to strategic reserves of agricultural raw materials as well as intermediate goods delivered to the defence industry for assembling weapon systems. Before 1972 and after 1981 this residual also contained defence construction, which during the years 1972–81 was subsumed under additions of inventories (unfinished production) in construction. The second residual undoubtedly contains current material purchases of the armed forces which in the official statistics are treated as part of the total Soviet population. The third residual contains state expenditures on all social services rendered to the military and their families. The existence of the fourth residual is most puzzling to economists. This investment, here believed to be connected to additions of capital stock in defence industries and space centres, cannot be explained by the traditional view of how planners disguise military expenditures in national income.

As estimated in tables 2.1.2 through 2.1.5, during the years 1970–82 the total investment residual increased from 13.7 to 29.5 billion roubles (b.r.), current consumption by the armed forces—from 6.5 to 13.0 b.r., military machine and equipment (M&E) commissions—from 1.7 to 2.6 b.r., capital outlays in defence industries and space centres—from 2.6 to 6.2 b.r., and social services rendered to the military—from 4.4 to 9.9 b.r. As estimated in table 2.1.2, defence construction remained around 4 b.r. The investment residual without military construction equalled 9.7 b.r. in 1970 and 25.5 b.r. in 1982. The derived estimate for 1982 constitutes only 45–50 per cent of the CIA figure for total Soviet weapon procurement (see below).

It is clear that estimates of Soviet weapon production based on published national income statistics cannot be reconciled with CIA estimates. One must thus conclude either that CIA analysts greatly overestimate prices of Soviet weapons or that the military component of the investment residual does not contain the total cost of weapons produced.

Table 2.1.1. Estimating total military expenditures and defence burden (in billions of current roubles)

	1970	1972	1975	1980	1982	1984
Total expenditures	54.3	61.5	73.8	97.2	108.1	118.6
Current material expenditures	19.9	23.4	28.0	38.7	43.6	48.8
Total wages	17.0	18.5	22.8	29.4	31.0	33.2
Social security deductions	1.6	1.8	2.1	2.8	3.8	4.1
Capital outlays	9.3	9.9	10.6	12.6	14.9	16.6
Total services	6.5	7.9	10.3	13.5	14.8	15.9
Weapon production and space	23.8	27.8	33.8	45.7	52.4	58.2
Current material expenditures	10.2	12.8	15.4	21.3	25.0	28.4
Total wages	9.6	10.4	13.0	17.0	17.9	19.0
Social security deductions	1.0	1.1	1.2	1.7	2.5	2.7
Capital outlays	2.6	3.0	3.6	5.1	6.2	7.2
Social services	0.4	0.5	0.6	0.7	0.8	0.9
Military administration	24.3	26.7	31.7	40.9	44.3	47.6
Current material expenditures	6.8	7.3	8.8	13.0	13.5	14.7
(a) Armed forces	6.5	7.0	8.4	12.6	13.0	14.2
(b) Central administration	0.3	0.3	0.4	0.4	0.5	0.5
Total wages	4.9	5.4	6.5	8.1	8.5	9.0
Social security deductions	0.5	0.5	0.7	0.8	1.0	1.1
Capital outlays	6.1	6.2	6.2	6.4	7.5	8.1
(a) Military construction	4.0	3.8	3.5	3.2	4.0	4.3
(b) Machines and equipment (M&E) commissions	1.7	1.9	2.1	2.4	2.6	2.8
(c) Housing	0.4	0.5	0.6	0.8	0.9	1.0
Transport and communication	1.6	1.9	2.5	3.5	3.9	4.2
Social services	4.4	5.4	7.0	9.1	9.9	10.5
(a) Pensions	1.4	1.8	2.4	3.3	3.6	3.8
(b) Services	3.0	3.6	4.6	5.8	6.3	6.7
Defence science	6.2	7.0	8.3	10.6	11.4	12.9
Current material expenditures	2.9	3.3	3.8	4.6	5.1	5.7
Total wages	2.5	2.7	3.3	4.3	4.6	5.2
Social security deductions	0.1	0.2	0.2	0.3	0.3	0.3
Capital outlays	0.6	0.7	0.8	1.1	1.2	1.4
Social services	0.1	0.1	0.2	0.2	0.2	0.3
Defence burden	0.144	0.149	0.151	0.153	0.152	0.153
Total GNP	376.1	412.4	490.3	632.9	711.2	777.6
Produced national income	289.9	313.6	363.3	462.3	523.4	569.6
Depreciation deductions	31.6	38.2	53.7	78.1	90.0	103.4
Non-production income less transfers	37.6	42.1	50.5	63.1	66.8	71.4
(a) Non-production labour outlays	35.0	39.3	47.0	60.4	64.8	68.4
(b) Non-production profit	7.8	8.8	11.0	12.7	12.7	14.5
(c) Production transfers	5.2	6.0	7.5	10.0	10.7	11.5
Defence wages	17.0	18.5	22.8	29.4	31.0	33.2

Sources: Tables 2.1.2–2.1.8, and text.

Table 2.1.2. Estimation of the investment residual (in billions of current roubles)

	1965	1970	1971	1972	1973	1974	1975	1982
1. Total fixed investment	52.7	87.4	93.6	95.3	99.4	106.8	115.0	154.4
2. (a) Construction	33.6	57.5	61.9	61.7	64.3	68.8	74.1	90.7
3. (b) M&E investment	16.0	25.3	26.7	28.6	30.0	32.5	35.6	57.4
4. M&E domestic	13.6	20.7	22.5	23.7	25.0	26.6	27.8	40.9
5. M&E imported	2.4	4.6	4.2	5.0	5.0	5.7	7.9	16.5
6. (c) M&E commissions	1.8	2.9	3.0	3.2	3.3	3.4	3.5	4.4
7. (d) Other investment	1.3	1.8	2.0	1.7	1.8	2.0	1.7	1.9
8. Uninstalled capital	4.0	6.5	7.1	9.2	4.2	6.3	7.0	3.4
9. (a) Unfinished construction	2.9	4.5	6.1	7.8	2.4	5.1	5.6	0.9
10. (b) Investment write-offs	1.1	2.0	1.1	1.4	1.8	1.2	1.4	2.5
11. Replaced capital	17.3	25.7	28.6	31.0	35.0	38.8	45.8	75.4
12. Estimated NFI (1-8-11)	31.4	55.1	57.9	55.2	60.2	61.6	62.2	75.6
13. Official NFI	27.9	51.1	53.7	55.2	60.2	61.6	62.2	n.a.
14. 12-13	3.5	4.0	4.2	0.0	0.0	0.0	0.0	4.0
15. Other expenditures (27)−[(13)+(28)+(9)]	12.5	13.7	13.6	9.3	14.2	14.0	14.9	29.5
16. Strategic reserves (15−14)	8.8	9.5	11.5	9.3	14.2	14.0	14.9	25.5
Supporting data:								
17. Construction GVO	40.0	67.6	74.7	77.4	80.9	86.4	91.7	115.1
18. Capital repair	6.2	9.5	10.4	11.0	12.0	13.0	14.0	20.8
19. Unfinished production	0.2	0.6	2.4	4.8	4.5	4.6	3.7	3.6
20. Investment construction	39.1	56.1	60.9	64.9	66.9	70.9	75.0	86.7
21. Construction price index (2−14):(20)	0.765	0.95	0.95	0.95	0.96	0.97	0.985	1.00
22. M&E investment construction	17.5	25.3	26.6	28.8	31.1	34.1	37.1	55.9
23. (a) Domestic	14.5	20.7	22.5	24.4	26.9	29.5	29.7	43.5
24. Domestic M&E price index	0.94	1.00	1.00	0.975	0.93	0.90	0.94	0.94
25. (b) Imported	3.0	4.6	4.1	4.4	4.2	4.6	7.4	12.4
26. Imported M&E price index	0.80	1.01	1.035	1.125	1.18	1.24	1.085	1.33
27. Total investment fund	50.2	84.2	87.1	85.3	97.6	98.2	96.6	134.4
28. Additions, inventories	6.9	14.9	13.8	13.0	20.8	17.5	13.9	32.4
29. (a) State co-operatives	5.1	12.8	11.7	12.1	18.3	15.5	13.3	29.8
30. (b) Collective	1.6	1.8	1.7	0.8	2.2	1.8	0.5	2.2
31. (c) Private	0.2	0.3	0.4	0.1	0.3	0.2	0.1	0.4

Table 2.1.3.   Estimation of consumption residuals (in billions of current roubles)

	1970	1972	1980	1982
1. Total consumption	201.3	225.4	345.5	378.5
2. Population current consumption	171.5	191.0	287.7	314.2
3. Household current consumption	165.0	184.0	275.7	301.3
4. (a) Retail trade	146.7	166.4	256.3	280.5
5. (b) Utilities	1.5	1.7	2.8	3.4
6. (c) Agricultural consumption-in-kind	15.9	15.1	15.0	15.9
7. (d) In-village consumption	0.6	0.5	1.1	1.0
8. (e) Other consumption-in-kind	0.4	0.4	0.5	0.5
9. Current consumption residual	6.5	7.0	12.0	13.0
10. (a) Wholesale trade	4.5	5.8	8.9	9.7
11. (b) Retail trade	1.8	2.0	2.8	3.0
12. (c) In-village consumption	0.2	0.2	0.3	0.3
13. Housing depreciation	6.3	7.2	11.5	12.5
14. Current material purchases	17.3	19.7	33.0	37.3
15. (a) Education, culture, health	7.5	8.4	14.0	15.8
16. (b) HC&E and T&C	4.6	5.1	10.4	11.7
17. (c) Science, administration	5.2	6.2	8.6	9.8
18. Depreciation in non-productive sectors	6.1	7.6	13.3	14.5
19. (a) Education, culture, health	2.0	2.3	3.5	3.8
20. (b) HC&E and T&C	2.3	2.9	4.9	5.2
21. (c) Science	0.6	0.8	1.4	1.6
22. (d) Administration	1.2	1.6	3.5	3.8
23. ——State administration	0.3	0.4	0.5	0.6
24. ——Non-productive depreciation residual	0.9	1.2	3.0	3.2
Supporting data:				
25. Total retail trade	159.4	181.0	278.0	304.3
26. (a) Population	151.4	172.1	265.5	290.8
27. ——Second-hand goods	0.8	1.5	3.8	4.5
28. ——Producer goods	2.1	2.2	2.6	2.8
29. ——Consumer goods	148.5	168.4	259.1	283.5
30. (b) Institutions	8.0	8.9	12.5	13.5
31. Private agricultural income	23.5	23.6	26.9	28.9
32. (a) Monetary	7.1	8.3	11.5	12.1
33. (b) Non-monetary	16.4	15.3	15.4	16.8
34. Residual housing stock	179.7	202.9	333.1	366.0
35. Total depreciation rate	3.5	3.5	3.5	3.4

Some economists suggest that 'other expenditures' contain only net additions to weapon stocks.[14] If these economists are correct, then one must search for weapon depreciation within the limits of published national income. This depreciation must equal the difference between the total value of weapons produced and net additions to weapon stocks. All available evidence indicates that there is simply no place for weapon depreciation in Soviet national income accounts. The depreciation residual found in the total for public consumption cannot represent weapon depreciation for two reasons: it is too small, and it contains replacement and repair of mounted M&E that are included in the

Table 2.1.4. Estimation of investment in defence fixed capital (in billions of roubles)

	1970	1972	1975	1982	1984
Constant 1969, 1973 and 1984 prices					
Total investment	24.8	26.8	29.9	37.2	47.6
(a) Construction	22.6	24.4	26.9	31.4	41.0
(b) M&E	2.2	2.4	3.0	5.8	6.6
Housing—communal	16.1	17.5	19.6	24.2	32.0
(a) Construction	15.8	17.2	19.2	23.5	31.1
(b) M&E	0.3	0.3	0.4	0.7	0.9
Education and health	4.8	5.0	4.8	4.1	5.3
(a) Construction	4.5	4.6	4.4	3.4	4.4
(b) M&E	0.3	0.4	0.4	0.7	0.9
Science	1.1	1.3	1.9	3.2	3.6
(a) Construction	0.6	0.8	1.1	1.5	1.7
(b) M&E	0.5	0.5	0.8	1.7	1.9
Other	2.8	3.0	3.6	5.7	6.8
State administration	0.5	0.5	0.6	0.9	1.1
Defence sectors	2.3	2.5	3.0	4.8	5.7
(a) Construction	1.1	1.2	1.4	2.1	2.8
(b) M&E	1.2	1.3	1.6	2.7	2.9
Current prices					
Defence sectors	2.2	2.4	2.8	4.8	5.7
(a) Construction	1.0	1.1	1.3	2.1	2.6
(b) M&E	1.2	1.3	1.5	2.7	3.1
Total M&E commissions	2.9	3.2	3.5	4.4	4.7
(a) Civilian	1.2	1.3	1.4	1.8	1.9
(b) Military	1.7	1.9	2.1	2.6	2.8

Table 2.1.5. Social services (in billions of current roubles)

	1970	1972	1975	1982	1984
Total social services	55.0	62.8	77.7	111.7	122.7
State-co-operative employees	44.8	50.7	62.7	92.7	102.6
Collective farmers	5.8	6.6	8.0	9.1	9.6
Military	4.4	5.4	7.0	9.9	10.5
Education and culture	18.7	21.2	25.1	34.0	36.2
(a) Civilian	17.1	19.3	22.8	30.9	32.9
(b) Military	1.6	1.9	2.3	3.1	3.3
Health and social sections	10.5	11.0	13.9	20.3	21.3
(a) Civilian	9.5	9.8	12.3	18.1	19.0
(b) Military	1.0	1.2	1.6	2.2	2.3
Pensions and allowances	22.3	26.3	33.6	49.6	56.4
(a) Civilian	20.9	24.5	31.2	46.0	52.6
(b) Military	1.4	1.8	2.4	3.6	3.8
Housing	3.4	3.9	4.9	7.9	8.8
(a) Civilian	3.0	3.4	4.2	6.9	7.7
(b) Military	0.4	0.5	0.7	1.0	1.1

Table 2.1.6. Structure of the investment residual (in billions of current roubles)

	Total supply	Intermediate	Consumption						
			house-holds	Organi-zations	Army	Investments & losses	Inventories	Exports	Strategic reserves
1972									
Heavy industry	323.2	209.0	24.6	11.4	3.8	42.2	5.9	13.5	12.8
Power	14.1	10.5	1.7	1.1	0.1	—	—	0.1	0.6
Fuels	39.7	32.6	1.6	1.6	0.4	—	0.4	2.7	0.4
Metals	45.7	40.7	—	0.8	—	—	0.2	3.6	0.9
Chemicals	32.2	24.6	1.9	1.5	0.5	—	0.4	1.1	2.2
MBMW	127.0	52.7	10.0	3.3	2.6	41.6	4.1	4.5	8.2
Wood	26.2	19.0	3.7	0.9	0.3	0.6	0.4	1.1	0.2
Construction	23.6	22.5	—	0.7	0.1	—	-0.2	0.1	0.3
Other	14.7	6.4	5.7	1.0	0.2	—	0.4	0.3	—
Light industry	99.4	47.7	43.6	2.2	0.9	0.2	3.0	1.8	—
Food industry	130.1	38.0	85.7	4.8	2.0	—	-2.2	1.8	—
Agriculture	101.3	69.3	27.9	0.9	0.3	4.4	1.3	0.7	-3.5
Construction	77.4	—	—	—	—	72.5	1.1	—	3.8
Other	5.3	2.5	2.2	0.8	—	—	0.1	—	—
Total	**736.6**	**366.5**	**184.0**	**19.7**	**7.0**	**119.3**	**9.2**	**17.8**	**13.1**
1982									
Heavy Industry	630.4	384.0	49.7	23.4	7.6	80.1	16.0	44.5	25.0
Power	27.8	19.7	3.5	2.5	0.2	—	—	—	1.4
Fuels	93.5	70.6	2.2	3.3	0.8	—	0.5	15.5	0.8
Metals	81.7	72.4	—	1.9	—	—	0.9	4.7	1.8
Chemicals	63.0	47.9	3.1	2.9	1.2	—	0.6	3.6	3.7
MBMW	250.8	94.3	20.7	6.6	4.1	79.4	12.3	17.6	16.0
Wood	44.1	29.9	7.2	2.1	0.6	0.9	0.7	2.1	0.7
Construction	42.1	38.7	—	1.1	0.3	—	1.0	0.2	0.7
Other	27.4	10.5	13.0	3.0	0.4	—	0.2	0.4	—
Light industry	165.7	77.1	74.4	4.2	1.7	—	5.2	2.7	—
Food industry	200.1	53.9	132.6	7.2	3.2	—	2.5	0.7	—
Agriculture	161.0	106.8	39.7	2.1	0.5	5.0	5.1	1.3	0.5
Construction	115.1	—	—	—	—	107.5	3.6	—	4.0
Other	8.3	3.4	3.9	0.6	—	—	0.3	0.1	—
Total	**1 280.6**	**625.2**	**300.3**	**37.5**	**13.0**	**192.9**	**32.9**	**49.3**	**29.7**

published fixed capital stock. All weapons, however, are excluded from fixed capital stock.

While it is impossible to determine whether CIA analysts grossly over-estimate prices on Soviet weapons without more information on how they arrive at these prices, there is much evidence to support the hypothesis that weapon production is excluded from published Soviet statistics: (a) 'other expenditures' contain outlays on materials produced by sectors which do not manufacture weapon systems; (b) households return more money to the state than they officially receive from it; (c) total revenues of the social security system significantly exceed payments made by sectors covered in the official statistics; and (d) the total labour force is larger than the official labour force.

IV.   Integration of national income with production, financial and demographic statistics

The military component of the total investment residual cannot be estimated using published national income statistics alone. It is necessary to integrate published national income with production statistics containing data on the supply and intermediate use of goods. The integration procedure is performed in table 2.1.6 for 1972 and 1982. The results indicate that the total value of intermediate products supplied to the defence industry increased from 12.8 to 25.0 b.r. Of these amounts, the value of MBMW and chemical products comprised 10.4 and 19.7 b.r. The remaining 2.4 and 5.3 b.r. represent materials produced by non-defence sectors. It is clear that the value of Soviet weapons could not be as low as 20.0 b.r. in 1982. One thus must conclude that most of the total investment residual consists of intermediate goods supplied to defence industries. The derived data on the structure of these supplies indicate that it changed little, despite large price increases on industrial materials in 1982.[15] Presumably, these price increases were offset by rapid technological changes in Soviet defence industries.

The fact that national income includes intermediate goods used in weapon production is confirmed by the compiled data on household budgets presented in table 2.1.7. Estimation results indicate that the total wages of defence sectors excluded from official statistics comprise more than 9 per cent of total annual wages. The traditional view is that the official statistics only exclude wages of the military and state security personnel. The proposed hypothesis is that the official statistics also exclude wages of employees engaged in the production of weapons for domestic use.

Total hidden wages increased from 14.4 b.r. in 1970 to 26.3 b.r. in 1982. These hidden wages clearly far exceed combined wages of all employees working for the military, the KGB and internal security. CIA analysts estimated that total military pay, including that received by draftees, equalled only 3.5 b.r. in 1970.[16] Draftees were paid 0.4–0.5 b.r., while the professional military received the remaining 3.0 b.r. The number of professional military equalled around 1.2 million; their average monthly salary was thus approx-

Table 2.1.7.   Soviet household budgets (in billions of current roubles)

	1970	1975	1982	1984
1. State-co-operative income from SCF	46.0	64.4	95.1	105.2
2. (a) State-co-operative families	44.9	63.1	93.4	103.4
3. (b) Collective families	1.1	1.3	1.7	1.8
4. One-time bonuses	1.2	1.7	2.5	2.6
5. 2–4	43.7	61.4	90.9	100.8
6. 7:5	3.35	3.25	3.01	2.87
7. Regular wages (5×6)	146.3	198.7	273.6	289.3
8. Official state-co-operative wages	131.3	178.2	244.7	258.6
9. (a) Productive	98.0	132.6	180.7	191.3
10. (b) Non-productive	33.3	45.6	64.0	67.3
11. Added state-co-operative wages	4.4	6.0	8.3	8.9
12. (a) Construction	3.0	4.3	5.9	6.2
13. (b) Agriculture	0.3	0.3	0.5	0.6
14. (c) Services	1.1	1.4	1.9	2.1
15. 8+11	135.7	184.2	253.0	267.5
16. (a) State-co-operative families	132.7	181.3	248.7	262.9
17. (b) Collective families	3.0	3.0	4.3	4.6
18. Hidden regular wages (7–16)	13.6	18.4	24.9	26.4
19. 18:7×100	9.3	9.3	9.1	9.1
20. Collective wages	14.5	15.9	18.4	20.6
21. Other official earnings	3.6	4.8	6.5	6.9
22. (a) Productive	3.0	3.9	5.3	5.6
23. (b) Non-productive	0.6	0.9	1.2	1.3
24. Total official wages (15+20+21)	153.8	204.9	277.5	295.0
25. Other hidden earnings	0.4	0.6	0.8	0.9
26. Draftees' pay	0.4	0.5	0.6	0.7
27. Total hidden wages (18+25+26)	14.4	19.5	26.3	28.0
28. Other monetary income	31.6	47.8	66.8	77.1
29. (a) Private income	6.3	9.2	10.1	12.6
30. (b) Pensions, stipends, etc.	23.6	35.7	52.1	59.1
31. (c) Interest on savings	1.1	1.9	3.3	3.9
32. (d) Other income	0.6	1.0	1.3	1.5
33. Total income (24+27+28)	199.8	272.2	372.1	401.1
34. Total outlays	186.4	253.4	357.6	382.3
35. (a) Retail trade and utilities	150.4	202.5	286.7	305.6
36. (b) Non-productive services	17.1	23.8	33.3	35.6
37. (c) Dues and insurance	3.5	5.4	6.8	7.9
38. (d) Budgetary receipts	14.4	20.3	28.8	31.1
39. (e) Other	1.0	1.4	2.0	2.1
40. Additions to savings (33−34)	13.4	18.8	14.5	18.8
41. (a) Official savings	8.2	12.1	8.6	14.6
42. (b) Unofficial savings	5.2	6.7	5.9	4.2

imately 205 roubles in 1970. State security personnel and employees of the Defence Ministry, also excluded from the official labour force, received wages totalling 1.2–1.5 b.r.

During the observed period average wages in the Soviet economy grew 1.5 times, while the size of the military apparently grew by no more than 0.5 million.[17] It thus can be estimated that total pay received by draftees and those employees of the military administration (Defence Ministry, KGB and

Ministry of International Affairs) who are excluded from official labour statistics increased from 4.7–5.0 b.r. in 1970 to 8.2–8.5 b.r. in 1982. The remaining wages—around 9.5 b.r. in 1970 and 18 b.r. in 1982—were received by defence industrial employees who are also excluded from the official labour force. Of these amounts, regular wages comprised around 9.0 and 17.5 b.r. and other earnings 0.3–0.5 b.r.

Table 2.1.8. Social security revenues (in billions of current roubles)

	1970	1972	1982	1984
Total state social security revenues	9.8	11.3	22.3	24.5
Revenues of published state sectors	8.3	9.4	18.8	20.7
Production sectors	6.5	7.3	15.4	16.9
Industry	3.9	4.2	9.2	9.8
Agriculture	0.5	0.6	1.2	1.4
Transportation & communications	0.7	0.8	1.6	1.8
Construction	1.0	1.2	2.1	2.4
Trade & distribution and other production	0.5	0.5	1.3	1.5
Non-production service sectors	1.8	2.0	3.4	3.8
Revenues of unpublished state sectors	1.5	1.8	3.5	3.8

Table 2.1.9. Soviet demographic trends (in millions of persons)

	July 1970 total	Males	Females	July 1982 total	Males	Females
Total population	243.0	112.0	131.0	270.0	127.5	142.5
Outside labour force	124.0	52.5	71.5	127.5	54.5	73.0
Children under 16	70.0	36.0	34.0	67.5	34.5	33.0
(a) School	40.0			35.0		
(b) Pre-school	9.0			15.0		
(c) At home	21.0			17.5		
Full-time students	12.0	6.0	6.0	13.5	6.5	7.0
(a) High school	5.5			5.0		
(b) College	2.5			3.0		
(c) Technical school	2.0			3.0		
(d) Professional school	2.0			2.5		
Non-working pensioners	32.5	10.5	22.0	40.5	13.5	27.0
Dependent adults	9.5		9.5	6.0		6.0
Drifters	0.3		0.3	0.3		0.3
Official labour force	108.0	63.0	55.0	129.0	63.0	66.0
Public sectors	107.0	62.5	54.5	128.0	63.0	65.0
Self-employed	1.8	0.2	1.6	0.7	0.1	0.6
Net unemployment	2.5	1.0	1.5	3.0	1.3	1.7
Unemployment	3.5	1.5	2.0	4.0	1.8	2.2
Double-counted persons	1.0	0.5	0.5	1.0	0.5	0.5
Unaccounted persons	8.5	7.0	1.5	10.5	8.7	1.8
Non-working prisoners	0.8	0.7	0.1	0.8	0.7	0.1
Armed forces	4.0	3.8	0.2	5.0	4.8	0.2
State security	0.5	0.3	0.2	0.5	0.3	0.2
Defence industries	3.2	2.2	1.0	4.2	2.9	1.3

These findings are confirmed by the discovery of demographic and social security gaps presented in tables 2.1.8 and 2.1.9. The demographic gap points to the existence of the defence industrial labour force outside the official labour force. During 1970–82 defence industries employed between 3.2–3.5 and 4.2–4.5 million persons. Their average monthly salary increased from 215 roubles in 1970 to 325 roubles in 1982. In comparison, the average monthly salary in the civilian MBMW sector increased from 135 to 200 roubles during 1970–82. Hidden state social security revenues increased during the observed period from 1.5 to 3.5 b.r., indicating the increase of social security deduction rates from 10 to 14 per cent. The increase took place in 1982 as in most other sectors of the Soviet economy.

V.   Estimating outlays on defence science

In Western systems of national accounts, total defence budgets usually (though not always) include outlays on military RDT&E which are called 'defence science' in Soviet national accounts. Western economists have had difficulties estimating outlays on defence science because of the absence of any data on extra-budgetary financing of military research. The thesis that defence industries are budget-supported suggests that all defence science is financed from the All-Union budget.

Total current outlays on civilian and defence science financed from the All-Union budget increased from 5.8 b.r. in 1970 to 10.3 b.r. in 1982. Most applied civilian research is on so-called '*khozraschyot*' (self-financing), which implies the absence of budgetary financing. Total outlays on basic research increased from 1.2 to 2.3 b.r. during the observed period.[18] At least half of basic research is in the area of weapon production and military-related space. It thus follows that most All-Union budgetary allocations on science must be included in total Soviet military outlays. If one assumes that applied civilian research financed from All-Union budgets is equal in size to basic research financed from All-Republic budgets, then outlays on defence science equalled 5.2 b.r. in 1970 and 9.4 b.r. in 1982. Some outlays on defence science, amounting to 0.3–0.6 b.r., are also hidden within budgetary outlays on geological works. Total current outlays on defence science then increased from 5.5 b.r. in 1970 to 10.0 b.r. in 1982 or 45 to 50 per cent of total current outlays on science. Capital outlays on both civilian and defence science are hidden in budgetary outlays on industry, while capital outlays on space fall under budgetary outlays on transportation and communication (T&C) services.

VI.   Do Soviet armament industries earn profit?

A final issue that must be resolved before estimating total Soviet military expenditures is whether Soviet defence industries producing weapons for domestic use earn a profit. D. Burton and other former US intelligence analysts claim to have incontrovertible evidence that prices of Soviet weapons include profit.[19] It would be difficult to dispute their claim if they revealed documents containing data on the structure of prices in the defence industry. But such documents do not exist, because planners make their own estimates based on enterprises data on total output, including defence, and the cost of total production input. Secret sections of these reports specify what portion of total production input was involved in weapon production. By analysing these reports, planners are able to compute production costs for the output of producer, consumer and defence goods. In the absence of covert information on the structure of prices of Soviet weapons, Western intelligence analysts thus can derive their knowledge only from the open Soviet literature or the testimony of *émigrés* who once worked in defence production plants.

Burton indeed quoted one Soviet writer, Sokolov, to the effect that defence enterprises began to receive profits after the price reforms of the late 1960s.[20] But Soviet writers cannot mention current practices in the defence production sector. The one notable exception was made by General Secretary Brezhnev himself, when he revealed that consumer goods comprise 42 per cent of the total defence industrial output.[21] The defence enterprises that Sokolov and other Soviet writers refer to are production units subordinated to the USSR Defence Ministry, which produce civilian goods for the armed forces.[22] These goods are registered in the same way as consumer goods produced by civilian ministries.

Defence industries reap large profits but from the production of consumer durables. Some of these profits may be used to finance weapon production. It is doubtful, however, that planners would allow defence industries to use these profits to finance armament production because planners need to maintain centralized control over defence finances. The profits must instead be extracted to the state budget, just like profits earned by civilian consumer industries. Defence industries in turn must receive funds directly from the state budget to finance weapon production—rather than from the USSR Defence Ministry, which never receives funds to pay for weapons.[23] In contrast, foreign trade organizations pay directly for armaments produced for export.

Since no evidence can be marshalled to verify the intelligence analysts' view that prices on Soviet weapons contain profit, the view must be checked for consistency with the conceptual framework of Soviet national accounts. It is clear that prices of weapons produced for export purposes must include profit, as do prices of any other unsubsidized export product. Export of weapons brings foreign trade revenues and hence must be included in the published statistics. However, if planners treat production of weapons for domestic consumption in the same way as non-productive services, then the issue must be settled by analysing planners' treatment of revenues received by non-productive sectors.

In the service sector of the Soviet economy only services financed by households receive any sizeable profit. Since the price reforms of the late 1960s, science organizations serving production sectors must sign enough contracts to finance their current expenses. The available evidence indicates that these organizations earn negligible profit in excess of their current expenses. All other Soviet non-production sectors serving public rather than private needs are budget-supported, that is, they receive most of their funds from the state budget. Thus, applied research organizations serving budget-supported sectors are themselves budget-supported. Since planners treat production of weapons as a non-productive activity performed for the Defence Ministry, enterprises making these weapons are themselves budget-supported. Hence, prices on weapons exclude profit. With this accounting trick, planners are able to reduce significantly the total value of produced weapons that appears in their own version of Soviet national accounts.

VII.   Estimating total military expenditures

The presented evidence uniformly supports the hypothesis that the value of weapons produced for domestic use is excluded from the published statistics. This conclusion invalidates traditional approaches to estimating total Soviet military expenditures as well as the size of the Soviet defence burden. In order to compare the size of the Soviet economy and defence burden with that of other countries, Western economists expand the published total for national income by the sum of value added in non-production services and military pay. Western economists thus underestimate the size of the Soviet economy by labour outlays included in prices on weapons produced for domestic use. These labour outlays are also excluded from published national income.

Total Soviet military expenditures are estimated in table 2.1.1 in two ways: as the sum of total outlays on weapon production and space, military administration and science; and as the sum of total material, capital and labour outlays in defence sectors. Current material purchases of weapon producers and defence construction are estimated in table 2.1.2, consumption of goods and social services by the armed forces in tables 2.1.3 and 2.1.5, capital outlays on defence industry, space and M&E commissioned by the armed forces in table 2.1.4, and total wages and social security deductions of defence sectors excluded from the official statistics in tables 2.1.7 and 2.1.8. These totals are disaggregated into defence industry and military administration using published intelligence data on the size and pay of the Soviet military.

There is no information on the structure of defence science outlays. It is assumed here that ratios between applied and basic research and between current and capital outlays are the same for civilian and defence science. This assumption makes it possible to apply the estimated structure of total outlays on science to disaggregating the derived total into material, capital and labour outlays.

There are some additional items in the total Soviet defence budget that still have not been discussed. The military administers an extensive T&C network, whose functions include transporting weapons and troops, servicing military communication lines and many other military-related functions. In the official statistics, military T&C is aggregated with sectors serving households as non-production T&C services. It is possible to estimate outlays on military T&C as the difference between the total volume of non-production T&C services and non-military purchases of these services.[24]

Capital outlays on science are relatively small in size and cannot possibly contain construction expenditures on space facilities, whose function is predominantly military. At the same time, capital outlays on budget-supported T&C sectors are relatively large in size and are likely to contain capital outlays on space. It is also likely that some construction of space facilities run by the military are hidden with defence construction.[25]

Total military expenditures also include current material purchases by the central military administration (probably no more than 0.3–0.5 b.r.), hidden with those of the state administration, and the construction of military housing facilities.[26]

VIII.   Estimating the defence burden

Economists estimate defence burden as the ratio between total military expenditures and GNP. The difference between GNP and the official Soviet national income (without planned losses) equals the sum of depreciation deductions, labour outlays and profit of non-production sectors, reduced by transfers from production to non-production sectors, and defence labour outlays. These transfers are estimated here as residual revenues of civilian production sectors.[27] The above estimates indicate that the defence burden increased from 14.4 per cent in 1970 to 15.1 per cent in 1972 and to 15.3 per cent during 1980–84.

IX.   CIA estimates of Soviet military expenditures

The CIA offers the most widely accepted estimates of the Soviet defence burden. According to the most recent CIA publication, the Soviet defence burden increased from 12–14 per cent in the early 1970s to 15–17 per cent in the early 1980s.[28] CIA analysts supposedly arrive at their results following two independent methods of calculation, both of which have never been revealed in detail in the openly published literature. The main CIA method, which apparently led to the above-quoted results, is based on pricing individual weapon systems. The second CIA method is based on published Soviet statistics which CIA analysts 'translate' into the GNP format familiar to Western readers.

As estimated by CIA analysts, Soviet GNP increased from 383.3 b.r. in 1970 to 720 b.r. in 1982, while total Soviet military expenditures increased from 45–54 to 108–122 b.r. during the same years.[29] CIA estimates for 1970 were confirmed by an intelligence report said to have been received from a source within the Soviet Defence Ministry. According to this report, total military expenditures (probably excluding military pensions and some social services) were around 50 b.r. As estimated by the CIA, weapons comprised no less than

18 b.r., military construction 3 b.r., defence science and space 10 (5+5) b.r., operations and maintenance 9 b.r., and military personnel 10 b.r.[30] By 1982, the cost of weapons estimated by CIA analysts should have reached 46–51 b.r., military construction 4–5 b.r., defence science and space 23–26 b.r., and military personnel, operations and maintenance 35–40 b.r.[31]

It is impossible to compare these CIA estimates of Soviet weapons with other CIA estimates that are based on reconstructed Soviet national accounts for three reasons. First, the CIA still has not published its analysis of the Soviet GNP by end-use in current 1982 prices. Second, the published analysis for 1970 contains only one explicit reference to weapons as being contained in the residual for the GNP by end-use.[32] This residual declined to 7 per cent of the GNP estimated in constant factor cost prices during the 1970s; a non-credible proposition.[33] Third, the reconstructed GNP accounts presented by the CIA contain unidentified gaps in both incomes and outlays that make it difficult to establish the Soviet weapon procurement bill with any certainty.[34]

X.   Conclusion: comparison of NEB-based and CIA estimates

The NEB-based estimates of total military expenditures are within the upper bound of CIA estimates for the early 1970s and are within the lower bound of CIA estimates for the early 1980s. The NEB-based and CIA estimates of the total Soviet GNP are quite close in size if account is taken of the fact that CIA analysts include transfers in the GNP. The NEB-based approach, then, leads to a figure for the defence burden (in 1982) that is also within the lower bound of CIA estimates.

Factors causing this discrepancy between NEB-based and CIA estimates are difficult to analyse for several reasons. First, the CIA has never publicly confirmed the structure of its estimates of total military expenditures in current roubles. Second, whereas most outlays on the military space programme are hidden in Soviet national accounts outside the science sector, CIA analysts group space and science outlays into one expenditure item. Third, it is unclear whether CIA analysts account for outlays on social services provided to military sectors, including military education, health, culture and pensions. Fourth, CIA analysts account for a rate of profit which they believe is included in the total price of weapon systems produced for domestic use. As was emphasized above, in Soviet national accounts, profit is excluded from the total price of these weapons.

Before CIA analysts reveal more details about their methodology, it is possible to make only a tentative comparison between NEB-based and CIA estimates of particular types of Soviet military expenditure. If one assumes that most outlays on the military space programme are treated by planners as part of outlays on weapon production, then NEB-based and CIA estimates of the weapons bill are the same. NEB-based estimates of outlays on military administration also corroborate CIA estimates. It appears, however, that CIA analysts overestimate the growth of expenditures on defence science.[35] The comparison of NEB-based estimates with the upper bound of CIA estimates points to two possibilities: either CIA analysts overestimate inflation in Soviet defence industries or the NEB data lead to estimates that are intentionally deflated by Soviet planners. The latter possibility is more likely, given the Soviet policy of artificially lowering official prices on weapons.[36]

Notes and references

[1] Refer to *Soviet Military Relations*. Proceedings of a workshop on 7–8 July 1982, sponsored jointly by the Subcommittee on International Trade, Finance and Security Economics of the Joint Economic Committee (JEC) of the US Congress and Congressional Research Service of the Library of Congress (US Government Printing Office: Washington, DC, 1983), pp. 208–9. Richard Kaufman, who serves on the staff of the JEC, wrote in his submitted note that: 'The CIA says that its direct cost estimates have a 10–15 percent range of error. A much greater range of error, 35 percent or higher, is assigned to a complementary methodology involving the analysis of Soviet published statistics to derive the implicit cost of defense. The usefulness of the latter methodology is seriously limited partly because of the large margin of error.' (p. 8). His note corroborates a view expressed by Paul Welsh, a senior CIA official, who said that: 'The residual approach is subject to much greater uncertainty than our direct cost estimates [as it leads to] something that is not at all precise and in some instances influenced more by the assumptions made than by the information base'. (p. 208).

[2] First, Lee, W., *The Estimation of Soviet Military Expenditures, 1955–1975. An Unconventional Approach* (Praeger: New York, 1977); and then, Wiles, P., 'Soviet military finance', in *The Economics of Soviet Arms*, STICERD Occasional Paper 7 (Imediaprint Limited: London, 1985), attempted to challenge the traditional view with the understandable aim of reconciling Soviet national accounts with the mounting evidence of Soviet military buildup. Lee introduced the method of estimating defence machinery as the difference between the total supply of machinery products and their civilian end-use. While Lee's work appeared to confirm many intelligence assessments of Soviet military preparations, it poorly withstood a test for estimation errors. Lee was correctly criticized for either omitting or grossly underestimating several large end-uses of machinery that cannot be attributed to weapon procurement, such as capital repair, consumption and exports. After enhancing Lee's approach, this researcher still finds a considerable gap, though much smaller than that discovered by Lee.

   While researchers focused on numerous estimation errors found in Lee's work, they paid little attention to the narrow scope of Lee's approach, which is its main weakness. Any gap found in the end-use of machinery products must be compared with gaps found in Soviet national income accounts. National income constitutes the total amount of resources available for consumption, net investment and defence. If national income contains the total value of produced weapons, then by definition any gap found by Lee in his analysis of final demand for machinery products must be smaller than gaps found in national income. Otherwise, Soviet national accounts lose all their inner logic based on the equality between supplied and purchased goods. In sum, gaps found in Soviet national income accounts must serve as control totals for users of Lee's approach rather than the other way around.

   In an attempt to reconcile essentially Lee's approach with national income accounts, Wiles suggested dividing weapon production into two parts: net additions to weapon stocks that he found in other expenditures and weapons write-offs that, as he speculated, are hidden in depreciation accounts of production enterprises. Wiles's original argument of treating weapons as capital stock was based on the idea (here believed to be fallacious) that Soviet planners treat soldiers as productive workers and their weapons as fixed capital stock engaged in the production of national income. It is unclear how weapons can be used to produce or to deliver goods to their end-users. Who is the consumer of soldiers' destructive activities? While in his revised work Wiles admits that there is no place for soldiers' wages in total income of productive employees, he still insists that planners siphon from depreciation accounts to pay for weapons write-offs.

It appears to this author that on the one hand Wiles confuses production and financial statistics and on the other hand does not acknowledge the interconnection between these two statistics. Published depreciation accounts belong to the financial statistics. Even assuming that planners siphon some money from these accounts to pay for weapons write-offs, Wiles would still have to find how planners hide these write-offs in final demand for produced goods. For example, the Soviet industry produces 100 weapons, of which 70 are entered as net additions to weapon stocks. All 100 weapons must appear as final demand for produced goods. Otherwise, the value of produced goods would exceed the value of supplied goods. By definition the remaining 30 weapons cannot be found in the intermediate product.

As Wiles suggested, the only place where these 30 weapons can possibly be found is depreciation of capital stock engaged in the production of national income. But all depreciations of productive capital can be accounted for in input-output rows registering components of prices on particular goods. Weapons write-offs cannot be part of capital depreciated in the process of producing weapons. Moreover, the comparison of financial and input-output statistics indicates that most depreciation funds formed by production enterprises are entered as payments to replace or repair productive capital.

Is published Soviet national income purposefully underestimated? A positive answer implies a discrepancy between production and national income statistics which destroys the entire inner logic of Soviet national accounts. To preserve that logic, planners would have to remove the assembly of weapons from production as well as from national income statistics. But in this case Lee would not find his huge gap anyway because the entire value added of defence production sectors would remain outside published statistics and thus outside Lee's scrutiny.

[3] Refers to paper 2.3 by economist Gérard Duchêne and paper 2.4 by economist Kiichi Mochizuki, both in this volume.

[4] See note 1. The estimation error apparently results from uncertainties in the CIA's knowledge of Soviet prices on weapons and defence science outlays.

[5] For example, see Bor, M., *Effektivnost' Obshchestvennogo Proizvodstva i Problemy Optimal'nogo Planirovaniya* (Mysl': Moscow, 1972), p. 72; and Zalkind, A. (ed.) *Dva Podrazdeleniya Obshchestvennogo Produkta* (Statistika: Moscow, 1976), p. 24.

[6] Zalkind (note 5), p. 24.

[7] Zalkind (note 5), p. 135. Also see Sobol', V., *Ocherki Po Voprosam Balansa Narodnogo Khozyaistva* (Gosstatizdat: Moscow, 1960).

[8] *Vestnik Statistiki*, no. 4, 1966, p. 96.

[9] For example, see Turetskiy, Sh., *Planirovanie i Problema Balansa Narodnogo Khozyaistva* (Ekonomizdat: Moscow, 1961), pp. 252–3.

[10] See Sokolov, P. (ed.), *Voyenno-Ekonomicheskie Voprosy v Kurse Politekonomii* (Voenizdat: Moscow, 1968), and Wiles (note 2), pp. 59–61. For the exposition of Strumilin's view, refer to his 1950 lecture on the NEB printed in Strumilin, S., *Statistiko-Ekonomicheskie Ocherki* (Gosstatizdat: Moscow, 1958), pp. 132–3.

[11] This can be ascertained by the overview of quotations on the subject after 1962 compiled in Zalkind (note 5), p. 23.

[12] Wiles, P., 'Soviet military expenditures: where the skeletons lie buried', paper delivered at the Third World Congress for Soviet and East European Studies, Washington, DC (Oct. 1985), p. 16.

[13] See Freidmunt, Ye. and Eydel'man, M., *Ekonomicheskaya Statistika* (Statistika: Moscow, 1976), pp. 92–3.

[14] See note 2.

[15] For data on price changes refer to *Vestnik Statistiki*, no. 9 (1985), p. 80.

[16] US Central Intelligence Agency (CIA), *USSR: Measures of Economic Growth and Development, 1950–1980*, studies prepared for the use of the Joint Economic Committee, Congress of the United States, 8 Dec. 1982 (US Government Printing Office: Washington, DC, 1982).

[17] This assumption is based on the study of demographic trends presented in table 2.1.9.

[18] According to Zhamin, V., 'Yedinstvo Naucno-Tekhnicheskoy Politiki', *Voprosy Ekonomiki*, no. 12 (1984), p. 21, the ratio between outlays on basic science and total science outlays equalled 9–10 per cent. It is assumed here that this ratio actually decreased from 10 to 9 per cent.

[19] See Burton, D., 'Estimating Soviet defense spending', *Problems of Communism* (Mar.–Apr. 1983), p. 87.

[20] Sokolov, P. (ed.), *Politicheskaya Ekonomiya: Pervaya Faza Kommunisticheskogo Sposoba Proizvodstva* (Voenizdat: Moscow, 1974), p. 287.

[21] *Pravda* (31 Mar. 1971).

[22] For example, refer to Shermenev, M. (ed.), *Gosudarstvennyi Byudzhet SSSR* (Finansy: Moscow, 1978), p. 87.

[23] Suvorov, V., *Inside Soviet Military Intelligence* (The Macmillan Press Ltd: New York, 1984), p. 35.

[24] The total volume of non-production T&C services can be estimated as the difference between total T&C services (material, depreciation, labour outlays and profit) and the GSP produced in these services which is regularly reported in *Narkhoz*. The derived total apparently includes budgetary outlays on news media, which in budgetary statistics are financed together with the culture and arts sector. For data on household purchases of these services refer to *Narkhoz 1985*, p. 488, and Rutgeizer, V., *Resursy Neproizvodstvennoy Sfery* (Nauka: Moscow 1975), pp. 158 and 164. The published data on household purchases apparently excludes budgetary subsidies of urban transportation and purchases of T&C services by foreign tourists, whose combined size is assumed to be below 10 per cent of household purchases.

[25] Indeed, as estimated in table 2.1.4, total capital investment into the entire science complex averaged only 2.5 b.r. a year during the 1970s. It is inconceivable that construction of all Soviet research facilities and space centres could be of such a small size.

[26] These estimates are based on the assumption that 25 per cent of all state administration activities are in the military area and that the share of military housing corresponds to the share of military consumption in the total consumption by the Soviet population.

[27] In Soviet national income accounts total revenues received by production enterprises consist of four parts: (*a*) net revenues (net profit, turnover tax less subsidies, foreign trade revenues in domestic roubles, added taxes and various penalty payments); (*b*) social security deductions and insurance payments; (*c*) other earnings in agriculture and construction; (*d*) additions to foreign currency earnings converted into domestic roubles; and (*e*) transfers to science, education and other non-production service sectors financed by production enterprises. Total revenues are estimated as the difference between produced national income and total income of production labour. Net revenues are estimated using the regularly published *Narkhoz* data on financial accumulation. Deductions and payments are estimated using published rates and secondary Soviet sources. Other earnings are derived from secondary Soviet sources. Additions to foreign currency earnings are converted from gold to domestic roubles using the derived export and import conversion coefficients ('e' and 'i'). As specified by Soviet authors, 'e' is used when the balance of trade in gold roubles is positive, 'i' is used when it is negative. The derived total transfers must be reduced by the amount of material outlays of financed service sectors, since these outlays are excluded from the GNP. Total transfers are divided into these outlays and labour outlays using the derived data on the structure of total outlays on service sectors financed by the state.

[28] US Central Intelligence Agency and Defense Intelligence Agency, *The Soviet Economy Under a New Leader*, a Report Presented to the Subcommittee on Economic Resources, Competitiveness, and Security Economics of the Joint Economic Committee, US Congress, 19 Mar. 1986, p. 35.

[29] Note 28, p. 33. For 1970 estimates refer to US CIA (note 16), pp. 39 and 123.

[30] Rosefield, S., *False Science: Underestimating the Soviet Military Buildup. An Appraisal of the CIA's Direct Costing Effort*, 1960–1980 (Transaction Books: New Brunswick, 1983), p. 35.

[31] Estimated on the basis of trends published in US Central Intelligence Agency, *Soviet and US Defense Activities, 1970–1979: A Dollar Comparison*, a research paper (Jan. 1980), p. 6.

[32] US CIA (note 16), pp. 39.

[33] US CIA (note 16), p. 78.

[34] US CIA (note 16), p. 39.

[35] The brief description of the estimation procedure presented by CIA analysts (note 16, p. 121) points to the fact that outlays on science and space (and capital investment) are the most difficult to estimate with technological means of intelligence.

[36] This policy has two relevant facets: the absence of profits in prices on weapons, and the suppressing of prices on good quality capital resources supplied to the defence industry.

Appendix 2.1A.   Supporting tables

The supporting tables, included in paper 2.1, have been extracted from a larger study of the reconstructed Soviet national accounts for 1965–85. As is evident from this paper's discussion of total Soviet military expenditures, any reliable estimate must be based on the reconstruction of the entire system of Soviet national accounts. This is a cumbersome endeavour requiring the analysis of more than 100 source tables published in *Narkhoz*, other official statistical publications and in works written by Soviet economists. Such an analysis certainly oversteps the limits of the present discussion. The discussion of support tables will therefore focus only on major estimation steps leading to residuals that comprise components of total military expenditures. A bibliography of cited sources is listed at the end of this appendix.

Table 2.1.2.   Estimation of the investment residual

The investment residual (row 15) equals the difference between total investment fund (row 27) that is regularly published in *Narkhoz* and the sum of NFI (row 13), additions to unfinished construction (row 9) and additions to inventories (row 28). The NFI was published until 1975. The independently estimated NFI (row 12) equals the difference between total fixed investment (row 1) and the sum of uninstalled capital (row 8) and replaced capital (row 11). Total fixed investment equals the sum of new construction (row 2), M&E investment (row 3), M&E commissions (row 6) and other investment (row 7). New construction is estimated as the difference between total construction GVD (row 17) that is regularly published in *Narkhoz* and the sum of capital repair (row 18) and additions to unfinished production in construction (row 19). Capital repair of buildings and installations is estimated using data on repair rates (published by Senchagov, p. 124), *Narkhoz* data on the structure of fixed capital and depreciation deductions, and budgetary data on financing capital repair works. Additions of unfinished production in construction are estimated using *Narkhoz* data on inventories. Even though data on the structure of inventories in construction were last published for 1980, it can be estimated after that year by continuing established trends.

Total investment in M&E (row 3) equals the sum of investment in domestic (row 4) and imported (row 5) M&E. Domestic M&E is converted from constant prices (row 23) using the domestic M&E price index discussed below. Domestic M&E in constant prices equals the difference between total M&E in constant prices (row 22) that is regularly published in *Narkhoz* and imported M&E in constant prices (row 25). The latter equals the ratio between the derived imported M&E in current prices (row 5) and the derived price index for imported M&E (row 26). Data on imported M&E were estimated by combining data on imports of M&E in current (published in the VT) and constant (published by Sel'tsovskiy, p. 45) gold roubles with the derived data on the total import conversion coefficient (i), which was obtained using published national income data. The M&E 'i' decreased from 1.00 to around 0.85 in 1972–82. The comparison of *Narkhoz* editions indicates that in 1984 the combined 1973 M&E price index equalled 1.06. The derived M&E import price index equalled 1.45 in 1984, thus leading to the domestic M&E price index—0.94. There was little official price change in the domestic M&E production during 1982–84. In fact, most changes in the official MBMW price index that took place after 1973 happened in 1975–76. It is thus assumed that the domestic M&E index remained almost unchanged after 1976. In comparison, the official MBMW price index decreased 10 per cent during the same period.

M&E commissions were first obtained for the late 1960s and early 1970s as the difference between total additions of non-production capital (published by Rutgeizer, p. 127) and capital investment (converted into current prices using the derived price indices) in these sectors, reduced by additions of unfinished construction in these sectors. The trend established before the early 1970s is extrapolated for later years. Other investment (row 7) primarily consists of agricultural investment in gardening and additions of livestock that are published in *Narkhoz*. Uninstalled capital (row 8) equals the sum of additions to unfinished construction in state-co-operative and collective-private sectors (row 9) that is regularly published in *Narkhoz* and investment write-offs (row 10). The latter were first estimated in constant prices as the difference between capital investment and the sum of published installed capital and additions to unfinished construction. The conversion from constant to current prices is performed using the derived construction price index. Replaced capital (row 11) was estimated as the sum of depreciation deductions for capital replacement and 10 per cent of depreciation deductions for capital repair, both of which are regularly published in *Narkhoz*, the unamortized value of liquidated capital (using rates given by Masal'skiy, p. 44), capital replacement financed by the state budget (using rates given by Senchagov) and replacement of housing that was estimated as the difference between total depreciation and capital repair discussed above. Total depreciation rate for housing was first estimated for 1972 using the input-output data on total depreciation of non-production capital (estimated by Gallik, p. 5) and depreciation of capital operated by service sectors (published by Rutgeizer, p. 157). This rate was then extrapolated for other years using data on the trend in ownership of residential housing (published by Rutgeizer, p. 154).

The independently estimated NFI (row 12) can be successfully tested for 1972–75 by comparing it with the official NFI (row 13). The test fails before 1972, thus indicating that some new construction is excluded from the NFI. This is confirmed by comparing new construction in current prices (row 2) and in constant prices (row 20). It is assumed that these excessive construction works are performed in the defence area. The above test proved successful in 1972–75 because defence construction began to be treated as part of unfinished production (see the jump in 1971–72 in the size of row 19). During 1980–81 the derived construction price index was around 1.00. Since there was no price reform in 1982, it is assumed that this price index was also around 1.00 during that year. This leads to the value of new construction in current prices that contributes to the official NFI. It is thus possible to estimate defence construction as a residual after accounting for all other components of the construction GVO. In 1982, additions of strategic reserves (row 16) equalled the difference between the investment residual and defence construction (row 14). During 1972–81 defence construction can be estimated only approximately using established trends and the *Narkhoz* data on inventories.

Table 2.1.3.   Estimation of consumption residuals

There are two consumption residuals: in consumption by the total population (row 9) and in public consumption (row 24). The first residual equals the difference between current consumption by the total population (row 2) and consumption by households (row 3). Row 2 was estimated until 1975 as the difference between consumption by the total population that was published in *Narkhoz* and housing depreciation (row 13). The latter is estimated using the derived data on the housing stock (row 34) and the depreciation rate (row 35). Row 2 was estimated after 1975 as the difference between total consumption (row 1) that is regularly published in *Narkhoz* and the sum of the derived current material purchases (row 14) and depreciation (row 18) in non-production sectors. The second residual is estimated until 1975 as the difference between published total public consumption and the sum of current material purchases and depreciation in non-production service sectors. It is estimated after 1975 by extrapolating the ratio between depreciation and capital investment in defence industry (see notes to table 2.1.4) established before 1976.

Consumption by households (row 3) equals the sum of household purchases through retail trade for current consumption (row 4), purchases of utilities (row 5), consumption-in-kind (rows 6 and 8) and in-village consumption (row 7). Row 4 is estimated as the difference between total retail trade turnover (row 25) that is regularly published in *Narkhoz* and the sum of household purchases of second-hand goods (most sales of used cars published by Lokshin, p. 80), producer goods (see CIA, p. 130) and institutional purchases by civilian organizations (published by Zaitseva and Moroz, p. 37, and Kharlamov, p. 96) and the military purchases of food products that were estimated using the share of the military in the total population. Data on utilities were also reported by Soviet authors (see Sverdlik, p. 71). Consumption-in-kind in agriculture is estimated as the difference between non-monetary income of private agricultural producers (row 33) and additions of their livestock, gardening and inventories (primarily young livestock). Row 33, in turn, is estimated as the difference between their total (row 31) and published monetary (row 32) income. Row 31 equals the difference between the GVO in private agriculture and material outlays which comprise 20–30 per cent of this GVO (see Gallik, p. 40, and Tikhonov, p. 499).

Military purchases through the wholesale trade network are estimated after accounting for retail trade and in-village (subsidiary farm) purchases. Current material purchases of education, culture, health and science are estimated as the difference between total expenditures that are regularly reported in *Narkhoz* and the sum of capital and labour outlays. The same approach is used for housing-communal services after independently deriving total expenditures as the sum of rent payments and subsidies. Data for T&C and administration services are extrapolated by continuing the trend established in the late 1960s and early 1970s (see Rutgeizer, pp. 157–58). Depreciation of capital operated by these services is estimated as the sum of capital repair and replacement by combining published data on depreciation deductions, rates and budgetary allocations with the derived data on capital stock.

Table 2.1.4.   Estimation of investment in defence fixed capital

All data on capital investment are published in constant prices. The structure of capital investment in all non-production sectors is determined by comparing the published structures of total and production investment, while that in household services is determined by using the published structure of capital stock operated by these services (see *Narkhoz 1972*, p. 66). The structure of investment in science is assumed to be the same as the published structure of investment in industry. Data on investment in state administration and civilian M&E commissions are determined by analysing budgetary data. Data on investment in defence industry and space are then estimated as residuals. The conversion into current prices is performed with price indices derived in table 2.1.1. Data on total M&E commissions are also from table 2.1.1.

Table 2.1.5.   Estimation of military social services

Social services are presented in the official statistics together with vacation payments and one-time bonuses as social consumption funds (SCF). The SCF are divided into three groups: families of state-co-operative employees, families of collective farmers, and the military. Wage statistics include data on the SCF (without vacation payments) received by state-co-operative employees. Published family budgets of collective farmers include an entry for the SCF. Data on one-time bonuses were published by Garbuzov, 1977, p. 161. It is thus possible to estimate the SCF allocated to the military as a residual. Military pensions are estimated using the published data on military pension recipients. Other military SCF were disaggregated proportionately to the total.

Table 2.1.6.   The structure of the investment residual

Estimates for 1972 were obtained using published input-output data on the structure of the intermediate product and delivery charge by sector and *Narkhoz* data on production and end-use of goods. Total supplies are estimated as the GVO plus the delivery charge, turnover tax less subsidies, and imports in domestic roubles. The GVO of most industrial sectors is estimated as the sum of published production outlays and net revenues. The GVO of non-ferrous metallurgy is estimated first for 1972 using the input-output data. Estimates for 1972 are then combined with published growth rates. The GVO of light and food industries is estimated using VS (no. 9, 1985, p. 80 and no. 2, 1986, p. 77) data on price indices and the output of mining and manufacturing industries. The GVO of other heavy industries is estimated using *Narkhoz* data on the production of consumer goods and producer goods manufactured in these industries. The total industrial GVO contains a residual which is assumed to pertain to hidden MBMW sectors (exports of armaments, etc.). Hidden MBMW GVO is added to the published MBMW GVO to derive the total MBMW GVO. Data on turnover tax collected in light and food industries and on subsidies are periodically published by Soviet planner Semenov (see his 1983 book, pp. 119, 142, 154–57). The total turnover tax for heavy industries is disaggregated into sectors using the published data for the early 1970s control total for obtaining imports of particular goods.

Inventories of heavy industrial materials are disaggregated into sectors of production using the derived data on the structure of the intermediate product. It is determined that these inventories include state reserves. The latter are hidden in the official statistics as part of commodities held in reserve. Inventories of light and food industrial products are estimated as residuals. Investment is discussed in notes to table 2.1.2, consumption in notes to table 2.1.3. The structure of consumption is determined by combining *Narkhoz* retail trade data, the derived data on consumption-in-kind, published data on public consumption and surveys of institutional retail trade purchases. Assumptions cannot be avoided in disaggregating total purchases of heavy industrial goods by the armed forces. Finally, additions to strategic reserves (the investment residual) is disaggregated into sectors of production using a residual method.

Table 2.1.7.   Household budgets

Household budgets contain two residuals: total hidden wages (row 27) received by defence industrial employees and the military, and additions to unorganized savings (row 42). Row 27 is estimated as the sum of regular hidden wages (row 18), other earnings of all defence sectors' employees (row 25) that are estimated as 3 per cent of their regular wages and draftees' pay (row 26). Row 18 equals the difference between regular wages received by households headed by all state-co-operative employees (row 7) and regular wages received by households of state-co-operative employees (row 16) whose number is published in *Narkhoz*. Row 7 is estimated using *Narkhoz* data on household budgets of families headed by state-co-operative employees. Published household budgets include entries for income received from the SCF (row 5) and regular wages (row 7). Even though many entries in published household budgets contain a sizeable margin of error, the ratio between regular wages and income from the SCF is part of the regular statistics and hence does not depend on the quality of data collected from household surveys. Row 5 equals the difference between total income from the SCF received by state-co-operative employees (row 1), which is published in *Narkhoz*, and the sum of income from the SCF received by employees who are members of collective farmers' families (row 3) and published one-time bonuses (row 4). Row 3 is estimated using the derived data on wages of these collective farmers (row 17), which is obtained from the *Narkhoz* data on household budgets of collective farmers.

Regular wages received by state-co-operative employees (row 15), whose number is published in the official statistics, equals the sum of official wages (row 8) and added wages (row 11). Row 8 is estimated by multiplying the *Narkhoz* data on average annual employment and average monthly salaries by sector. Aggregated wages of production employees are first estimated for 1972 and 1977 using published input-output data and then extrapolated for other years in relation to regular wages. Aggregated wages in services are first estimated for the early 1970s as the difference between the *Narkhoz* data on total current expenditures and the sum of official wages and current material purchases reported by Rutgeizer. The results obtained are then extrapolated for later years in relation to regular wages.

Collective wages are from *Narkhoz*. The published input-output data indicate that the ratio between other earnings and total wages of non-farm labour is around 3 per cent. It is assumed that this ratio is around 1 per cent for farm and service sectors and 3 per cent for hidden defence sectors. Other monetary income (row 28) equals the sum of monetary income received by private producers (row 29), pensions, allowances and stipends (row 30), interest on savings (row 31), which is estimated as 3 per cent of average annual savings held in state banks, and other income (row 32). Row 29 is estimated as total monetary income received by private agricultural producers from sales to the state and at ex-village markets covered in *Narkhoz*, reduced by non-monetary wages received by farmers (6 per cent of total wages). Total monetary income (row 33) equals the sum of rows 24, 27 and 28.

Total monetary outlays (row 34) equal retail trade purchases and production-type utility payments (row 35), which are estimated in table 2.1.3, plus published (see *Narkhoz* 1985, p. 488) purchases of non-production services (row 36) plus derived membership dues (see CIA, p. 130) and published outlays and profits of insurance agencies (row 37) plus published budgetary receipts (row 38) plus other outlays (row 39), which consist primarily of investment in co-operative housing and in-village purchases that are excluded from the retail trade data. Total additions to savings (row 40) are estimated as the difference between total income (row 33) and total outlays (row 34). Official or organized savings are reported in *Narkhoz*. Additions of unofficial savings are then determined as a residual.

Table 2.1.8.   State social security revenues

The *Narkhoz* table on the state budget has two entries for revenues of the social security system. One entry is presented as part of budgetary revenues, while another entry is presented as a component of total outlays of the state social security system that is financed with received revenues. The author believes that until 1981 the second entry represented total revenues of the state social security system, while the first entry represented revenues received from sectors published in the official statistics. This can be ascertained by independently estimating revenues received from sectors published in the official statistics as the sum of deduction payments made by each production and service sector. Such payments are estimated by applying published deduction rates to the derived wages of production and service sectors. It is believed that until 1974 the gap between total and official revenues equalled deduction payments made by unpublished state sectors, i.e., defence industry and military administration. After 1974 there were jumps in this gap, which are difficult to explain. It is possible that the budget began to receive other revenues that helped finance the growing deficits of the state social security system. In 1982, the above two entries become almost equal in size, thus indicating a change in accounting practices. New deduction rates are still not published, thus making it impossible to make precise calculations of deduction payments made by production and service sectors. Payments made by industrial sectors are estimated using the *Narkhoz* table on industrial production outlays. The average deduction rate in industry increased from 7.4 to 10.4 per cent. It is assumed that in defence sectors the rate increased from 9 to 13 per cent.

Table 2.1.9.   Demographic trends

The Soviet population has a large number of unaccounted persons who in census returns are registered as receiving support from the state but who are excluded from the official labour force. Part-time employees must also be accounted for. Total population consists of two groups: (*a*) persons outside the labour force and (*b*) persons who under Soviet law must be part of the labour force. The first group includes children under 16 (students above 7 and children under 7 are estimated using *Narkhoz* data on students and newborns), full-time students (reported in *Narkhoz*), non-working pensioners (estimated as the difference between all pensioners and working pensioners—see Notkin, p. 255, and census returns), drifters (persons without income who are reported in census returns) and dependent adults (primarily women). The latter are estimated as the residual for the female population. *Narkhoz* includes data on total female population, female students and females in the official labour force. The VS (no. 1, 1977, p. 84) includes data on non-working female pensioners and females in the total labour force. Among children the ratio between males and females is 1.05 : 1.00 (see Volodarskiy, p. 17).

The difference between females in the total and official labour force consists of part-time employees who are unemployed part of the year and females working in defence sectors. Planners estimate unemployment in terms of lost working days that come to 1 per cent unemployment for the non-farm labour (see Antosenkov and Kupriyanova, 1977, p. 191) and 10 per cent in the farm sector (estimated on the basis of the derived unemployment among female collective farmers). Net unemployment is the difference between all lost working days and the number of double-counted labour. The latter are pensioners who are engaged in full-time study (2.2 million students received pensions according to the 1970 census returns—see TSU, 1973, p. 146) or part-time employees. There are also registered non-working pensioners who work part-time. The number of double-counted persons is assumed to be at least

1 million. It is also assumed that the overwhelming majority of prisoners work (as specified in the labour code) and that the number of non-working prisoners is below 1 million. The number of persons in the armed forces and state security is taken from published Western intelligence estimates. Persons employed in defence industries are then estimated using a residual method.

Bibliography

1. Antosenkov, V. and Kupriyanova, Z., *Tendentsii v Tekuchesti Rabochikh Kadrov* (Nauka: Novosibirsk, 1977).

2. US Central Intelligence Agency (CIA), *USSR: Measures of Economic Growth and Development, 1950–1980*, studies prepared for the use of the Joint Economic Committee, Congress of the United States, 8 Dec. 1982 (US Government Printing Office: Washington, DC, 1982).

3. Gallik, D., *Consumption in the 1972 Soviet Input-Output Table*, a working paper (US Department of Commerce, Bureau of the Census: Washington, DC, 1983).

4. Gallik, D., Kostinsky, B. and Treml, V., *Input-Output Structure of the Soviet Economy: 1972*, Foreign Economic Report No. 18 (US Department of Commerce: Washington, DC, 1983).

5. Garbuzov, V. (ed.), *XXVI Syezd KPSS i Sotsialiasticheskie Finansy* (Finansy i Statistika: Moscow, 1982).

6. Kharlamov, A., *Statistika Sovetskoy Torgovli* (Ekonomika: Moscow, 1982).

7. Lokshin, P., *'Stoimost'i struktura roznichnogo tovarooborota'*, *Voprosy Ekonomiki*, no. 10 (1981).

8. Masal'skiy, A., *'K voprosu o nachislenii i ispol'zovanii amortizatsii'*, *Finansy SSSR*, no. 4 (1974).

9. Ministerstvo Finansov SSSR, *Gosudarstvennyi Byudghet SSSR* (Finansy i Statistika: Moscow, 1977 and 1982). (Budgetary statistics.)

10. Ministerstvo Vneshney Torgovli, *Vneshnyaya Torgovlya SSSR* (Finansy i Statistika: Moscow, 1970–). (VT)

11. Notkin, A., ed., *Voprosy Intensifikatsii i Sbalansirovannosti Rasshirennogo Vosproizvodstva v Period Razvitogo Sotsializma* (Nauka: Moscow, 1981).

12. Rutgeizer, V., *Resursy Razvitiya Neproizvodstvennoy Sfery* (Mysl': Moscow, 1975).

13. Sel'tsovskiy, V., *'Sovershenstvovanie analiza effektivnosti vneshney torgovli SSSR'*, *Vestnik Statistiki*, no. 6 (1983).

14. Semenov, V., *Finansovo-Kreditnyi Mekhanizm v Razvitii Sel'skogo Khozyaistva* (Finansy i Statistika: Moscow, 1983).

15. Senchagov, V., *et al.*, *Amortizatsionnyi Fond v Usloviyakh Intensifikatsii Pro-izvodstva* (Finansy: Moscow, 1975).

16. Sovet Ekonomicheskoy Vzaimopomoshchi, *Statisticheskiy Yezhegodnik Stran-Chlenov Soveta Ekonomicheskoy Vzaimoposhchi* (Finansy: Moscow, 1970–1984). (CMEA)

17. Sverdlik, S., *Obshchestvennyi Produkt i Denezhnyi Oborot* (Social Products and Money Circulation) (Nauka: Novosibirsk, 1981).

18. Tikhonov, V. (ed.), *Agrarnye Problemy Sotsializma* (Nauka: Moscow, 1980).

19. Treml, V. and Kostinsky, B., *Domestic Value of Soviet Foreign Trade: Exports and Imports in the 1972 Input-Output Table*, Foreign Economic Report No. 20 (US Department of Commerce, Bureau of the Census: Washington, DC).

20. TSU SSSR, *Itogi Vsesoyuznoy Perepisi Naseleniya v 1970 Godu* (Statistika: Moscow, 1973). (Analysis of census returns.)

21. TSU SSSR, *Narodnoe Khozyaistvo SSSR* (Statistika: Moscow, 1965–1984) (*Narkhoz*)

22. Volodarskiy, L. (ed.), *Naselenie SSSR* (Politizdat: Moscow, 1983).

23. Zaitseva, A. and Moroz, R., '*Izuchenie vyborochnym metodom pokupok tovarob organizatsiyami, uchrezhdeniyami i predpriyatiyami roznichnoy seti i na kolkhoznom rynke*', *Vestnik Statistiki*, no. 5 (1971).

Paper 2.2.   How Soviet defence expenditures fit into the national income accounts

PETER WILES

I.   Basic methodological approach

Duchêne and Steinberg (see paper 1.2) have explained the Material Product Accountancy (MPA), with its distinction between productive and unproductive and its division of material production into Departments I, II and possibly III. It suffices to add that the budgetary accountancy is, in its basic concepts, of the normal Western kind: the Minister of Finance must enable the Minister of Defence to pay for the services he buys as well as the material products, and for the wages (not just material consumption) of his own civilian employees, the personal services, as well as the food, enjoyed by servicemen, and so on.

There is thus little reason for the budgetary accounts to resemble the national income (hereafter NMP) accounts. Indeed in the short period (about 1960–70) when they did, the object was deception. The NMP accounts are not traditionally deceptive, merely peculiar. They are the 'modern' sector of Soviet statistics. The definitions are published, consistent and reasonable. There is evidently a large internal lobby for them, keeping them 'clean'. It is much harder to conceal military expenditures among them, as we shall see.

Sovietologists straddle two attitudes to Soviet deception, the author and Steinberg standing at opposite extremes:

Wiles: They practice 'minimal untruthfulness': they detest mendacity and use it only as a last resort. In particular, the net material product total does still include all 'net' defence expenditures, according to the narrow official functional definition of defence, which excludes 'science' and pensions. The NMP omits services as it *should*, and—since 1959 or 1963—the weapons write-off (below). But the latter is included in such concepts as global social product and final product, which incorporate gross, not net, investment. So there is deception here but no untruth. However, the budget, which published that same number, 'NMP defence', as the OBDA, i.e. as if it did include services and the weapons write-off, is not telling the truth.

Steinberg: Few holds are barred. Weapons output (Department III) is simply not included anywhere at all, which is of course an untruth. But the laws of accountancy survive the untruth, and so we get 'rational mendacity': *everything* connected with factories directly producing weapons must go (though the inputs into those factories remain) and indeed is excised so far as is humanly possible. But it is not humanly possible: hence Steinberg's residuals, with which he hopes to catch out the Central Statistical Office.

I, too, of course operate with residuals, but believe that serious professional people in Moscow, engaged in national income and input/output (I/O) statistics, are not lying, merely deceiving me as to the names of sub-totals: the totals are always correctly stated. This is probably true even of the budget as a total. My assumption is the ordinary Sovietological assumption, and Steinberg's is the exception. Sovietology, however, is a career and has an establishment: it has always operated on my kind of assumption. Steinberg, though extreme, is nevertheless acceptable. But, if Soviet statistics were random numbers, there would be little point in paying our salaries. The assumption of Soviet non-randomness is our *déformation professionnelle*. Happily, between 'rational' and 'minimal' mendacity, we have work and plenty to spare.

There are also questions of ideology. Accountancy is a particularly ideological subject in the USSR, and I have stayed within its rules. But I question whether Steinberg has: notably in calling weapon factories unproductive labour. For since weapons are material objects, Marx himself, had he thought of it, would beyond any question at all have called these factories productive, the *material* nature of the productivity of labour being for him a matter of high philosophy. This fact should weigh heavily upon students in this field. After all, Department II is productive.

II.   The historical sequence of national income and budgetary accountancies

1.   In the 1930s, and possibly until after Voznesenski's post-war book (1948), they followed the normal Western rule: defence is a part of public consumption. It has only buildings for its capital, since public buildings are treated as capital in all countries. But weapons are public consumer durables and so written off, like private consumer durables, at the moment of delivery. This fits well with, but is not actually entailed by, the apparently best previous source, the '*Materialy*'.[1]

In this period, the overt budgetary defence allocation (OBDA) told the truth. The 'true' budget must of course at any time include the unproductive wage payments to servicemen, and so on, so the budget cannot afford to respect the MPA.

Moreover, there was at that time no talk of a Department III. Since defence was firmly inside public consumption (PuC), weapon manufacture should have been (but was it?!) firmly inside Department II, like that of sausage (private consumption) and pharmaceuticals (public consumption). For instance, Strumilin, whom the problem of accounting for defence haunted all his life, simply had defence as productive in 1926,[2] and gave no hint of a Department III as a notion being entertained by himself or anyone else.

2.   A brief proleptic detour is intellectually necessary here. When Hungary was drawn into the Soviet sphere after the war, this was the defence account-ancy that the Russians imposed. Hungarian defence is still squarely ensconced, for national income and I/O purposes, in PuC, indeed specifically the column 'administration'; but this is concealed, and there is, as in the USSR, practically no mention of it in other than budgetary statistics. In recent years, however, Hungarian statistics have evolved in two ways. The first is the 'Magyarization' of PuC: the calculation, publication and emphasizing of the unproductive wages and profits of PuC industries, so that they look, in an I/O table, indistinguish-able from the productive industry columns. Thus the Hungarians today calculate in an I/O context and used to publish yearly not only the NMP but also the national 'total' product, or as we would say the NNP at market prices.

These unproductive columns are each summed at the bottom as material inputs plus depreciation plus wages plus profits plus taxes, into a word that is translated into Russian as '*Produktsia*'. So the unproductive labour has a production! As one particularly scholarly Hungarian said to me when I drew his attention to this: 'That is not a Marxist concept'. This is what I call the Magyarization of PuC, the gradual rehabilitation of unproductive labour from the curse laid upon it by Adam Smith and Karl Marx. Soviet scholars follow this tendency, but hesitatingly (see below). Rutgaizer,[3] perhaps its principal importer, quotes Hungarian sources.

It is possible to deduce, or rather infer, a Hungarian defence *produktsia*. It includes servicemen's pay and maintenance (SPM), weapon deliveries (not capitalized but treated as MOI). It is—unless I am absurdly optimistic—open to anyone in the world to decompose, helped by not much guesswork, 'administration' into 'administration and defence'. That very title alternates with mere 'administration' in official Hungarian publications, presiding over the self-same numbers. It is also a profoundly Soviet title, and crops up in Soviet statistics, economic writings and budget speeches from at the latest 1930 down to the present day. But by no means all Soviet defence expenditures are any longer treated like that. It cannot be denied that Hungary's armed forces have sought the shelter of its administrators. Indeed the latter are otherwise impossibly numerous and impossibly well supplied with 'machinery'.

Meanwhile budgetary honesty has sharply deteriorated, and the Hungarian OBDA appears to be a straight untruth of unusual magnitude: the 'true' budgetary defence allocation (BDA), even on the narrow Soviet definition, seems to have been almost twice the OBDA in 1970. This possibility sheds a radical and baleful light on all Western calculations of all non-Soviet Warsaw Pact defence expenditures, which appear to be based on budgetary data and have surely been very passive and careless.

3.   Reverting to our main argument, in or at least just after World War II, Voznesenski initiates the notion, common in the West since the middle of the war, of the defence burden: the percentage of war expenditures to national income. But he restricts himself in two important ways: he must of course confine his burden to material products, and he must respect the division of

NMP into 'consumption' and 'accumulation'. He achieves this later by adding a third division, 'war'. There is not the slightest indication that 'war' is a form of investment. On the contrary, it seems to have been merely an activity lifted out of PuC on account of its monstrous size and given separate but similar treatment. This might well be an early application of the notion of Department III: factories making weapons would have been distinguished from both those making the means of production (I) and those making the means of consumption (II), and they would have delivered these out of their new Department to a newly separate end-use called war. However, no overt recognition is given to Department III.

Characteristically of Soviet thinking, servicemen's incomes, or rather their PMC, are retained under 'consumption' and not moved to 'war'. This is precisely the fate of the PMC of PuC employees, like doctors and teachers, at all times. But some of Voznesenski's followers shift to a true Western 'defence burden' concept (though a narrow one) by transferring this item to 'war'.[4] This issue at least is settled by the early 1950s; but if 'war' now contains some evident consumption, how can it not contain some investment?

The details of Voznesenski's accountancy are obscure and do not concern us. Under Voznesenski, Kosygin (in his brief term as Finance Minister) and the early Zverev (the Finance Minister of that very Malenkov who had had Voznesenski shot), the OBDA remained an honest figure.[5] Indeed the execution of the senior economist in the land inhibited all kinds of fresh economic expression. Moreover, Malenkov was a 'dove': the most dovish leader the USSR ever had except, in certain phases, Stalin himself (died April 1953). But in February 1955 Malenkov stepped down. Khrushchev was an adventurist and so a rearmer.

4.   Already in 1950 new ideas began to stir, and it is at this point that I part company with all of my colleagues in the field. What the reader now gets is not the received version. We are at peace, so Voznesenski's name of 'war' for the defence item becomes inappropriate. The word 'reserves' (*rezervy*)[6] is used more and more: we keep central stocks of gold and (possibly) wheat as civilian reserves outside commercial channels: they are not work-in-progress or trade stocks (*oborotnie sredstva*), and they are not agricultural stocks (*zapasy*). Then too we keep military reserves. But if 'reserves' means military fuel, just where do you put weapons? The answer gradually gains ground: in here too. Weapons are public, not private, consumer durables (my phrase) and should not be automatically written off on delivery (as in the whole of the rest of the world), but stocked, depreciated, replaced and repaired, all in money terms.

So while Voznesenski had a wartime military accounting concept, we have now a peacetime one. The word 'war', indeed the word 'defence', is avoided. It is merely that unpleasant military eventuality against which we pile up military reserves, just as we pile up gold and wheat against the unpleasant civilian eventuality of a bad harvest. Voznesenski could hardly have treated weapons as capital stock since battlefield losses would have turned net military expenditures negative.

This rethinking is greatly stimulated by the determination—we do not know exactly whose—to create an I/O table and to publish the NMP in current prices. Before that comes to pass (1959), a *deceptive* defence accountancy (which shall allow Comrade Khrushchev to rearm quietly) must be developed, which yet fits in with the 'reserve' idea. The solution is to recognize that:

(i)   Stocks of durables depreciate and are repaired and replaced—that is definitional, it cannot be escaped. No stock of named objects consists of the sum of gross additions for ever and ever, since it only contains what it actually contains, not rubble or scrap or rust.[7]

(ii)   Weapon repair is a *major* economic activity in any country, and weapon replacement about equally big. So the growth of the weapon stock accounts for only a fraction of weapon procurement. And we shall only report this growth, because we have had, since *Das Kapital* at least, a net investment concept. Gross investment and GNP are capitalist nonsenses, introduced into the capitalist world about 1949 because capitalists are too finicky about the exact meaning of depreciation. Only the increase in the weapon stock *can* figure in NMP.

But then it will pay us to play around with the OBDA. Capitalist countries, believers in the concept of the defence burden, simply divide the 'true' BDA by GNP. We are entitled to do the same with NMP underneath and our new OBDA on top: *material* personal military consumption + materials currently consumed for defence purposes + the *net* increase in the weapon stock. Obviously that pushes other items out of the OBDA into, say, Financing of the National Economy (FNE) and/or extra-budgetary sources. But then the budget never was a wholly honest document. Whereas the components of the OBDA fit the material national income accountancy to a T.

The capitalization of weapons appears to be an original Soviet idea. But, as a theory, it has not been without (perfectly independent) Western supporters, and US tax-evaders have also been able to exploit it once in actual fiscal practice, while a UK Government has used it in political argument.[8]

If one single sentence is to tell us all, it is this: Voznesenski kept weapons as ordinary traditional consumer durables, written off on delivery and so indistinguishable from fuel or other non-durable MOI; the new accountancy treats them as capital and so must distinguish them from fuel. There is now military investment as well as direct military consumption (quite apart from PMC of course).

5.   Incidentally, *military buildings* have always been investment. They were treated as part of national investment in the days of the dual accountancy, which put defence in PuC and recognized only national consumption and national investment. In Voznesenski's triple accountancy (defence is outside PuC but resembles it), there is still only one investment fund, so the buildings stay where they were. In the modern accountancy, military buildings are still left behind, and that deserves an excursus.

As part of the traditional concept of investment, buildings are not 'reserves' but 'basic funds' (*osnovniye fondy*). The huge majority of Soviet capital is 'basic funds' if fixed, or 'circulating means' (of production: *oborotniye sred-stva*) if not fixed. The only exceptions are the civilian 'reserves' *sensu stricto* and the new military capital, which is also called 'reserves'. The creation of basic funds has always been called 'capital investment' (*kapital'noe vlozhenie*, here KV), which is also, by a curious but highly traditional confusion, the heading in *Narkhoz* for the statistical achievements of the construction industry. Now bricks and mortar usually enclose machinery, whether it be a passenger lift or a giant turbine; so KV includes the value of machinery installed plus the installation labour, and 'capital investment' is exceedingly difficult to disentangle from construction.

But what of loose machines, for example, vehicles? No builder touches them, yet they go down in KV if delivery is to *khozraschyotni* activities (nearly all productive labour, and unproductive labour for the market). But the delivery of loose machines to budgetary organizations (PIEBO) is no part of KV, and this has created controversy, as well it might. What differentiates the minister's limousine (and the surgeon's scalpel) from the director's limousine? One is reminded of the identical conundrum in the West, brought out for the amusement and puzzlement of generations of students of national income accountancy. The answer is the same everywhere: public bodies have only buildings as capital, private bodies depreciate their limousines too. The minister's limousine is a consumer durable. The anomaly was corrected in the USSR in 1965, when PIEBO was held to go towards the increase of basic funds, but not to be KV (there are one or two other small things in this category anyway).

Now the minister's limousine resembles uncannily a nuclear submarine: loose machinery procured by a budgetary organization. No builder ever touched either, yet they are durable. It seems as if the new solution for weapons (introduced in 1959?) sparked off this (unpublished) controversy over the similar civilian case. But of course the limousines are by no stretch of imagination 'reserves', so they have to be 'basic funds'. And of course PIEBO is very unimportant as a magnitude,[9] but it is a magnificent illuminator.

So PIEBO is a type of machine-building that is not KV. But KV by long tradition excludes weapons,[10] and weapons are 'reserves' instead. Therefore, as I understand it (not without logical strain), we confine our new military accountancy to those things that are truly reserves and keep those things that are truly basic funds (and KV too!) like military buildings in their accustomed place. So the net increase of military buildings is not counted into the OBDA. To the writer this is best called a falsehood, since it is part of the 'true' budgetary defence allocation (BDA), and military too. But one wonders whether the anonymous authors of the 1959 reform saw it that way, whether indeed they had their minds on the matter at all. Military buildings had long ago been satisfactorily placed, they were not a big item; why not let sleeping dogs lie?

Where precisely does this item go? I have never discovered. Presumably it is somewhere in PuC to this day. The phrase 'administration and defence' has been and is extremely common in all sorts of contexts in the USSR (and in Hungary 'administration' *contains* 'defence', as we saw). One looks first here, but administrative basic funds are not very big.[11] In the UK, KV in military buildings seems to be about one-tenth of weapon procurement including spare parts,[12] and I have proceeded on this analogy.

III.   The documentary evidence for the capitalization of weapons

I owe the first two quotations to Sokoloff,[13] who was of course the pioneer in the West. Firstly, is Ryabushkin's 'increment':[14] 'Everything connected with consumption by the army—food, uniforms—enters into consumption whereas the increment of arms, military equipment etc. (*prirost voyennykh sredstv i tak dalee*) can only be attributed to accumulation'. It is, of course, since he is a Soviet Marxist, a net increment—there is no gross investment in Marx, and very little in the USSR today outside I/O tables. Besides, the word 'increment' (*prirost*) entails the increase in a capital stock, even to a non-Marxist. So, unconsciously and indirectly, but still very strongly, Ryabushkin is telling us that W_w exists. The heading of this chapter in his textbook is 'the national income'. He does not mention the budget.

Secondly and most curiously of all—this reference is also due to Sokoloff— what Ryabushkin says is exactly what the Russians told the expert committee of the UN Economic and Social Council (*EcoSoc*) on (1) the *Gosrezervy* (State reserves) and (2) the 'defence fund':[15]

1.   Please find enclosed the definitive version of the material product accountancy . . .

The accumulation of material means of circulation [doubtless *sredstv*—PJDW] and stocks represents the increase of reserves of material goods, and notably of the following:

a) Stocks of raw materials, fuels, spare parts and semi-fabricates in the hands of consumers;

b) Uncompleted production;

c) Residual stocks of finished products and merchandise [doubtless *tovary*] in pro-ducers' warehouses and distributive expenses;

d) Merchandise in transit;

e) Young livestock and livestock being fattened [working stock is a fixed asset, including *cows*];

f) The material reserves of the state (including defence).

Under this last rubric there figure also reserves of precious metals and precious stones belonging to the state.

2.   A further difference between SNA and MPA is that in the former expenditure on fixed assets used for military purposes is treated as final consumption expenditure, whereas in the latter it is included in fixed capital formation. This difference is likely to be of sufficient importance to be taken into account in inter-system comparisons . . .

Expenditures on fixed capital used for military purposes. In the Western accountancy expenditures are treated as intermediate consumption by the producers of the services of the public administrations, while in the (Soviet accountancy) they are included in the formation of capital . . .

Expenditure on Military Equipment. In the (Western accountancy) expenditure on military equipment is treated as intermediate consumption of producers of government services, and therefore enters final consumption expenditure, whereas in the (Soviet accountancy) it is included in fixed capital formation.

But stocks of durable assets logically entail a write-off procedure, as we have seen.

Background sources on the meaning of the word 'reserves' are very numerous. There is an important early one from the period of the semi-secret pre-1959 discussion:[16]

[Defence is extremely important for us . . .]

How does the necessity of large defence expenditures influence the allocation of the national income? . . . [Stalin prepared for World War II: paragraph] . . . But military readiness is defined not merely by the general dimensions of social production. A certain part of the productive apparatus must be specialized in peacetime in supplying the army with equipment (*vooruzhenie*), the *creation (sozdanie) of reserves of equipment*, and must serve as an experimental base for the developing war technology etc. A certain part of economic resources must be set aside for the formation and growth of *special state reserves of productive capacities*, equipment, raw materials, fuel and food.

All this means that in peace-time part of the fund of socialist *accumulation* is destined for the *sphere of the production of the means of defence*, just as part of the consumption fund must cover the direct needs of servicemen's maintenance. This is why it is clearly necessary to set aside a part of the funds of accumulation and consumption, spent on war needs, into the special defence fund [the reader is reminded that in Communist Russian 'fund' often means 'annual flow'!].

The first two phrases in italics represent respectively the Sokoloff/Wiles view: weapons are capitalized and their net growth is in other expenditures (OE) in the NMP case, while the gross flow into this stock is in OE in Sverdlik— and the Steinberg view that weapons are not capitalized and that OE contains mainly current flows of material into weapon factories (here 'productive capacities'). Notkin, writing very early, confuses the two concepts. But in either case he is a clear enthusiast for capitalizing *something* in the defence sector! Indeed he goes further in the third phrase italicized, where investment in weapon factories is mentioned but it is not really clear what happens to their MOI (their current inputs, which Steinberg holds to be precisely the I/O column OE), nor indeed whether such investment should be added to the previous items or somehow sums them up.

Thirdly, there appears to exist one single Soviet direct admission of the existence of such a thing as the weapons write-off (W_w). It is very indirect, and almost dishonest—but that of course is the name of the game. In his table 2.1 (reproduced here as table 2.2.1), before he gets down to his actual numbers,

Table 2.2.1. Expanded scheme of the inter-branch balance of the production and re-distribution of the social product in the national economy of the USSR (in 1972) in money terms

Branches producing \ Branches consuming	Branches of material production 1	Personal consumption 2	Branches of the unproductive sphere 3	Accumulation, replacement of the retirals of basic funds and capital repair 4	Other expenditure, replacement of losses and export 5	Total 6
1. Branches of material production	1.1 Quadrant I 1.1	1.2 1.4 2.2	1.3 Quadrant II	1.4	1.5	1.6 1.6
2. Amortization	2.1		2.3 (2.3)		2.5	
3. Pay and net income	3.1		3.3 (3.3)		3.5	
4. Import	4.1				4.6	
5. Total production	5.1		5.3 (5.3)			

Source: Sverdlik's table 2.1: Sverdlik, S. B., *Denezhni Oboroti Obshchestvenni Produkt* (Novosibirsk, 1980) (p. 38).

Notes:

The column in brackets shows the location of the misprint. The column to the left of it shows my correction. The meaning and placing of the numbers underlined is nowhere explained; I have neglected them. They are placed exactly as in the original.

On row 2 Sverdlik says (p. 39): 'Indicators of the amortization of productive basic funds, which in the expanded scheme are counted between the first and third quadrants, are included in block 2.1; the *iznos* of the housing stock and other unproductive basic funds, counted in the expanded balance between the second and third quadrants, is included in blocks 2.2 and 2.3'. He is referring, of course, to amortization in the sloppy Soviet sense of the depreciation of productive basic funds: the annual contribution of fixed assets to gross value added.

Sverdlik gives us a symbolic treatment of his main concepts. This treatment contains the mysterious item 2.5 in the box 'amortization/OE'. Now OE, as he defines it, contains exports. But these cannot be amortized, since they are a final product, leaving the country within the year. It also contains the mysterious element 'losses', which must indeed be replaced; but he says explicitly (page 129) that losses are replaced in his book out of *net* national product, simply in order not to differ gratuitously from the official methodology. So 2.5 is not that either.

The mysterious item, therefore, must come under OE, the third thing mentioned in the title of the column. But OE is the name in all I/O tables for 'reserves'; and weapons are the only depreciable item in OE. This interpretation is reinforced by the fact that although every other item in Sverdlik's table 2.1 gets a further mention in the pages of explanatory text that follow (especially his table 2.6 which is his convenient summary lists of all the symbols he has used), this one does not! It is never mentioned again: therefore it constitutes a security problem. This argument is not certain however. For instance on pages 45 and 46, Sverdlik offers us schematic breakdowns of gross investment and $\triangle$ stocks in the truncated form without mentioning OE at all. It is not clear why he has omitted it here. Again the sentence that implies that box 2.5 cannot be the replacement of 'losses' comes 91 pages later in the book. The undoubted fact of a misprint in the table (not common in this book) also reduces our confidence in it.

Above all, the appearance of W_w here *entails* that there be two military columns between which the OE that we know is divided: an investment one including $\triangle$ stocks, where it cannot figure by definition (cf. column 4), and one for current operations, with military MOI (fuel, bullets, etc.) figuring as non-capital material inputs, soldiers' pay as the wage, and—of course—W_w as depreciation. This latter column will add up like those of PuC in a 'Magyarized' treatment, to an 'unproductive *produktsia*'—which is *not* published!

Bor[17] gives us, closer to the 'kick-off' date of 1959–63, what we would call an I/O row and column for industry alone, in conventional magnitudes:

			Sold to:	
Global product	5900	(=total in	Other producers for inputs	3200
Material costs	3100	row and	End uses: consumption	2300
Net product	2800	column)	accumulation	400
(i.e. value added				——
by productive				5900
labour)				

He has evidently abstracted from foreign trade.

His exact words for the 400 are 'for the accumulation of basic and circulating funds, *state reserves* (*gosudarstvenniye rezervy*) *of uninstalled equipment* [weapons?], the increase of stocks (*zapasy*) of fuel, materials, raw materials, *gosrezervy*, etc. (for the most part by means of FNE in the budget)'; [italics added]. The apparently otiose distinction between '*gosrezervy*', an obvious stock item, and '*gosudarstvenniye* (which is but an expansion of the abbreviation) *rezervy*', which is equipment, is that the latter is secret and military, while the former is so much common knowledge. We are even told where to look for it in the budget (as budget textbooks confirm). Bor keeps coming back to the subject and clearly finds it important. Reserves are clearly, but too briefly, distinguished on pages 36 and 81–82. But on pages 95–97 Bor has his most extended, crystal-clear passage:

> In its final use the national income is divided into the funds of accumulation, reserves and consumption . . . [He goes on to put cattle herds; 'circulating funds' in industry, agriculture and construction; and 'stocks' (*zapasy*) in trade all into 'accumulation'] . . . The reserve fund within the national income is specially distinguished in the plan balance of the national economy. This is because reserves are the potential expression of future productive and consumption funds. The accumulation of reserves is an obligatory condition, flowing from the demands of the law of the planned, proportional development of the national economy. If there are not in the hands of the government large reserves of metal, coal, petroleum products, industrial and agricultural raw materials, bread, manufactured goods and groceries for mass consumption we cannot assure the uninterrupted development of the socialist economy and culture or protect the country from accidents of all kinds. [But] the reserve fund includes only state reserves. Reserves formed in artisanal and consumer co-operatives and also in *kolkhozy* are counted into the general sum of the accumulation of the co-operative-*kolkhoz* sector. The reserve fund combines, first, state material reserves having a long-term character; secondly, the reserves of the means of defence, which have a special character; thirdly, the current operative reserve of the Council of Ministers, used in the course of filling the annual plan to satisfy ever-arising current needs.

Much of this is inaccurate if the *EcoSoc* document is to be believed. But the presence of weapons in the reserve, and so in accumulation, is pretty definite. For the rest, Bor may be taken to be making up his own ideal version. It avoids, at least, Notkin's basic confusion.

Finally in 1967, so well into the classic period of weapons capitalization, Albert Vainshtein, the distinguished national income expert, says: 'The growth of expenditure for defence could not raise at all the proportion of accumulation in the national income, since a considerable (*znachitel'naya*) part of them is included in consumption and only a part in accumulation'.[18] Thus in the 1960s Voznesenski's doctrine (above) that military PMC is, for national income but not budgetary purposes, 'consumption', while weapons are 'war', has been abandoned definitively: 'defence' includes both.

It is very dangerous, but illuminating, to take Vainshtein quite literally. If he is referring to 1966, accumulation was 24 per cent of NMP. Therefore $\triangle R_w$ was 24 per cent of the BDA (which is not true). Otherwise a (balanced) increase in defence would have changed the consumption/accumulation ratio! But this is to put too much weight on an *obiter dictum*. Perhaps Vainshtein simply meant that consumption was about a half of the BDA. In 1951 Allakhverdyan[19] utters the same kind of thought: 'To the consumption fund also belongs the dominant (*preobladayushchaya*) part of expenditures for the state's defence and security needs'. *Preobladayushchaya* is very much stronger than *znachitel'naya*, and this indicates some such shift between 1950 and 1966 as from 60:40 to 40:60. Such a move is not dissonant with our numbers here for the later year. As to the earlier year, it is obvious from the production index for heavy industry in the post-war years (the so-called Department A, which includes weapons) that Stalin accepted military inferiority and was producing few weapons. He also notoriously kept millions of men under arms simply to feed them at East European expense; so an excess of 'consumption' over 'investment' is quite possible.

IV.   Some actual numbers on weapon capitalization

Our last documentary evidence for the existence of W_w is numerical as well. It cannot be emphasized enough that we must not consider any accounting schema proved to be the one in use until the numbers have clicked. Prose is much inferior to arithmetic. We shall turn shortly to examine the Soviet I/O tables for the 'three glorious years' 1959, 1966 and 1972. These are the only years in which I/O tables were published. They are a greatly superior source to the *Narkhoz*. Their beauty for the residual-hunter is of course that they yield both a row and a column residual, and this is a sharp curb on imaginative error. They have the further beauty of being so very detailed. It is, we may conclude, a breach of security to publish any input/output table anywhere, ever.

We have two sources for the final-use wings of these I/O tables: Gillula and Sverdlik. The beauty of these sources is that Gillula presents every column net of depreciation and then sets up the whole of national replacement and repair into a single separate column, equal to the row total of depreciation, while Sverdlik gives us every column gross, including the military column. So all Gillula's columns, except R and R, are net and all Sverdlik's are gross. Therefore in the military column, in the form of a slogan, 'Sverdlik − Gillula = Wiles', and we have actual Soviet numbers for W_w.

Before we get to the I/O tables themselves, many warnings are in order. Gillula still somewhat mistrusts his own results, heroically labour-intensive as they have been. He has been forced, here and there, to bet upon his own definitions and so arbitrarily allocate certain items to certain boxes. Sverdlik is at least as heroically labour-intensive, but cannot, naturally, tell us exactly what he has done or what the exact definitions are of his rows and columns. Indeed he is quite deceptive, beyond the calls of ordinary discretion: the word defence (*oborona*) does not occur in his book—which is nevertheless a mine of information, a veritable counter-*Narkhoz*.

Especially it is clear that Sverdlik's military column (OE) includes the *EcoSoc*'s l.f. (see below), the special state reserves or *Gosrezervy*, as can be seen from its small scattered items, many of them negative, since of course the NMP concerns only increments of stocks. But Gillula (private correspondence) admits to having cleaned his military column of all such items, making it solely military. This seems to me to be most regrettable. But it can hardly affect the contribution of the engineering MBMW row (Gillula) and/or the heavy industry row (Sverdlik) to the column, except maybe in what concerns the increment of military fuel stocks. Along this row, evidently, Gillula gives us the net accumulation of, and Sverdlik the gross expenditures on, weapons. W_w is thus fairly certain, but there is nevertheless a doubt about the meaning of $\triangle R_w$: to repeat, it probably includes the current consumption of bullets, fuel and whatever other material objects procured by the Ministry of Defence (MoD) are defined as being current inputs, or military MOI. We return to this in section VII, where we see that $\triangle R_w$ should include these uninvested military end-products, but maybe they constitute the residual in servicemen's consumption.

We now approach the OBDA through its single significant treatment in the *Narkhoz*: the 'new' table in the NMP section, which appeared in *Narkhoz* 1971–75 only, without proper introduction, immediately after the usual, and continuing, 'old' table. The former is in 1965 roubles and distinguishes defence, but it is still NMP used and has the same total value. The latter is in current roubles and does not distinguish defence.

We sort out below the shifts in the 'accumulation' part, which are simple. The definitions that follow the new table in the *Narkhoz* text are a brief recapitulation of those given for the 'old' table. The consumption definitions read: 'first on the consumption of material goods by workers in the productive sphere *on account of their pay*';[20] 'secondly on the collective satisfaction of the requirements of the population and on general administration (material costs of their current functioning of institutes of cultural and daily-life service to the population and general administration; here too is included the consumption of material goods by the workers so engaged)'; 'thirdly on maintenance of those unable to work (pensioners, the temporarily disabled etc.)'; fourthly on science [as in 'secondly' above]; 'the consumption of workers in all branches of the national economy *includes* that of their families'.[21]

There is thus no direct mention of defence in the definitional discussion in the *Narkhoz*.

Now a good first question is, where has the 'new' table put servicemen's PMC? For this is not the NMP produced, in which the incomes of unproductive workers play no part. This is NMP used, and in a version that specifically tells us it has allocated PMC according to its users. The 'new' table's 'productive labour' entry is simply the personal material consumption of the workers engaged in such labour (and their families). The 'unproductive labour' entry is, as is normal in the MPA, the personal consumption of material goods by PuC labour plus the material inputs it uses in the course of its work (MOI). This is because such goods (pharmaceuticals, textbooks) are deemed to be indirectly consumed by the population, and so part of final-use. Productive workers, by contrast, are down just for their personal material consumption (and not, of course, their value added, for that pertains to NMP produced, not used).

The rationale of the 'new' table, then, is: let us look in another way than the orthodox one in the 'old' table at the same question—how do we allocate the net national material product? The very Marxist answer is: let us divide it into seven categories, net investment and gross consumption (the latter is gross because it includes the *iznos* of housing and PuC fixed capital) by the three great types of activity that use them, plus consumption by the inactive. Thus:

i.   direct material consumer goods in such-and-such proportions to: productive workers and their families; unproductive workers and their families (very probably including the KGB [Committee for State Security] internal and frontier troops);[22] economically inactive people; servicemen, including construction troops, and (? in the case of non-conscripts only) their families; and here too very probably the MoD's civilian employees.

ii.   the MOI of service institutes, including their *iznos*, to be 'consumed' by the relevant workers, to perform services with (in addition to their allocation under (i)—actual services are of course excluded by the definition of NMP; the MOI of defence should logically be treated in the same way but in a separate place (section VII);

iii.   net investment to: productive branches; defence (hitherto definitely included in the productive total: see table 2.2.2; but possibly the accounts published show military MOI on the same line, which is therefore not all investment; unproductive branches (very probably including the KGB, etc.).

Table 2.2.2.   Productive investment (R md., current prices)

	(i) In new table (1965 prices)	(ii) In old table	(iii) Implied deflator $(ii \div 39.8) \div$ $(i \div 33.1)$	(iv) $\triangle R_w = (ii) -$ $(i) \times (iii)$
1961	23.8	33.2	113.6	6.16
1962	24.3	34.8	115.2	6.81
1963	22.8	31.7	115.6	5.34
1964	32.0	39.6	105.9	5.71
1965	33.1	39.8	100.0	6.70
1966	34.7	43.4	104.0	7.31
1967	35.6	47.0	109.8	7.91
1968	36.7	51.5	116.7	8.67
1969	38.0	54.9	120.1	9.26
1970	41.0	65.1	132.0	10.98
1971	43.0	66.9	124.8	10.74
1972	42.6	64.8	126.2	11.04
1973	48.4	76.4	131.0	13.00
1974	49.0	77.0	130.4	13.10
1975	48.0	73.4	126.9	12.49

As to (i), the consumption figures in the 'new' and 'old' tables are easily reconcilable, as can be seen from table 2.2.3. The gap between the two subtotals called 'consumption' is of extreme importance. It tells us that the 'new' table transferred in the inflation-free year of 1965 some R 5.9 bn. from the four items listed by me under '? consumption' to the rest. Where did it go? Of the other items, as we can see, the 'service institutions' investment is defined the same way in both tables, so it clearly neither lost nor gained. Productive accumulation plus stocks actually lost. That leaves defence; the consumption gap is of course military.

So if both our larger consumption items really are consumption, they will yield us a price index. Indeed a very great supplementary charm of table 2.2.3 is its information about prices; compare note k to that table. But in this case we have also the published index (for prices of goods in state shops) to worry about. The indices run parallel: both faithfully reflect the great rise in meat prices in July 1962 (the occasion of the Novocherkassk riots). For 1.4 per cent over the whole year, with all other items steady, implies a very great rise in the one item, however important. It reinforces our confidence to find the implicit index doing the same thing. Exactly why the two indices diverge between the years 1965 and 1971, in years unaffected by the meat price crisis, is unclear.

Note, however, the writer's strong motivation: his whole insistence on 1959 as a year of low, if any, W_w depends on a low consumption gap in that year (table 2.2.4).

Turning from consumption to investment, we look for the accumulation of arms, $\triangle R_w$. We find it easily enough in the productive investment gap, also a feature of table 2.2.3. This number is very nearly equal to Gillula's own $\triangle R_w$. And of course military PMC plus military net investment add up to the OBDA.

So the OBDA is the sum of the defence items that enter the NMP: $\triangle R_w +$ *military PMC.* This unusual identification of budgetary with national income concepts enables any propagandist to say, hand on heart, that we only spend 7 per cent of NMP on defence. The remainder is either in R and R (no part of NMP) or in other items like science and pensions (the natural and honest result of having a restricted definition of defence, which has often been published).

This is our basic position. Note that it seems that the OBDA's own deflator, on 1965=100, is 100 throughout. We return to this below, and try to develop a temporal series for weapons first, marrying or failing to marry our $\triangle R_w$ (OBDA—consumpton gap) with Gillula's $\triangle R_w$ (the box MBMW/OE). 1966 presents no problem. 1959 seems very small since our $\triangle R_w$ is almost as big as Sverdlik's gross procurement, but that is only to be expected as the new accountancy begins. 1972 is evidently wrong but, in the words of Jean-Paul Sartre, 'it is right to be wrong': the OBDA has ceased to have meaning since it has become the 'Brezhnevian Number' (see section XI). Only the 'productive accumulation gap' is now reliable (table 2.2.2), while in earlier years its performance is not superior.

It is superfluous to stress here our uncertainty as to the appropriate deflators for weapons. Apart from all the usual conceptual difficulties, Soviet civilian machinery prices always tend to fall after the first year of model introduction, and the price index chains together the succeeding new models very badly, so that the machine-price index itself often falls. The unpublished weapon-price

Table 2.2.3. The 'new' table disaggregated (R bn., 1965 prices) (The large numbers between lines are the original five-year totals.)

	1961	1962	1963	1964	1965	1966	1967	1968	1969	1970	1971	1972	1973	1974	1975
CONSUMPTION (PMC + MOI)[a]															
Productive	69.8	74.0	389 / 77.5	81.0	86.7	91	97	518 / 103	110	117	122	126	133	139	147
'Service Institutions'[b]	19.8	22.5	126 / 25.1	27.9	30.8	33.8	36.8	199 / 39.8	42.8	45.8	49	56	60	66	70
Science	3.4	3.8	22 / 4.3	4.9	5.6	6.4	7.3	41 / 8.2	9.1	10	11	13	14	15	14
Economically Inactive	10.1	10.3	53 / 10.5	10.8	11.3	12.2	14.4	80 / 16	17.9	19.5	21	22	23	25	28
Σ above[c]	103.1	110.6	117.4	124.6	134.4	143.4	155.5	167.0	179.8	192.3	203	217	230	245	259
Total of definitely[d] consumption, old table, current prices	108.1	117.5	124.1	130.4	140.3	150.0	162.1	174.8	187.3	201.3	213.0	225.4	237.3	250.3	266.6
Deflator, deduced[e]	100.4	101.8	101.3	100.2	100	100.2	99.9	100.3	99.8	100.3	100.5	99.5	98.8	97.9	98.6
Index of state goods prices[f]	98.6	100.0[g]	100.7	100.7	100	99.3	99.3	99.3	99.3	99.7	99.6	99.4	99.4	99.3	99.3
ACCUMULATION[a]															
Productive plus stocks	23.8	24.3	136 / 22.8[h]	32.0	33.1	34.7	35.6	186 / 36.7	38	41	44.6	42.7[i]	48.5	49.1	48.1
'Service Institutions'[j]	9.5	10.0	50 / 10.5	9.6	10.4	10.5	11.6	62 / 12.2	13.1	14.6	16.0	16.6	17.4	18.4	19.6
Defence[j]	11.6	12.6	64 / 13.9	13.3	12.8	13.4	14.5	80 / 16.7	17.7	17.9	17.9	17.9	17.9	17.7	17.4
Σ above	44.9	46.9	47.2	54.9	56.3	58.6	61.7	65.6	68.8	73.5	78.5	77.2	83.8	85.2	85.1
Total of definitely[d] accumulation & other, old table, current prices	42.9	45.0	42.5	49.3	50.2	54.2	59.4	64.8	69.4	84.2	87.1	85.3	97.6	98.1	95.8
Ditto 'Service institutions' only	9.7	10.2	10.8	9.7	10.4	10.8	12.4	13.3	14.5	18.0	20.2	20.5	21.1	21.1	22.4
Deflator 's.i.' only[k]	102.1	102.0	102.9	101.0	100	102.9	103.3	109.0	110.7	123.3	126.3	123.5	121.8	114.7	114.3
NMP 'Used'[e] Σ above	148.0	157.5	840 / 164.6	179.5	190.7	202.0	217.2	1166 / 232.6	248.6	265.8	281.4	294.2	313.8	330.2	344.1
By direct interpolation[l]	150	158	164	178	190	200	216	235	247	268	282	293	315	330	343
At current prices, old table	151.0	162.5	166.6	179.7	190.5	204.2	225.1	239.6	256.7	285.5	300.1	310.7	334.1	348.4	362.4

Official NMP[m] growth, index	78	82	85	93	100	108	117	127	133	145	153	159	174	184	191.4
Deflator[n]	101.8	102.7	101.0	100.8	100	101.0	103.5	102.9	103.2	107.3	106.5	105.6	106.5	105.5	105.3
CONSUMPTION GAP (old–new, by the deduced deflator)															
Current prices	4.6	4.9	5.2	5.5	5.9	6.3	6.8	7.3	7.9	8.4	9.0	9.5	10.1	10.4	11.2
1965 prices						6.3						9.5			

Source: Narkhoz, 1973, pp. 603–6; and various other editions.

Notes:

[a] The subheadings are mine. The authors of the 'new' table would not like them, and very significantly do not use subheadings at all.

[b] This is a narrower concept than 'unproductive': 'education, health and the satisfaction of other cultural everyday life needs of the population and of social needs'. It may or may not include unproductive transport and communications (see text).

[c] The principal component of the officially recognized inflation is the official price reform of investment goods between 1969 and 1970.

[d] The old table does use these subheadings.

[e] The 100.4 in 1961 = $\frac{108.1}{103.1} ÷ \frac{140.3}{134.4}$, and so on.

[f] This is the official index, pieced together from various sources. I have used only figures based on 1940 = 100 (1965 = 140), since the rounding error is smaller than in the two-digit numbers based on 1950 = 100 (1965 = 75). From 1970, however, the original data go into one place of decimals.

[g] Rise in meat prices (see text).

[h] The fall is due to a run-down in agricultural stocks: bad harvest.

[i] 'Service institutions' (same as our PuC) are the only accumulation item completely comparable in the new and old tables.

[j] Taken to one place of decimals from the budget statements, which are identical to this row.

[k] The new and old tables both explicitly concern the 'used' not the 'produced' NMP.

[l] I have used the official annual growth rates to aid interpolation.

[m] This is the official volume index. It slightly outpaces the two series in 1965 roubles.

[n] Using the row 'Σ above'.

Table 2.2.4. The OBDA, servicemen's pay and $\triangle R_w$ (current R md., mn. men)

	1950	1955	1956	1957	1958	1959	1960	1961	1962	1963
OBDA[a]	8.28	10.74	9.73	9.12	9.36	9.37	9.30	11.59	12.64	13.87
FNE residual[b]	1.43	2.61	2.35	2.92	5.02	5.33	4.17	2.57	4.99	4.86
Men under arms, mn.[c]	3.3	5.7	4.7	3.9	3.6	3.6	3.5	3.3	3.3	3.5
Pay and maintenance[c]	3.6	6.0	5.0	4.2	3.9	4.2	4.1	4.3	4.5	4.8
Consumption gap						(?7.0)[e-g] (?5.0)[e,h]	? ?4.4	(6.4)[g] (4.6)[h]	(6.9)[g] (4.9)[h]	(5.9)[g] (5.2)[h]
OBDA-gap						(2.4)[g] (4.4)[h]				
$\triangle R_w$ when known	—	—	—	—	—	?4.7[i]	—	—	—	—

	1964	1965	1966	1967	1968	1969	1970	1971	1972	1973
OBDA	13.28	12.8	13.4	14.5	16.7	17.7	17.9	17.9	17.9	17.9
FNE residual	4.70	7.83	7.8	9.7	11.3	11.6	15.8	18.2	20.1	21.6
Men under arms	3.6	3.8	3.9	4.0	4.1	4.2	4.3	4.4	4.5	4.6
Pay and maintenance	5.1	5.6	5.9	6.1	6.7	7.0	7.4	7.8	8.2	8.9
Consumption gap	(4.9)[g] (5.5)[h]	5.9	(7.6)[g] (6.3)[h]	6.8[h]	7.3[h]	7.9[h]	8.4[h]	9.0[h]	(9.7)[g] (9.5)[h]	10.1[h]
OBDA-gap			5.8[g] 7.1[h]						8.2[g] 8.4[h]	
$\triangle R_w$ when known	—	—	6.73[d]	—	—	—	—	—	11.04[f]	—

	1974	1975
OBDA	17.7	17.4
FNE residual	25.6	25.4
Men under arms	4.7	4.8
Pay and maintenance	9.3	9.7
Consumption gap	10.4[h]	11.2[h]
$\triangle R_w$ when known	—	—

Notes:

[a] Tables 2.2.1 and 2.2.16.

[b] Lee p. 309; *Gosudarstvenny Byudzhet 1971–5*, p. 22. This is the 'residual by headings' (*glavy*).

[c] Lee (note b), pp. 274–5.

[d] Table 2.2.15, column 5, cf. table 2.2.2.

[e] Guessed. Khrushchev began reducing the number of men under arms in 1960, but did not get very far. The items marked g and h in this year are simply my extrapolations from the respective series.

[f] From table 2.2.2, column iv, cf. also the MBMW item in OE, table 2.2.15, last column. On the unsatisfactory case of 1972 cf. section IX.

[g] Based on the published state index of goods prices. See text. This series is on all grounds much to be preferred.

[h] Based on the implicit deflator in table 2.2.3. See note g, and text.

[i] In the absence of a net estimate by Gillula, this is the *gross* figure in Sverdlik. The reasonableness of the number is our main evidence that W_w did not yet exist.

index must do the same. So since the cost-of-living index is also fallaciously stable, there should be no surprise if the OBDA deflator stands always at 100 (current prices = 1965 prices).

V.   The magnitude of gross procurement, and hence of W_w

We have established in table 2.2.5, mainly from non-I/O sources, the magnitude and (in part!) the exact definition of $\triangle R_w$ over many years. Gillula's number for net OE is much the same, it does refer to defence, and it originates overwhelmingly in the rows for MBMW and fuel. We reproduce in table 2.2.6 his final-use wings for the USSR in 1966 and (in part) 1972. Unfortunately he has not been able to tackle 1959, but we have already established $\triangle R_w$, by an act of minimal extrapolation, for that year. In table 2.2.7, we give Sverdlik's gross magnitudes for all three years. To save printing expense, we give his 1966 table in full, including the first quadrant, and simply his OE column in 1959 and 1972.

Table 2.2.5.   Some estimates of $\triangle R$ compared (R md., current)

	1960	1961	1962	1963	1964	1965	1966	1967
OBDA-PMC[a]	4.9	7.0	7.7	8.7	7.7	7.1	7.0	7.6
$\triangle R$ in I/O tables	—						7.4[b]	
Productive accumulation-gap[d]	—	6.2	6.8	5.3	5.7	6.7	7.3	7.9
$\triangle R$ in Sokoloff[e]	5.9	6.9	7.4	7.1	8.2	9.1	10.5	9.4
$\triangle R$ in Mochizuki	—	5.7	7.1	6.2	8.4	13.2	10.4	9.3

	1968	1969	1970	1971	1972	1973	1974	1975
OBDA-PMC[a]	9.4	10.8	9.5	9.0	8.4	7.7	6.2	6.0
$\triangle R$ in I/O tables					$\left\{\begin{array}{l} 12.9^c \\ 11.9 \end{array}\right.$			
Productive accumulation-gap[d]	8.7	9.3	11.0	10.7	11.0	13.0	13.1	12.5
$\triangle R$ in Sokoloff[e]	12.7	15.1	11.8	16.2	14.7	18.2	18.5	19.1
$\triangle R$ in Mochizuki	11.9	15.9	12.8	14.7	7.3[f]	11.8	11.7	11.6

[a]Refer to table 2.2.4. Note that this line is $\triangle R_w$, not $\triangle R$.
[b]Refer to table 2.2.6.
[c]Refer to table 2.2.6. This is the estimate Gillula (in correspondence) thinks is too big, followed by my arbitrary correction.
[d]Refer to table 2.2.2.
[e]Sokoloff, G., *L'Economie de la Détente* (Fondation National des Sciences Politiques: Paris, 1983), pp. 55–60, 195–7, 281.
[f]Clearly Mochizuki has included some negative harvest-related element in his 'reserves'. This was a crisis year in agriculture. Cf. Mochizuki, K., *Voyennie Raskhody SSSR* in *Japanese Slavic and East European Studies*, no. 4, 1983.

Table 2.2.6.   The author's final verdict on W_w (R md., current)

	1959	1966	1972
$\triangle R_w$, including military MOI	?4.40[a]	6.73[b]	?10.33[b]
Gross procurement, including MOI			
but excluding foreign trade	4.70[c]	9.20[c]	17.80[c]
W_w (residual)	?0.00	2.50	7.50

[a]Table 2.2.4.
[b]Gillula (see table 2.2.15).
[c]Sverdlik (see table 2.2.7).

Looking at Gillula's more detailed 'net' breakdown, it is clear that Sverdlik's 'heavy industry' includes Gillula's MBMW and fuel, but little else. It is thus very probable indeed that Sverdlik gives us gross procurement and Gillula $\triangle R_w$, so that the difference is W_w (see table 2.2.6). In table 2.2.7, the only strictly comparable numbers are for gross procurement. In particular $\triangle R_w$ in 1959 is not on the same definition as in 1972, and 1966 is probably on some intermediate definition.

So doubtful a series should be checked by all possible means. Here, then, are the opinions—so diverse!—of the Washington intelligence community (table 2.2.8).[23] The figures seem to be for MBMW's military *output*, not the MoD's *procurement*. They presumably include, out of military MOI, bullets but not fuel; and certainly include foreign trade.

We agree, it seems, very well with Lee and Rosefielde earlier, but the US Central Intelligence Agency (CIA) later. This is in several ways not very satisfactory. First, our interpolated figure for gross procurement in 1970 is R 14.7 md., while the CIA's celebrated espionage coup says R 18.5 md. (Pitzer, p. 33).[24] The origin, credibility, exact definition or margin of error of this number is unknown to this author. Furthermore, the CIA itself disregards it. Quite possibly it is for the MoD's budgetary estimate and so includes military building.

We must also compare rates of growth (table 2.2.9). It is particularly striking that $\triangle R_w$ alone does not grow as much as NMP in 1959–66. Since our figures for $\triangle R_w$ are entirely independent of all our other workings, this would be a very serious matter indeed, making nonsense of recent Soviet economic and diplomatic history, were it not for the superior growth of the weapons write-off. The CIA makes nonsense of both economic and diplomatic history by undershooting NMP. None the less, the relation of gross procurement to the global value of output (GVO) of MBMW is problematical, because a GVO is a global figure, which includes a great deal of double counting within the MBMW sector. Procurement, however, is a net figure since it is a final use entering into NMP—or at least into the Western GNP.

Table 2.2.7.   Input/Output for 1966 (in milliards of current roubles)

MOI (products of branches)	The branches of material production [See the numbers in the down column]											Σ material branches	Private consump-tion	The unproductive sphere The service branches *Khoz raschyotni*	Science	B ta
	1	2	3	4	5	6	7	8	9	10	11	12	13	14	15	
Industry																
1. Heavy	72.4	2.2	2.4	77.0	21.3	5.7	0.0	5.7	3.9	1.2	0.6	109.7	14.7	3.1	2.9	
2. Light	1.9	27.0	0.5	29.4	0.6	0.3	0.0	0.3	0.2	0.3	0.0	30.8	27.5	0.0	0.0	
3. Food	0.9	0.7	22.1	23.7	0.1	0.9	0.0	0.9	0.0	0.3	0.0	25.0	62.0	0.0	0.0	
4. Σ Industrial	75.2	29.9	25.0	130.1	22.0	6.9	0.0	6.9	4.1	1.8	0.6	165.5	104.2	3.1	2.9	
5. Construction	—	—	—	—	—	—	—	—	—	—	—	—	—	—	—	
Agriculture																
6. Socialized	0.7	5.2	27.9	33.8	0.0	6.4	2.9	9.3	0.0	0.1	0.0	43.2	3.7	0.0	0.0	
7. Private	0.0	0.2	3.3	3.5	0.0	0.0	8.3	8.3	0.0	0.0	0.0	11.8	17.4	0.0	0.0	
8. Σ Agricultural	0.7	5.4	31.2	37.3	0.0	6.4	11.2	17.6	0.0	0.1	0.0	55.0	21.1	0.0	0.0	
9. Transport & Communications	15.9	0.4	1.5	17.8	0.1	0.9	0.0	0.9	—	0.1	0.1	19.0	—	—	—	
10. Trade, procurement and supply	3.9	1.7	7.0	12.6	0.0	2.8	0.0	2.8	0.0	0.0	0.3	15.7	—	—	—	
11. Other [productive] branches	0.7	0.0	0.0	0.7	0.5	0.1	0.0	0.1	0.0	0.1	0.0	1.4	2.4	0.0	0.0	
12. Σ MOI	96.4	37.4	64.7	198.5	22.6	17.1	11.2	28.3	4.1	2.1	1.0	256.6	127.7	3.1	2.9	
13. Amortization	9.9	0.5	1.0	11.4	1.8	4.0	0.4	4.4	2.7	1.2	0.0	21.5	5.6	1.9	0.4	
14. Primary incomes of workers	30.4	4.5	3.5	38.4	15.9	20.0	18.0	38.0	6.5	7.2	2.7	108.7	—	4.6	3.9	
15. Primary incomes of enterprises	30.2	14.6	21.4	66.2	3.2	12.3	—	12.3	5.7	5.2	0.3	92.9	—	0.9	0.2	
16. Σ net *produktsia*	60.6	19.1	24.9	104.6	19.1	32.3	18.0	50.3	12.2	12.4	3.0	201.6	—	5.5	4.1	
17. Total *produktsia*	*166.9*	*57.0*	*90.6*	*314.5*	*43.5*	*53.4*	*29.6*	*83.0*	*19.0*	*15.7*	*4.0*	*479.7*	—	*10.5*	*7.4*	
18. Imports	5.8	5.1	2.4	13.3	—	2.0	—	2.0	—	—	0.0	15.3	—	—	—	
19. Grand total	*172.7*	*62.1*	*93.0*	*327.8*	*43.5*	*55.4*	*29.6*	*85.0*	*19.0*	*15.7*	*4.0*	*495.0*	—	*10.5*	*7.4*	

*Sverdlik's table 2.9.

Table 2.2.8.   Some US estimates of gross weapon procurement (current R bn.)

	1960	1965	1970	1975
CIA 1982/3	9.9	12.8	16.2	21.5
Lee	5.5	12.5	18.8	33.4
Rosefielde	5.5	10.1	18.5	33.9

Source: Parker, P. J. and Rosefielde, S., 'Soviet Arms Procurement—Strategy in the Eighties', draft of Nov. 1984 (unpublished).

	Accumulation and OE														Column 29 in 1959/1972	
	Gross fixed investment						Δ stocks									
	productive			unproductive			in productive branches			in unproductive branches						
Σ all uses	public	private	Σ	public	private	Σ	public	private	Σ		OE	Σ 19–29	Exports	Grand Total		
18	19	20	21	22	23	24	25	26	27	28	29	30	31	32		
22.6	17.7	0.0	17.7	2.2	0.2	2.4	3.4	—	3.4	0.4	9.2	33.1	7.3	172.7	4.7	17.8
28.8	0.0	0.0	0.0	0.0	0.0	0.0	0.2	—	0.2	0.0	1.4	1.6	0.9	62.1	1.2	−0.3
64.3	0.0	0.0	0.0	0.0	0.0	0.0	1.7	—	1.7	0.0	1.0	2.7	1.0	93.0	1.4	−0.3
115.7	17.7	0.0	17.7	2.2	0.2	2.4	5.3	—	5.3	0.4	11.6	37.4	9.2	327.8	7.3	17.2
—	24.0	—	24.0	16.5	3.0	19.5	—	—	—	—	—	43.5	—	43.5	—	—
4.4	0.4	0.0	0.4	—	—	—	6.2	—	6.2	0.0	0.8	7.4	0.4	55.4	−1.9	−1.9
17.4	0.0	0.4	0.4	—	—	—	—	0.0	0.0	—	0.0	0.4	—	29.6	—	0.0
21.8	0.4	0.4	0.8	—	—	—	6.2	0.0	6.2	0.0	0.8	7.8	0.4	85.0	−1.9	−1.9
—	—	—	—	—	—	—	—	—	—	—	—	—	—	19.0	—	—
—	—	—	—	—	—	—	—	—	—	—	—	—	—	15.7	—	—
2.6	—	—	—	—	—	—	0.0	—	0.0	0.0	0.0	0.0	0.0	4.0	−0.1	−0.2
140.1	42.1	0.4	42.5	18.7	3.2	21.9	11.5	0.0	11.5	0.4	12.4	88.7	9.6	495.0	5.3	15.1
9.9																
—																
—																
—																
—																

Table 2.2.9. Some annual rates of growth from table 2.2.8 (current prices, except CIA)

		MBMW		Gross procurement and the like		
	$\triangle R_w$	GVO	NMP	Wiles	Rosefielde	CIA
1959–66	6.1[a]	15.5[b]	6.5	9.9	14.6[c]	5.4[c]
1966–72	7.4[a]	10.0[d]	6.5	11.7	12.9[e]	4.8[e]

[a]See table 2.2.6.
[b]Treml, V., Kostinsky, B. and Gallik, D., in *Soviet Economic Prospects for the Seventies* (Joint Economic Committee of Congress: Washington, DC, 1973), back flap.
[c]1960–65.
[d]R 117, 127 mn. in 1972 (Gallik, D., Kostinsky, B. and Treml, V., *Input-Output Structure of the Soviet Economy 1972*, Foreign Economic Report no. 18 (Department of Commerce: Washington, DC, 1983); R 66.2 md. in 1966 (Kostinsky, B., in ed. V. Treml, *Studies in Input-Output Analysis* (New York, 1977), pp. 52–4).
[e]1965–70.

VI. How is W_w financed?

So W_w exists and is big. In its accounting aspect, however, it corresponds to a serious economic activity in the real world, absorbing 2 per cent of NMP: the replacement and repair of weapons, whether in the MoD's own repair shops or in the civilian enterprises of the military-industrial complex. Have we discovered then a new output, which we must add to all existing outputs, thus increasing overall Soviet productivity?

Nothing of the sort. The sum of gross fixed investment, stock change and OE is identical in Sverdlik and Gillula. The sum of amortization payments and *iznos* is also the same. Therefore, simply, different things are being depreciated in our two sources, and some replacement and repair hitherto thought to be civilian is in fact military—even though our estimates of net military and civilian investment are unchanged. We illustrate this by comparing two Soviet sources (table 2.2.10): they yield different gross totals for civilian and military fixed investment.

But it does follow that amortization payments are being drained away into the maintenance of budgetary, that is public, capital. For none of our work suggests that these must be lowered and *iznos*, in the strict sense of replacement and repair financed out of FNE, raised. It is possible that the new drain goes towards PuC fixed assets like hospitals and schools. It is probable that it goes to the MoD. In any case, note that an amortization payment is a *payment*, an admitted part of the (central) Financial Plan. The payer has no claim to get it all back. Part of it is redistributed, extra-budgetarily. Thus, part of the work of the tax system and the Ministry of Finance is and has always been done by *khozraschyotni* enterprises.

Nay, more, on 1 January 1963 amortization rates were raised by about 25 per cent (see table 2.2.11). This was within two years of Khrushchev's rearmament drive. True, there were many complaints in 1962 of the insufficiency of amortization payments; but that might well be precisely because of the new military claims. We have reverted to something like the wartime system, when amortization payments actually went into the budget.[25] Our next two tables (2.2.12 and 2.2.13) assure us that Sverdlik's gross investment is of the same size as Gillula's, so that we really do have to deal with a shifting of its components between classifications.

Finally in table 2.2.10, the *Metodicheskie Ukazania* (Methodological Instructions),[26] a very authoritative source, present the same contrast to Sverdlik as does the US I/O school. In the 1969 edition, a table, in 'conventional' numbers of R md. and an unnamed year, very clearly omits all mention of W_w, where it would be most appropriate. I reproduce it with a slight clarification by differently indenting the items in the left-hand margin and inserting some dashes (—), meaning 'inapplicable'. Figures in brackets are Sverdlik's for 1966. Duchêne, who drew my attention to this table, comments on the closeness of its conventional (*uslovni*) numbers to those of 1966. They are indeed close, with discrepancies of: exports + 20 per cent, productive

Table 2.2.10. *Metodicheskie Ukazania* versus Sverdlik (bn. roubles)

	Consumption	KY = net accumulation + replacement	Capital repair	ΔS + OE	Export	Import	Losses	Final product
NMP used	140	30	7	17				200 (204.2)
Consumption	140	4[a] (——9.9——) 32	6[b])	—				150
Accumulation			1[d])	17				50
of which: Δ basic funds		30	—	—				30
Δ circulating funds, stocks, reserves and other elements of accumulation		2[c] (——3.3——) (+10%)	1[d])	17				20
Amortization of productive funds and not fully amortized value		14[e]	11[f]	—				
Exports				—	8		25 (21.5) (−14%)	8
Imports						−15		−15
Losses							2	2
Final Product	140	50[g] (——64.4——)	18	17	8	−15	2	220
(Sverdlik for 1966)	(140.1)	(−5.3%)		(24.3)	(9.6)	(−15.3)	(?)	(223.1)
(Percentage discrepancy)				(+42.9%)	(+20%)	(+2%)		(+1.4%)

Notes in original: [added by Wiles]

[a] Replacement of unproductive [basic] funds.
[b] Capital repair of unproductive [basic] funds.
[c] Δ uncompleted building.
[d] Δ uncompleted capital repair. [This is not expressly in Sokoloff, G., *L'Économie de la Détente* (Fondation Nationale des Sciences Politiques: Paris, 1983); Mochizuki, K., *Voyennie Raskhody SSSR* in *Japanese Slavic and East European Studies*, no. 4, 1983; and Sverdlik, S. B., *Denezhni Oboroi i Obshchestvenni Produkt* (Novosibirsk, 1980). I assume it is normally part of Δ uncompleted building, and the name 'growth of unfinished building' cover both items.]
[e/f] Replacement and capital repair, respectively.
[g] At *smetny* prices, KV in 1966 was R 52.4 bn.

Table 2.2.11.   The 1963 jump in amortization deductions

1959	1960	1961	1962	1963	1964	1965	1966	1967
Deductions as a percentage of industrial *khozraschyotni* basic funds								
?	?	?	5.9	7.6	7.3	7.4	7.3	7.4
The absolute sum of nationwide deductions (R mn.)								
7943	9095	10 208	11 300	15 553	17 045	18 805	20 584	22 380

1968	1969	1970	1971	1972	1973	1974	1975
Deductions as a percentage of industrial *khozraschyotni* basic funds							
7.4	7.3	7.4	7.4	7.5	7.4	?	?
The absolute sum of nationwide deductions (R mn.)							
24 257	26 551	29 105	32 080	35 291	38 923		

Sources: Narkhoz: The general introduction to the industrial section; and the financial section. See especially *Narkhoz*, 1963, p. 653.

amortization − 14 per cent, $\triangle$C + 10 per cent (and that one only rounding error), . . . but $\triangle$S + OE has + 43 per cent! This is the largest percentage and even the largest absolute discrepancy. It obviously conceals W_w, and the writer emerges greatly reinforced from this trial—a trial by fire and water, since one does not lightly take on the *Metodicheskie Ukazania*, which for the rest has been 'pathologically discreet' over defence.

The next biggest discrepancy in absolute terms is that Sverdlik's gross investment (64.4) is R 3.6 md. too small. This is no accident: take away W_w = R 2.3 bn. (see table 2.2.6) from Gosplan's civilian capital repair, and Sverdlik's number becomes a mere R. 1.3 md. too small.

What has happened is the very same thing that the writer first suspected on contemplating Gillula: on the left in his tables too (table 2.2.15 here) is (net) accumulation (here KV), on the right is (net) OE and in the middle is, in Gillula's case R&R, but here only capital repair, the second R. Who tells us how much of that goes left and how much right? No one. Capital repair other than that part of it in budgetary branches' *iznos* is financed, to repeat, by amortization *payments*. These are made by *khozraschyotni* branches, but they do not necessarily receive them all back.

Moreover, these payments are specified as part replacement and part repair (on the incomplete *Narkhoz* reckoning, in 1966 R 10 154 and 10 430 mn.—*Narkhoz*, 1967, p. 883). And the Soviet literature tells us that it is precisely the capital repair part that is centralized into the financial plan. So even this small point is confirmed by the table.

Finally let us disaggregate $\triangle$S + OE. Sverdlik has R 11.9 bn. for $\triangle$S and R 12.4 md. for OE. Suppose that, true to form, the *Gosplan* wrote $\triangle$S =

Table 2.2.12. Gross investment in various versions

US versions,[a] R mn., current   Sverdlik,[b] R md., current, Σ gross investment in many detailed columns, here summarized

	Losses	R and R nationwide (= amortization + iznos)	+ net fixed investment	ΔS[a] +	OE heavy industry	OE other	Total	production fixed	unproduction fixed	ΔS[b]	OE heavy industry	OE other	Total
1966	1574	32 712	29 700	17 348	7410	0	88 744	42.5	21.9	11.9	9.2	3.2	88.7
1972	1691	52 272	55 200	17 200	12 900	0	139 263	78.2	37.5	8.8	17.8	−2.7	139.6

We now arrange these numbers to show the most likely locations of the discrepancies

1966

		ΔC[c]	discrepancy	
32.7	+ 29.7	3.3	−1.3	= 42.5 + 21.9 = 64.4 (gross fixed investment)
	− 17.3	3.3	−2.1	= 11.9 (civilian stock movements)
1.6	+ 7.4		+3.4	= 9.2 + 3.2 = 12.4 (reserves and losses)
	88.7		+ 0	= 88.7

1972

		ΔC[c]	discrepancy	
52.3	+ 55.2	8.3	−0.1	= 78.2 + 37.5 = 115.7 (gross fixed investment)
	− 17.2	8.3	−0.1	= 8.8 (civilian stock movements)
1.7	+ 12.9		+0.5	= 17.8 − 2.7 = 15.1 (reserves and losses)
	139.3		+0.3	= 139.6

Notes:

[a] Table 2.2.9 here: ΔS includes ΔC.

[b] Table 2.2.7 here for 1966; Sverdlik, S. B., *Denezhni Oborot i Obshchestvenni Produkt* (Novosibirsk, 1980), pp. 86–9 for 1972: ΔS excludes ΔC.

[c] This is the growth of the stock of uncompleted buildings. ΔC is here calculated à la Sverdlik (note b; pp. 90–1), not à la Sokoloff, to preserve cohesion. In 1972 it is 7.353 (the increase in this magnitude in state and cooperative enterprise) × 94.3/83.8 (the proportion that the national total bears to this magnitude—*Narkhoz*, 1973, pp. 545, 554, 558). In 1966 it is 2.9 × 52.4/45.8 (*Narkhoz*, 1967, pp. 619, 621, 629).

	1972			1966		
	Sverdlik[a]	*Narkhoz*[a]	*Gallik et al.*[c]	*Sverdlik*[a]	*Narkhoz*[d]	*Kostinsky*[e]
Productive:						
Industrial	20.10	18.73	20.20	11.40	11.11	11.63
Agricultural—public	6.50	3.75	7.00	4.00	2.15	4.78
—private	0.60			0.40	—	—
Transportation and communications, all	6.47[f]	6.47	4.70	3.80[f]	3.80	—
Transportation and communications, productive	4.40	4.40[f]	—	2.70	2.70[f]	2.85
Building	3.60	2.89	3.60	1.80	1.45	1.84
Trade and distribution	1.90	1.47	1.80	1.20	0.71	1.19
Consumer cooperatives	—	0.43	—	—	0.24	
Other	0.00	0.00[g]	0.00	0.00	0.00[g]	
Σ productive branches	37.10	31.67	37.30	21.50	18.36	22.31
Khozraschyotny unproductive services	3.50[h]	3.64	3.30[i]	1.90	1.95	1.86
Communal economy	0.79			0.40	0.72	
'Other'	0.78[g]			0.45[g]		
Unproductive transport and communications (UTC)	2.00[i]	2.07[i]		1.10[i]	1.10[i]	1.14
Σ *Khozraschyotny*	40.60	35.31	40.60	23.40	20.31	24.17
Budgetary services	4.10		11.54[f]	2.40		2.58
In personal consumption	7.80			5.60		5.56
Σ all	52.50	52.14	31.40			32.31[e] / 32.71[c]

Notes:

[a] Sverdlik, S. B., *Denezhni Oborot i Obshchestvenni Produkt* (Novosibirsk, 1980), pp. 83 and 87.

[b] *Narkhoz*, 1973, p. 777.

[c] Gallik, D., Kostinsky, B. L. and Treml, V. G., *Input-Output Structure of the Soviet Economy: 1972*, Foreign Economic Report no. 18 (US Department of Commerce: Washington, DC, Apr. 1983).

[d] *Narkhoz*, 1967, p. 883.

[e] Kostinsky, B., in ed. V. Treml, *Studies in Input-Output Analysis* (Praeger: New York, 1977), pp. 52–4, as in table 2.2.9.

[f] From the next column.

[g] All 'other' has been arbitrarily assigned to *khozraschyotny* (unproductive services).

[h] Sverdlik (note a) also gives these numbers for 1970 (p. 74): Communal economy 1.1, Entertainment 0.1, UTC 2.1.

[i] The 14.84 in the source has been distributed among these two items in Sverdlik's proportion (note 1).

R 11 md.—a moderate discrepancy. Then their OE figure was R 6 md. and it was net, as its presence in the top line confirms. Their W_w was R 2.3 bn. And those two are within close range of Gillula's R 7.4 md. (net), but Sverdlik's R 12.4 md. (gross) is a big discrepancy.

The *Gosplan*, be it noted, has in no way been deceptive. They have given us an honest accounting of capital repair: they have simply not told us what is being repaired. Why should they?

VII. Other items in the budgetary defence allocation (BDA)

The author has discussed this one issue of weapon depreciation at such length because of its great interest and importance, and because it illustrates what is and what is not good Sovietological evidence. There are many other problems, with which we shall be brutally short, putting off the more inquisitive reader with 'workings available on request'.

Servicemen's pay must be rigorously distinguished from servicemen's main-tenance, and both servicemen's pay and maintenance from the wages of the MoD's civilian employees. The large PMC figure in table 2.2.3 (the 'consump-tion gap') is no doubt more maintenance than pay, but participates of both; it also includes the PMC of civilian defence employees. This is logical since the consumption gap is part of the OBDA, which is by definition some part of the estimates (*smeta*) of the MoD. The extremely approximate and doubtful numbers in 1965 (not 1966) are shown in table 2.2.14. They leave, according to the author's latest reworking of new evidence, a substantial residual within the

Table 2.2.14. Servicemen's pay and maintenance (SPM) in 1965

	Number of people, thousands	Per head R per annum	Total income, mn. R	PMC ÷ money income[a]	PMC element, mn. R
Servicemen's pay	3900[b]	600[c]	2340	78[d]	1825
Servicemen's maintenance	3900	480[c]	1872	95[d]	1778
Civilian employees' pay	390[e]	1241[f]	484	86	416
Discrepancy	0	—	—	—	1881
Totals	4290	1095	4696	—	5900[g]

Notes:

[a] In 1965 an industrial worker's family received 13 per cent of its global income in social services in kind, and spent 61.3 per cent of the same on PMC plus 2.5 per cent on rent (*Narkhoz*, 1973, p. 632). $(61.3+2.5)/(100-13.8)=86$ per cent. This is 86 per cent of money income, of course.

[b] Table 2.2.3.

[c] Workings available on request. The sources are quite bad and contradict each other.

[d] These percentages are designed to average 86.

[e] Figures exist up to 1945 (4.4% of servicemen). I assume 10% by 1965 because of the increasing demands for repair workers and minor bureaucrats.

[f] 12 × the average wage nation-wide (R 96.5 p.m.: *Narkhoz*, 1973, p. 586).

[g] Table 2.2.3; i.e., the quasi-official figure out of *Narkhoz*.

total of military consumption. The best, but by no means proven, explanation is that this is military MOI, which then has been treated in table 2.2.3 exactly like PuC MOI.

Military MOI might, however, be in $\triangle R_w$, the other part of the OBDA. Since it is not investment, unlike weapons, it would then be the element that necessitates the technically honest phrase 'Accumulation and Other Expenditures'. That phrase includes, alike in the *Narkhoz* and in Sverdlik:

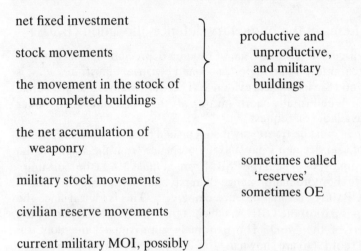

net fixed investment

stock movements

the movement in the stock of
   uncompleted buildings

productive and
unproductive,
and military
buildings

the net accumulation of
   weaponry

military stock movements

civilian reserve movements

current military MOI, possibly

sometimes called
'reserves'
sometimes OE

Of all these, only the last is not investment. It certainly contains the fuel burned—and must have increased many times with Afghanistan (December 1979). It must also include stationery, civilian transport and communications when paid for, and—why not?—bullets. But if bullets, why not shells? And if shells, why not atom bombs? We have no answers to these questions.

Military stock movements will be in the same objects plus perhaps food. Looking at Gillula's fuel/OE box, we see that it is far too big to contain only the stock movement: current consumption must also be there. He gives us (current R mn.):

	OE	Final use	GVO	
1966	330	3700	19000	(table 2.2.15[27])
1972	1570	7100	49000	

Nine per cent, let alone 22 per cent, of final use is an extremely large slice for the growth of military stocks. It is clear that the OE figures cover mostly military use.

The remaining items must be compressed into footnotes in our summary.

Table 2.2.15. Components of gross investment in the USSR: 1966 (millions of roubles)

Accumulation fund

Branch	Gross investment (1)	Total (2)	Net fixed investment (3)	Inventory change (4)	Other expenditures (5)	Capital replacement (6)	Losses (7)	Column 5 in 1972
Total	88 744	54 458	29 700	17 348	7 410	32 712	1 574	12 900
Industry	37 344	22 883	8 845	6 628	7 410	14 461	0	12 900
Metallurgy	400	400	0	400	0	0	0	0
Fuel	670	670	0	340	330	0	0	1 570
Power	0	0	0	0	0	0	0	0
MBMW	31 399	17 160	8 642	1 788	6 730	14 239	0	11 330
Chemical	1 055	1 055	0	705	350	0	0	0
Wood & paper	451	229	203	26	0	222	0	0
Construction materials	310	310	0	310	0	0	0	0
Textiles & apparel	967	967	0	967	0	0	0	0
Food	2 012	2 012	0	2 012	0	0	0	0
Industry NEC	80	80	0	80	0	0	0	0
Construction	43 360	24 073	19 789	4 284	0	18 251	1 036	0
Agriculture & forestry	7 995	7 457	1 030	6 427	0	0	538	0
Transport & communications	0	0	0	0	0	0	0	0
Trade & distribution	0	0	0	0	0	0	0	0
Other branches	45	45	36	9	0	0	0	0

Source: Gillula, J., *Components of Gross Investment in 1966 and 1972*, Data Resources Inc. (US Department of Commerce: Washington, DC, 1984).

VIII.   The BDA, all items

Our estimates and guesses for 1965–66 (current mn.) are summed up in table 2.2.16.

Table 2.2.16.   The Soviet budgetary defence allocation (BDA) in 1966 (in millions of current roubles)

Common to all definitions:

$\triangle R_w$	6730		
W_w	2500		
Gross weapon procurement			9230
Servicemen's pay[a]		?	2360
Servicemen's maintenance[a]		?	1900
Civilian employees' wages[a]		??	500
Civilian employees' social security[b]		??	28
Fuel consumed or stocked			330
Other operations and training[c]		??	330
Construction at 1/10 of gross weapon procurement (as in UK)		??	923
Machinery for MoD enterprises (double-counted)[d]			—

In NATO but not in Soviet definition:

Military R&D (60 per cent of official total)[e]	?	4440
Military health		?
Military pensions (but not those of civilian employees: 7 per cent[f] of current pay and maintenance as in UK)	??	298

In Soviet but not in NATO definition:

Suvorov and Nakhimov Schools[g]	?	2
General expenses of construction, railway, etc., troops	?	included above

Excluded from both definitions:

Services rendered to the civilian economy: all payments are assumed to be deducted above already, along the appropriate line. Security, public order, frontier troops (KGB and MVD); weapon factories' expenses not covered by MoD procurement,[h] DOSAAF, the voluntary civil defence organization.

Resulting totals (current prices unless otherwise stated)

On NATO definition (my work)		20 339
On Soviet definition (my work)		15 603
OBDA + W_w (mixed work) [Bear in mind that this definition omits services.]		15 800
CIA (in 1970 roubles)	[Work of author shown, exact definition not published.]	40 000[i]
Lee	,,	28 000[i]
SIPRI (in later versions)	,,	31 000[i]
Rosefielde (in 1970 roubles)	,,	23 700

These chaotic numbers are not such as to make any scholar proud of his field. Our own numbers for weapon procurement and pay/maintenance are within the general 'ballpark'; our big shortfall seems to stem from elsewhere.

Notes:

[a]Includes all such fringe benefits as special tourist resorts. I assume that civilian employees participate only a little, and on the whole depend upon their trade unions.

[b]At the usual 5.5 per cent. This explains their absence from military pensions.

[c]This is non-fuel MOI, plus the service supplies also bought. It is guessed, without any knowledge at all, as equal to the item above it.

[d]This item is entered as a warning. We assume that both British and Soviet statistics treat productive machinery installed in the MoD's repair shops as a part of construction. In the USSR, at any rate, it is barely conceivable that the hallowed definition of KV would be changed at this point. At stake are about R 100 mn.

[e]This is far bigger than Acland-Hood's number (see paper 2.5), which I unhesitatingly reject as based on the improbable assumption that the USSR spends on military R&D the same proportion of money to output, branch by branch throughout the economy, as the USA. My basic assumption is that the USSR spends a slightly higher proportion of R&D money on each unit weapon (knowing that its R&D is very inefficient), and so as a residual radically less on civilian outputs, branch by branch, than is commonly supposed. But there are other factors: workings available on request.

[f]This figure was 14 per cent in the USA in 1966 (Statistical Abstract, 1968, pp. 248 and 267: \$52 818 mn pay; 1591 'retired pay' on MoD vote; 5691 on Veterans Administration vote). But US veterans live longer than Soviet ones, and the US system is notoriously over-generous by everyone's standards, including those of most Americans.

[g]These are basically orphanages that discharge their protégés into the forces. Their expenses might overlap, on the wages side, with civilian employees. The figure of R 2 mn. is a quite well-informed guess. (Workings available from this author on request.)

[h]The weapon factories (and probably the MoD repair shops) are on *khozraschyot* (cost accounting) and therefore not extrabudgetary (Julian Cooper, private correspondence, Oct. 1986). The former make civilian goods well and in large quantities. Presumably, they use the profits, with Treasury permission, to cross-subsidize weapon production. Presumably, too, they all get investment finance direct from the budget, so never have to borrow it from the bank at interest and pay a low or no rate of the tax on working fixed assets. All this will be reflected in low weapon prices.

[i]As quoted by Abraham S. Becker, 'Sitting on Bayonets?', revised version of that in *Soviet Union*, 1983, privately circulated.

IX.   A fantasia on the Brezhnevian Number

Since 1972, at the latest, the OBDA has consistently declined (until 1984). The chance of so consistent a decline in a random series is one in 120; yet the face story is impossible to take seriously. It deprives the OBDA of all meaning, and so our previous work of very much of its value. For the 'old' OBDA was full of serious information deceptively packaged, and it was very valuable to understand its meaning.

Already in 1972 our net procurement figure, taken from Gillula (table 2.2.15), is definitely too big for the OBDA, considering the figure for military PMC (table 2.2.3). Also it shows suspiciously little growth from 1971. So let the new OBDA be a code for the 'true' or old OBDA from 1 January 1972, so that falls mean rises. A convenient simple code is: $(X+Y)(2-Y)$, where X is the number of whole billions and Y is the decimal point and the number of millions. So the old OBDA in 1972 was:

$$17.9 + 17.9\,(1-0.900) = 19.69.$$

If we look back at table 2.2.4, we see how much more plausible this is in terms of $\triangle R_w$.

By 1981, the Brezhnevian Number had fallen, often in 'steps' of more than one year, to R 17.054 bn. This yields R 33.19 bn, and the Number sticks there for four years! What is wrong? Why do they pile absurdity on absurdity by freezing their number? The reason may be that for a year or two one can secretly expand W_w at the expense of $\triangle R_w$ (depreciation always lends itself to fiscal evasion!), so the long 'steps' are tolerable; but in the end, the R 34 bn. barrier must be broken; for by our formula the 17 billions new OBDA cannot yield over 34.0 billion old OBDA at the maximum. So in 1984 the Russians took a deep breath and chose a new value for X: 19. 18 was wisely avoided since it could not last beyond an 'old' OBDA of R 36 bn. The new number actually chosen was 19.063, implying R 36.80 bn. Our suggested formula has then survived a very awkward crisis with flying colours, even explaining the long hesitation. There must be very many formulae that can conjure 5 per cent per annum growth out of small declines, but not many can simultaneously explain the upward jump, right over 18, to a low 19—and still deliver roughly 5 per cent growth. However, R 38 bn (for the items in the 'old' OBDA of course) is not far away, so numbers in 19 will not flourish long either. Indeed, regretfully, the author would advise a new code.

Our new numbers yield a growth rate of 5 per cent since 1972. This is about the US Defense Intelligence Agency (DIA)'s growth rate in current roubles: our number is always about one-third of theirs. This too is a test that any interpretation of the Brezhnevian Number must pass, though of course it might be a little lower or indeed higher.

Yet my solution for the problem of the Brezhnevian Number, though surprisingly successful, remains, it must be said, fantastic. Above all, in practical administrative terms, *why* do all this?

Notes and references

[1] Voznesenski, N. A., *Voyennaya Ekonomika SSSR* (Moscow, 1948); *Materials for a Balance of the Soviet Economy*, 1928–30, English translation and edition by S. G. Wheatcroft and R. W. Davies (Cambridge University Press: Cambridge, 1985), p. 165. The original was an informal collection of papers by the *Gosplan*.

[2] Strumilin, S. G., in *Planovoye Khozyaistvo* (8/1926), pp. 148 and 162.

[3] Rutgaizer, V. M., *Resursy Razvitia Neproizvodstvennoi Sfery* (*Mysl'*: Moscow, 1975).

[4] Note that no Soviet or Western statistician goes further and transfers investment in weapon factories to 'war': except (in both cases) in MoD repair shops. Note too that eventually in the 1970s the 'new' NMP table (section 4) transfers unproductive workers' PMC to PuC, according them equal treatment with servicemen.

[5] E.g., in 1941, for which we have good data. This author hopes to deal with Voznesenski and the *Materialy* in the detail they deserve in a subsequent publication.

[6] It is of great importance that Poland uses the 'reserves' for weapons. But the Polish OBDA engages in far less deception than the Hungarian, let alone the Soviet.

[7] Many of my colleagues have extreme difficulty with this point! They try to accept the capitalization of weapons in view of the many literary sources—and then they try to

reject the weapons write-off. Would they do that to their own cars? Don't they repair and replace them? Do they keep all the cars they ever had out in the street?

[8] Cf. Kuznets, S. S., *National Product in Wartime* (National Bureau of Economic Research: New York, 1945); Moss, M. (ed.), *The Measurement of Economic and Social Performance* (National Bureau of Economic Research: New York, 1973) (F. Thomas Juster on p. 70, Robert Eisner on p. 100, Richard Tobin and Walter Nordhaus on pp. 515–6); 'Adam Smith', 'If the Navy sells the fleet who pays the bill?', *Esquire*, Aug. 1984; and for UK note 12 here.

[9] Sverdlik's guesstimate is R 1 md. in 1970 (pp. 91–2): Sverdlik, S. B., *Denezhni Oborot i Obshchestvenni Produkt* (Novosibirsk, 1980), pp. 91–2; see also Gillula, J. W., *Components of Gross Investment in 1966 and 1972 I/O Tables*, Data Resources Inc. (US Department of Commerce: Washington, DC, 1984).

[10] I have only one reference for this: Strumilin, S. G., *Voprosy Ekonomiki*, 7/1959, p. 128. But the point is sufficiently obvious, since weapons used not to be capitalized, and the KV statistics sail through that event (1959 or 1963) without a hiccup.

[11] A great deal of work went into this statement—available on request from this author.

[12] Her Majesty's Treasury, *Economic Progress Report* (Her Majesty's Stationery Office: London, Feb. 1984), p. 3. *The Public Expenditure White Paper*, also a Treasury document (Her Majesty's Stationery Office: London), contains the same data every year. The numbers, both for weapon procurement and for building procurement, are called gross investment. The reason is that the monetarist ruling party, disappointed by the negative effect of its policies on civilian capitalist investment, wishes to show that 'investment' remains high. The Central Statistical Office however, in a truly Soviet departmental quarrel, does not recognize this manoeuvre.

[13] Sokoloff, G., *L'Economie de la Détente* (Fondation Nationale des Sciences Politiques: Paris, 1983), pp. 55–60, 195–7 and 281.

[14] Ryabushkin, T. V., *Ekonomicheskaya Statistika* (Moscow, 1976), p. 176.

[15] Item 1: Economic and Social Council E/CN.2/396 of 25 July 1969 (from Russian into French, courtesy of Georges Sokoloff), section 56.
Item 2: Economic and Social Council E/CN.3/397/REV. of 6 July 1970 (English version), sections 38; 38 (iv); and 71 (ii), respectively.

[16] Notkin, A. I., *Ocherki Teorii Sotsialisticheskogo Vosproizvodstra* (Moscow, 1948), p. 195 (italics added).

[17] Bor, M. Z., *Balans Narodnogo Khozyaistva S.S.S.R.*, 1956, pp. 57–8.

[18] Vainshtein, A., in *Ekonomika i Matematicheskie Metody*, 1/1967.

[19] Allakhverdian, D. A., *Nekotoriye Voprosy Teorii Sovetskikh Finansov* (Moscow, 1951), p. 30.

[20] This extremely awkward concept must be supposed, since the total adds up to the national total PMC, to include the PMC they finance out of lottery winnings, interest and so on.

[21] The second and other workers in a family are ranged under the classification of the head [PJDW].

[22] This author's more recent workings on Poland and Hungary leave little doubt that all security and police formations are ordinary unproductive labour recorded as Administration.

[23] Parker, P. J. and Rosefielde, S., 'Soviet Arms Procurement—Strategy in the Eighties', draft of Nov. 1984 (unpublished).

[24] Pitzer, J., *Reconciliation of GNP and SNI* (Office of Research, US Central Intelligence Agency: Washington, DC, Dec. 1977), photocopy.

[25] Campbell, R., *Accounting in Soviet Planning and Management* (Harvard University Press: Cambridge, MA, 1963), p. 94.

[26] *Gosplan, Metodicheskie ukazania* (Moscow, 1969), p. 591.

[27] See Gillula (note 9).

Paper 2.3.   How much do the Soviets spend on defence?

GÉRARD DUCHÊNE

I.   Introduction

Any estimate of Soviet military expenditure makes sense only in relation to a consistent accounting of the total economic activity of the USSR. The purpose of the present paper is: first, to give a general picture of the difficulties involved in estimating Soviet economy aggregates and their defence component; and second, to propose a method of estimation of the defence burden using the Soviet accounting framework of material product accountancy (MPA) and avoiding at the same time the 'residual methods'.

II.   The use of Soviet statistics for purposes of economic and defence studies

Uncertainty of Soviet data

Practically all users of Soviet data complain about the lack of consistency and the cumbersome or secret methodology. A quick glance at Soviet statistics can be deceiving due to numerous incompatibilities between different sets of data, such as the various kinds of manpower; the manpower, income and consumption series; and the investment, capital and production series, not to mention the non-inexistent monetary and financial data.[1] The only relatively solid basis of consistent data has been given by the input-output tables (the latest dates from 1972 and confirms the gross consistency of input-output methodology and MPA).

This situation of uncertainty has led to several attempts at reconstructing systems of national accounts on the basis of the fragmentary information delivered. Unfortunately, these attempts, although they may provide interesting insights on some aspects of the Soviet economy, can be criticized when they pretend to give a comprehensive picture of it.

The demographic gap

The excellent unpublished study presented by D. Steinberg at the 1985 Gleneagles Meeting insists convincingly on the existence of gaps in practically all sectors of Soviet statistics. Above all, he suggests a general explanation of these pervasive gaps: a complete sector of production (defence production) with its inputs, incomes, production and so on is excluded from most of the published aggregates. Let us examine the most impressive of his tables: Demographic trends (table 11A of his study).

Conceptually, Steinberg tries to show that if one deducts from the total population figure (which is not contested for the moment) all known categories of the population (children under 16, pensioners, the labour force, students and so on), this leaves an 'unaccounted residual' of 17.2 million persons in 1983. This residual is supposed to contain such categories as the unemployed (1.7 million), prisoners (1.0 million), the armed forces (7.8 million) and those engaged in defence production (6.7 million). This method has the merit of showing that the Soviet Union, in the simplest of its dimensions (population), remains mysterious. Nevertheless, one cannot accept the type of calculation proposed by Steinberg for several reasons.

1. There is a misconception regarding the 'pensioners' category. The figures mentioned, drawn from the Soviet *Statistical Yearbooks* (*Narkhoz*), refer to a complex concept grouping many different categories of so-called pensioners,[2] a great part of whom are of working age (or even children under 16). As a result, a percentage of these 'pensioners' is already accounted for by Steinberg in other categories of the table; the number of working pensioners is undervalued. Above all, many people above the ages of 55 to 60 did not until very recently receive any pension nor work, and they are missing from the table. (These amounted to at least 6 million people in 1970.)

2. The labour force proposed by Steinberg includes as one of its components the figure of the mean annual number of wage-earners (*srednegodovaja cislennost rabocikh i sluzascikh*) as given by *Narkhoz*. This is again a conceptual gap since this figure represents jobs (full-time equivalents) and not persons. A mere glance at the census data from 1970 and 1979 shows that there is a large gap between the number of persons (*zanjatoe naselenie*) and the number of full-time equivalents, due to seasonal work, part-time jobs, temporary inability to work, fractional unemployment and so on.

3. Several minor elements of the demographic table lack precise support: labouring youth, non-working mothers, dependent persons (?), prisoners and so on. This accumulation of approximate data is a weakness because the architecture of the table is to refine a residual. For instance, Steinberg states that there are 0.5 million non-working mothers (a constant figure from 1970 to 1983). But there are approximately 2 million mothers with 4 children or more receiving aid (*posobie*) and most probably not working. Replace the figure of 0.5 with 2.0 and the defence production population drops from 6.7 to 5.2 million (or –22 per cent).

To sum up, the method used to construct the 'democraphic gap' seems too imprecise to provide convincing results. The only years to which a Steinberg-type methodology can be applied are the census years (1970 and 1979).

Comparing the census data of 'employed population' with the adjusted *Narkhoz* series does lead to a residual. This is, in fact, the manifestation of what the Soviet planners call the 'excluded category' (*iskljucaemyj kontingent*) in regional employment or living standard forecasts.[3] But it is difficult to say that the employed part of this *kontingent* (appearing in the residual) is much superior to what we know (for instance through IISS publications) of Soviet armed forces and internal security forces. If there is a 'secret defence production sector', it would be quite small.

In the later versions of his contribution, Steinberg drastically reduces his estimation of manpower involved in defence production first to 4.5 and then to 4.0 million persons in 1982 (the last estimation is the one given in paper 2.1 in this book), compared to 6.5 million previously. The method used to compute these numbers is through the estimation of female manpower and the population; the first of these versions gave a rather idyllic vision of the Soviet woman, who was totally excluded from the ranks of prisoners, the unemployed, the armed forces and those working in defence production. The version given in paper 2.1 allows for all these categories, which gives a more realistic picture; but, as Steinberg recognizes, there are still some rather unavoidable margins of uncertainty in the conversion between man-hours and persons, in the estimation of prisoners and so on. Even the figure of 5.5 million armed forces and state security personnel is disputable: compare to 7.7 million in the initial document and 5.2 million in the first revised version. One puzzling fact is that comparing the 4.0 million persons employed in defence production with their estimated revenues (18.5–19.0 billion roubles) gives a nearly 400 roubles-per-month wage, which is more than twice the average wage.

Falsification of categories

Another type of problem with Soviet statistics is the falsification of certain categories. The Soviet statisticians give insufficient methodological explanations of their concepts and it is probable that some of the figures listed under a 'peaceful' heading may have at least a partial military content. Nevertheless, one must not exaggerate this practice and, here again, Steinberg seems to push the game a little too far, for instance in his table 'Consumption funds of national income' (table 24A of the Gleneagles paper).

In 1975 the Soviets presented the consumption fund of national income as indicated in column 1 of table 2.3.1. Steinberg asserts that personal consumption (according to the Soviet concept) includes a hidden allocation to the armed forces, in addition to the part of personal consumption of defence households, as indicated in column 2 of table 2.3.1.

It is not explicit what this allocation represents concretely (it is much too large to include only the food and clothing of conscripts). In fact, the figure seems to be a kind of residual which Steinberg deduces from the reconstitution of the personal consumption line. To obtain the total of 217.2 for this line, Steinberg makes a calculation of the type shown in column 1 of table 2.3.2. The

Table 2.3.1. Consumption fund of national income, 1975 (in billions of current roubles)

	Narkhoz figures	Steinberg figures
Consumption fund	266.4	266.4
Personal consumption	231.6	217.2
of which: defence households	—	19.0
Consumption of goods by institutions	34.8	34.8
of which: welfare	24.1	—
R&D administration		
of which: defence	10.7	—
science	—	3.1
Armed forces	—	14.4

Table 2.3.2. Personal consumption, 1975 (in billions of current roubles)

		Steinberg	Duchêne	Steinberg 'gains'
1.	Turnover of all forms of retail trade	215.6	215.6	—
2.	Sales of administrations (*mel'kij opt*)	11.9	9.0	2.9
3.	Second-hand sales (commission trade)	2.3	1.7	0.6
4.	Producer goods	2.6	2.0	0.6
5.	Consumer goods sold to the army	2.3	—	2.3
6.	Sales of goods to households			
	(=1–2–3–4–5)	196.5	202.9	6.4
7.	Utilities	2.4	4.6	2.2
8.	Consumption in kind (in fact other			
	elements are also included)	12.7	14.6	1.9
9.	Housing depreciation	5.6	9.5	3.9
10.	**Total household consumption**			
	(=6+7+8+9)	**217.2**	**231.6**	**14.4**

Source:

Explanation of Duchêne column: our estimates of *mel'kij opt* are based on detailed and explicit data given by Soviet specialists for certain years.[1] Our estimate of utilities is based on a detailed Lithuanian study of the consumption fund[2] giving implicit prices for electricity, gas and other expenditures. The same source and method is used for housing depreciation, and corresponds to a reliable Soviet source on other non-productive depreciation (*iznos*) for the USSR as a whole.[3] Our estimates for line 8 are the sum of self-consumption on private plots, wages in kind of *kolkhoz* and *sovkhoz* members and a small residual supposed to account for fishing, gathering, hunting and so on; the private plot self-consumption is based on the gross social product of agriculture, minus the part produced by *kolkhoz* and state farms, minus the sales on the market and the procurements to state and co-operative trade.

Notes:
[1] These data are referred to by Birman, pp. 250–51 and by CIA 1975, pp. 39 and 61–2. The 1970 figure is projected with three explicative factors: the number of children in pre-school institutions; gross income of *kolkhoz* and administration wage-earners.
[2] Misjunas and Rajackas, p. 52–60.
[3] Rutgajzer, p. 157.

problem here is the estimation of each of the lines except the first one: lines 2.3.2 to 5 are exaggerated by Steinberg while lines 7 to 9 are undervalued. Column 2 of table 2.3.2 presents a different picture, which can be used for the purpose of reconstructing the consumption fund for the years after 1975.

This author considers, therefore, that the officially announced figure of personal consumption should not be reduced by any allocation to the armed forces. The same view was shared by the Central Intelligence Agency (CIA 1975, p. 18). There certainly *is* consumption by the armed forces but not in the way nor in the amount proposed by Steinberg. His argument in itself seems quite strange: why should the Soviets include an allocation to the armed forces in the consumption fund, when they could present equilibrated accounts of consumption and income?

In the revised version of his estimation in paper 2.1, Steinberg has greatly reduced the amount of consumption funds allocated to the 'armed forces'. Although he does not present data for 1975, an interpolation between 1972 and 1980 gives a rough estimate of 8.5 billion roubles instead of the 14.4 billion roubles previously presented. Nearly all of the 'gaps' between column 1 and column 2 of table 2.3.2 have been reduced, see especially lines 2 (sales of administrations) and 9 (housing depreciation).

CIA reconstruction of accounts

Another use of Soviet statistics which aims at the reconstruction of accounts is the extensive work done by the CIA specialists.[4] In contrast with Steinberg, this line of research denies that material product accounts give workable data, because the concepts are too poorly defined. The CIA reconstructs gross national product (GNP) accounts on the basis of a large number of fragmentary Soviet statistical and budget data, between which important gaps appear.

The basic architecture of the CIA accounts is a two-sector economy (households–public sector), each sector having income and outlays which must equilibrate. As expected, outlays in the household sector are superior to income (leaving room for unidentified money income other than defence incomes) and income in the public sector is superior to outlays (leaving room for unidentified outlays, including 'defence not elsewhere classified'—NEC). The sum of the outlays of both sectors is the basis of the end-use presentation of GNP, the total income is the basis of a presentation by type of income, further refined in a sector of origin presentation.

The gap on the household side is quite acceptable, and can be at least partly explained by various wage-type bonuses or expenses not included in normal monthly wages: in Lithuania, these supplements account for 3.3 to 4.2 per cent of total monetary wages for the period from 1965 to 1980 (*dokhody rabocikh i sluzascikh ot predrijatiij i organizacii krome zarplaty*). The gap may also be explained by the wages of the unenumerated population other than the armed forces, such as internal security personnel, non-permanent personnel (*nespisocnij sostav*) or working prisoners. The essential problems with the CIA GNP methodology lie in the public sector accounts.

The gap on the public sector side is questionable, because the budget data—of which the CIA makes extensive use—are hardly more adequately explained and defined by the Soviets than is MPA data. This appears crudely with the inclusion, in the income of the public sector, of a 'miscellaneous charges' line (24.386 billion roubles in 1970) corresponding in part (12.831 billion roubles) to 'the unidentified budgetary income which is received from current production activities'. The CIA researchers honestly recognize that 'in the absence of information on the content of the revised residual [i.e., what is left of the budget income from the socialist sector after deducting more or less identified components], we assume that 90 per cent (12.831 billion roubles) represents income derived from current production of goods and services' (CIA 1982, p. 135). The basic methodology used by the CIA in 1975 presented a range of other possible percentages which implied a ± 5.6 billion rouble margin of uncertainty (CIA 1975, p. 16), but these doubts no longer appear in 1982. Another CIA publication (CIA 1977) suggests that the budget incorporates bank loans as an income based on the savings of the population; such funds might well exceed the 12.8 billion roubles mentioned above and would already be included in public sector income. Thus, one could replace the arbitrarily fixed share of 90 per cent by 0 per cent, which reduces public sector income by 12.8 billion roubles and provokes a drop of 'unidentified outlays' (including defence NEC) by nearly one-half in 1970.

In conclusion, the CIA GNP accounts seem as weakly based as Steinberg's accounts.

CIA factor—cost adjustment procedure

There is still another important and critical point in the CIA methodology which requires clarification, namely, the constant assertion that direct estimation of military spending (an exclusivity of the Agency) is compatible with the set of reconstructed GNP accounts. This assertion is of course necessary if the CIA desires to evaluate the *burden* of defence. Unfortunately, the Agency has never published the scheme of compatibility between the two sets of data. We are told only that:

. . . if we [CIA] have correctly constructed Soviet GNP of end-use, then all purchases of goods and services for defence must be included in it somewhere under either consumption, investment or government expenditure. One part of other government expenditure is the residual element—outlays not elsewhere classified. By its method of construction, this element should be made up almost completely of defence expenditures . . . . The following categories seem [also] likely to include defence expenditures:

- Communal services probably include defence expenditures for education, health and physical culture;

- Government administration probably includes defence expenditures for administration;
- Investment probably includes defence expenditures for (a) common-use durables (machinery and equipment that are similar in design and use to items that would be considered investment in a civilian sector); (b) construction of new facilities; and (c) capital repair of equipment and facilities;
- R and D probably includes defence expenditures for R and D (CIA 1983, p. 24).

It would be useful to check this CIA assertion because in the published GNP accounts, outlays NEC, unlike military expenditures, show a dramatically stagnant trend from 1967 to 1980. The check is complicated by the fact that the Agency publishes different sets of GNP accounts with differing degrees of detail.

Table 2.3.3 synthesizes the principal results published by the CIA for the years 1970 and 1980. There are accounts in 'established prices' (that is, prices actually used by the Soviets) and in factor-cost prices (theoretical prices which eliminate the effects of taxes and subsidies and equalize rates of return on capital in various sectors of the economy). There are also accounts in current prices and in 1970 constant prices. It is uncertain whether defence expenditures have been published in factor-cost prices before the CIA's 1982 publication (as, for instance, in CIA 1978); in any case they have never been published in current prices except for the year 1970. It can be assumed that all CIA defence expenditure figures are calculated at the 1970 factor-cost prices, that their composition (partially revealed in CIA 1978) refers also to factor-cost prices, and that military pensions are included in the total. In contrast, outlays NEC have never been published in the 1970 factor cost prices (even for 1970), but are given in current established prices.

Converting outlays NEC from one step of prices to another is possible if we convert other elements of the line 'other expenditures' (net exports and inventory change).[5] The resulting figures are the one in parentheses in table 2.3.3.

The problem is then the following: in 1970 there were 49 billion roubles devoted to military expenditures (direct costing by the CIA), composed of 31.3 billion roubles in outlays NEC and parts of the categories of education, health, investment, state administration and research and development (R&D) for a total of 17.7 billion roubles. On the basis of approximate information given by the CIA about the composition of military spending,[6] all defence expenditures can be categorized as investment, R&D and outlays NEC, without including education, health and state administration. But the picture is totally different in 1980, where outlays NEC drop drastically to 27 billion roubles (1970 factor-cost prices) and military expenditures jump to 71 billion roubles. In that case, one would have to deduct from education, health and administration some 18 billion roubles to complete military spending, which is clearly not realistic.

Paradoxically when we try to convert defence expenditures from factor-cost prices to established current prices, the new figures fit quite well with the GNP

Table 2.3.3. CIA GNF accounts by end-use (in billions of current roubles)

	1970		Current established prices	1980	
	Established prices	Factor-cost prices		Factor-cost 1970 prices	Established 1970 prices
Consumption	211.1	207.8	346.7	281.8	296.4
Goods	166.5	133.1	274.8	179.2	232.6
Durables	14.3	9.4	38.8	21.5	32.0
Services	44.6	74.6	71.9	102.6	64.1
Education	14.4	17.2	23.1	22.0	18.3
Health	8.6	9.9	13.7	12.4	10.8
Investment	109.2	108.2	175.9	173.3	174.5
Machinery	26.0	25.6	52.2	53.5	53.5
Construction	59.8	59.6	85.1	83.0	83.2
Capital repair	19.0	18.5	38.4	36.7	37.5
Other government					
Expenditures	63.0	67.3	111.2	70.3	54.9
Government administration	9.0	10.7	17.2	14.9	12.5
State administration	3.8	5.1	6.6	6.8	5.1
R&D	10.3	12.0	18.5	18.9	16.2
Other expenditures	43.6	44.5	77.5	36.4	26.8
Net exports	1.0	(1.0)	5.2	(−4.3)	(−4.3)
Inventory change	15.1	(12.2)	20.7	(13.7)	—
Outlays NEC	27.5	(31.3)	51.6	(27.0)	—
GNP	383.3	383.3	635.8	525.4	525.4
Defence expenditures	—	49	—	71	—

Notes and sources:

Elements may not add up to totals due to rounding. Figures in parentheses are our own estimates. First and third columns are from CIA 1983, p. 18. Second and fourth columns are from CIA 1982, p. 67. Fifth column is calculated from data in CIA 1983, pp. 18 and 23. Last line is based on CIA 1982, p. 123: following instructions in CIA 1978, the mean of lower and upper bounds corresponds approximately to the minimum estimate of the Soviet concept of defence and to the maximum estimate of the Western concept of defence expenditures.

In April 1986 the CIA, together with the Defense Intelligence Agency (DIA), released new figures for 1982. In then current factor-cost prices GNP amounted to 720 and defence expenditure to 115 billion roubles. Unfortunately, the details of the structure of these two aggregates are not given, and the method of calculation is not explained.

accounts. The result of this estimation[7] is 51 billion roubles or 13.3 per cent of GNP in 1970 (in current established prices, instead of 49 billion roubles and 12.8 per cent in factor-cost prices), and 81 billion roubles or 12.7 per cent of GNP in 1980 (instead of 71 billion roubles or 13.5 per cent in factor-cost prices). The 81 billion rouble figure for 1980 would be quite consistent with the 51.6 billion roubles of outlays NEC. We must nevertheless recall, as mentioned above, that this author finds outlays NEC to be much overvalued, and that also recent work by the CIA indicates a 15–17 per cent burden of defence in 1982 prices (which would lead to a 100 billion rouble figure of defence expenditure in 1980).

In conclusion, it seems that there is some problem in the factor-cost adjustment procedure used by the CIA. Inconsistencies between direct costing of defence and GNP accounts cannot simply be solved by changing the price basis, and while a new methodological work on 1982 accounts has not been published, it is difficult to consider the Agency's estimation of burden as a firm basis.

Use of material product accounts

Whereas Steinberg makes extensive use of material product accountancy but considers defence production as essentially external to this system of accounts, the CIA rejects the use of MPA but considers that defence production is included by the Soviets in published input–output data, and thus implicitly in gross social product (GSP) and net material product (NMP).

The 1972 input–output table very explicitly isolates a residual sector (called 'Radio and other Machine-Building' by Gallik, et al. in their reconstructed table) representing about 30 per cent of the machinery sector in 1972. This residual sector is supposed to contain a large part of military production (but not all of it). Such a practice seems again in contradiction with Steinberg's hypothesis: if the Soviets had a 'secret sector' producing armaments with basic inputs received from conventional sectors, and if the activity of the defence production had to be completely hidden from statistics, then, would they have concentrated all the basic inputs in one line of an input–output table? On the contrary, they would have deleted all these inputs (deleting as well the final demand column of uses), or they would have matched the inputs with their sector of origin (maintaining the final demand column of other uses), thus masking completely the existence and magnitude of the 'secret sector'.

Thus, it seems wise to accept Steinberg's use of MPA but to reject his hypothesis of an outside defence production sector. The advantage of MPA is that it gives a consistent year-by-year picture of the Soviet perception of their economy as a whole, with stable methodological explanations which are, in fact, more detailed than the budgetary ones. The drawback is that the data are not detailed (the degree of detail having been further reduced since 1976) and that here, too, a reconstruction of the accounts is necessary. But at least, we have the framework and the totals.

Filling up the framework requires the use of many other sets of data which are published by the Soviets. To what degree are all of these sources consistent? The consistency of the consumption fund of national income with retail sales turnover and other data (see the 'falsification of categories' section above) has already been examined. Let us turn now to the production side of national income and check the consistency of the sources for industry.

For this sector, *Narkhoz* as well as others present data on input (wage-earners and capital), on income and costs (monthly wages, social security rates, total profits, amortization rates, turnover taxes), on the structure of costs, on total production in 'enterprise' and 'industry' current prices and on national income.

At first glance, all of these data are not consistent, as the following observations make clear.

1. Wage-earners do not exhaust the personnel of the sector, since there is a *kolkhoz* industry, quite apart from the very small private sector; moreover there may exist a discrepancy between the definitions of the sector by labour statistics and MPA.

2. Capital data are given in comparable 1973 prices whereas amortization rates apply to current price data; the capital of budgetary organizations is unknown, though not amortized.

3. Monthly wages include all sorts of bonuses and benefits, part of which are included in profits, but they do not include some other forms of income or bonuses such as 'the incomes of population from enterprises and organizations, other than wages'; and we do not know the *kolkhoz* labour income of industry.

4. Social security deductions depend on trade unions, and there can be a discrepancy between industrial trade unions and the industrial sector of MPA; moreover the new rates applied since 1 January 1982 are not known with certainty.

5. 'Total profits' probably refers to industrial ministries, not to the MPA definition of the sector.

6. Industrial amortization rates have not been published since 1977; total amortization deductions are published but probably on a ministry basis.

7. Turnover taxes do not exhaust the numerous taxes, fees and penalties paid by industry, nor do they take account of the subsidies received, though all these elements should enter the national income.

8. The structure of industry does not cover the budgetary organizations; the definition of total costs is not precisely established, nor is the definition of each element of the structure; 'other costs' include elements of material cost, but also some labour and socialist sector income, in an unknown and changing proportion (last change in 1982).

Nevertheless, one can show that despite all these inconsistencies there is a gross compatibility between all these sets of data, including the various concepts of production. The basis for this gross consistency is the cost structure of industry as applied to approximate total costs; these are defined very crudely as total production (in enterprise current prices) minus total profits. The resulting costs breakdown gives a gross confirmation of a direct costing approach: for amortizations; for wages and social security deductions, with the wages reduced by the amount of bonuses from incentive fund; for total material costs, defined as the difference between industrial GSP and industrial NMP (40 per cent of 'other costs' must then be included in material costs computed from the cost structure). The NMP (national income) of industry can be easily reconstructed by adding (a) wages (without bonuses) and social security deductions; (b) the non-material-cost part of 'other costs'; (c) gross profits; and (d) a composite sum representing all taxes minus subsidies (this last element is the difference between the total production of industry in industrial prices and in enterprise prices). The approximate implicit amount of subsidies (turnover taxes minus the last element just defined) matches quite closely the amount of subsidies precisely accounted by V. Treml.

The 'behaviour' of these various statistical sources satisfies our purpose: the officially (and regularly) published data, though incomplete, are grossly consistent. If, as we believe, the inputs of defence production (labour and capital) are nearly all accounted for in published data, then defence production is accounted for in total production. Conversely, if defence production is accounted for in total production (as the input-output tables testify), then, defence production labour and capital are all (or nearly all) accounted for in published data. This enables us to estimate the defence burden on the basis of MPA without modification.

III.   Estimating the Soviet burden of defence through material product accountancy

Overview of the method

The basic principle of analysis of the defence burden of any country is the establishment of two consistent accounting concepts: one for the global economic activity, another for defence spending: the second one must be a part of the first one. The method we use to determine this burden has been described earlier in a French publication,[8] and has not been modified profoundly since then, except on some minor points motivated by constructive critiques from P. Wiles as well as other academics or officials of the military establishment. These modifications do not affect the basic finding which is that the Soviet military burden is estimated at a level appreciably inferior to CIA estimates. The comparison is nevertheless hazardous since our method proceeds in current prices, without factor-cost adjustments.

In contrast to the residual methods, it is proposed here to determine, in each element of the final uses of a global aggregate, which part goes to military aims. In the framework of material product accountancy, this means that we seek to determine which part of the production of the so-called productive sectors is used by the military non-productive institution. Considering the peculiarities of the framework used, it is of course rather difficult to follow the classification of defence expenditures used by Western countries (as for instance the one described in note 6). It is also not possible to refer to a Soviet official set of expenditures (for instance, budgetary fixed expenditure) since, apart from the one item in the published budget, no such set of expenditures appears in any presently available Soviet document. Thus, we will refer to a rather theoretical conception of military expenditures, as described below.

The term 'global aggregate' refers to a variant of the usual Soviet concept of net material product; in this paper a global aggregate is defined as an intermediate between the Soviet NMP and Western gross domestic product (GDP), which we will call gross material product (GMP), defined as the NMP *plus* productive depreciation. The aggregate of GMP is useful, first, because it eases the perception of the place of investment (gross-Soviet concept) in MPA; and second, because it favours the determination of both NMP and GDP in further elaborations of the defence burden. The GMP concept can be clarified by comparison with the Soviet concept of 'end product'.[9]

As in the case of NMP, there is a produced GMP and a used GMP (which differ by the same amount: losses plus external balance in foreign trade roubles). Table 2.3.4 gives the content of the used GMP to which we refer and compares each element with NMP content. Note on line 4 the agreement with Gillula's distinction between 'reserves' and 'other expenditures'.

The Soviet military institution appears as a non-productive activity (as for instance a welfare service) implying the use of current material expenditures, the realization of investments (gross of depreciation including capital repair), and the coverage of personnel costs. This activity is constituted of three basic or direct parts: the strictly military activities, administrative activities and 'scientific' (R&D) activities, each having the three types of cost defined above.

The personnel costs must reflect, to fit in the GMP framework, the value of the goods consumed by the personnel of the three basic sub-activities. In an earlier presentation by this author of military expenditures,[10] the assumption was made that this value was in proportion to the population (or active population) concerned. This evaluation has been modified and the proportion of population replaced by the proportion of income received.[11]

Income is spent not only on goods, but also on non-productive welfare services. As in the earlier presentation, allowance is made for a kind of direct or indirect employment of welfare services personnel by the military institution: whether health services are consumed by an officer's child in a civilian hospital or by a conscript in an Army hospital, the value of the goods consumed (material expenditures of various hospitals, investment in new hospitals,[12] and goods consumed directly and indirectly by the doctors and nurses) is assumed to be in proportion to the income of the officer or conscript.[13] The same reasoning applies to all kinds of welfare services (including current military and civilian education, housing, transport of personnel and so on). In total, the military share of individual consumption was 5.9 per cent in 1975, 6.1 per cent in 1980 and 1982 and 6.0 per cent in 1984.

Table 2.3.4.   Comparison of GMP and NMP

---

1. *Consumption of goods*
(= consumption fund of national income minus non-productive depreciation − amortization and *iznos* including capital repair).

(a) Individual consumption of goods (= individual consumption of NMP minus *iznos* of housing, see 'Falsification of categories' section above);

(b) Net material consumption of welfare services (= gross material consumption of welfare services of NMP, minus amortization and *iznos* of non-productive welfare capital excluding housing); and

(c) Net material consumption of science-administration services (R&D administration) (= same as for welfare services).

2. *Investment*
Same concept as used in planning and statistics, plus budgetary financed equipment, plus cattle inventory change (= accumulation of fixed capital in NMP, plus amortization and *iznos* of productive and non-productive capital aimed at the replacement of the capital stock, plus construction in progress, plus non-amortized value of liquidated capital).

(a) Productive investment;
(b) Non-productive welfare investment; and
(c) Non-productive R&D administration investment.

3. *Capital repair (buildings and equipment)*
(= part of the replacement fund of productive capital aimed at capital repair, plus capital repair of non-productive capital which is included in the consumption fund of national income).

(a) Productive capital repair;
(b) Non-productive welfare capital repair; and
(c) Non-productive R&D administration capital repair.

4. *Inventory change, reserves and other expenditures*
(= change in circulating capital, in reserves and other expenditures of NMP, minus construction in process).

(a) Inventory change;
(b) Reserves change; and
(c) Other expenditures.

5. *Total GMP (1 + 2 + 3 + 4)*
(= Total NMP plus replacement fund of productive capital.)

As for the material expenditures and investments in R&D and administration services, a global 60 per cent share of the corresponding GMP lines has been used.[14] This share, as in the previous contribution, is assumed to be constant.

Thus far, all of the sub-activities of military R&D and military administration (personnel costs, material expenditures and investments) and the strictly military personnel costs have been taken into account; all personnel costs include direct and indirect consumption of goods, as defined above. The problem of material expenditures and investments of strictly military activities has not yet been tackled. These include: procurement (and capital repair) of weapons and communications systems; construction (and capital repair) of military facilities, mainly ports, airports and so on, that is, transport infrastructure; material expenditures for the operating of forces, mainly fuel and current repair of military equipment. The first and third elements are included in the 'other expenditures' line of the GMP, and the second in the non-productive welfare investment and capital repair lines of the GMP (table 2.3.4). This is dealt with to a greater extent below.

Reconstruction of the GMP

A rather lengthy process of computations is necessary to reconstitute the data presented in table 2.3.4. Summing up this process, the following stages must be followed.

Computation of investment in current prices

This stage begins with the determination of the elements of the construction sector output. An index of prices of construction work is established on the basis of gross social product data (construction less capital repair and drilling in current prices) and investment data (in comparable prices). A price index for machinery and equipment is separately established, and the combination of the two indexes gives the price index for investment (on a 1973 = 100 per cent basis, this index gives the following values: 100.4 per cent in 1975; 101.2 per cent in 1980; 105.4 per cent in 1982 and 113.2 per cent in 1984). The distribution in current prices between productive and non-productive investment is made on the basis of comparable prices data, taking into account the specificities of transport and communications investment, of budgeted equipment and of cattle.

Reconstitution of fixed capital in current prices

Gross commissioning of capital (*vvod v dejstvie osnovnykh fondov*) is deduced in current prices from preceding investment series, and construction in process. Scrapping of capital is determined separately in 1973 prices. Starting from the 1972–75 values of fixed capital (in current prices, after re-evaluation), the 1976–85 values of fixed capital in current prices are computed year by year by adding gross commissioning in current prices and deducting scrapping in 1973 (re-evalued) prices. The mid-1984 value of fixed capital amounts to 2191 billion roubles. Fixed capital in current prices is then distributed between productive and non-productive capital (of which housing capital stock is presented separately).

Determination of capital replacement fund

On the basis of the series of mid-year fixed capital in current prices and adjusted depreciation rates (comprising amortization, *iznos* and unamortized write-offs), one can compute the productive capital replacement fund, the non-productive capital depreciation (including *iznos* of housing) and the total capital renewing fund (replacement minus capital repair).

Filling up the GMP structure

All the elements of table 2.3.4 can be determined, except for the subcategories of line 4 (inventory change, reserves change and other expenditures). The treatment of this part of GMP is straightforward: inventories and reserves will be considered as containing two parts, one partly published in *Narkhoz* ('material circulating means' which must be adjusted to include *kolkhoz*), and another not published which is supposed to maintain a null value over the long period. This means that 'other expenditures' are determined by the trend of variable which is equal to the difference between line 4 of table 2.3.4 and published inventory and reserves change. The result of this procedure gives 17 billion roubles of 'other expenditures' in 1975; 24 billion roubles in 1980; 27 billion roubles in 1982 and 32 billion roubles in 1984.[15]

The assumption is made that 'other expenditures' represent the main part of investments and material expenditures of the strictly military part of the Soviet defence institution, discussed in the preceding section. We maintain that construction (and capital repair) of military facilities (transport infrastructure) is included as a part of transport and communications investment and capital repair.[16] Part of this sector's investment and capital repair (its non-productive 'welfare' part) accounts for construction of military facilities (2.6, 3.3, 3.8 and 4.2 billion roubles for 1975, 1980, 1982 and 1984 respectively).

Most of 'other expenditures' are then composed of procurement of weapons and communications systems. It has been suggested by P. Wiles, as well as by officials of the military establishment, that the value appearing in 'other expenditures' could be the net of depreciation, and thus could underestimate the real value of the procured weapons. Two arguments should prove that such a view—although it would bring estimates of procurement closer to what is suggested by the CIA—is not founded. We may proceed to a first check on depreciation of 'normal' fixed capital: published rates of depreciation fit fairly well with the total value of capital and input-output data on productive and non-productive depreciation. A second check can be carried out by computing what share of the machinery sector final demand can be assigned to weapons procurement; applying the 1972 ratio of final demand to national income for the machinery sector leads, for recent years, to levels of final demand consistent with the data on invested equipment, net exports, consumer durables, inventory change, capital repair of equipment and computed procurement figures. It should be noted that other lines of military expenditure also include products of the machinery sector, more or less similar in design and use to civilian products. Table 2.3.5 gives a summary of the military shares of various components of the GMP.

Conversion to GDP and final remarks

It is possible to modify GNP in a GDP concept. For that, we have to add to produced-GMP the value added by 'non-productive' (according to Soviet

Table 2.3.5. Military elements of the GMP (in billions of current roubles)

	1975	1980	1982	1984
1. Consumption of goods	246.3	318.5	348.4	372.6
(a) Individual	222.3	284.1	314.1	340.6
Defence	13.1	17.3	19.3	20.6
(b) Welfare services	14.9	21.1	20.5	18.3
Defence	0.9	1.3	1.3	1.1
(c) R&D administration services	9.1	13.3	13.8	13.7
Defence	5.5	8.0	8.3	8.2
2 & 3. Investment and capital repair	138.9	171.1	192.8	224.6
(a) Productive	95.2	118.9	136.5	154.5
(b) Military infrastructure	2.6	3.3	3.8	4.2
(c) Welfare services	38.4	45.7	48.9	61.7
Defence	2.3	2.8	3.0	3.7
(d) R&D administration services	2.6	3.2	3.6	4.2
Defence	1.6	1.9	2.2	2.5
Depreciation fund of productive capital	(52.4)	(75.4)	(86.7)	(99.5)
4. Inventory and reserves change				
Other expenditures	29.6	39.9	58.4	64.5
(a) Published change	13.0	20.2	32.2	28.3
(b) Complementary change	0	−4	−1	+4
(c) Other expenditures	17	24	27	32
5. Total GMP	414.8	529.5	599.6	661.7
Total defence	43	59	65	72
NMP used	363.0	454.1	512.9	558.6
Total defence in per cent of NMP used	11.8	13.0	12.7	12.9

concepts) services. This added value is composed of the gross earnings of non-productive manpower (including social security and income 'other than wages'), plus the gross earnings of the 'excluded category' and the profits and other socialist sector income of non-productive sectors. In the view of this author, 'revenues of foreign trade' in internal roubles should not be included in the GDP, since they correspond to the commercial balance of the country. One should thus deduct them from produced-GMP, but for purposes of comparison with the methodology of the CIA, a variant of the GDP including foreign trade revenues (which could be assimilated to a custom duty) has been presented. In this GDP framework, the computation of military expenditures remains valid. The final results are presented in table 2.3.6.

As can be seen from the table, military expenditures are sensibly inferior to the results of the CIA (even in constant 1970 prices), whereas the aggregate of global activity is very close to the CIA figures (2 per cent less) in current established prices. Even if one assumes that the CIA's calculation of military expenditure includes military pensions (which is not explicit), one should add about 0.3 per cent to the burden percentage, which is then still under the 10 per cent level. Two comments may be made.

Table 2.3.6. Soviet Union GDP and military expenditures (in billions of current roubles)

	1975	1980	1982	1984
GDP (domestic concept)	463.6	575.8	643.5	701.2
GDP (with foreign trade incomes)	482.2	621.6	700.4	765.7
Military expenditures (pensions excluded)	43	59	65	72
Per cent of GDP–2	*8.9*	*9.5*	*9.3*	*9.4*

The first comment is that, although comparisons with CIA estimates are difficult because of the different pricing systems used, the difference between the two results can be essentially attributed to the estimations of the procurement of weapons. The conclusion at which one arrives is, in fact, close to the previous (pre-1976 revision) estimation of the Agency.

The second remark concerns international comparisons. This author's estimation of the burden is 'only' 50 per cent above the equivalent US figure, but current views estimate that this does not correspond to the superiority of Soviet military forces and to the relatively low economic development attained by the USSR. Previous CIA estimates led to the thesis of a super-productive Soviet defence production sector in comparison to the rest of the economy. This paper suggests another type of explanation, relying on the super-overcosting of the US defence production sector. Verification of such an assumption would lead far beyond the scope of the present paper. But in the debate one should consider the argument that the mysteries of Soviet defence expenditures might be disclosed in Washington's budgetary procedures.

Notes

[1] On manpower, see Rapawy. On consumption, savings and income, see Birman. Soviet authors, such as Sverdlik, also shed light on some inconsistencies.

[2] There are four categories of pensioners: (a) war invalids and their survivors (somewhat different from 'military pensioners'); (b) retired wage-earners; (c) retired *kolkhoz* members and (d) others. This last group contains the following elements: (a) invalid wage-earners; (b) invalid *kolkhoz* members; (c) seniority pensioners (*za vyslugu let*: physicians, professors, scientists, pilots, artists and so on); (d) 'personal' pensioners (*apparatchiki*); (e) military and internal security pensioners and (f) survivors of all the categories of pensions except for war invalidity.

[3] Reference to this concept may be found in Misjunas and Rajackas, p. 26; and in Imanov, p. 12.

[4] CIA 1975, CIA 1982 and CIA 1983.

[5] A rather crude estimate of the conversion factors for inventory change could be obtained by supposing that inventories are composed roughly of one-half industrial products, one-quarter agricultural goods and one-quarter consumption goods. CIA data on value-added of industry and agriculture (GNP by sector of origin) and on goods consumption end-uses have been used. For conversion of net exports, no

adjustment for factor-cost prices is necessary since this line is valued in foreign-trade roubles. Exports and imports of 1980 have been converted to 1970 values using the indexes given by *Vnesnjaja Torgovlja*.

6 From CIA 1978, we know that the composition of defence spending (in an imprecise system using 1970 prices) between 1967 and 1977 is greater than 50 per cent for investment (of which 90 per cent is procurement and 10 per cent construction); greater than 25 per cent for operating expenses (60 per cent for military personnel including pensions, the rest for other operations and maintenance expenses) and 20 per cent for research, development, testing and evaluation (RDT&E). These rates are applied to the 1970 and 1980 total expenditures given in table 2.3.3. CIA 1982, p. 244, states that one-third of the machinery sector final demand is military machinery 'deducting common-use durables' (which are part of procurement); this implies that around one-quarter of procurement expenditure corresponds to equipment (or repair) 'similar in design and use to civilian equipment', a fairly large sum for motor cars, trucks, typewriters and even computers and transport aircraft. This author assumes that this part of procurement and military construction is included in the announced total investment, as the CIA suggests.

7 The conversion from factor-cost price to current established prices uses the following ratios (applied to the figures defined in note 9): procurement: ratio for machinery sector value added; construction: ratio for construction sector value added; military personnel: ratio for 'other branches' sector (including military personnel) value added; other operating and maintenance (OM) expenses: ratio for transportation sector value added and RDT&E: ratio for end-use R&D. All conversion ratios are calculated from CIA 1982 and CIA 1983.

8 See Duchêne, pp. 100–5.

9 The reference for the concept of end-product is the following excerpt translated from *Methodological Instructions for the Establishment of the State Plan of Development of the National Economy of the USSR* of 1969, p. 591.

Computation of the end-product and its elements (in billions of roubles, conventional figures)

Indicators of the national economy balance	Elements of the final product							
	(A)	(B)	(C)	(D)	(E)	(F)	(G)	(H)
National income (used)	140	36	7	17	—	—	—	200
Consumption fund	140	4^1	6^2	—	—	—	—	150
Accumulation fund	—	32	1	17	—	—	—	50
Increment of fixed capital	—	30	—	—	—	—	—	30
Increment of circulating capital, stocks, reserves and other elements of accumulation	—	2^3	1^4	17	—	—	—	20
Amortization of productive capital and unamortized value	—	14^5	11^6	—	—	—	—	25
Export	—	—	—	—	8	—	—	8
Import	—	—	—	—	—	−15	—	−15
Losses	—	—	—	—	—	—	2	2
Total end-product	**140**	**50**	**18**	**17**	**8**	**−15**	**2**	**220**

(A)   Consumption fund
(B)   Investment
(C)   Capital repair
(D)   Increment of circulating capital, inventories, reserves and other elements of accumulation
(E)   Export
(F)   Import
(G)   Losses
(H)   Total end-product

[1]Amortization of non-productive capital, aimed at replacement.
[2]Amortization of non-productive capital, aimed at capital repair.
[3]Increment of unfinished construction.
[4]Increment of unfinished capital repair.
[5]Amortization and unamortized value of productive capital, aimed at replacement.
[6]Amortization of productive capital, aimed at capital repair.

The 'conventional' figures indicated in the table look very much like the 1966 real input-output table ones. Our concept of GMP does not take into account the three lines and columns export, import and losses. With the conventional figures above, the GMP would equal 225 $(220 - 2 + 15 - 8)$ instead of 220 billion roubles.

Gillula's presentation can be easily compared with the table above: his column 'Replacement and repair' includes the figures (conventional): $4 + 6 + 14 + 11$; his column 'Accumulation of circulating capital and reserves' includes the figures for unfinished construction $(2 + 1)$ and inventory change which in the table above is mixed with 'other expenditures' (17). See also Sverdlik for comparison.

[10]   Duchêne, pp. 101–2.
[11]   In this new context, we consider the income of conscripts as a shadow-wage representing 75 per cent of the mean-value of wages; this takes into account that neither the 3.80 roubles per month received in cash by servicemen nor the allocation for food and clothing cover the real consumption of these people (including housing, various services, transport and so on); the 75 per cent share reflects the share of wages received by one member of an average Soviet family, which seems to be closer to the actual consumption of a conscript.
[12]   The military share of income is applied to gross investment in non-productive welfare capital. One could have argued that only the depreciation part of that capital is really consumed, but this would not have accounted for the 'profit' part of the service. Considering that, for instance, gross investment (with capital repair) of housing is 'consumed' by military personnel leads to the inclusion in the cost of the military institution, of construction of barracks and of flats 'built on their own account' (Soviet terminology) by permanent military (or defence R&D . . .) staff and of flats rented at a very low rent to this staff but costed at their full value.
[13]   It may seem questionable that the use of free services is in proportion to income. In fact, the results of our earlier estimations—using population or employment shares— lead to results very similar to those obtained here by using income shares.
[14]   This takes into account an 80 per cent military share of total R&D activity (which seems excessive, but is in line with most Western estimations, including recent direct costing by the CIA) and a 20 per cent military share of administration activity. This last share is based on an estimation of military-administrative (in fact civilian) personnel equal to 10 per cent of the military staff as reported by the Institute for International Strategic Studies. Published administrative employment is approximately one-half of scientific employment, which leads to the 60 per cent military share for the entire R&D administration sector.

[15] For 1972, the distribution between 'other expenditures' and 'inventory and reserves change' is a little different from the one published by J. W. Gillula in 1984; but all other elements of GMP are practically identical.

[16] This is justified by an analysis of the composition of the total stock of capital published for the years 1966 and 1972, (see *Narkhoz* 1968 and 1974): the only sector for which yearly published data differ from detailed capital stock published for 1966 and 1972 is the transport and communications sector (by an amount of approximately 17 per cent).

References

Birman, I., *Secret Incomes of the Soviet State Budget* (Martinus Nijhoff: The Hague, 1981).

CIA 1975, Abbreviated citation of *USSR GNP Accounts 1970* A (ER) 75–76, Nov. 1975 (US Government Printing Office: Washington, DC, 1975).

CIA 1977, Abbreviated citation of *The Soviet State Budget Since 1965* (US Government Printing Office: Washington, DC, 1977).

CIA 1978, Abbreviated citation of *Estimation Soviet Defence Spending: Trends and Prospects*, SR 78–10121 (US Government Printing Office: Washington, DC, 1978).

CIA 1982, Abbreviated citation of *USSR: Measures of Economic Growth and Development 1950–1980*, Joint Economic Committee, Congress of the United States (US Government Printing Office: Washington, DC, 1982).

CIA 1983, Abbreviated citation of *Soviet GNP in Current Prices 1960–1980*, Sov 83–10037 (US Government Printing Office: Washington, DC, 1983).

Duchêne, G., 'Place of the defence effort in the Soviet national accounts', *The Socialist Reality*, eds. W. Andreff and M. Lavigne (Economica: Paris, 1985) pp. 83–109 [in French].

Gallik, D. M., Kostinsky, B. L. and Treml, V. G., *Input-Output Structure of the Soviet Economy: 1972*, Foreign Economic Report no. 18, US Department of Commerce (US Government Printing Office: Washington, DC, 1983).

Gillula, J. W., *Components of Gross Investment in the 1966 and 1972 Soviet Input-Output Tables*, CIR Staff Paper no. 7, Department of Commerce (Mimeographed: Washington, DC, 1984).

Imanov, K. D., *Models of Economic Systems* (Elm: Baku, USSR, 1983) [in Russian].

Methodological Instructions for the Establishment of the State Plan of Development of the National Economy of the USSR, Planning Agency of the USSR (Economika: Moscow, USSR, 1969) [in Russian].

Misjunas, A. and Rajackas, R., *Analysis and Forecast of Non-Productive Consumption* (Mintis: Vilnjus, USSR, 1983) [in Russian].

Narkhoz, Abbreviated citation of *The National Economy of the USSR in 19–. Statistical Yearbook*, Central Statistical Administration of the USSR (Finansy i Statistika: Moscow, USSR), generally published the year after the year appearing in the title, last issue 1985 [in Russian].

Rapawy, S., *Estimates and Projections of the Labor Force and Civilian Employment in the USSR 1950 to 1990*, Foreign Economic Report no. 10, US Department of Commerce (US Government Printing Office: Washington, DC, 1976).

Rutgajzer, V. M., *Resources of Development of Non-Productive Sphere* (Mysl': Moscow, USSR, 1975) [in Russian].

Sverdlik, S. B., *Social Product and Monetary Circulation* (Nauka: Novosibirsk, USSR, 1961) [in Russian].

Treml, V. G., 'Subsidies in Soviet agriculture: record and prospects', *Soviet Economy in the 1980's: Problems and Prospects*, Joint Economic Committee, Congress of the United States (US Government Printing Office: Washington, DC, 1982), Part 2.

Paper 2.4.   Estimating Soviet defence expenditures from national accounts

KIICHI MOCHIZUKI

I.   Introduction

In this paper an attempt is made to derive an estimate of Soviet defence expenditures from Soviet national accounts as defined by Soviet authorities. Three approaches are possible: the first looks at production data; the second looks at final demand categories; and the third examines final expenditures.

In view of the limitations of Soviet statistical data, no single approach can suffice. For instance, if we use the production viewpoint, there are input-output tables for some years, but these are far from sufficient for the purpose of estimating military expenditures. In the final expenditure figures we have the *pro forma* defence budget but few believe that it covers all defence expenditures. Many specialists think that the larger part of military expenditures is included instead under 'national economy expenditure' budget items and that another part may be found under 'social-cultural expenditures'. But such identifications are speculative and inconclusive.

The final demand data for national accounts are plagued by similar problems. Yet this accounting approach appears more fruitful for our purpose. It subdivides the main military expenditure items as follows: (*a*) consumption by soldiers; (*b*) science research expenditures (R&D) for military purposes; (*c*) non-productive investment for military purposes (arms production and military construction) and (*d*) increase in the state reserve for military purposes.

II.   Consumption by soldiers

Soviet conscript soldiers receive 3.8 roubles a month. However, this is not enough to cover all living expenses (food, lodging, clothing, and so on). One method of estimating soldiers' real living costs might view the living costs per capita as equal to the average annual wage of the national economy. Following this procedure, we can calculate the total consumption by the soldiers by multiplying their number by the average wage. Alternatively, the average wage plus the *per capita* social consumption fund provides another estimation variant. Since most soldiers are single, adding 'the social consumption fund per capita' to the average wage clearly produces too high a figure. In view of the soldiers' youth, the average wage in the service sector, which is lower than the average for the national economy as a whole, is a more appropriate yardstick with which to calculate their living costs.

As regards the number of soldiers, there are at least three categories, namely, the regular armed forces, frontier security (KGB), and internal security troops (MVD). All contribute to the economic burden of defence in the USSR (for purposes of international comparison, however, one must note that many nations exclude para-military or quasi-military formations from defence tabulations).

III.   Science research expenditures (R&D)

Official information on R&D is poor. For example, *Narkhoz* provides expenditures on sciences from all sources, including the state budget. But it is not clear what percentage is related to military purposes. Professor Sh. B. Sverdlik provides R&D expenditures for the non-self-financing sector.[1] R&D expenditures in the non-self-financing sector are more likely to relate to military R&D than are the figures of *Narkhoz*. For as far as the R&D in a production sector are concerned, they are sooner or later counted as an element of production costs. R&D expenditures in a self-financing sector need not be counted in the production stage. Professor Sverdlik shows that the R&D expenditure in the non-self-financing sector was 2.0 billion roubles (b.r.) for 1959, 4.6 b.r. for 1966, and 7.4 b.r. for 1972, while *Narkhoz* shows the following averages: 15.4 b.r. for 1971 to 1975; 19.6 b.r. for 1976 to 1980; and 25.6 b.r. for 1981 to 1984.

The 'estimates of Soviet military and space R&D expenditure' (highest plausible) in Mary Acland-Hood's paper 2.5 in this book are very close to Sverdlik's figures for R&D expenditures in the non-self-financing sector. For example, Mary Acland-Hood's figures are 2.1 b.r. for 1959; 4.2 b.r. for 1966; 8.1 b.r. for 1972; and so on. The average of her figures of 'most likely range' are used in table 2.4.4, line 2.

IV.   Investment and defence expenditures

In Soviet statistics, national income consists of consumption and accumulation. Part of defence expenditures is consumption, and the rest belongs to accumulation. Consumption includes food and clothing (barracks belong to investment); increases in military goods and armaments belong to accumulation. Accumulation consists of increases in fixed assets and increases in circulating assets and reserves. The latter covers increases in raw materials, fuels in storage, uncompleted construction and government reserves (see below). The former—increases in fixed assets—is covered by investment finance. Western analysts assume that Soviet investment data also include military outlays:

Defense expenditures are contained in several components of GNP. Investment probably includes the procurement of common-use durables, such as trucks and transport aircraft, and the construction of military facilities. Science probably is very heavily weighted toward defense expenditures. Other defense expenditures could well be contained in administration, education, and health expenditures.[2]

Another standard source remarks: 'Expenditures on fixed assets for military purposes are treated in the MPS as a part of net fixed capital formation'.[3]

Investment is divided into two parts, productive and non-productive. According to Soviet statistical practice, military expenditure must be included in non-productive investment. Statistical dictionaries define non-productive fixed assets to include the following items: housing; municipal services and utilities; cultural consumer and health services; education; science; art; administration; *defence* structure (military installations, equipment, machinery, etc.); and means of transportation.[4] But construction of military factories is also productive investment, because they are means of production that produce weapons. Military expenditures should be measured at the final stage of flow of goods in order to avoid double counting.

Professor J. Vaňous and B. Robert have pursued this approach in 'PlanEcon Report'.[5] Their work can be developed, with profit, especially by incorporating the concept of non-productive investment. They looked at three categories of machinery production: (*a*) durable consumption goods; (*b*) domestic investment machinery production; and (*c*) domestic machinery defence production. The first of these consists of consumer goods (group B) produced by heavy industry. The division of remaining machinery production into 'investment machinery production' and 'domestic defence machinery production' is decisive. They employ a statistical concept that defines machinery production as investment end-use, after adjustment for uncompleted investment and foreign trade (see figure 2.4.1). If this is generally appropriate, it should be applied to the defence machinery production, though they do not do this. A flow chart on foreign trade would be analogous. Foreign trade plays a role similar to that of uncompleted investment, in that it represents leakage between total production and total domestic usage (investment).

Applying this method to official statistical data for 1975–84 produces 'a flow chart of estimates of defence machinery production' (see figure 2.4.2). Three check points show discrepancies between Vaňous's and Robert's calculations and the results of the approach pursued here (see table 2.4.1): between lines 25 and 26; lines 28 and 29; and lines 32 and 34 (or 22). The differences for 1975 to 1979 in line 27, for 1980 to 1984 in line 30, and in line 35 (except 1975 and 1981) are smaller. While Vaňous and Robert use constant price series based on the production index, I apply current prices series. However, the differences derive not from the methods but, rather, from variation of the investment valuation based on different price bases between the periods 1975 through 1979 and 1980 through 1984, and also from the fact that my conversion coefficient ($\beta = 1.06$) relating constant price to current price cannot be applied to such a lengthy period (1975 through 1984) without some modification.

The adopted approach extends the application of the Vaňous–Robert method, integrates defence machinery production and non-productive invest-

Figure 2.4.1.   Flow chart on uncompleted investment

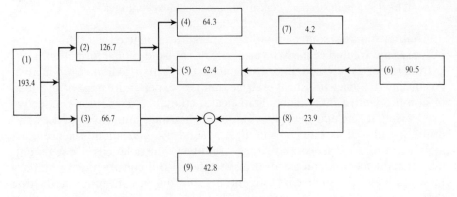

Notes:
1. Total capital investment (193.4).
2. Productive investment (126.7).
3. Non-productive investment (66.7).
4. Procurement of productive machinery products (64.3).
5. Productive construction (62.4).
6. Constructive investment (90.5).
7. Uncompleted construction (or investment) (4.2).
8. Non-productive construction (23.9); if uncompleted construction (7) is not separated, then this item appears as 28.1.
9. Non-productive machinery products=procurement of defence machinery in constant prices (42.8); if uncompleted construction (7) is separated, this figure becomes 38.6. Uncompleted investment shows the leakage between investment and durable goods production (including machinery).

ment, and thus provides a closed loop schema joining machinery production and investment.

Using table 2.4.1 and the flow chart (figure 2.4.2), one can follow the argument and track the *Narkhoz* data. Yet, problems remain:

1. We use an expanded concept of capital investment which adds to the standard investment data the supplementary investment figures found in footnotes to the total investment statistical data pages of *Narkhoz*. The supplementary investment figures provided by the footnotes (with accompanying explanation) are comparatively large. Its size was 19.3 billion roubles in 1984, almost as much as the budget defence provision. Yet Soviet sources never indicate where this expenditure is located within the system of national accounting. In the above treatment, this supplementary investment is included in the accounting system, because it provides reasonable scope within which to allocate shares of non-productive investment to defence expenditures; without the addition, unproductive investment appears too small to permit allocation of an investment share to defence expenditures. The chosen course is dictated not by theory, but rather by practical considerations and ramifications.

2. The data on intermediate items (balance of foreign trade *in domestic prices* and uncompleted investment) between production and domestic use

Figure 2.4.2. Flow chart of estimates of defence machinery

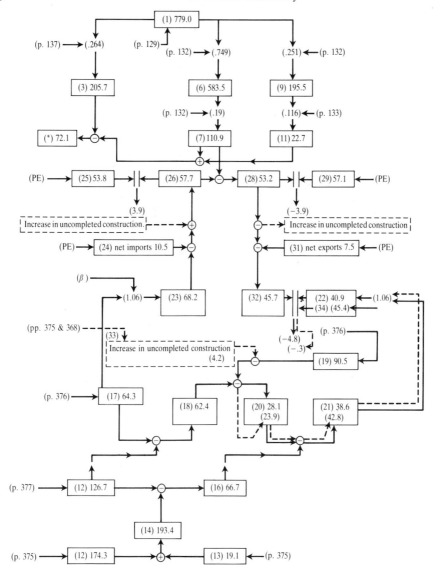

Notes:
1. ( ) means the difference between two elements.
2. 'page' shows the page in *Narkhoz 1984*.
3. * stands for intermediate machinery production; this designation avoids doublecounting, the problem of (civilian) machinery used as inputs within the machinery sector. Machinery end-use is divided into civilian and military machinery, whereupon the former is divided again into producer and civilian durables.
4. Figures in a parenthesis coincide with the line number in table 2.4.1
5. (PE) means 'PlanEcon Report'.
6. Dashed line shows a case including 'increase in uncompleted construction'.

Table 2.4.1. Estimate of domestic production and use of defence machinery (in billions of roubles)

Narkhoz 1984			1975	1976	1977	1978	1979	1980	1981	1982	1983	1984
1.	129	Industrial production	519.2	527.9	553.7	579.7	595.1	616.3	635.3	721.5	751.3	779.0
2.	137	Ratio of domestic machinery production	0.201	0.251	0.259	0.268	0.279	0.243	0.248	0.254	0.258	0.264
3.		Machinery and metal production	142.1	132.5	143.4	154.8	116.0	149.8	157.6	183.3	193.8	205.7
4.	132	Group A production (%)	0.737	0.740	0.929	0.940	0.740	0.738	0.737	0.751	0.749	0.749
5.		Group A production	376.8	390.6	409.2	427.5	440.4	454.8	468.2	541.8	562.7	583.5
6.	132	Labour means production (%)	0.194	0.195	0.196	0.197	0.202	0.203	0.206	0.186	0.187	0.190
7.		Labour means production (%)	73.1	76.2	80.2	84.2	89.0	92.3	90.4	100.8	105.2	110.9
8.	132	Group B production (%)	0.263	0.260	0.261	0.260	0.260	0.262	0.263	0.249	0.251	0.251
9.		Group B production (%)	134.4	137.3	144.5	150.2	154.7	161.5	167.1	179.7	188.6	195.5
10.	133	Machinery production in group B (%)	0.104	0.105	0.108	0.112	0.115	0.118	0.120	0.114	0.114	0.116
11.		Durable consumption goods	14.0	14.4	15.6	16.8	17.8	19.1	20.1	20.5	21.5	22.7
12.	375	Capital investment	112.9	118.0	122.3	129.7	130.6	150.9	156.5	161.9	171.0	174.3
13.	375	*Supplementary* capital investment in footnote	11.9	12.5	12.9	13.7	13.8	16.5	16.2	16.3	18.0	19.1
14.		Total capital investment	124.8	130.5	135.2	143.4	144.4	167.4	172.7	178.2	189.0	193.4
15.	377	Productive capital investment	91.8	96.0	99.4	105.5	106.2	111.2	115.0	118.6	124.9	126.7
16.		Non-productive capital investment	33.0	34.5	35.8	37.9	38.2	56.2	57.7	59.6	64.1	66.7
17.	376	Machine-equipment investment	37.1	40.7	43.0	46.6	48.3	53.9	56.6	59.3	63.4	64.3
18.		Productive construction investment	54.7	55.3	56.4	58.9	57.9	57.3	58.3	59.3	61.5	62.4
19.	376	Total construction investment	66.2	67.0	68.4	69.5	69.1	82.7	84.4	86.0	89.6	90.5

No.	PE	Item										
20.		Non-productive construction investment	11.5	11.7	12.0	10.6	11.2	25.4	26.1	26.7	28.1	28.1
21.		Defence machinery investment	21.5	22.8	23.8	27.3	27.0	30.8	31.7	32.9	36.0	38.6
22.		Defence machinery investment (current prices)	22.8	24.2	25.2	28.9	28.6	32.6	33.6	34.9	38.2	40.9
23.		Machinery-equipment investment (current prices)	29.3	43.1	45.6	49.4	51.2	57.1	60.0	62.9	67.2	68.2
24.	PE	Productive machinery net import	5.5	6.1	6.1	7.8	6.7	6.6	6.5	9.2	11.3	10.5
25.	PE	Productive machinery domestic production (1)	33.9	37.2	39.5	41.8	44.7	47.0	50.1	50.1	52.1	53.8
26.		Productive machinery domestic production (2)	33.8	37.0	39.5	41.6	44.5	50.5	53.5	53.7	55.9	57.7
27.		Difference between (25) and (26)	-0.1	-0.2	0	-0.2	-0.2	3.5	2.4	3.6	3.8	3.9
28.		Defence machinery domestic production (1)	39.3	39.2	40.7	42.6	44.5	42.1	43.0	46.9	49.3	53.2
29.	PE	Defence machinery domestic production (2)	27.6	30.8	34.7	37.3	40.2	41.8	43.6	48.9	51.9	57.1
30.		Difference between (28) and (29)	11.7	8.4	6.0	5.3	4.3	+.3	-.6	-2.0	-2.6	-3.9
31.	PE	Defence machinery net export	3.4	3.7	5.5	6.1	6.0	5.4	6.4	7.9	8.1	7.5
32.		Defence machinery investment	35.9	35.5	35.2	36.5	38.5	36.7	36.6	34.0	41.2	45.7
33.		Uncompleted investment	9.7	11.6	12.5	10.2	11.2	2.0	7.1	4.7	4.5	4.2
34.		Adjusted defence investment	30.9	34.4	36.3	37.5	38.2	34.7	41.0	39.9	42.9	45.4
35.		Difference between (32) and (34)	5.0	1.1	-1.1	-1.0	0.3	2.0	-4.4	-0.9	-1.7	-0.3

Notes:

1. The figures of the first column show the pages of *Narkhoz 1984*, which are only available for 1980 through 1984.
2. PE stands for 'PlanEcon' 27 June 1986 (paper of Jan Vaňous and Bryan Roberts).
3. 1984 price for the period 1980 through 1984 and 1975 price for 1975 through 1979 are available for line 2.
4. All figures of investment for 1980 through 1984 are applied for the 1984 price and for 1975 through 1979 are applied for the adjusted 1969 price.
5. Line 34 is calculated by [(16)−(20)+(33)] × 1.06.
6. Additional capital investment in the footnote is calculated as 0.1056 × (main capital investment) for 1975 through 1979.
7. Average ratio of productive investment for 1975 and 1984 (73.5%) is used as the productive investment ratio for 1976 through 1979 of line 15.

(investment) may not reflect the actual size of the items. More research is needed.

3. Statistical investment data were converted to 1984 prices in *Narkhoz 1984*. As Vaňous and Robert suggested, we can derive a unified time series of investment data by applying the *Narkhoz* index. But the footnoted supplementary investment figures cannot be converted to 1984 prices.

4. Here investment is regarded simply as consisting of only two parts—construction and machinery procurement. But *Narkhoz 1984* informs us that other investment elements (including design and planning costs) add up to about 10 per cent of total investment costs. Room must be found in our accounts in order to incorporate this fact.

V.   Estimate of the state reserve

State reserves are generally acknowledged to cover military materials (as well as precious minerals, jewels, etc.)[6] in Soviet budgetary terminology, state reserves consist of production means and consumption goods available for emergency production and defence purposes. In estimating state reserves, it is necessary to separate the periods before and after 1975, because of the concealment of statistical data that occurred that year.

Before the year 1975

The symbols employed in the calculations correspond closely to the lines of table 2.4.2; they are: Y = productive national income; Yu = national income used in domestic economy; AM = amortization; C = consumption; Vf = gross fixed capital formation in current prices (fp); Vc = gross fixed capital formation in constant prices (cp) (fixed assets put into operation); MO = increase of inventory; S = (export-import) + losses; U = increase of uncompleted investment in fp; Uc = increase of uncompleted investment in cp; $M1$ = increase of working assets (except *Kolkhoz*); $M2$ = increase of working assets of *Kolkhoz*; P = the state reserve; and K = gross fixed investment.

The value added of the national economy (Y) plus amortization (MO) equals final demand (equation a):

$Y + AM = C + Vf + MO + S$ (in fp)
hence
$Vf = Y + AM - C - MO - S$
  $= AM + (Y-C-MO-S)$ (see table 2.4.2, line 11)

Furthermore, $(Y - C - MO - S)$ = 'the net increase of fixed assets' in fp. Hence (equation b):

$Vf = AM +$ 'the net increase of fixed assets' (see table 2.4.2, lines 11 and 9).[7]

It should be pointed out that national accounts data are usually published in current prices, but data on capital formation are given in constant prices. A conversion coefficient is required. The coefficient relates 'gross fixed capital formation in current prices' (Vf) to the same concept in constant prices (Vc). The former is available in equation b and the latter is given in *Narkhoz*, as 'fixed capital put into operation' (equation c):

Vc = 'gross fixed capital formation' (in cp, see table 2.4.2, line 12).

Hence equation b = equation c; Vf = $\beta \cdot$Vc, where β stands for the conversion coefficient from constant to current prices (see table 2.4.2, line 13).

The uncompleted construction project figure (U) is the difference between gross investment (K) and gross fixed capital formation (Vc: assets put into operation), both of which are given directly in *Narkhoz*. However, the figure obtained is expressed in constant prices. Using coefficient β, we convert it into current prices (equation d : U = $\beta \cdot$Uc) in order to put it into the next equation e: MO = U + M1 + M2 + P. Increases in material circulating assets and stock (MO), which consists of increases in the stock of enterprises in the material production sphere, including wholesale and retail trade units (M1), increases in the circulating assets of *Kolkhoz* (M2), uncompleted construction in current prices (U), and the increase in government stockpiles (P) were published until 1975 in *Narkhoz*, in a section on national income used in the domestic economy (Yu). Equation e was thus applicable until then.

Thereafter, the increase in material circulating assets of *Kolkhoz* (M2) has to be estimated, while the increase in similar assets of enterprises and other units (M1) continued to be provided by *Narkhoz* (see table 2.4.2, line 17). As regards *Kolkhoz*, there are very few data in *Narkhoz*. But part of 'the *annual* increment in indivisible assets of *Kolkhoz*' can possibly be used. 'The indivisible assets of *Kolkhoz*' consist of both 'circulating assets' and 'fixed assets'. These must be separated. The ratio of fixed assets to the whole is available in *Narkhoz*. If we assume the *Kolkhoz* ratio to be similar, then we can extrapolate a ratio of 'circulating assets' to total *Kolkhoz* assets (see table 2.4.2, lines 18 and 19). We need not convert this concept, in constant prices, into current prices, because of the negligible difference that this would entail. Now we have all the data necessary to calculate 'the increases in government stockpiles (P)' as shown in line 20 of table 2.4.2.

After the year 1976

After 1976 further publication of 'increases in material circulating assets and stock (MO)' ceased. Equation a can therefore no longer be used. However, provided coefficient β is given, MO can be derived through Vf, as determined by $\beta \cdot$Vc (see table 2.4.2, line 13).

Figures 2.4.3 A and B are flow charts of decision procedure. There are, however, still aspects that are less than clear:

1. It is not clear whether the 'increases in material circulating assets and

Table 2.4.2. Increases in government reserve (in billions of roubles)

Narkhoz	1960	1961	1962	1963	1964	1965	1966	1967	1968	1969	1970	1971
1. 80: Productive national income 379 (Y)( )=(1)/(6)%fp	145.0 (86.1)	152.9	164.6	168.8	181.3	193.5 (83.0)	207.4	225.5	244.1	261.9	289.9 (82.8)	305.0 (82.4)
2. 80: National income used 380 Yu=7+8, fp	142.8	151.0	162.5	166.6	179.7	190.5	204.2	221.0	238.7	256.7	285.5 (81.5)	300.1
3. s=(1)−(2),( )=(3)/(1)(%)	2.2 (1.5)	1.9 (1.2)	2.1 (1.3)	2.2 (1.3)	1.6 (0.9)	3.0 (1.6)	3.2 (1.5)	4.5 (2.0)	5.4 (2.2)	5.2 (2.0)	4.4 (1.5)	4.9 (1.6)
4. Excess value of ( )=(4)/(6)(%) non-material services	14.3 (8.5)	15.5	16.3	16.9	18.6	20.7 (8.9)	21.2	25.2	28.0	29.4	31.1 (8.9)	33.3 (9.0)
5. 80: Amortization (AM)( )=(5)/ 521 (6)(%)	9.1 (5.4)	10.2	11.3	15.6	17.0	18.8 (8.1)	20.6	22.4	24.3	26.6	29.1 (8.3)	32.1 (8.7)
6. Conditional GNP (1)+(4)+(5)fp	168.4 (100.0)	178.6	192.2	201.2	216.9	233.0 (100.0)	249.2	273.1	296.4	317.8	350.1 (100.0)	370.3 (100.0)
7. 80: Consumption fp 380	104.5	108.1	117.5	124.1	130.4	140.3	150.0	162.1	174.8	187.3	201.3	213.0
8. 80: Accumulation & others (fb)(8)/ 380 (6)%	38.3 (22.7)	42.9 (24.0)	45.0 (23.4)	42.3 (21.0)	49.3 (22.7)	50.2 (21.5)	54.2 (21.7)	59.4 (21.8)	64.8 (21.9)	69.4 (21.8)	84.2 (24.1)	87.1 (23.5)

#	Item	1	2	3	4	5	6	7	8	9	10	11	12
9.	75: 566 Net increase of fixed assets (fb)	25.3	25.3	28.4	28.2	28.9	27.9	29.7	31.8	34.0	40.0	51.1	53.7
10.	75: 566 Increase of inventory (MO) (fb)	13.0	17.6	16.6	14.1	20.4	22.3	24.5	27.6	30.8	29.4	33.1	33.4
11.	$V_f=(1)+(5)-(3)-(7)-(10)=(5)+(9)$ (fp)	34.4	35.5	39.7	44.0 (43.8)	45.9	46.7	50.3	53.7 (54.2)	57.4 (58.3)	66.6	80.2	85.8
12.	80: 327 Gross fixed capital formation (Vc) (cp)	37.7	38.0	42.5	46.4	49.3	51.4	55.0	59.5	61.6	66.6	76.4	81.3
13.	$\beta = 11\ /\ 12$	0.9125	0.9342	0.9341	0.9483	0.9310	0.9086	0.9145	0.9025	0.9318	1.0000	1.0444	1.0554
14.	80: 333 Gross investment (cp)		42.9	44.9	47.2	51.4	56.0	59.9	64.8	70.0	72.3	80.6	86.5
15.	Increase of unfinished investment $(U_c)(14)-(12)$(cp)		4.9	2.4	0.8	2.1	4.6	4.9	5.3	8.4	5.7	4.2	5.2
16.	$U=\beta \cdot U_c$(cp→fp)		4.6 (2.6)	2.2	0.8	1.9	4.2	4.6	4.8	7.9	5.7	4.4 (1.3)	5.6
17.	80: 510 Increase of working assets except *Kolkhoz* (M1) (fp)	6.9 (4.1)	7.3	7.3	7.1	10.1	4.9 (2.1)	9.5	13.5	11.0	7.0	14.6 (4.2)	11.8
18.	80: Indivisible assets of *Kolkhoz* in year-end						42.3		52.7		55.5	60.0	64.2
19.	254 $M2=0.3[(18)_{-1}-(18)_0]$										0.84	1.35	1.26
20.	Increase of state reserve $(P)=(10)-(16)-(17)-(19)(\ )=(20)/(6)\%$		5.7 (3.2)	7.1 (3.7)	6.2 (3.1)	8.4 (3.9)	13.2 (5.7)	10.4 (4.2)	9.3 (3.4)	11.9 (4.0)	15.9 (5.0)	12.8 (3.7)	14.7 (4.0)
21.	80: 379 Index (1960=100) of Y	100.0 (145.0)					136.4 (197.8)					197.7 (286.7)	
22.	Deflators$=(1)/(21)(\%)$	100.0					97.8					101.1	

Table 2.4.2. Continued

	Narkhoz	1972	1973	1974	1975	1976	1977	1978	1979	1980	1981	1982	1983	1984	
1.	80: 379 Productive national income (Y)( )=(1)/(6) % fp	313.6 (81.6)	337.8 (81.4)	354.0 (80.9)	363.3 (79.7)	385.7 (79.7)	405.6	426.3	440.6	458.5 (78.5)	486.7	523.4	548.1	569.6	Y
2.	80: National income used Yu=7+8, 380 fp	310.3	334.1	348.2	363.0 (79.6)	383.0	399.4	420.6	432.9	450.8 (77.2)	477.9	512.9	536.4	558.6	Y_u
3.	s=(1)−(2),( )=(3)/(1)(%)	3.3 (1.1)	3.7 (1.1)	5.8 (1.6)	0.3 (0.1)	2.7 (0.7)	6.2 (1.5)	5.7 (1.3)	7.7 (1.7)	7.7 (1.7)	8.8 (1.8)	10.5 (2.0)	11.7 (2.1)	11.0 (1.9)	S
4.	Excess value of ( )=(4)/(6)/(%) non-material services	35.5 (9.2)	38.4 (9.2)	40.8 (9.3)	42.7 (9.4)	43.6 (9.0)	46.4	49.6	50.4	53.3 (9.1)	55.74 (9.0)	58.0 (8.7)	60.3 (8.6)	62.5 (8.6)	—
5.	80: 521 Amortization(AM)( )=(5)/ (6)(%)	35.3 (9.2)	38.9 (9.4)	42.7 (9.8)	49.9 (10.9)	54.2 (11.9)	58.6	63.1	68.1	72.1 (12.3)	78.2 (12.6)	83.9 (12.6)	90.1 (12.9)	96.4 (13.2)	AM
6.	Conditional GNP (1)+(4)+(5) fp	384.4 (100.0)	415.2 (100.0)	437.5 (100.0)	455.9 (100.0)	483.6 (100.0)	510.6	539.0	559.1	583.9	620.6	665.3	698.5	928.5	—
7.	80: Consumption fp 380	225.4	237.0	250.3	266.4	279.7	292.5	307.9	323.6	343.6	364.9	398.5	393.0	406.5	C
8.	80: Accumulation & others (fb) (8)/ 380 (6)%	85.3 (22.2)	97.6 (23.5)	98.1 (22.4)	96.6 (21.2)	103.3 (21.4)	106.9 (20.9)	112.7 (20.9)	109.3 (19.5)	107.2 (18.4)	113.0 (18.2)	134.4 (20.2)	143.4 (20.5)	152.1 (20.4)	—
9.	75: 566 Net increase of fixed assets (fb)	55.2	60.2	62.0	61.2	59.8	59.0	64.7	59.7	66.4	80.2	82.7	86.4	83.9	(8)
10.	75: 566 Increase of inventory (MO)(fb)	30.1	37.4	36.1	34.6	43.5	47.9	48.0	49.6	40.8	32.8	51.7	37.0	68.2	−(10) MO
11.	Vf=(1)+(5)−(3)−(7)−(10)= (5)+(9)(fp)	90.1 (90.5)	98.6 (99.1)	104.5 (103.9)	111.9 (111.1)	114.0	117.6	127.8	127.8	138.5	158.4	166.6	176.5	180.3	V_f
12.	80: 327 Gross fixed capital formation (Vc)(cp)	84.0	92.9	97.3	105.6	107.1	110.5	120.1	120.1	130.2	149.4	157.2	166.5	170.1	V_c

		(1)	(2)	(3)	(4)	(5)	(6)	(7)	(8)	(9)	(10)	(11)	(12)	(13)	
13.		β= 11 / 12	1.0726	1.0614	1.0740	1.0568	1.0640	1.0640	1.0640	1.0640	1.0640	1.0640	1.06	1.06	1.06	—
14.	80: 333	Gross investment (cp)	92.6	97.0	103.9	112.9	118.0	122.3	129.7	130.6	133.5	156.5	161.9	171.0	174.3	K
15.		Increase of unfinished investment	8.6	4.1	6.6	7.3	10.9	11.8	9.6	10.5	3.3	7.1	4.7	4.5	4.2	U_c
16.		$(U_c)(14)-(12)(cp)$ / $U=β·U_c(cp→fp)$	9.2	4.2	7.1	7.7 (1.6)	11.6	12.5	10.2	11.2 (2.0)	3.5	7.5	5.0	4.8	4.5	U
17.	80: 510	Increase of working assets except Kolkhoz (M1)(fp)	12.1	18.3	15.6	13.3 (2.9)	17.8	17.2	17.2	16.1	20.8 (3.6)	38.5	29.8	30.8	22.5	M_1
18.	80: 254	Indivisible assets of Kolkhoz in year-end	69.2	79.4	85.0	91.7	95.4	99.7	103.7	107.5	109.8	113.5	113.1	121.8	?	—
19.		$M2=0.3[(18)_{-1}-(18)_0]$	1.50	3.06	1.68	2.01	1.11	1.29	1.20	1.14	0.69	1.1	0	2.6	?	M_2
20.		Increase of state reserve / $(P)=(10)-(16)-(17)-(19)(\ )=(20)(6)\%$	7.3 (1.9)	11.8 (2.8)	11.7 (2.7)	11.6 (2.5)	13.0 (2.7)	16.9 (3.3)	19.4 (3.6)	21.2 (3.8)	15.8 (2.7)	-14.3	16.9	18.8	41.2-d_1	P
21.	80: 379	Index (1960=100) of Y				250.0 (362.5)	275.0 (398.8)	286.4 (415.2)	302.3 (438.3)	309.1 (448.2)	320.5 (464.7)				—	—
22.		Deflators=(1)/(21)(%)				100.2	96.7	97.7	97.3	98.3	98.7				—	—

Notes:

1. fp stands for 'current price' and cp 'constant price'.
2. 0.3 (line 19) is calculated as follows: 0.3 = 1 − a, where a = fixed assets/all assets in *Kolkhoz* (data from *Narkhoz 1975*, p. 329 and *Narkhoz 1980*, p. 213).
3. 1.0640 or 1.06 in line 13 is calculated as: $1/5Σβ$; ($i = 1971 ∼ 1975$).
4. $(2) = V_f = βV_c$
5. $(3) = (1) + (5) − [(3) + (7) + (11)] = MO$
6. $(4) = (8) − (10)$

Figure 2.4.3. Decision procedure

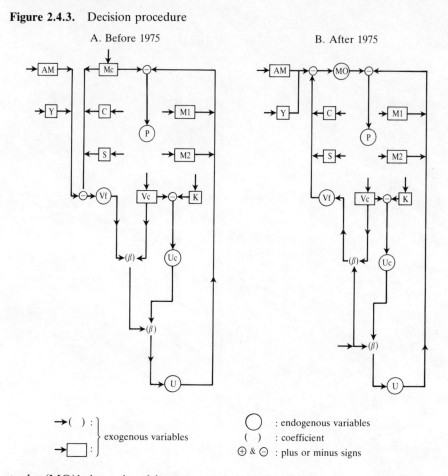

A. Before 1975   B. After 1975

→( ) : ⎫
        ⎬ exogenous variables
→▢ :   ⎭

◯ : endogenous variables
( ) : coefficient
⊕ & ⊖ : plus or minus signs

stocks (MO)', in national income used, include 'the increases in circulating assets' of *Kolkhoz*.

2. There are two data series of uncompleted construction projects (U). One shows the value of increases of uncompleted construction at year-end (excepting *Kolkhoz*) compared with the previous year. The other gives the difference between gross capital investment and the fixed assets put into operation. The former is expressed in terms of actual value at year-end. The latter is shown in constant prices. The coverage of the two concepts is also different. While the former covers only uncompleted construction, and probably excludes the value of machinery and equipment prior to the start of the work in question, the latter includes these values with the value of uncompleted construction (see table 2.4.3).

3. The last but most important problem is that we have no information to help us separate increases in defence resources from those in other categories of state reserves, including food, fuels, precious and non-precious metals, and jewellery. What we get as 'p' includes the other elements in addition to

Table 2.4.3. The comparison of two data series on uncompleted construction (in billions of roubles)

Year	1961	1962	1963	1964	1965	1966	1967	1968	1969	1970	1971	1972	1973	1974	1975	1976	1977	1978	1979
1	24.8	26.1	26.2	27.1	29.6	32.5	35.8	41.8	48.6	52.5	57.9	65.2	67.1	71.7	76.7	84.1	92.5	99.0	106.4
2	3.4	1.3	0.1	0.9	2.5	2.9	3.3	6.0	6.8	3.9	5.4	7.3	1.9	4.6	5.0	7.4	8.4	6.5	7.4
3	4.9	2.4	0.8	2.1	4.6	4.9	5.3	8.4	5.7	4.2	5.2	8.6	4.1	6.6	7.3	10.9	11.8	9.6	10.5

Notes:

1. The value of uncompleted construction at year-end.
2. The increases in that value during a year (except *Kolkhoz*).
3. New uncompleted construction = the difference between the gross fixed investment and fixed assets put into operation (see table 2.4.2, line 15).

Table 2.4.4. Estimate of defence expenditures (in billions of roubles)

	1975	1976	1977	1978	1979	1980	1981	1982	1983	1984
1. Number of soldiers (in thousands)	4763	4871	4872	4856	4827	4837	5275	5182	5274	5418
Consumption by soldiers	6.6	6.6	6.8	7.2	7.5	8.0	8.9	8.8	9.0	9.5
2. Military R&D	6.0	6.0	6.2	6.5	6.8	7.6	7.7	7.8	8.2	9.3
3. Procurement of arms Non-productive investment	30.9	34.4	36.3	37.5	38.2	34.7	41.0	39.9	42.9	45.4
4. Military construction	2.1 } 6.3	2.3 } 6.8	2.3 } 6.8	2.3 } 6.8	2.3 } 6.8	2.6 } 7.8	2.6 } 7.8	2.6 } 7.8	2.9 } 8.6	2.8 } 8.5
5. Military state reserve	3.9 } 11.6	4.3 } 13.0	5.6 } 16.9	6.5 } 19.4	7.1 } 21.2	5.3 } 15.8	−143	5.6 } 16.9	6.3 } 18.8	13.7 } 41.2

6. Total of defence expenditures	49.5 ⌡ 61.4	53.6 ⌡ 66.8	57.2 ⌡ 73.0	59.9 ⌡ 77.4	61.8 ⌡ 80.5	58.2 ⌡ 73.9	— ⌡ 51.1	64.7 ⌡ 81.2	69.2 ⌡ 87.5	80.8 ⌡ 113
7. Conditional gross national product	455.9 ⌡ 472.1	483.6 ⌡ 500.7	510.6 ⌡ 528.3	539.0 ⌡ 558.1	559.1 ⌡ 580.6	583.9 ⌡ 606.8	620.6 ⌡ 644.1	665.3 ⌡ 689.0	698.5 ⌡ 721.5	728.5 ⌡ 752.0
8. Share of defence expenditures in GNP (%)	10.5 ⌡ 13.4	10.7 ⌡ 13.7	10.8 ⌡ 14.2	10.7 ⌡ 14.3	10.6 ⌡ 14.3	9.6 ⌡ 12.6	— ⌡ 8.2	9.4 ⌡ 12.2	9.6 ⌡ 12.5	10.7 ⌡ 15.6

Notes:

1. Number of soldiers is cited from *US–Soviet military balance: assessments and statistics 1980–85*, Report Nos. 85–89 S (US Library of Congress: Washington, DC), p. 296. The figures include security forces: frontier security (KGB) and internal security (MVD).
2. The consumption by soldiers is calculated as follows: (number of soldiers) × (average wages of commerce and distribution industry for each year).
3. Line 2 is cited from M. Acland-Hood's paper 2.5, table 2.5.3, column 4.
4. Line 3 comes from my table 2.4.1, line 34.
5. Line 4 is calculated as: upper figures—capital investment in constructing facilities of sciences, culture, art and education', with the lower limit estimated as one-third of it.
6. Line 5 comes from my table 2.4.2, line 20; the lower limit is estimated as one-third.
7. The lower limit of 'conditional gross national products' comes from my table 2.4.2, line 6. As a revised GNP, the surplus value of the non-productive sector is calculated as a proportion of the share of profits to the total wage income of the whole economy.

defence. We thus measure an extreme upper limit of defence resources in these stocks.

VI.   Estimate of defence expenditures

Thus far we tried to estimate defence expenditures by the main items. In this section, we sum them up (see table 2.4.4). In order to try to ascertain the reality of defence expenditures and calculate their 'burden', we added two items to table 2.4.4: line 4 (military construction) and line 7 (conditional gross national product). Military construction is derived from 'capital investment in constructing facilities of sciences, culture, art and education'. This is the only item with room for military expenditures that accords with Soviet statistical terminology. The item does not, of course, equal defence expenditures. We estimate that the defence expenditures component's lower limit constitutes one-third of its value.

VII.   Conclusion

The estimation of defence expenditures is imprecise because of the scarcity of data and the obscurity of statistical information and methodology concerning some items.

The true size of Soviet military expenditures has often been distorted for political purposes. Soviet authorities minimize spending messages in order not to cause Western powers to take countermeasures. Western powers often manipulate people to support increased defence expenditures by raising exaggerated spectres of Soviet military efforts. Scientists must avoid political distortion.

In spite of its many defects, the statistical approach is the only scientific approach to estimates of the national burden of military expenditures; it also forces people to recognize how military expenditures erode the welfare of the nation. Statistical comparisons of the respective values of two countries' military expenditures, however, are technically and theoretically very difficult. It requires extraordinary finance, time and numbers of specialists to arrive at any significant results in terms of international, statistical comparisons. Attempts to assess military ability through comparisons of military expenditures also have little significance, because the size of military expenditure hardly reflects destructive power.

It must be admitted unreservedly that statistical estimates are conditional. In addition to the unresolved problems mentioned earlier, there are others. Calculating real military burdens demands consideration of the opportunity cost of defence, the hidden cost and indirect negative effects (see Introduction, pages 3–10).

Notes and references

[1] Sverdlik, S., *Obshchestvenny i Produkt i Denezhnyi Oborot* (The social products and money circulation) (Nauka: Novosibirsk, 1981).

[2] US Central Intelligence Agency (CIA), *USSR: Measures of Economic Growth and Development, 1960–1980*, studies prepared for the use of the Joint Economic Committee, Congress of the United States, 8 Dec. 1982 (US Government Printing Office: Washington, DC, 1982).

[3] United Nations, *Yearbook of National Accounts Statistics, 1981*, Vol. 1, individual country data, p. XX.

[4] Ezhov, A. I. and Bojarckij, A. Ya., *Statistical Dictionary* (Moscow, 1965).

[5] *PlanEcon Report*, nos. 25 and 26 (27 June 1986).

[6] United Nations (note 3).

[7] Ts SU SSR *Narodnoe Khoziaistvo SSSR v 1975* (National economy of the USSR) (Finansy i statistika: Moscow, 1975), p. 566.

Paper 2.5.   Estimating Soviet military R&D spending[1]

MARY ACLAND-HOOD

I.   Introduction

Soviet secrecy about its military effort is particularly effective at concealing the current military research and development (R&D) part of it. Its results—new or improved weapon systems—only show after delays of considerable, but not precisely known, length. Moreover, the results depend not only on the scale of the effort, but on its efficiency.

There are a number of possible, but not equally good, approaches to estimating the scale of Soviet military R&D spending. One is only open to intelligence services. This is to calculate from observed facilities, usually making the assumption that they are fully employed. The reliability of this method is doubtful because it is not easy to assess how much the military, in fact, use the facilities. (However, if it really works, it ought to make possible a high degree of verification of suitable agreements to control military R&D.)

The other approaches are as follows:

1. To make an assessment of its likely size in relation to total military expenditure (itself an uncertain figure). This approach has been used by Forsberg as a check[2] and, in a rather odd way, by the US Defense Intelligence Agency (DIA).[3]

2. To examine aggregate budget and other expenditure data. This method was used by Korol,[4] Lee,[5] and by Nimitz as a check on her main method.[6]

3. To infer it from examination of weapon developments, especially compared to US developments, allowing for the effects of technological lags. This approach has been used, in varying depths, by the US Central Intelligence Agency (CIA),[7] the DIA[8] and Forsberg.[9]

4. To estimate the military share of R&D outlays sector by sector, in as much detail as possible, starting from the disaggregated Soviet science data. This method was used by Nimitz[10] and is the one used in this paper.[11]

5. To attempt to identify the military element of total R&D employment and to assess the significance of changes in it. This method has been used in this paper rather crudely as a check.[12]

Almost all methods include some assumptions based on analogies with the

USA. It is not valid to treat these assumptions as if they were estimates in subsequent calculations or in drawing conclusions.

The reasons for choosing the methods used in this paper are outlined below and are given in greater detail in Acland-Hood[13] together with some of the detailed calculations.

The first two methods—examinations of aggregates—are best used as checks on other methods: the potential errors are huge. Total military expenditure is itself uncertain (as much of the rest of this volume indicates) and the evidence on the defence and space shares of the science budget is highly ambiguous and depends much on the examination of residuals.

The third method—inference from examination of weapon developments— works back to input from output and so necessitates making assumptions about efficiency. Assumptions about efficiency are, as Nimitz says, 'a central issue in evaluating the military burden in the USSR'.[14] Estimates made in this way can therefore only be used to support propositions about efficiency if they are compared with independent estimates made by another method or methods. Moreover, this method can only produce estimates for the past—and, given the considerable time needed from conception to production of weapons, not the very recent past. Changed trends in the R&D effort will not be picked up for many years, when the results in more or fewer new weapons are apparent.

The disaggregated method developed and described by Nimitz[15] seems the best. In essence, the method is, first, to derive an estimated distribution of R&D outlays sector by sector. For this, the available information about disaggregated science expenditure and breakdowns of various types of scientific worker by type of training are used to estimate the distribution of the total number employed in R&D in each sector, assuming a similar distribution of the ratio between scientists and support staff (but not similar actual ratios) in the USSR and the USA. The second part of the method is to assess the most likely military shares in each sector individually, using analogies with US shares, and to assess the highest plausible military shares in each sector, given the nature of each sector. As Nimitz says, use of this method reduces the risks of overlooking civilian activity and also makes use of analogies with the USA less risky, since each area can be separately examined to see whether the results are plausible and consistent with whatever pieces of evidence exist. Up to the mid-1970s Soviet statistical sources gave breakdowns of science expenditure and employment. These have been exhaustively analysed and interpreted by, among others, Nolting and Feshbach[16] and Campbell,[17] and, while neither complete nor wholly unambiguous, they are good enough to make estimation by this method or a similar method possible.

Therefore this is the method employed in this paper. Nimitz's last estimate was for 1968. My estimate is for 1974, the last year for which similar disaggregated data for scientific employment is available. I followed Nimitz closely, except where differences in the available data invited or forced variations. (These variations are not of a kind to make my estimate non-comparable with Nimitz's 1968 estimate, although it is less certain whether it is comparable with her 1965 and 1960 estimates.) Table 2.5.1 gives the results of the estimation.[18]

For 1977, I used Cooper's analysis of Plekhov's distribution of scientific workers serving and in industry.[19] 1977 is the last year for which this information is available. It was not obvious whether the resulting estimate was comparable with the 1974 one. I therefore recalculated Nimitz's 1968 estimate, substituting Plekhov/Cooper figures for the distribution of scientific workers serving and in industry, but otherwise making no changes. This indicated that the Plekhov/Cooper data resulted in lower estimates—a military share of $33\frac{1}{2}$ to 47 per cent of R&D instead of Nimitz's 39 to 55 per cent. Consequently, the 1977 estimates cannot be compared with earlier years without adjustment of some kind. I have therefore made adjustments on the basis of the 1968 comparison in both directions, arriving at a series consistent with the 1977 estimate and a series consistent with the Nimitz 1968 estimate.

My estimates of the military shares of total R&D, unadjusted, are shown in table 2.5.2, together with Nimitz's estimates, and the US military and space shares of total R&D for the years covered by the estimates of Soviet shares plus 1982 and 1984. Both Nimitz's and my Soviet medium estimates (but not the 'highest plausible' estimates) depend on strong analogy with US sectoral shares of military and space R&D in total R&D. These US sectoral shares change significantly from year to year. There are two reasons for these changes. One is that the particular industrial (or other) sector has increasing military importance because of changing military technology. The other is that there is a general reduction, or increase, in the relative importance of military technology as a whole.

The first type of change is one which is unlikely to be specific to any one country; developments in technology tend eventually to be much the same in the Soviet Union as in the United States. The second type of change, however—the general trend in the military share in US R&D—is obviously one which should not be imported into any process of estimating the Soviet figures.

It therefore seemed reasonable to adjust the estimates to avoid importing a US trend into them. Since there is a lack of decisive information about which year or years to adjust towards, and whether to adjust towards Nimitz or Plekhov/Cooper, I adjusted in both directions to arrive at a range of probable estimates. It does come out clearly that, whatever way the adjustments are made, the share of military and space R&D in total R&D was falling from 1960 to the early 1970s and falling or constant from then until 1977—but probably falling. It is the changes in the distribution of outlays between sectors that determines this. This falling trend also shows in the 'highest plausible' shares, which are not dependent on US sectoral or other shares of total R&D. The falling trend was accompanied by rising actual expenditure.

For the estimates, I chose to adjust the post-1968 data to a basis equivalent to the Nimitz 1968 estimate, using the relationship between the US military and space shares in 1968 and in later years. This is an arbitrary decision. However, it seemed less reasonable to adjust towards remoter years than 1968; 1968 is a

Table 2.5.1. Estimation of the defence and space share of Soviet R&D outlays in 1974 (Shares in parentheses are derived totals)

	Estimated R&D outlays (million roubles)	Estimated percentage defence and space shares				Estimated defence and space outlays (million roubles)	Estimated highest plausible defence and space outlays (million roubles)
		Defence	Space	Defence & space	Ceiling: highest plausible share		
Academies of Science	818	13	4	17	50	142	409
Higher educational institutions	1 500	13	4	17	50	260	750
Geology	148	2	13	15	40	22	59
Construction	85	4	1	5	10	4	9
Health	258	6½	—	6½	15	17	39
Agriculture	314	1	—	1	5	3	16
Transport	151	1	—	1	10	2	15
Communications	15	1	1	2	10	—	2
Education and culture	190	1	1	2	10	4	19
Other non-industrial	296	3	1	4	10	12	30
Total non-industrial	**3 775**	**(9)**	**(3)**	**(12½)**	**(35½)**	**465**	**1 346**

Electric and thermal power	107	1	1	2	5	2	5
Coal	56	1	—	1	5	1	3
Petroleum and minor fuels	77	2½	½	3	20	2	15
Ferrous metals	91	2	½	2½	5	2	5
Non-ferrous metals	89	3½	1	4½	15	4	13
Chemicals	925	7½	2	9½	25	88	231
Machine-building and metal-working	8 313	(35)	(8½)	(43½)	(72)	3 622	982
Electrical and power M&E	788	37½	9½	47	65	370	512
Machinery	1 268	12	3	14½	40	186	507
Precision instruments and computers	1 000	15	3½	18½	60	186	600
Ships and railroad M&E	254	—	—	—	—	—	—
Automobiles and bearings	586	10	2½	13	40	107	336
Fabricated metal products	226	3½	1	4½	20	10	45
Machinery NEC	4 191	52½	13	66	95	2 762	3 982
Wood and paper	251	—	—	—	5	—	13
Construction materials	136	½	—	½	5	1	7
Light and food industries	294	—	—	—	5	—	15
Other	86	3	1	4	10	3	9
Total industrial	**10 425**	**(28½)**	**(7)**	**(35½)**	**(60½)**	**3 725**	**6 298**
Total	**14 200**	**(23½)**	**(6)**	**(29½)**	**(54)**	**4 190**	**7 644**

Source: Acland-Hood, M., *Military Research and Development: Resource Use and Arms Control*, SIPRI (Oxford University Press: Oxford, 1987, forthcoming), chapter 4 and appendix 4.

Table 2.5.2.   Initial estimates of the Soviet military and space shares of total R&D expenditure, compared to Nimitz and to US shares

	Nimitz's estimates, for comparison		Acland-Hood (Similar method to Nimitz's)		Acland-Hood (Similar method to Nimitz's, using Plekhov/ Cooper distribution of scientists)		US shares, for comparison	
	Medium	High	Medium	Highest plausible	Medium	Highest plausible	Total of military and space	Space alone
1960	48	62					55	3
1965	45	57					54	21
1968	39	55			33½	47	48	13
1974			29½ᵃ	54			35	8
1977					23	43½	33	8
1982							32	7
1984							35	6

ᵃMilitary 23½ per cent, space 5 per cent.

Sources: Nimitz, N., *The Structure of Soviet Outlays on R&D in 1960 and 1968*, Rand Report R-1207-DDRE (Rand Corporation: Santa Monica, CA, June 1974), p. v; Cooper, J., *Scientists and Soviet Industry: A Statistical Analysis*, Centre for Russian and East European Studies, Birmingham University, UK, informal discussion paper (Nov. 1981); Acland-Hood, M., *Military Research and Development: Resource Use and Arms Control*, SIPRI (Oxford University Press: Oxford, 1987, forthcoming), chapter 4 and appendix 4.

year for which Soviet information is relatively good, and the US military and space share of total R&D was not much below the high levels of the early and mid-1960s, so lessening the chance of underestimating the Soviet share.

It is necessary to estimate the total R&D expenditure that the estimated shares are to be applied to. I have added something to the total reported science outlays for omitted development (OKR). The particular adjustments I made are shown in table 2.5.3, and the reasons for them are described in Acland-Hood.[20]

Table 2.5.3 shows the resulting estimates: years for which there are detailed estimates are shown in bold print, other years are interpolations. The probable range is shown as shares in column 1 and in billions of roubles in column 3. The low end is Cooper/Plekhov-based (and equivalent) shares, not adjusted to remove the effect of US share changes, applied to total reported science expenditures increased by one-tenth. The high end is Nimitz-based (and equivalent) shares, adjusted to remove the effect of US share changes, and applied to total reported science expenditures increased by one-fifth. These are the most extreme assumptions short of taking the largest plausible shares sector by sector, which is done to arrive at the 'highest plausible' estimates in columns 2 and 5.

The 'most likely' range shown in column 4 is the range between the Plekhov/ Cooper-based and Nimitz-based estimates, adjusted to remove the effects of the US share changes and applied to total reported science outlays increased by one-tenth.

Columns 7 and 8 show the 'most likely' estimates as percentage shares of Soviet GNP (as estimated by Campbell[21]) and of a range of Soviet military expenditure estimates. These are included as a check on the reasonableness of the estimates: they do not seem unreasonable. (The reasons for rejecting higher estimates of the R&D share of total military expenditure are given in Acland-Hood.[22])

In addition to these estimates, I also made some rough estimates based on method 5, attempting to identify the military element of total R&D employment, using data on specialities to assess the significance of changes in the military element. The results depend rather heavily on analogy with the USA for each sector, but show an overall Soviet share a little, not a lot, higher than the US share. Given the higher labour intensity in the USSR, this is consistent with similar shares of expenditure in both countries.

II.   Problems and possible improvements

There are a number of improvements that could be made. First, the estimates could be refined and improved by including extra bits of information as they become available. Second, these trends are expenditure trends. A suitable price index is necessary for volume trends to be identified. It would then be possible to see if there was any sign of a slowing down during the 1970s in the rate of increase of the volume of military R&D. If inflation in the USSR followed or shadowed Western experience to any significant extent, this might be so. Evidence of restraint in this period would be highly significant.

The principal problem is that 1977, the last year for which adequate disaggregated data is available, is 10 years ago now, and it is difficult to see how any more recent estimates can be made by this method. It will probably eventually be necessary to use method 3 working back from output. Work could be done on lags between R&D and production of various types of weapon, in order to see how estimates made in this way could be linked to the disaggregated-method estimates up to 1977. However, this method cannot, in the nature of things, provide up-to-date estimates of expenditure in Soviet military R&D. It could lead to some continuing ability to estimate past trends in Soviet military R&D.

The Grishaev information

Finally, as a curiosa, one might mention the information provided by E. E. Grishaev in 1973.[23] He declared that if certain construction and research support costs were excluded, then remaining Science (R&D) expenditures could be broken down as follows: fundamental research—14 per cent; applied research—22 per cent; development—64 per cent. 'However, if we exclude from that general volume a significant part of the Ministries of heavy industry,

Table 2.5.3. Estimates of Soviet military and space R&D expenditure: shares of total expenditure and billion roubles, 1959–84

Years[a]	Percentage shares of total R&D		Estimated expenditure, billion roubles			Most likely range of expenditure as a % of:	
	Probable range[b]	Highest plausible[c]	Probable range[d]	Most likely range[e]	Highest plausible[f]	Soviet GNP[g]	Soviet military expenditure[h]
1959	41–48	62		1.3–1.6	2.1	—	—
1960	41–48	62		1.5–1.9	2.2	—	7–9
1961	41–48	61		1.7–2.2	2.8	1.0–1.2	—
1962	40–47	60		1.9–2.4	3.1	1.1–1.3	—
1963	40–46	59		2.2–2.7	3.5	1.0–1.3	7–9
1964	39–45	58		2.3–2.9	3.8	1.0–1.2	—
1965	39–45	57	2.5–3.1	2.5–2.9	4.0	1.0–1.2	7–10
1966	37–43	56	2.6–3.3	2.6–3.0	4.2	1.0–1.2	—
1967	35–41	56	2.8–3.5	2.8–3.2	4.8	1.0–1.1	—
1968	$33\frac{1}{2}$–39	55	2.9–3.7	2.9–3.4	5.2		—
1969	$32\frac{1}{2}$–39	55	3.1–4.0	3.2–3.7	5.7	1.0–1.1	—
1970	31–39	55	3.5–4.7	3.8–4.3	6.7	1.0–1.2	7–10
1971	$30–39\frac{1}{2}$	55	3.7–5.3	4.2–4.9	7.4	1.1–1.2	8–11
1972	28–40	54	3.9–6.0	4.7–5.5	8.1	1.2–1.4	8–13
1973	$27–40\frac{1}{2}$	54	4.0–6.7	5.3–6.1	8.9	1.2–1.4	9–14
1974	$25\frac{1}{2}–40\frac{1}{2}$	54	4.0–6.9	5.5–6.3	9.2	1.2–1.4	9–14
1975	25–40	53	4.1–7.1	5.5–6.5	9.4	1.2–1.4	8–14
1976	24–39	52	4.0–7.0	5.6–6.4	9.4	1.1–1.2	8–14
1977	23–39	51	3.9–7.3	5.7–6.7	9.5	1.1–1.3	8–14
1978	23–39	51	4.1–7.7	6.0–7.0	10.0	1.1–1.3	8–15
1979	23–39	51	4.4–8.0	6.2–7.4	10.5	1.1–1.3	8–15
1980	23–39	51	4.8–8.9	6.9–8.2	11.6	1.1–1.3	8–17
1981	23–39	51	4.9–9.3	7.1–8.3	12.2	1.1–1.3	8–17
1982	23–39	51	4.9–9.5	7.1–8.4	12.5	1.1–1.3	8–17
1983	23–39	51	5.2–10.2	7.5–8.9	13.3		—
1984	23–39	51	5.8–11.3	8.7–9.9	14.7		—

Source: Acland-Hood, M., *Military Research and Development: Resource Use and Arms Control*, SIPRI (Oxford University Press: Oxford, 1987, forthcoming), chapter 4 and appendix 4.

[a]Years for which detailed estimates exist are bold: all others are interpolations and extrapolations. The detailed estimates for 1960 and 1965 are Nimitz's (Nimitz, N., *The Structure of Soviet Outlays on R&D in 1960 and 1968*, Rand Report R-1207-DDRE (Rand Corporation: Santa Monica, CA, June 1974), for 1968 they are Nimitz's and mine, and for 1974 and 1977, mine. The broad lines of the 1974 estimation are given in Acland-Hood, M., *Military Research and Development: Resource Use and Arms Control*, SIPRI (Oxford University Press: Oxford, 1987, forthcoming), appendix 4.

[b]These estimates are derived from table 2.5.2. Lower estimates are based on data including Cooper's analysis of Plekhov's distribution of scientists supporting industry and without any adjustment to compensate for the possible effect of changes in the overall military and space share of US R&D. Higher estimates do not use Plekhov's distribution and, after 1968, are crudely adjusted to remove the effect of the lower overall military and space share of US R&D after that date.

[c]Based on the highest plausible-seeming shares sector by sector, weighted by estimated total R&D outlays for each sector.

[d]Lower figures are the lower percentage shares from the probable range in column 1 applied to total reported science expenditure (excluding capital) increased by one-tenth up to and including 1980, by 7½ per cent for 1981 and by 5 per cent from 1982 to allow for development (OKR) omitted according to Soviet definitions. Higher figures are the higher percentage shares from column 1 applied to total reported science expenditure (excluding capital) increased by one-fifth to allow for development (OKR) omitted according to Soviet definitions.

[e]Lower figures are the lower percentage shares from the probable range in column 1 adjusted crudely to remove the effect of the lower overall military and space share of US R&D, applied to total reported science expenditure increased by one-tenth up to and including 1980, by 7½ per cent for 1981 and by 5 per cent for 1982 to allow for development (OKR) omitted according to Soviet definitions. Higher figures are the higher percentage shares from column 1 applied to total reported science expenditure increased by one-tenth as above.

[f]Highest plausible shares applied to total reported science expenditure increased by one-fifth as above.

[g]GNP estimates are from Campbell, R. W., *Reference Source on Soviet R&D Statistics 1950–1978, Soviet R&D Statistics, 1977–80, Soviet R&D Statistics 1975–1982* (University of Indiana for National Science Foundation: Washington, DC, 1978, 1980 and 1982, respectively).

[h]The size of Soviet military expenditure is uncertain: these shares can only be viewed as a rough check on the plausibility of the estimates. The Soviet military expenditure figures taken here are estimated CIA figures and (currently unpublished) SIPRI figures.

the proportion of all expenditures on fundamental science is 29%, applied science 40% and development only 31%.' The 'significant part of the Ministries of heavy industry' may well refer to military R&D. If so, they reflect the fact that rigorous military procurement standards and quality control procedures had no civilian analogue, and the consequent fact that the final development stage of military production constituted a relative burden that was dramatically higher than that in civilian production. The figures also suggest that military R&D takes an absolute minimum of 51.73 per cent of the Science budget (pure research—?) as defined by Grishaev; this assumes that none of the fundamental science expenditures are charged to the military. If 50 per cent of fundamental science is assigned to the military, then their total share rises to 75.86 per cent; nine-tenths would translate into 95.17 per cent. The exercise is speculative. And the context is not at all clear. The suggested military R&D budget may refer to weapon procurement alone, in which case it would not be exhaustive. The category excluded from Grishaev's science budget may also constitute a very high portion of the base budget. Suggested military share conclusions may therefore be grossly misleading. The Grishaev information is thus intriguing, but not particularly helpful. It does not provide sufficient information to allow alternative calculations of substance, nor can it be used to check the validity of those presented here.

Notes and references

[1] The estimates and methods are given in greater detail in Acland-Hood, M., *Military Research and Development: Resource Use and Arms Control*, SIPRI (Oxford University Press: Oxford, 1987, forthcoming) chapter 4 and appendix 4.

[2] SIPRI, *Resources Devoted to Military Research and Development: An International Comparison* (Almqvist & Wiksell: Stockholm, 1972).

[3] See the discussion in Acland-Hood (note 1), referring particularly to *Allocation of Resources in the Soviet Union and China: 1984*. Hearings before the Subcommittee on International Trade, Finance and Security Economics of the Joint Economic Committee, Congress of the United States, 98th Congress, 2nd session and 99th Congress, 1st session, part 10, executive sessions, 21 Nov. 1984 and 15 Jan. 1985 (US Government Printing Office: Washington, DC, 1985).

[4] See Korol, A., *Soviet Research and Development: Its Organization, Personnel and Funds* (MIT Press: Cambridge, MA, 1965).

[5] See Lee, W. T., *The Estimation of Soviet Defense Expenditures, 1955–75: An Unconventional Approach* (Praeger: New York, 1977).

[6] See Nimitz, N., *The Structure of Soviet Outlays on R&D in 1960 and 1968*, Rand Report R–1207–DDRE (Rand Corporation: Santa Monica, CA, June 1974).

[7] *Estimated Soviet Defense Spending: Trends and Prospects*, National Foreign Assessment Center (CIA: Washington, DC, June 1978).

[8] See Acland-Hood (note 3).

[9] See SIPRI (note 2).

[10] See Nimitz (note 6).

[11] See Acland-Hood (note 1).

[12] See Acland-Hood (note 1).

[13] See Acland-Hood (note 1).

[14] See Nimitz (note 6), p. v.

[15] See Nimitz (note 6).

[16] Nolting, L. E. and Feshbach, M., 'R&D employment in the USSR: definitions, statistics and comparisons', in *Soviet Economy in a Time of Change*, Vol. 1, US Congress, Joint Economic Committee (US Government Printing Office: Washington, DC, 10 Oct. 1979).

[17] Campbell, R. W., *Reference Source on Soviet R&D Statistics 1950–1978, Soviet R&D Statistics, 1977–80, Soviet R&D Statistics 1975–82* (University of Indiana for National Science Foundation: Washington, DC, 1978, 1980 and 1982, respectively).

[18] The detailed calculations for 1974 are given in Acland-Hood, M., (note 1), appendix 4.

[19] Cooper, J., *Scientists and Soviet Industry: A Statistical Analysis*, Centre for Russian and East European Studies, Birmingham University, UK, informal discussion paper (Nov. 1981).

[20] See Acland-Hood (note 1).

[21] See Campbell (note 17).

[22] See Acland-Hood (note 1).

[23] Grishaev, E. E., in ed. D. M. Gvishiani, *Osnovnye Printsipy i Obshchie Problemy Upravleniya Naukoi* (Nauka: Moscow, 1973), p. 143. The author is grateful to Dr Julian Cooper of the University of Birmingham for drawing attention to this book.

Part 3.   Historical context—future prospects

Paper 3.1.   The Soviet defence burden through the prism of history

DAVID R. JONES

I.   Introduction

As we approach year three of what may become known as the 'Gorbachev era', the Soviet Union's stagnating economy is still a matter of primary concern. Although there has been talk of 'revolutionary' change, the steps towards this goal have thus far been partial and halting. In the view of most Western economists, economic growth will not be sustained until a number of fundamental innovations are introduced into this highly centralized system with its ageing industrial plant.

Changes must deal with much more than decentralization of the planning structure, the introduction of realism into the pricing structure, and measures to ensure higher productivity from the existing plant and the workers using it. If the Soviet Union is to regain its position as a leading industrial nation, it must somehow acquire and absorb the modern technologies now being applied by its Western and Japanese rivals. This, in turn, seems to require considerable capital investment at a time when funds are tight. This last concern raises the questions of the burden that defence expenditures place on the economy and of the extent to which some of these funds might be converted into capital for use in other ways. Although there is little agreement among Western analysts on the exact amounts being spent on the military-naval establishment, all agree that the levels are high, however they are measured. And many, especially during Brezhnev's last years, suggested that policies of restraint in this area would meet serious opposition from within the Soviet defence community.[1]

Equally important, however, is the fact that many of the same technologies needed to spark an industrial renewal are just as essential for maintaining the USSR's position as a 'superpower' in an age when the decisive battles of any future war may be fought with sophisticated, precision-guided, 'high-tech' weaponry. For in an age of 'nuclear parity', the use of nuclear weapons has become impossible owing to the fact that each side would inevitably damage the other so severely that victory has become a meaningless concept.[2] For this reason, then, the military's needs parallel those of the civilian economic reformers.

From another point of view, however, this situation has been a recurring one in the history of Russia and the Soviet Union. Having struggled to gain parity, as they perceive it, with their US rival in the 1950s and 1960s, the Soviet leaders suddenly found themselves falling behind. Once again their nation had to play 'catch-up ball' in a world fraught with danger. Once again, Russia's pretensions to 'Great (Super) Power' status were threatened by the old problems of cultural and technological 'backwardness'. And once again, Western trade barriers complicated efforts to acquire the necessary technologies from abroad, while the implications of these technologies in themselves threatened to transform drastically the existing political and social system. In this sense, Gorbachev and his military leaders are heirs to similar problems to those that faced Ivan III in the 1470s, Ivan IV in the 1550s, Alexis in the 1650s, Peter the Great in the early 1700s, Alexander II in the 1860s and Stalin in the 1930s.

Although many refuse to accept the past as a useful guide to the possible handling of present problems, the parallels noted are intriguing. Yet, as the present author has argued elsewhere, there are strong strands of continuity linking today's Soviet military with their Tsarist forebears in terms of social and political traditions, nationalist ethos, style of organization, system of military administration, and attitude to the external world.[3] In addition, there also appear to be certain similarities in the structure of Imperial and Soviet budgets, both with regard to the broad range of activities included under defence and in other areas. For example, a comparison of the figures for 1913 and 1965 shows that direct and indirect taxes represent very similar proportions of the state's revenues (47.9 per cent in 1913 compared to 45.3 per cent in 1965).[4] While much has of course changed, such recurring patterns suggest that past bureaucratic styles and practices have continued to influence the conduct of public affairs in areas outside the military establishment *per se*. During the Middle Ages, Werner Philipp once observed, 'Russia became the conservative country *par excellence* in Europe'.[5] And despite the events and continuing rhetoric of 1917, in many ways his statement seems as applicable to Gorbachev's Soviet Union as to Ivan III's Grand Principality of Moscow.

For this reason, what follows is a brief analysis of the traditional Russian attitudes towards security and their nation's subsequent rise as a great power, the nature of the burden they have borne to achieve these goals, and the interaction between the civil and military leadership over the size and justification of that burden. As suggested, the themes of backwardness and power are persistent issues, as is that of the misery endured by past Russians to ensure their state's military prowess. Taken together, these themes provide a backdrop of attitudes and actions against which General Secretary Gorbachev's efforts will be enacted, and the basis on which his fellow citizens—the military included—will judge and possibly support his initiatives.

II. The Muscovite experience

As Daniel Galik once observed, the influence of the Soviet 'defence burden' on policy depends on the leadership's recognition of it and 'on official perceptions of the offsetting benefits that flow from Soviet military efforts'.[6] Such benefits may be social, political, military, strategic, economic or even psychological.

This last is particularly important for this discussion, since 'security', or *bezopasnost'*, is at least in part a psychological state. Yet since it is also a state that is buttressed by physical strength, a strength that is purchased by the expenditure of economic means, it may also be regarded as a vital and precious 'product of social consumption'.

Although usually translated as 'security', *bezopanost'* is closer to the meaning of such English expressions as 'the absence of threat' or 'absolute security'.[7] That the realization of this mirage has been a consistent goal of the Great Russians should cause no surprise. Russia's history has been a chronicle of almost continuous conflict:[8] the 'basic continuous elements of Russian history are the people, the Great Russians, surrounded by real or imagined enemies in a country without suitable natural frontiers and without adequate resources—material or human—for their own defense'.[9] One may argue that in reality many of these enemies were imaginary, but the Russians thought otherwise; the theme of repelling invasions has dominated their historical military studies both before and after 1917.[10]

The roots of this almost pathological concern with security can be found in the historical experiences of Kievan Rus' and of Muscovy. Thus the ancient Kievan ballads or *byliny* are full of the glorious combats of Rus' knights (*bogatyri*) against the infidel steppe nomads; Aleksandr Nevskii won lasting recognition for defeating the Swedes and Teutonic Knights while Russia lay prostrate under the Mongol heel; and Dmitrii Donskoi joined him as a national hero for inflicting his country's first major defeat upon these same Tatars. All in all, the Imperial nationalist historian S. M. Solov'ev argued that, between 1055 and 1462, Russia suffered 245 'attacks' and that 200 of these occurred between 1240 and 1426.[11] By the late 15th century, matters had improved but little. Describing Muscovy's geopolitical position, a Soviet scholar noted that the state remained isolated and 'hemmed in by a ring of hostile neighbours':

> the eastern and southern frontiers were assaulted by the Tatar khanates that had been founded after the collapse of the Golden Horde; on the western frontier, the struggle for the old Russian lands continued with the Grand Duchy of Lithuania, while the Livonian Order and Sweden were sources of constant danger to the northeastern Russian territories.[12]

Even after the victories over the Khanates of Kazan and Astrakhan under Ivan IV had more or less secured Moscow's eastern borders, wars continued in the south where the frontier remained 'a terrible gaping wound through which Russia's strength poured out'.[13] Here the enemy was the *Krimtsy* (Crimean Tatars) who, as beneficiaries of the 'cavalry revolution' of the 8th and 7th centuries BC, lived by slave-raiding and dominated the steppes until well into the 1700s. Between 1601 and 1655 they reportedly captured 150 000–200 000 Russian, Polish and Ukrainian prisoners and, as late as 1710–18, still managed to seize 14 000 prisoners from the Kharkov district. Small wonder that, as another Imperial historian recorded, '[e]ach year one waited for an attack, spoke of war. . . . A year rarely passed without raids, fires, devastation'.[14]

It is obviously simplistic to explain the growth of Russian autocracy on this situation alone. None the less, it was one 'which kept the whole military establishment of *Rus'* in a state of combat readiness', and a major source 'of the tremendous material burden which lay heavily on the peasant and urban population'.[15] The development of the 'garrison state', directed by an 'autocratic-bureaucratic government' and supported by a military 'service class', was one obvious way of mobilizing Muscovy's scarce resources for the struggle.[16] Or as the great liberal historian P. N. Miliukov described it, the principality of Moscow became 'a military-national state [founded] on a primitive economic basis', one that in practice existed as 'a permanent armed camp'. Its main concern, he argues, was 'how to obtain money and troops'. This means that, from the late 15th century onwards, questions of war and finance 'entirely absorbed the attention of the central authorities and all other central reforms, especially reforms of the state administration, . . . were in the end always called forth by these two demands'.[17]

Apart from an autocratic and centralized government, the early reforms also brought a bureaucratic system which saw the populace become regimented into legal 'estates' that either performed military service or supported those that did. By the mid-17th century, the peasantry had become almost fully enserfed and tied to their land. This was a result of the Muscovite Government's first great military innovation, 150 years earlier—the creation of a mounted gentry militia (the *dvorianstvo*) which, as a service class or 'estate', obtained the sole right to ownership of lands (*pomestie* grants or fiefs) farmed by peasant-serfs. In return, these gentry-militiamen were obligated to render military service for life. In this manner Muscovy became more 'organized for warfare' than was any other European state, with all its 'principal resources . . . channelled into military purposes'.[18]

III.   The Petrine transformation

It was on the basis of this 'service state' that Peter the Great created his Westernized empire and won it a place as a great power. The 'crucial element' that enabled Russia to retain this status until the 1850s 'was the pre-Petrine political and social system that permitted the effective mobilization of human and material resources from a large poor country in a manner that no European country could equal, at least until the French Revolution'.[19] But at the same time, as a great power Russia has traditionally presented outsiders with the paradox of undeniable military force, backed by apparently vast resources, on the one hand, and a crude, savage, barbaric and above all else backward social system; both perceptions are correct, if incomplete.

At the same time, it must be stressed that Peter's modernization of his realm did little to shift the primary focus of state concern from the needs of the armed forces. Indeed, his reforms began with the military and only subsequently turned to other spheres of state life as he sought to maintain his new armed forces more efficiently. Or to put it differently, his 'military organization preceded the Senate and gave birth to it, and senatorial government evolved as a continuing response to the interaction of the new army (and navy) with Russian society'. For the fundamental purpose of the governmental system that emerged after 1711 'never ceased to be the creation and maintenance of a domestic administration that could furnish a steady, predictable quantity of men and supplies for the purposes of war'.[20] And it is to the credit of Peter the Great that, despite continuing problems, he left his successors a state and fiscal system that meant that future governments were not caught unaware by military necessities and forced into the hasty reorganizations so characteristic of the Muscovite period.[21] (See table 3.1.1.)

As for the burden imposed by Peter's reformed military establishment, after

Table 3.1.1.   Army manpower, 1680–1914

Year	Numbers	Year	Numbers
1680	216 000	1830	1 051 484
1700	50 000	1835	1 073 539
1707	145 000	1840	1 151 813
1711[a]	174 000	1845	1 293 918
1720	178 049	1850	1 316 803
1725	304 500	1855	1 843 463
1731	205 549	1856	1 742 000
1734	196 511	1862	859 000
1740	111 583	1866	·779 257
1754[a]	325 673	1871	734 000
1756	330 000	1876	737 000
1761	335 375	1878	1 511 000
1763	274 667	1880	884 000
1765	303 529	1885	814 000
1795	413 473	1890	850 000
1796	507 538	1897	1 033 153
1801	446 057	1898	1 059 000
1806	391 000	1900	1 075 000
1808	663 000	1907	1 345 000
1809	520 000	1909	1 348 769
1812	597 000	1911	1 100 000
1815[b]	709 603	1914	1 185 482
1826	1 055 107		

[a]This figure represents the established manpower as set down by law but is not adjusted for existing manpower shortages.
[b]Manpower of 1st and 2nd (Field) Armies only.

Sources: Numbers are taken from Beskrovnyi, L. G., *Russkaia Armiia i Flot v XVIII Veke (Ocherki)* (Voenizdat.: Moscow, 1958); Beskrovnyi, L. G., *Russkaia Armiia i Flot v XIX Veke: Voennoekonomicheskii Potentsial Rossii* (Nauka: Moscow, 1973); Bogdanov, L. P., *Russkaia Armiia v 1812 godu. Organizatsiia, Upravlenie, Vooruzhenie* (Voenizdat.: Moscow, 1979); Keep, J. L. H., *Soldiers of the Tsar, Army and Society in Russia, 1462–1874* (Clarendon Press: Oxford, 1985); Pintner, W. H., *Russia as a Great Power, 1709–1856: Reflections on the Problem of Relative Backwardness, with Special Reference to the Russian Army and Russian Society*, Occasional Papers No. 33 (Kennan Institute for Advanced Russian Studies: Washington, DC, 1978); and Rostunov, I. I., *Russkii Front Pervoi Mirovoi Voiny* (Nauka: Moscow, 1976).

peaking in the early 18th century, it fell to acceptable levels throughout the rest of that century. Indeed, it can be argued that owing to demographic and economic growth, as well as territorial expansion, it was actually somewhat lightened. For while defence expenditures grew in terms of absolute current roubles, their proportion of total state spending had dropped by 1781 to 34.3 per cent, from the estimated 62 per cent of a century earlier (see table 3.1.2). So while funding did not always meet the military-naval establishment's perceived needs, and while the state might experience fiscal difficulties in meeting the current expenses of a crisis like the Seven Years' War (1756–63), Westernization clearly reduced the fiscal pressure placed by defence on the state's resources.[22]

Fair enough, critics might respond, but this does not answer the charge that Peter's empire none the less began the practice of maintaining 'the largest standing army in the world', or that this placed a disproportionately large burden on its populace relative to that found elsewhere in the Europe of the day.[23] Or as John Keep recently noted, the great tsar's successors were continually preoccupied with maintaining 'an overwhelmingly large force—the largest on the European continent' to bolster their foreign policies, preserve domestic security and satisfy some undefined 'deeper psychological need'.[24] At this point, such critics are fond of quoting the somewhat self-serving lament of a later Minister of Finance, Sergei Witte, whose policies are referred to below. 'In truth, what is it that has essentially upheld Russian statehood', he asked. 'Not only primarily, but exclusively the army', he replied, and then sadly

Table 3.1.2. Percentage distribution of state budget expenditures in selected years, 1680–1874

Year	Army	Fleet	Defence total	Remainder
1680	62	—	62	38
1701	73.58	3.24	76.82	23.18
1710	81.89	13.85	95.74	4.26
1725	50.40	14.10	64.50	36.50
1734	58.09	13.34	71.43	28.57
1762	56.03	7.27	63.30	36.70
1764	40.40	5.70	46.10	53.90
1767	42.20	5.40	47.60	52.40
1773	34.50	4.00	38.50	61.50
1781	26.30	8.00	34.30	65.70
1796	28.40	9.00	37.40	62.60
1808	39.70	12.30	52.00	48.00
1820	39.60	5.10	44.70	55.30
1830	38.60	8.20	46.80	53.20
1840	36.20	7.20	43.40	46.60
1850	30.70	6.20	36.90	63.10
1862	29.00	5.80	34.80	65.20
1870	27.90	6.10	34.00	66.00
1874	31.90	4.26	36.16	63.84

Source: See table 3.1.1.

concluded: 'The world bowed not to our culture, not to our bureaucratized church, not to our wealth and prosperity. It bowed to our might.'[25]

Here in full is the Western model of Great Russia, the militarized autocracy, which continues to shape perceptions to this day. Yet despite the importance placed on military power by St Petersburg and other capitals throughout the 1700s, this view of Russia's military burden does not accord with reality. Even if Keep is correct in implying that, for the most part, the military men had little problem in imposing their view of the army's needs on the monarch and his or her civilian advisers, this says little about the validity of the assessment of those needs. While this question is too complex and contentious for a full discussion here, a few comments may provide a context for judgement. First, it must be remembered that a series of wars with Turkey, and that empire's Crimean Tatar allies, continued throughout the century, even after the Crimea itself had fallen in the 1770s and 1780s. Whether or not this conquest, and the opening of the agriculturally rich steppe lands of the Ukraine to full Russian colonization, was historically 'necessary' or 'justified' must remain a matter of opinion. The same is true of both Russia's participation in the partition of Poland, and its intermittent wars with its neighbours to the west, which—owing to abominable communications—led to the permanent stationing of large field forces along the empire's western frontiers. But if necessity entered the question, it now arose not only from direct threats to the security of the Russian heartland, but also from the empire's new status as a great power. And if some might later argue that such a status was an expensive illusion, one can hardly expect to find St Petersburg's rulers and military planners drawing similar conclusions in the Europe of the 18th century.[26]

Second, given the empire's expanding frontiers, vast internal areas that required policing, and the growing complexity of its external relations, were the armies they fielded excessively large? According to General A. N. Kuropatkin, during this century the empire grew by 65 000 square miles to include a total area of 331 000 square miles. In the meantime, the population had risen from an estimated 12 million in 1700 to about 50 million in 1800. But in spite of such growth and the associated increase in its responsibilities, by 1801 the army numbered only 446 000 men. This may indeed appear large in comparison to other European nations (e.g., France's 350 000 and Austria's 325 000). None the less, the figure represents only a 107 per cent increase over Muscovy's some 215 000 men of 1680, and a modest 47.5 per cent increase over the 304 500 men of the Petrine army of 1725. Further, table 3.1.4 demonstrates that a half-century earlier the army's manpower level had dipped to 292 000, which was below both the Petrine establishment and the 330 000 men then being fielded by the French monarchy.[27]

Before leaving the 18th century, a few points concerning the true nature of Russia's defence burden deserve to be stressed. In the first place, the expansion of the armed forces between 1750 and 1800 parallelled a *decrease* in the defence portion of state expenditures. For example, in 1763 the army reportedly had in its ranks 274 667 men and in the following year consumed 40.40 per cent of the state's funds. With an additional 5.70 per cent added for the fleet, the total defence portion represented 46.10 per cent (see table 3.1.2). In 1796, however, when the army had swollen to some 507 500 men, it consumed only an estimated 28.4 per cent, and the newly expanded navy an additional 9 per cent. So despite the increased manpower, the relative burden of expenditure had actually slipped to 37.4 per cent of state spending. It therefore seems obvious that in this period Russia was capable of fielding even larger armies than it did without incurring major fiscal penalties.[28]

Although the evidence is less straightforward and cannot be discussed at length here, the same appears to be true of the human burden as well. To be sure, recruitment was a numbing and horrifying experience for those who underwent it. Until 1793, it meant leaving one's home for a lifetime of service, and after 1793, for a mere 25 years—which usually amounted to the same thing.[29] None the less, owing to demographic growth, the horror was not as widespread as one might expect. Official data of the Ministry of War suggest that between 1726 and 1800, in only two five-year periods (1736–40 and 1786–90) did the recruit levy affect more than four eligible males out of every hundred (see table 3.1.3). Further, as table 3.1.4 illustrates, in 1750 the Imperial Army represented a smaller percentage of the total populace than it did in either France or Prussia, and that in 1800 the figure equalled that of France but was well below those of Prussia and Austria. So in an age when the limiting factor on the size of a military establishment 'was the ability of a poor agricultural country to feed and clothe men who were making no productive contribution to the society', and when problems of transport and logistics made it difficult to supply large armies in the field, Imperial Russia had little difficulty

Table 3.1.3. Average number of recruits per 100 males, 1726–1873

Period	Number/100	Period	Number/100
1724	0.4	1801–05	1.8
1726–30	1.5	1806–10	3.4
1731–35	1.9	1811–15	6.6
1736–40	4.5	1816–20	1.6
1741–45	2.8	1821–25	0.4
1746–50	1.3	1826–30	2.4
1751–55	1.0	1831–35	2.1
1756–60	2.9	1836–40	2.1
1761–65	0.0	1841–45	1.9
1766–70	2.3	1846–50	2.4
1771–75	3.7	1851–55	6.4
1776–80	1.0	1856–60	0.0
1781–85	2.7	1861–65	2.1
1786–90	4.0	1866–70	2.7
1791–95	1.4	1871–73	3.9
1796–1800	1.1		

Source: Pintner, W. M., 'The burden of defense in Imperial Russia, 1725–1914', *Russian Review*, vol. 43 (1984), p. 250.

Table 3.1.4.   Comparative manpower burdens, 1750–1900

Period and country	Population (thousands)	Army (thousands)	Army as percentage of population
c. 1750			
Russia	23 230	292	*1.3*
France	22 000	330	*1.5*
Austria	18 300	201	*1.1*
Prussia	3 659	155	*4.2*
c. 1800			
Russia	37 414	446	*1.2*
France	29 107	350	*1.2*
Austria	21 695	325	*1.5*
Prussia	5 704	109	*1.9*
c. 1850			
Russia	56 882	1 118	*2.0*
France	37 382	404	*1.1*
Austria	35 109	269	*0.8*
Prussia	30 367	345	*1.2*
c. 1900			
Russia	126 367	1 033	*0.8*
France	38 133	573	*1.5*
Austria	41 286	337	*0.8*
Prussia	49 428	492	*0.9*

Source: Pintner, W. M., 'The burden of defense in Imperial Russia, 1725–1914', *Russian Review*, vol. 43 (1984), pp. 246–47.

in retaining its seat at the table of the great powers.[30] Indeed, it was not until Europe became convulsed by the Napoleonic Wars that Peter's system was fully tested and Russia had to discover just how many men it could throw into the fray. And to the great Tsar's credit, Russia emerged victoriously and, in the process, gave substance to his views of the military burden.

After 1801, the threatening international situation led to a rapid buildup of Russian military strength. Between 1802 and 1805, for example, a further 50 000 men were added to the army, and by 1808 that service numbered an unprecedented 663 000 men (an increase of 48.75 per cent over 1801). Even in 1809, a year of presumed peace with Napoleon, 520 000 men were under arms. Then, as relations with France worsened and the Turkish war dragged on, St Petersburg again hastened to expand its armed forces. By the time Napoleon entered Russia, Alexander I had an army of 597 000 men in 169 infantry, 66 line-cavalry and 84 irregular-cavalry regiments, backed by 49 artillery battalions and other gunnery and engineer units. Not only was the army about 34 per cent larger than that of 1801, but the government had also raised a militia to provide an additional 420 000 combatants. And in August 1812, at the height of the emergency, it called another 180 000 men to the colours.[31]

This effort quite naturally drastically increased both the financial and human burden borne by the Russian state. By 1808, for example, the defence portion of the budget had risen from the 37.40 per cent of 1796 to 52 per cent. Taken in five-year periods, this portion averaged 49.7 per cent during 1804–1809, and 61.2 per cent during 1810–14.[32] As for the human burden, the figure remained at the comparative low of 1.8 per 100 men during 1801–1805, rose to 3.4 per 100 during 1806–10, and climbed to an all-time high of 6.6 per 100 men during the hostilities of 1811–15.[33] None the less, the state both survived and, by 1815, emerged as the greatest land power in Europe.

St Petersburg's appreciation of the responsibilities entailed by this position is evidenced by the fact that, with the cessation of hostilities in 1815, the military establishment did not return to its earlier levels of manpower. In 1815 the Active Army was not disbanded, but deployed as the separate First and Second Armies in the Warsaw and Kiev regions, respectively. Taken together, but excluding garrison and other units elsewhere, they represented a strength of 709 600 men (159 per cent more than the total of 1801). Equally revealing, by 1826 the army as a whole contained 1 055 107 men, and by 1856—the end of the Crimean War—had reached 1 742 000 men. These figures represent increases of 136.5 and 290.9 per cent, respectively, over 1801, and naturally are reflected in higher defence expenditures. Between 1820 and 1840, the five-year averages ranged from a high of 45.8 per cent (1820–24) to a low of 41.1 per cent (1835–39). Ironically, it was only on the eve of the Crimean conflict (1850–54) that these expenditures again fell to the level of 1796 (37.4 per cent), which was still higher than during much of the 1770s and 1780s. As for recruit levies, after having fallen as low as 0.4 men per 100 during 1821–25, call-ups affected between 1.9 to 2.4 men per 100 during the next two decades, and then rose to 6.4 at the time of the Crimean conflict.[34]

Unlike the sacrifices of 1812–15, those of 1853–56 proved insufficient to save Russia from a humiliating defeat on its own territory. It therefore spurred the authorities to face up to the new military and naval reality then being wrought by railways and other technological advances. But before turning to the reorganization of the post-Crimean era, it is worth examining briefly the exact nature of the costs incurred by Russia's army during the years 1700–1855, and the impact of technology on these costs.

As part of his reforms, Peter the Great had set out to provide for his military and naval establishment solely from domestic production. Owing in part to the efforts of his predecessors, he was largely successful in areas such as arms and munitions, but somewhat less so with regard to the 'soldiers' cloth' used for uniforms. None the less, by his death Russia was relatively self-sufficient in most vital regards. That this was the case is largely to be explained by the static military technology of the period under consideration. Or to put it differently, between 1700 and 1850 the major changes were in the sociology, not the technology, of war. So while the French Revolution brought an age of mass armies, and while tactics changed as a consequence, the weapons used by the army of Alexander I were of the same type as those carried by Peter's initial conscripts of the early 18th century. Indeed, in 1802 one Russian regimental commander reported that some of his men were actually using weapons dating from the early 1700s.[35] And since small arms were seldom lost on the battlefield, stocks could be easily built and maintained. This was more or less true with regard to cannon and munitions as well: 'Russia was . . . able to field a highly effective army without significantly changing her economic or social system or developing anything that could be called a modern industrial capacity'.[36]

Maintaining an army 'was not a matter of equipment but of men (and horses), and the costs were largely those of subsistence'.[37] The pioneering work of D. I. Zhuravskii demonstrated that in 1731 'muskets and accoutrements' consumed only 6 per cent of an infantry regiment's funds and 10 per cent of those of a heavy cavalry regiment. Soldiers' pay, food and clothing constituted 89 per cent of remaining infantry expenses; the same items, plus horses and fodder, consumed 87 per cent of cavalry funds. When examining the army's statutory budget, with artillery and uniforms excluded, in 1798 Zhuravskii concludes that 30 per cent went on pay, 24 per cent on provisions, 17 per cent on fodder, and only 28 per cent on weapons and other equipment.[38] More striking still is the War Ministry's official account of its spending in 1803, a time of military expansion. In that year, the state's expenditures totalled 81 081 671 roubles, of which the ministry received 35 563 154. Of this, only 15 per cent was devoted to weapons, other equipment, horses and medical services. Of the remainder, 31 per cent went to pay, 38 per cent to provisions and 11 per cent to uniforms. The ministry's official history goes on to conclude that in 1803 equipping, provisioning and paying the army absorbed 92–95 per cent of the army's funds (equal to 40–44 per cent of total state treasury expenditures); over the five-year period 1802–1806, 92 per cent of the ministry's funds went to clothing, provisions and pay.[39]

Other data confirm the pattern: by 1763, 95.8 per cent of a regiment's annual costs went to subsistence, only 3.5 per cent to weapons and artillery practice; of the army's actual expenditures in 1829 and 1835, the Artillery Department spent 1.8 and 5.2 per cent, while uniforms, pay and provisions consumed 79.3 and 91.4 per cent, respectively; in terms of per capita cost per soldier in the years 1847 and 1857, the shares expended on weapons and training were 2.6 and 2.7 per cent, respectively.[40] These last figures go far to explaining why, in the army of Nicholas I (1825–55), 'parade mania' went side-by-side with an 'underestimation of fire power and reluctance to technical innovations' (such as adopting the breech-loading musket, which critics worried would simply mean that the troops would run out of cartridges).[41] So while Peter's transformation had provided his empire with a system that, in the face of the Napoleonic threat, permitted the raising of a million-man army, this took place in an environment in which few funds were needed once the men had been clothed, equipped and fed. And in 1800, the impact of the coming 'technological-economic challenge to Russia was still more than fifty years away', and many of the Tsar's military men would happily ignore all signs of its onset until the humiliation of their proud army in the Crimea.[42]

IV.   Imperial Russian modernization and the military burden

There has been considerable discussion of the pressures and motives that brought Alexander II (1855–81) to adopt a course of reform, of which liberation of the serfs served as a centrepiece. But while many have argued that this last was perceived as a military imperative, it still may be true that 'more than marginal military reform . . . would have been possible even under serfdom'.[43] None the less, the failure of Nicholas I's army to successfully expel maritime invaders from the Crimea discredited the 'most vital justification for the conservative and even reactionary bureaucratic order that the Tsar had imposed upon Russia for nearly 30 years—military invulnerability'.[44]

In 1855 it remained 'far from clear that Russia's marginal inferiority in quality and quantity of equipment at that time was related to the backwardness of Russian industry, or whether it was simply the result of poor planning by those in charge'.[45] Those examining the state of the land forces could easily put the blame for defeat on the bureaucratic obscurantism that had prevented the building of sufficient rail connections to the Crimea, and on the inefficiency and incompetence displayed by individual generals and officials. And even if the need for more modern small arms and artillery was recognized, many soldiers still had yet to recognize the new technological age that was upon them. As a result, the views of military reformers like D. A. Miliutin, who wished to create a mass army, on the Prussian model, composed of cadres fleshed out with short-term citizen conscripts and reservists, were far from universal among Russian generals. However, once Alexander II had himself accepted the need for liberating the serfs, such reformers could 'sell their cause to conservatives by stressing the military advantages to be gained: more prosperous and self-reliant peasants would make soldiers more able to comprehend orders, handle modern equipment, and take the initiative on the battlefield—aptitudes that were now essential, as the Crimean War had abundantly shown'.[46]

Strangely enough, given its reputation as a bastion of conservatism, the navy was much more aware of the demands being made by modern technology. Until Grande Duke Konstantin Nikolaevich took charge on the eve of the war, appeals of progressive sailors for the building of modern steam warships, and the yard facilities for their maintenance and construction, went unheeded (the Black Sea Fleet fared somewhat better, reflecting competent and inspired leadership, and distance from the corruption, formalism and extreme central-ism that stifled Baltic developments).

The Tsar 'did not understand the full ramification of the introduction of steampower on war at sea. He considered the screw-propeller a fad, and even thought it feasible to send armed galleys against the modern warships of the Allies' Baltic squadron'; the war's end found the Naval Ministry a hot-bed of enthusiasts for new approaches and techniques.[47]

Not unexpectedly, then, this ministry's absolute expenditures on matériel rose considerably after 1856, and especially after 1862, when the building of a fleet of screw-powered vessels began in earnest. But while absolute increases appear impressive, table 3.1.2 indicates that total funds assigned to the fleet as a percentage of the state budget decreased. From 1863 to 1894, funding for the navy remained below 20 per cent of the army's, although by the 1890s it reached 17–19 per cent, up from 12–15 per cent during the earlier years.

The army, too, spent considerable funds on new matériel. As a result of re-equipment programmes mounted at the end of hostilities, by 1859 each infantryman and the majority of the cavalry had a modern rifle, while the artillery was receiving more efficient and longer-ranged guns of bronze (and later of steel). Indeed, in that year alone 7 500 000 roubles went on such 'special objects', a figure which nearly doubled in 1860.[49] Yet table 3.1.2 illustrates that the army's overall funding also dropped significantly after the 1850s.

In some ways, of course, this was to be expected. The Crimean War had quite naturally placed a heavy burden on the Russian state. According to the Ministry of Finance its cost, expressed as combined military-naval expenditures as a percentage of state expenditures, had taken the following course: 1853, 36.2 per cent; 1854, 51.9 per cent; 1855, 51.4 per cent; and 1856, 42.0 per cent. Or to put it differently, the War Ministry's expenditures alone in 1854–56 were 652 million roubles, a rise of 237 per cent over the period 1851–53, and other sources place the real figure at closer to 800 million roubles.[50] The result was a massive deficit, which meant considerable pressure on all sections of government, and especially the military-naval establishment, to make reductions. Indeed, the Ministry of Finance concluded that the defence budget should revert to 71 923 300 roubles, the level of 1847. But while the Ministry of War remained resistant to many of the proposals put forth as a means to this end, cuts were made so that its expenditures fell to 30.6 per cent of state expenditures during 1859–64, hovered between 28 to 29 per cent during the subsequent three five-year periods, and then dropped to 26.8 per cent during 1880–84 (see table 3.1.5).

During 1857–61 funding of the armed forces fell by 13.7 per cent, while civilian expenditures grew by 76.2 per cent, compared to 1854–56.[51]

F. A. Miller, a critic of the War Ministry of this time, asserted that the army achieved these savings 'only by taking the drastic step of consuming its own reserve supplies', and that it 'had no effective plan for reducing its size in peacetime'.[52] But cut-backs were made. In 1856, for example, several Cossack units and the militia were disbanded completely, 421 000 regulars were sent on indefinite leave and another 69 000 were discharged completely. Further, the Ministry refrained from call-ups until 1862, and began the process of reducing the period conscripts served in the ranks, which had been set at 20 years in 1834. This now dropped to 15 years, then to 12, and in 1868 to 10 years. As a result of such measures, the army's strength fell from some 1.7 million men in 1856 to 1 million in 1858 and a low of 850 000 men in 1859. In the 1860s it again began to grow, slowly: to 859 000 in 1862, 734 000 in 1871, and 737 000 on the eve of the war with Turkey in 1876 (see table 3.1.1). During this period (1859–74), absolute military expenditures increased by 54 per cent. But, as noted, this growth also parallelled a drop in military spending as a percentage of state

Table 3.1.5. Percentage distribution of state budget expenditures in 5-year periods, 1804–1914
(Figures are quinquennial averages, with those for 1875–84 and 1904–1909 excluding war expenses.)

Period	Army	Fleet	Total defence	Remainder
1804–09	40.1	9.6	49.7	50.3
1810–14	55.2	6.0	61.2	38.8
1815–19	46.1	5.0	51.5	48.9
1820–24	40.3	5.5	45.8	54.2
1825–29	37.8	6.6	44.4	55.6
1830–34	35.1	6.8	41.9	58.1
1835–39	34.4	6.7	41.1	58.9
1840–44	33.8	6.6	40.4	59.6
1845–49	33.1	5.9	39.0	61.0
1850–54	31.2	6.2	37.4	62.6
1855–59	35.6	5.4	41.0	59.0
1860–64	30.6	5.5	36.1	63.9
1865–69	29.0	4.3	33.3	66.7
1870–74	28.0	4.0	32.0	68.0
1875–79	28.8	4.2	33.0	67.0
1880–84	26.8	3.9	30.7	69.3
1885–89	22.8	4.4	27.2	72.8
1890–94	23.8	4.3	28.1	71.9
1895–99	18.7	5.5	24.2	75.8
1900–04	17.3	5.2	22.4	77.6
1905–09	18.9	4.4	23.3	76.7
1910–14	19.0	6.2	25.2	74.8

Source: Pintner, W. M., 'The burden of defense in Imperial Russia, 1725–1914', *Russian Review*, vol. 43 (1984), p. 248.

expenditures, at a time when military spending in Germany and Turkey grew by 164 and 73 per cent, respectively.[53]

This round of military reforms was crowned by Minister of War Miliutin's conscription law of 1874, 'the most radical social measure of the reform era' (the emancipation of the serfs excepted).[54] Inspired in part by Prussian developments, he and his colleagues sought to introduce universal conscription and convert the old standing army into a 'nation in arms'. From that year on, this law provided the basis on which the army replenished itself and sought to maintain a large reservoir of reservists for use in case of war. This was first tested during the Turkish war of 1877–78, when the number of those called up rose from 737 000 men, in 1876, to 1 511 000, in 1878. Thereafter, the numbers actually serving fell, to 884 000 in 1880, and a low of 814 000 in 1885, before rising slowly to 850 000 men in 1890, 1 033 153 in 1897 and 1 075 000 men in 1900 (see table 3.1.1).[55]

At first sight this suggests a return to the burden of Nicholas I. However, given Russia's accelerated economic expansion after 1860, and a parallel demographic trend, this is far from the case. Although figures vary, the empire's population expanded from an estimated 56 882 000 in 1850 to

126 367 000 inhabitants in 1900. This meant, as table 3.1.4 demonstrates, that the army represented 2.0 per cent of the population in 1850 but only 0.8 per cent in 1900, and that the former consumed close to 30 per cent of state monies as compared to the latter's 18 per cent. As for the fleet, its programmes did increase somewhat in the latter 1890s and early 1900s, and rose to equal 30 per cent of the military's spending in these years. None the less, if defence spending as a whole is compared for 1845–49 and 1895–99, it dropped from 39.0 per cent of state expenditures in the first period to 24.2 per cent in the second. In terms of the financial and human burden, the reforms of 1856–74 reduced the weight placed on Russian society by its defence establishment, and significantly improved the latter's capability.[56]

Despite this consideration, critics still charge that the Imperial establishment was larger than necessary in 1900. Others note that its size reflected 'inertia, the tradition of having a large army', 'the unchanging geographical reality, the great distances and the extensive frontiers', and the perhaps more important point about Russian backwardness, that the authorities:

believed, rightly or wrongly, that Russian peasant recruits needed longer training than the better educated conscripts of Western Europe. Hence, at any given time, proportionally more men had to be in uniform. In turn, the problem of size was exacerbated by a crucial change, the development of railroad networks, which permitted the deployment of men in much larger numbers than before.[57]

Consideration of these points suggests that inertia and tradition had little to do with the large armies maintained by Imperial Russia during its last decades, or subsequently by the Soviet Union. In the first place, the existing frontiers of 1900, along which Russia faced at least four potential enemies (Germany, Austro-Hungary, Turkey and Japan) meant that any Russian Government not bent on committing national suicide was (and is) bound to maintain significant armed forces. And table 3.1.4 suggests that the army fielded by St Petersburg at that time was arguably necessary, from the point of view of prudent military planning, if the existing threat was to be countered successfully. Further, owing to the railroad developments, Russian generals knew that their German counterparts could mobilize and deploy much more rapidly, 'and therefore believed that they had to deploy a greater number of men on active duty than Germany, and additionally had to place a great number of them in the West in order to compensate for Germany's mobilisation superiority'; these factors, as well as the dream of converting the armed forces into a 'school' of national patriotism, and the perceived difficulty of training peasants for modern war, provided ample motives for St Petersburg's military policies.[58]

Here it should also be noted that, while the Russian Army was Europe's largest in 1900, it still ranked with that of Austria as representing only 0.8 per cent of the population, and thus lagged behind those of Prussia and France, where the comparable figures were 0.9 and 1.5, respectively (see table 3.1.4). Indeed, given demographic growth, the above considerations and a system of universal conscription, the question arises as to why the army was not even larger. Indeed, by 1905 it was estimated that only some 20 per cent of the adult males of the major social groups (peasant householders, artisans, factory workers, small proprietors, lower officials, merchants, tradesmen, and so on) had passed through the ranks. In part this reflected the numerous exemptions given for educational, family, religious and ethnic reasons, which meant that the army always inducted only a portion of the physically fit. In 1874, for example, a mere 150 000 recruits were accepted, which figure had risen to 235 000 in the 1880s, 320 000 by 1900 and 450 000 in 1906. Even the 585 000 envisaged by the 'Grand Programme' of 1914 would still have represented a bare one-third of the men available.[59]

Furthermore, these shortfalls were the result of deliberate policy. The motives behind this, in turn, were largely based on fiscal considerations. Here two factors deserve stress. First, the changing technology of war forced military planners into cruel dilemmas of whether to spend the funds available on maintaining men, on re-equipping a smaller number with more modern weaponry, or on building the industrial plant to produce such weapons and the railways by which to mobilize and deploy the men that had been raised and the reservists who back them. Second, the parameters within which such decisions were made depended on the funds available which, from the military's standpoint, were woefully inadequate throughout most of the 1880s and 1890s.

With regard to the first point, the large sums spent before 1855 on feeding, clothing, paying and otherwise simply maintaining the troops should be recalled. With industrialization and the shorter term of conscription, these costs can be expected to have dropped somewhat. Yet research suggests that subsistence items continued to consume about 60–70 per cent of the total military budget from 1863 to 1891 (about the same as a century earlier), hovered around 55 per cent from 1891 to 1912, and only dropped slightly below 50 per cent in 1913–14; while a decline of 15–20 per cent of the total share is admittedly significant, it is far 'from a transformation of the pattern of military expenditure'.[60]

Other studies concur. Of the annual average of 172 million roubles allocated to the army in the 1870s, 19 million went to 'administration' and over 100 million to *indententstvo* (food, fodder, clothes, etc.); in 1913–14 these categories still consumed 450 million of a budget of 580 million roubles.[61] In 1909 the War Ministry estimated that it cost some 350 roubles per annum to support each enlisted man, considerably less than comparative figures for France and Germany.[62] Meanwhile, 'despite the advent of a wide range of new weapons', the sum allocated for their purchase 'wobbles above and below 10 per cent, reaching a peak of 12 to 15 percent on three widely separate occasions: 1870–73 (12–13 percent), 1893–97 (13–16 percent), and 1904–14 (12–15 percent)'; apart from these periods of 'special effort', one discerns 'no steady upward trend in weapons expenditures as a share of the total, but rather a relatively level of expenditure'.[63]

Imperial military men clearly had to accept that the more men they called up for training, the fewer funds would be available for other purposes. Their problems were further complicated by the fact that after 1881 a succession of Ministers of Finance gained the backing of Alexander III and Nicholas II to curtail military expenditures. As table 3.1.5 demonstrates, after 1880 defence expenditures as a whole declined from 30.7 per cent in 1880–84 to 22.4 per cent in 1900–1904, and the army's share in particular from 26.8 to 17.3 per cent. The details of the bureaucratic politics involved, and refutation of the argument that the funds expended on railways were really military expenditures, have been presented elsewhere.[64] Suffice it to say that, at a time when the European arms race was gathering steam and the great-power balance was being upset by the arrival of upstarts (most notably Prussia-Germany), Russia's military clearly found themselves hampered by fiscal restraint.

In 1900 Russia was spending 54 per cent more than France and 28.3 per cent more than Germany 'on an army that by no means was as well trained or equipped as the armies of these two powers'; to maintain its armed forces 'even at the unsteady preparedness level of 1900', Russia had to pay a proportion of its national income that was two to three times larger than that of France or Germany.

None the less, Russia could not 'simply withdraw from international military competition'.[65] Accepting their obligations as an ally of France, and believing that Germany would soon launch an aggressive war, military men could only deplore the army's diminishing share of state expenditures.

The reality behind the military's complaints became painfully apparent on the battlefields of Manchuria during 1904–1905. True, a number of other factors also contributed to Russia's defeat at the hands of the Japanese in a conflict that ended by costing the empire over 2.5 billion roubles in war expenditure alone.[66] None the less, the humiliation brought home to the authorities, and to Russian-educated society at large, the necessity of instituting another round of military-naval reforms. The unthinkable alternative was to risk seeing the once proud empire slip to the status of a second-rate power. Fortunately, during the years 1900–13, the national income rose by 80 per cent which, along with foreign loans, permitted a 93 per cent increase in the state budget. Even so, the official defence share averaged only 23.3 per cent during 1905–1909, and 25.2 per cent during 1910–14, and had risen to a high of 28.7 in 1913.[67]

On the basis of these figures one can conclude that the military-naval share of the overall budget 'rose to a peak of 55 percent during the Napoleonic wars and, most surprisingly, declined steadily throughout the nineteenth century and virtually until the outbreak of World War I'; during 1910–1914, owing to overall industrial and demographic growth and expansion of the state's own revenue-producing enterprises, 'the proportion of the total state expenditures devoted to the army was about half of what it was in the 1820's, despite a 25 percent growth in the standing strength of the army (1912 versus 1826), and some increased expenditure on more costly weapons'.[68]

Yet in this period of special effort the official figures do not tell the whole story. In fact, for the years after 1908 at least, they considerably understate the real defence effort. As indicated in tables 3.1.6 and 3.1.7 the Tsarist Government supplemented its regular budgetary estimates by the money it raised through loans for 'exceptional' expenditures. During 1904–1906 these amounted to a total of 3 260 million roubles, of which 2 260 million was quickly spent, largely on suppressing disorders and railroad construction. Although the latter (now more directly related to strategic goals) retained its priority in subsequent

Table 3.1.6. Analysis of Russian defence expenditures, 1909–12
(Figures are in millions of roubles.)

	1909	1910	1911	1912	1913	Total 1909–13
Direct defence expenditure[a]	565.59	597.64	618.73	703.95	825.95	**3 311.86**
of which War Ministry	473.37	484.91	497.77	527.87	581.10	**2 562.02**
of which Naval Ministry	92.22	112.73	120.96	176.08	244.85	**746.84**
Total regular budget	2 451.42	2 473.16	2 536.00	2 721.76	3 094.25	**13 276.59**
Total exceptional budget	156.13	123.50	309.69	449.30	288.67	**1 327.29**
Total expenditure	2 607.55	2 596.66	2 845.69	3 171.06	3 382.92	**14 603.88**

[a]Exceptional funds are excluded from military and naval figures.

Source: Sidorov, A. A., *Finansovoe Polozhenie Rossii v Gody Pervoi Mirovoi Voiny (1914–1917)* (Nauka: Moscow, 1966), p. 47.

Table 3.1.7. Analysis of government expenditures, 1913
(Figures are in millions of roubles.)

Regular budget expenditures		*Share*
War and Naval Ministries	825.9	*26.7*
Railways	586.9	*19.0*
Payments on loans	424.4	*13.7*
Alcohol monopoly	235.0	*7.6*
Remaining expenditures	1 022.0	*33.0*
Total	3 094.2	*100.0*
Total exceptional expenditures	288.67	—
On Army and Fleet	127.3	—
On railway construction	133.8	—

Source: Sidorov, A. A., *Finansovoe Polozhenie Rossii v Gody Pervoi Mirovoi Voiny (1914–1917)* (Nauka: Moscow, 1966), p. 43.

years, military and naval expansion came to take second place. If such exceptional funds are added to the regular expenditures, then during 1909–13 about one-third of the state's monies were absorbed by the armed forces. Indeed, Finance Minister V. N. Kokovtsov maintained that, during 1909–10, defence accounted for 43 per cent of the government's total spending.[69] As for the exceptional funds *per se*, the services usually received these as capital grants for such projects as the 'small' naval programme of 1908–1909, the army re-organization of 1910 and the Grand Programme of 1914. Some 700 million roubles had been allocated for the first two by 1914, while the third foresaw the expenditure of 140 million roubles per year on the ground forces, quite apart from the capital investment of another 432 million over a three-year period ending in 1917. In the meantime, the fleet received an additional 800 million roubles in 1913 for naval expansion, largely in the Black Sea.[70]

These developments increased both the state debt and the burden borne by the empire and its citizens. By 1913, for example, the average Russian's income was only 27 per cent that of the average Englishman, but he saw 50 per cent more of his money being appropriated for defence than did the latter.[71] Further, the concentration on defence also diverted attention from such categories as public health and education, as well as the further expansion of the transport net and the state's more general industrial infrastructure. In this way it detracted from the areas that comprised Russia's 'more fundamental backwardness', areas that in the long run could have had a major impact on the empire's military potential.[72] Meanwhile, within the government, Kokovtsov noted as early as 1908 the dangers inherent in the state's growing debt. None the less, he still insisted that it would be a mistake 'to propose that we seek in our regular budget sufficient funds to cover both the progressive growth of spending in all our civil departments and a further increase in expenditures on state defense'.[73] Outside of the Council of Ministers, others were equally concerned. In 1909, for example, the influential publicist Prince G. N. Trubetskoi openly warned that Russia's resources were insufficient for its military commitments, especially as these were conceived by the pessimists in the War and Naval Ministries. In the view of this and other commentators, the attempt to satisfy these commitments meant risking undermining the overall economy and bankrupting the treasury.[74] But as Kokovtsov's comments illustrate, it was a risk the Imperial Government felt it had to accept. And when the test of war came in 1914, the empire proved surprisingly resilient even though, in the end, the economic and social strains imposed by the prolonged struggle contributed much to the political crisis that led to revolution.[75]

V.   The Soviet dilemma

What, then, is the relevance of the preceding discussion for the leadership of today's Soviet Union? In the first place, it may tell us something about the specifics of the Soviet defence budget, a topic of considerable debate, especially since the mid-1960s. The figures Soviet writers have published on this topic are usually greeted with natural scepticism by Western observers, but a comparison with past patterns may help place them in perspective. For example, the claim that defence spending consumed 20.6 per cent of the state's total expenditure in the years 1950–55, a period of continuing reconstruction and political change, seems perfectly reasonable. Parallel claims that this figure fell to 14.4 per cent during 1956–60, and dipped to 12.58 in 1965, 11.55 in 1970, and 7.22 per cent in 1977, are much harder to credit. These were, after all, years of another special effort, as evidenced by expanding manpower and weaponry. On the other hand, the Central Intelligence Agency's estimate that defence and defence-related expenditure consumed 28–30 per cent of the state budget in 1970 is startlingly consistent with the figures for the period of modernization a century earlier (see table 3.1.5).[76]

Second, the historical analysis may tell us something about the manner in which the funds assigned to defence *per se* are expended. Given further industrial expansion and the advantages allegedly inherent in a command economy, one might argue that maintenance costs, which had fallen to just under 50 per cent by 1914, should have dipped still further. If these are subsumed within 'operating costs' as currently defined in CIA estimates, however, then the figure may now have risen again, to well over 60 per cent of the total defence budget. And when one realizes that the Soviet military establishment maintains more expensive matériel and now may conscript some 80–85 per cent of those eligible, such an increase is not remarkable. In any case, here again is an example where the study of past trends might provide useful insights into present practices.[77]

More generally, it also seems clear that the Communist state that emerged from the chaos of 1917–22 inherited much more than just the geographical area once occupied by its imperial predecessor. With it went the traditional problem of backwardness and age-old sense of insecurity, now expressed in terms of 'capitalist', later 'imperialist', encirclement. Together, they fuelled the Soviets' own first efforts at military modernization, carried out under the aegis of the first Five-Year Plans. That Stalin himself was not unmindful of this recurring imperative is clear from his declaration that 'those who fall behind get beaten . . . . Old Russia's history is one unbroken record of the beatings she suffered for falling behind, for her backwardness'.[78]

After Stalin's death, his successors—bent on retaining for the USSR its prestige as a great power, and determined to gain parity with the United States as a superpower—faced similar problems during the 1960s and early 1970s. Indeed, given the rapid pace of technology, they may well have found this a continuing process, much as their Tsarist predecessors did in the 1860s and 1870s. And like these latter in the 1880s, today's Soviet leaders may believe that the time has come to curtail current military spending in favour of investment in other areas—areas on which the state's future economic and military health may well depend. In other words, computers and the associated technologies mean to today's USSR what railways and their associated industries meant to the Russia of the 1880s and 1890s.

Marshal N. V. Ogarkov has made it clear that today's military leadership is fully aware of the need for the new technologies both in weaponry and the supporting industrial base. There is considerable evidence that he and other military reformers support the technology-intensive focus and cost implications of General Secretary Gorbachev's civilian economic reform programmes, recognizing that general economic health and dynamism are a prerequisite for sustainable military might. On the other hand, Ogarkov's 'reassignment' in September 1984 from the post of Chief of the General Staff has by others been interpreted as indicating that he was pushing too hard for greater defence expenditures: 'if the Kremlin had agreed to such an approach, it would have mortgaged a considerable part of the country's economic future to weapons systems'; this 'would obviously fly in the face of Gorbachev's efforts to modernize the country's economy'.[79] If this second interpretation is correct, then the new General Secretary is following the lead of Sergei Witte and his fellows of the last century. Such a course (whether or not supported by Ogarkov) means a 'zero-growth defense budget' at most, and conceivably even reductions in such spending. Many of the soldiers will no doubt grumble and resist cuts, but will only succeed in reversing the process when once again the international situation makes this an inescapable necessity. Western statesmen would do well, however, to remember that such reversals have been frequent in Russian history, and that both governments and citizens have willingly and repeatedly tightened their belts when faced with foreign threats to their status and security.

Notes and references

[1] See, for example, Ulsamer, E., 'Beyond Andropov', *Air Force Magazine* (Mar. 1984), pp. 62–67; and Currie, K., 'The Soviet General Staff's new role', *Problems of Communism*, no. 2 (Mar.–Apr. 1984), pp. 32–40.

[2] Fitzgerald, M. T., *Marshal Ogarkov and the New Revolution in Military Affairs* (Center for Naval Analysts: Arlington, VA, 1985), unpublished paper, *passim*; and Odom, W. E., 'Soviet force postures: dilemmas and directions', *Problems of Communism*, no. 4 (July–Aug. 1985), pp. 6–14.

[3] Jones, D. R., 'Russian military traditions and the Soviet military establishment', *The Soviet Union: What Lies Ahead? Military-Political Affairs in the 1980s*, eds K. M. Currie and G. Varhall (US Government Printing Office: Washington, DC, 1985), pp. 21–47.

[4] Kaser, M., *Soviet Economics* (McGraw-Hill: New York, 1970), p. 133.

[5] Philipp, W., 'Russia's position in medieval Europe', *Russia, Essays in History and Literature*, ed. L. H. Legters (E. J. Brill: Leiden, 1972), p. 36.

[6] Gallik, D., 'The military burden and arms control', *The Future of the Soviet Economy: 1978–1985*, ed. E. D. Hunter (Westview Press: Boulder, CO, 1978), pp. 133, 137, 139.

[7] For a fuller exposition of this view see Jones, D. R., 'Soviet concepts of security: reflections on KAL 007', *Air University Review* (Nov.–Dec. 1986), pp. 30–32.

[8] Pipes, R., 'Militarism and the Soviet state', *Daedalus: Journal of the American Academy of Arts and Sciences*, vol. 109, no. 1 (Fall 1980), p. 2.

9 Hellie, R., 'The structure of modern Russian history', *Russian History*, vol. 4, no. 1 (1977), p. 3.
10 Jones (note 7), pp. 32–36.
11 Solov'ev, S. M., *Istoriia Rossii s drevneishikh vremen* (23 vols. in 15; Izd. Sots.-ekonomicheskii Lit.: Moscow, 1959–1966), V. 2(4), pp. 514–15. On the *bogatyri, et al.*, see Kargalov, V.V., *Narod-bogatyr* (Voenizdat: Moscow, 1971); and Mirzoev, V. G., *Byliny i letopisi: Pamiatniki russkoi istoricheskoi mysli* (Izd. Mysl': Moscow, 1978).
12 Bazilevich, K. V., *Vneshniaia politika Russkogo tsentralizovannogo gosudarstva vtoraia polovina XV veka* (Izd. MGU: Moscow, 1952), p. 2.
13 Szameuly, T., *The Russian Tradition*, ed. R. Conquest (Secker & Warburg: London, 1974), p. 25.
14 Khlebnikov, N., *O vliianii obshchestva na organzatsiiu godudarstva v tsarskii period russkoi istorii* (Tip. A. Kotomina: St Petersburg, 1869), pp. 5–6. On the numbers of captives see Sumner, B. H., *Survey of Russian History*, 2nd edn (Duckworth: London, 1947), p. 41; Fisher, A. W., *The Russian Annexation of the Crimea, 1772–1783* (Cambridge University Press: Cambridge, 1970), pp. 19–22; and Novosel'skii, A. A., *Bor'ba Moskovskogo Gosudarstva s Tatarami v pervoi polovine XVII veka* (Izd. Nauka: Moscow, 1948), pp. 434–36. The basis of the Tatars military strength is discussed in McNeill, W. H., *The Pursuit of Power: Technology, Armed Forces and Society Since A.D. 1000* (University of Chicago Press: Chicago, 1982), pp. 18–19.
15 Bazilevich (note 12), p. 2.
16 Hellie (note 9), p. 3.
17 Miliukov, P. N., *Ocherki po istorii Russkoi kult'ury*, 5th edn, 3 vols (Tip. I. N. Skorokhodova: St Petersburg, 1904), vol. 1, p. 145.
18 Pipes, R., *Russia Under the Old Regime* (Weidenfeld and Nicolson: London, 1974), p. 115. The interaction between the need to maintain the strength of this gentry militia and the enserfment of the peasantry is the subject of Hellie, R., *Enserfment and Military Change in Muscovy* (University of Chicago Press: Chicago, 1971). See also Keep, J. L. H., *Soldiers of the Tsar. Army and Society in Russia, 1462–1874* (Clarendon Press: Oxford, 1985), pp. 13–55.
19 Pintner, W. M., *Russia as a Great Power, 1709–1856: Reflections on the Problem of Relative Backwardness, with Special Reference to the Russian Army and Russian Society*, Occasional Paper no. 33 (Kennan Institute for Advanced Russian Studies: Washington, DC, 1978), pp. 2–3.
20 Yaney, G. L., *The Systematization of Russian Government. Social Evolution in the Domestic Administration of Imperial Russia, 1711–1905* (University of Illinois Press: Urbana, 1973), p. 51.
21 Miliukov (note 17), pp. 148–49.
22 Pintner, W. M., 'The burden of defense in Imperial Russia, 1725–1914', *Russian Review*, vol. 43 (1984), pp. 246–51. For an example of the fiscal difficulties incurred in times of crisis, see the discussion of the period 1748–63 in Troitskii, S. M., *Finansovaia politika russkogo absoliutizma v XVIII veke* (Nauka: Moscow, 1966), pp. 230–31, 246–48.
23 See, e.g., Pipes (note 8), p. 3; and Miliukov (note 17), pp. 148–50.
24 Keep (note 18), pp. 144–45.
25 Vitte, S. Iu., *Vospominaniia*, 2 vols (Nauka: Moscow, 1960), vol. 2, p. 380.
26 On Russia's status as a Great Power see Nekrasov, G. A., 'Mezhdunarodnoe prizvanie rossiiskogo velikoderzhaviia v XVIII v.', *Feodal'naia Rossiia vo vsemirno-*

istoricheskom protsesse. Sbornik statei, posviashchennyi L'vu Vladimirovichu Cherepninu (Nauka: Moscow, 1972), pp. 381–88. Russia's military heritage during this period is detailed in Duffy, C., *Russia's Military Way to the West. Origins and Nature of Russian Military Power, 1700–1800* (Routledge & Kegan Paul: London, 1981); and Beskrovnyi, L. G., *Russkaia armiia i flot v XVIII veke (Ockerki)* (Voenizdat: Moscow, 1958).

[27] Kuropatkin, A. N., *Zapiski generala Kuropatkina o russko-yaponskoi voine. Itogi voiny* (J. Ladyschnikow: Berlin, 1909), pp. 16–19; Pintner (note 19), pp. 8–12, 29.

[28] Pintner (note 19), pp. 8–12, 26–30.

[29] Keep (note 18), p. 156.

[30] Pintner (note 22), p. 240.

[31] Bogdanov, L. P., *Russkaia armiia v 1812 godu. Organizatsiia, upravlenie, vooruzhenie* (Voenizdat: Moscow, 1979), pp. 46, 72, 87–93.

[32] Pintner (note 19), p. 28; and Pintner (note 22), p. 248.

[33] Pintner (note 22), p. 250.

[34] Beskrovnyi, L. G., *Russkaia armiia i flot v XIX veke. Voenno-ekonomicheskii potentsial Rossii* (Voenizdat: Moscow, 1973), pp. 14–16; Pintner (note 22), p. 250.

[35] Pintner (note 22), p. 232, 234–35; Beskrovnyi (note 26), pp. 74*ff.*

[36] Pintner (note 22), p. 235.

[37] Pintner (note 19), p. 26.

[38] Zhuravskii, D. I., 'Statisticheskoe obozrenie raskhodov na voennyie potrebnosti (s 1711 po 1826 god)', *Voennyi sbornik* (1859), no. 9, p. 30, and no. 11, p. 8.

[39] *Stoletie voennogo ministerstva 1802–1902. Kn. 5: Glavnoe intendantskoe upravlenie. Istoricheskii ocherk*, ed. D. A. Skalon, Part I: *Vvedenie i tsarstvovanie imperatora Aleksandra I* (Berezhlivost': St Petersburg, 1903), pp. 83–84.

[40] Pintner (note 22), pp. 238–39.

[41] Curtiss, J. S., *The Russian Army Under Nicholas I, 1825–1855* (Duke University Press: Durham, NC, 1965), pp. 120–21.

[42] Pintner (note 19), p. 27; Curtiss (note 41), pp. 115–16; McNeill (note 14), pp. 228–30.

[43] Beyrau, D., 'Leibeigenschaft und Militarverfassung', p. 211, as cited by Keep (note 18), p. 353 from an unpublished work.

[44] Kipp, J. W., 'Charisma, crisis and the genesis of reform: the Konstantinovtsy and Russian naval modernization, 1853–1858', in International Commission for Military History, *ACTA No. 2* (Washington, DC, 13–19 Aug. 1975), p. 85.

[45] Pintner (note 22), p. 235.

[46] Keep (note 18), pp. 352–53.

[47] Kipp (note 44), pp. 86–87.

[48] Pintner (note 22), pp. 243–44; Beskrovnyi (note 34), pp. 600–601.

[49] Keep (note 18), p. 354.

[50] Figures cited in Keep (note 18), pp. 353–54.

[51] Keep (note 18), p. 354; Pintner (note 22), pp. 248–49; Miller, F. A., *Dmitrii Miliutin and the Reform Era in Russia* (Vanderbilt University Press: Charlotte, NC, 1968), pp. 26–29; Zaionchkovskii, P. A., *Voennye reformy 1860–1870 godov v Rossii* (Izd. MGU: Moscow, 1952), pp. 62–67; and Beskrovnyi (note 34), pp. 483–86.

[52] Miller (note 51), pp. 27–28.

[53] Keep (note 18), p. 354; Zaionchkovskii (note 51), pp. 68*ff.*

[54] Wildman, A. K., *The End of the Old Army. The Old Army and the Soldiers' Revolt (March–April 1917)* (Princeton University Press: Princeton, 1980), p. 25.

[55] Rostunov, I. I., *Russkii front pervoi mirovoi voiny* (Nauka: Moscow, 1976), p. 52;

Zaionchkovskii, P. A., *Samoderzhavie i russkaia armiia na rubezhe XIX–XX stoletii, 1881–1903* (Mysl': Moscow, 1983), pp. 123–31; Beskrovnyi (note 34), pp. 82*ff*.

[56] Pintner (note 22), pp. 243–44, 246–47; Beskrovnyi (note 34), pp. 600–601; Fuller, Jr, W. C., *Civil-Military Conflict in Imperial Russia, 1881–1914* (Princeton University Press: Princeton, 1985), pp. 48–55; and Gregory, P. R., *Russian National Income, 1885–1913* (Cambridge University Press: Cambridge, 1982), pp. 86–87, 171–73.

[57] Pintner (note 22), p. 245.

[58] Fuller (note 56), pp. 52–53, 58; Pipes (note 8), p. 3; Pintner (note 22), p. 247.

[59] Jones, D. R., 'Imperial Russia's Armed Forces at War, 1914–1917: An Analysis of Combat Effectiveness' (Dalhousie University: Halifax, N.S., 1986), unpublished dissertation, pp. 58–60, 63–70.

[60] Pintner (note 22), pp. 241–43.

[61] Stone, N., *The Eastern Front, 1914–1917* (Hodder & Stoughton: London, 1975), p. 213.

[62] Rostunov (note 55), p. 52.

[63] Pintner (note 22), p. 243.

[64] Fuller (note 56), chapter 2.

[65] Fuller (note 56), p. 58. See also Jones (note 59), pp. 14–17, 87–89; and Lieven, D. C. B., *Russia and the Origins of the First World War* (St Martin's Press: New York, 1983), pp. 5*ff*.

[66] Podkolzin, A. M., *A Short Economic History of the USSR* (Progress: Moscow, 1968), p. 62.

[67] Podkolzin (note 66), pp. 76–77.

[68] Pintner (note 22), pp. 249–51.

[69] Sidorov, A. A., *Finansovoe polozhenie Rossii v gody pervoi mirovoi voiny (1914–1917)* (Nauka: Moscow, 1960), pp. 39, 48.

[70] Stone (note 61), pp. 28–29; Sidorov (note 69), pp. 48–50.

[71] Lieven (note 65), p. 13.

[72] Pintner (note 22), p. 249; Lieven (note 65), pp. 12–13.

[73] Sidorov (note 69), p. 32.

[74] Cited in Lieven (note 65), p. 12.

[75] On Imperial Russia's performance in World War I see Stone (note 61), and Jones (note 59), *passim*.

[76] Rabin, S. T., *The Soviet State Budget Since 1965. A Research Paper*, ER 77–10529 (Central Intelligence Agency: Washington, DC, Dec. 1977), pp. 14–17. For Soviet figures for the period before 1965, see Gladkov, I. A., *et al.* (eds), *Istoriia sotsialisticheskoi ekonomiki SSSR*, 7 vols (Nauka: Moscow, 1976–1980), vol. 6, pp. 511, 515; vol. 7, pp. 160–62.

[77] Compare Pintner (note 22), pp. 242–43, with *Soviet and US Defense Activities, 1980–9: A Dollar Cost Comparison*, SR 80–10005 (Central Intelligence Agency: Washington, DC, Jan. 1980), p. 8; and *Soviet and US Defense Activities, 1971–80: A Dollar Cost Comparison*, SR 91–10005 (Central Intelligence Agency: Washington, DC, Jan. 1981), p. 2.

[78] Stalin, J. V., *Problems of Leninism* (Foreign Languages Press: Peking, 1976), p. 528.

[79] Herspring, D. R., 'Marshal Akhromeyev and the future of the Soviet Armed Forces', *Survival* (Nov.–Dec. 1986), p. 531. One interesting interpretation of possible future trends in Soviet defence spending is given in Westwood, J. T., 'The USSR's 12th Five-Year Plan and its Zero-Growth Defense Budget', Unpublished paper, 1986.

Paper 3.2.   The defence burden—some general observations

ALEC NOVE

I.   The object of the exercise

Being to some extent responsible for initiating this discussion, it seems only right to begin by explaining the reason.

In the post-war years, this author detected a strong tendency to exaggerate the scale of Soviet military might and so also of its cost. In the early 1950s we were told of 175 Soviet divisions, a formidable force, showing such vast superiority in conventional force that only the nuclear deterrent kept them from sweeping on to the Atlantic. While there is indeed some evidence (e.g., from Czech, Hungarian and Polish sources)[1] that Stalin in his last years thought that war was likely, hardly anyone today would maintain that the 175 divisions actually existed, in the sense of actually being mobilized (a great many must have been skeleton formations, and skeletons do not fight wars). Then came the story of the missile gap, which, as Kennedy must have quickly discovered, did not exist, or rather existed in reverse: US superiority in nuclear weapons could have been of the order of 15 : 1 in 1960, and the Cuban missile crisis of 1962 occurred precisely because Khrushchev wanted to narrow it by installing medium-range missiles within range of the United States. It is an interesting question for historians how far the exaggerated estimates of Soviet strength were due to human error, how far they were deliberate (to help get money from the US Congress), and how far they were the consequence of the Soviet Union's own efforts to conceal weakness, to present itself as stronger than it really was. There was also the tendency—which still exists—to present the Soviets as hell-bent on aggression, aiming at superiority, and so on. All this developed in my mind an attitude of cautious scepticism about some published Western estimates.

On the Soviet side there was, and still is, almost complete silence. If their publications cite any figures on Soviet hardware, they usually come from US sources. This author is not competent to assess the quantity and quality of modern weaponry, having, in his army days, fired nothing more up-to-date than a Lee-Enfield rifle. But the burden to the economy, the scale of military expenditures, those are matters of evident interest to an economist. The only figure available was, and is, the Defence vote in the budget. This was supposed to cover 'the cost of weapons, ammunition, technical equipment, fuel, food and other equipment supplied to the Soviet armed forces', plus military schools, hospitals, sanatoria, sports, pay of those employed, 'the financing of capital construction', and so on, to cite one of several textbooks on the Soviet budget.[2] While vague at the edges (this seemed to exclude R&D and did not mention pensions), this definition would seem logically to cover the bulk of what is usually called military expenditures. But the budget total remained very low, it even fell slightly from 1970 to 1983, and it was in total and blatant contradiction with the Soviets' own claim that they were in the process of achieving parity with the United States. So, while Western propaganda may have overstated Soviet military strength and capabilities, Soviet sources were unusable, virtually non-existent: clearly, a large part of Soviet defence expenditure was not on the reported *smeta* (estimate) of the Ministry of Defence. Where, then, was it? What did the published *smeta* actually mean? Did its meaning and coverage change, and if so, when, due to what logic or sleight-of-hand? I agree with Peter Wiles (author of paper 2.2 in this book) that we must look for an accounting logic of some sort. To cite one of my own books, submarines are not likely to be disguised as expenditures on aid for lonely mothers.[3] They must be somewhere where they could be said to 'belong'.

II.   Some Western recomputations

Faced with increasingly incredible Soviet official figures, Western intelligence agencies made their own calculations, involving the conversion of their estimates of Soviet hardware and other expenditures into dollars and into roubles. This led to much controversy: what was the appropriate rouble–dollar ratio for defence goods? Is the high priority of the defence sector a reason for supposing it to be much more efficient and low-cost than civilian industry, or could the high priority be a reason for tolerating extravagance? The US Central Intelligence Agency (CIA), one recalls, had the embarrassing task of doubling their rouble estimate of Soviet military expenditure overnight, in 1976, not because they had discovered weaponry they had previously missed, but because they decided that they had grossly underestimated its cost. Then there was a further question, to which I will return: if we do compute a series in roubles, what price index is it appropriate to use? Finally, what can or should be the relationship between monetary magnitudes and the physical evidence of actual weapon development? In other words, suppose the growth indicated by these two measures is different, which is more likely to be wrong? For example, Steven Rosefielde arrives at a much higher growth figure in roubles than does the CIA.[4] This could mean: (*a*) Rosefielde's results overstate volume because of rising costs and prices; (*b*) these results are mistaken, because they are inconsistent with intelligence estimates of the weapons buildup; or (*c*) the intelligence estimates of weapons buildup are mistaken, either because the Soviets successfully conceal it or because the higher expenditure implies higher quality, accuracy, and so on. I would like to make clear that I do not agree with Rosefielde's methodology and reject his conclusions. But he is not alone in challenging the CIA's computations, and this cannot be ignored.

SIPRI also published estimates, but they were midway between the CIA's revised version and the official Soviet figures, and I was unaware of their methodology.

Other approaches existed, including Bill Lee's attempt to calculate the value of military hardware by identifying a residual in machine-building and metal-working (MBMW), subtracting all known civilian uses from the published total value of MBMW. This yielded a plausible total for 1970, and indeed was in line with the CIA's revised figure, and the method appealed to me at the time.[5] However, subsequently the figures ceased (in my view) to make sense; it is possible that Soviet statisticians made sure that they could no longer be used in this way. In any case, evidence is lacking on the use of MBMW within the MBMW sector itself, which renders calculation by residual subject to serious error.

Finally, there were two other approaches. One was to try to identify the military component in the input-output tables published for the years 1967 and 1972. The other was to analyse the Soviet national-income accounts. In both instances one had to look for residuals, items whose end-use was military but which did not appear as such. Peter Wiles's paper has much to say about the input-output tables, and he also refers to the work of Gillula and others, so I leave this aside, except to say that this is certainly a very useful approach which can also cross-check other calculations. As for national income, together with the late Alfred Zauberman I wrote an article, entitled 'A Soviet disclosure of rouble national income'.[6] We there reasoned that, since presumably there was no separate 'Annihilation fund' (S. G. Strumilin's phrase for the defence sector),[7] defence expenditures must be divided as follows:

- Material consumption of the Defence Ministry is part of 'Material consumption in institutions and enterprises of the non-productive sphere'.
- Consumption by military personnel is, of course, 'Personal consumption'.
- Accumulation (i.e., increase in numbers of weapons) appears as 'Investment in State reserves'.
- Some military construction (e.g., new barracks) is 'Investment in the national economy'.

We suggested that there was room in the figures we had computed for 'State reserves' for the increase in numbers of weapons. In my textbook on the Soviet economy, I had also surmised that some military hardware could be financed out of the budgetary heading 'Allocations to the National Economy', which also contains a sizeable item for 'State reserves'.[8] But it was clear that the national-income accounts and budgetary expenditures were two different ball games, since accumulation is a net figure (net of depreciation and/or retirements) and so is different from (smaller than) gross expenditures on capital investment or acquisition of weapons in any particular year.

Then, in 1970, the Soviet statistical annual began for several years publishing a utilization-of-national-income table which included explicitly an item for 'defence' (*oborona*). I duly noted that it was identical with the budget defence vote, but considered that this showed that it was meaningless.[9] Peter Wiles took a different view (see his paper 2.2), since it suggested to him that the defence vote is equal to what it seems legitimate to enter in the national accounts, that is, current consumption plus *net* additions to weapons (i.e., net of retirements, amortization). We will return to this question when discussing what the budget defence vote could or could not mean. Peter Wiles then tried to combine this interpretation of the budget vote with the defence elements hidden in the input-output tables. But in more recent years the *oborona* figure disappeared, along with the breakdown of national income utilized.

The Soviet national income tables divide the total into two main heads: 'consumption', and 'Accumulation *and other expenditures*' (my emphasis), which formulation gives rise to the attempt to compute the 'accumulation residual', possibly equal to non-consumption military expenditures (e.g., see Duchêne's paper 2.3).

By the mid-1970s it became abundantly clear to every serious observer that Soviet defence expenditures were very substantially in excess of the defence vote. But the higher rouble estimates began to be too big to 'fit' anywhere in the national accounts or in the state budget. For example, Rosefielde's figure for weapons acquisition for 1980,[10] 54 billion roubles, is roughly double the CIA's estimate, and Steinberg's figures for defence expenditures in total, given in this volume, are also well above CIA estimates, and he points out himself that such figures cannot be accommodated within the published Soviet totals. This raised two sorts of question. One, already mentioned, is whether these high figures, and the high growth rate calculated by Rosefielde, Lee and Steinberg, are consistent with the physical data on increases in military hardware which all the protagonists seem to accept. The other is whether the fact that the rouble figures seem too high to 'fit' into the accounts means that these figures are too high, or the accounts (and the budget) omit some significant part of military expenditure.

This last view is vigorously defended by Steinberg (see paper 2.1). Yes, he says, part of expenditures are not in the national income statistics, or in the budget, just as those engaged in producing weapons are not in the statistics of the labour force. This creates, in his view, demographic and expenditure inconsistencies which can be identified, and used to reconstruct the 'real' figures. Otherwise his methodology is open to the objection that, without an agreed total (e.g., of national income), the sky becomes the limit, since there is no total to subtract from, so to speak.

Steinberg's computations cannot be compared with the CIA's, or with those who claim that the CIA has too low an estimate, because, firstly, the CIA series (for some reason) are in what it describes as 1970 prices, not current prices (but note partial update in a joint CIA/DIA presentation in March 1986). Secondly, the authors of the higher estimates (or the CIA for that matter) have not tried to fit them into the Soviets' own national accounts (the CIA recomputes GNP, i.e., uses Western statistical categories). The comparison with Gerard

Duchêne's computations is a particularly interesting one to make, because Duchêne's considerably lower figures are capable of being fitted into various national-income residuals without having to assume that Soviet official stat-istics understate the national income (net material product), industrial produc-tion and budgetary expenditures (as Steinberg does). Steinberg's views are a challenge to everybody, and it is quite a formidable task to prove that he is wrong, if indeed he is wrong. (It is interesting to note that the notion that those engaged in the defence industries were omitted from the labour statistics also came to Abram Bergson, and may be found in a contribution written 40 years ago.[11] He was analysing the gap, also noted by Steinberg, between the total population reported as employed and their total disposable incomes, which is greater than the number employed multiplied by their average wage).

All of this still leaves multiple question marks, to the clarification of which the rest of this note will be devoted. But it is worth saying again, with regret, that any effort to prove that Western propagandists exaggerate 'the Soviet military build-up' has been hampered by the Soviet publication of increasingly incredible budgetary defence votes. One appreciates their embarrassment, however. Imagine the following conversation in the Kremlin:

Comrade A: 'Look, why not publish what we really spend? That will help to put a stop to some of the wilder overstatements of our enemies. We can blame Brezhnev, after all.'

Comrade B: 'Sorry, *tovarishch*, impossible. It involves admitting that the real figure is four times what we said it is. They will say we lied all these years.'

Comrade A: 'Oh well, I suppose you are right. Pity, though.'

III. The budgetary defence vote

So let us pass on to the meaning of the budget defence vote. Wiles, as we have seen, supposes that, for some years at least, it was equal to the value of the item *oborona* (defence) in the national accounts, and that this item included the increment in weapons, that is, the gross volume less depreciation (write-offs). But he too cannot fit the level of expenditures of recent years into the defence vote defined in this way, and, as his paper 2.2 shows, he supposes that additional concealment was occurring. Another interpretation is that the defence vote covers all current operational expenditures, such as pay, sub-sistence, administration, material utilization (e.g., fuel, heating, the use of practice ammunition, etc.), but that weapon production and stocks are separately financed, as is investment (and, of course, R&D).

Given the virtually unanimous view that the major part of defence expenditure is not in the budget defence vote, then where is it? Everyone agrees that most if not all military R&D is financed out of the Science vote (i.e., out of Social-cultural expenditure), and the paramilitary police troops out of the Ministry of the Interior vote. Where can the rest be more or less legitimately hidden? It is well hidden; so we do not know. One obvious 'candidate' is 'Allocations to the National Economy', the budget's largest item, and within it the allocation to Heavy industry—or, in another categorization, in the allocation to State material reserves. The accounting logic would be: not to sell weapons to the Ministry of Defence (unless it needs them in, say, Afghanistan), but to put them in special State stores. Also in the most recent years there has been a sharp rise in the overall budget residual, though this may have other explanations. But these are just hypotheses, which cannot be proved. It has also been argued that these residuals, when their other contents are allowed for, are too small. Thus the National Economy residual by use-category includes agricultural subsidies and foreign-trade expenditures, among others.

So—extra budgetary financing? If so, from where? One idea is Peter Wiles's: a transfer to Defence of a part of the civilian amortization account. Obvious objection: it is fully committed (indeed, real depreciation may well be higher), and such a transfer would simply create another gap which would have to be filled with other revenues. I am unconvinced. An alternative argument advanced by Igor Birman,[12] and in effect also by Dmitri Steinberg:[13] a large (even very large) concealed budgetary deficit, which contributes to inflationary pressure. Birman claimed that the State Bank issued extra money to the government, which appeared nowhere in the published accounts. Steinberg seemed to envisage the granting of credits, which are never repaid, which cover a large part of expenditures on weapons. Interestingly, the existence of fictional budget *revenues* has been pointed out by several Soviet economists,[14,15] but their point is a different one: that many sums paid into the budget by normal *khozraschyot* enterprises consist of turnover tax and profits in respect of goods not sold, so that the State Bank has to issue extra credits to cover the resultant gap in enterprise funds.

Presumably it is possible that direct grants are made to defence-industry enterprises (which Steinberg believes to be 'on the budget' in the same sense as, say, schools or hospitals, i.e., they make no profits and their expenses are covered by public funds). These *could* masquerade as long-term credits. But this seems a not-very-probable masquerade, which finds no precedent in what we know of Soviet accounting. The very large budget deficit which such procedures imply is *very* unsound finance. (True, Reagan tolerates a vastly bigger deficit! But it is not concealed.) So, speaking for myself, I am agnostic on this question. If extra sources of finance do exist, why not some of the proceeds of arms exports? But again, there is no proof.

Some estimates of Soviet military expenditures, notably the CIA's, put in a very high figure for R&D, and seem to be using a definition of R&D that is a good deal wider than that which the Soviets put into their budget statements. Otherwise one would reach the ridiculous conclusion that close to 95 per cent of all Soviet R&D expenditures are military. This definitional problem bedevils all such international comparisons. (Indeed, I recall being asked to fill in a form specifying how many hours a week I spent on 'research'. I had no idea of the answer! In writing this paper, am I engaged in 'research'?) There is also the point that much military-type research in the United States is undertaken by private firms and does not appear in US figures of military expenditure. But, as was pointed out in Mary Acland-Hood's paper 2.5, some of the estimates used by the CIA for Soviet military R&D are, to put it mildly, lacking in any solid basis and may well be substantially overstated.

IV.   How much?

To return to rouble estimates of Soviet military expenditures. As emerges clearly from the papers printed here, there is considerable difference of opinion as to the actual figures. But apart from this, one can have very differing views as to how they can be compared with US expenditure data in dollars, and also on the price trends which rouble figures reflect.

The first of these points was dealt with by Franklyn Holzman,[16] and there is no need for me to enlarge on it, other than to stress that his points are serious and cannot be ignored. It may also be apposite to cite SIPRI's own calculations, published in the 1986 Yearbook:

Table 3.2.1.   World military expenditures (billions of US dollars at 1980 prices and exchange rates)

	1977	1980	1985
USA	137.1	144.0	204.9
Other NATO	103.3	112.3	122.8
Total NATO	*240.4*	*256.3*	*327.7*
USSR	(126.1)	(131.8)	(146.2)
Other WTO	11.9	12.5	13.9
Total WTO	*(138.0)*	*(144.3)*	*(160.1)*

Source: SIPRI, *World Armaments and Disarmament: SIPRI Yearbook 1986* (Oxford University Press: Oxford, 1986), p. 231.

Notes:
Square brackets in original indicate estimate by the analysts.
NATO = North Atlantic Treaty Organization
WTO = Warsaw Treaty Organization

Those are the sort of figures that led Admiral LaRoque's publication, *Defense Monitor*,[17] to assert, contrary to what is seen as Pentagon propaganda, that NATO substantially outspent the Warsaw Pact. And indeed even if *Soviet* expenditures in real terms were equal to, or somewhat exceeded, the US figures, 'Other NATO' is vastly bigger, in total, than 'Other Warsaw Pact'. As Jacobsen pointed out in the same SIPRI volume[18] (p. 264), the CIA's own revisions, made in 1983, also effectively show Soviet military expenditures below US levels, and indeed, after allowance for R&D, show no growth since 1976, a conclusion which was bitterly attacked by Rosefielde.[19]

The growth (or non-growth) in question, to have meaning, should be in

Acknowledgements

The copyright in JCT 80, IFC 84 and the JCT Standard Form with Contractor's Design is held by RIBA Publications Ltd. The copyright in DOM/1, NSC/4 and NAM/SC is held by the Building Employers Confederation. The copyright in the ICE Conditions is held by the Institution of Civil Engineers. The copyright in GC/Works/1 is held by the Crown. The copyright in the ACA Forms of Building Agreement and Sub-contract is held by the Association of Consultant Architects Ltd. The copyright in the FCEC Form of Sub-contract is held by the Federation of Civil Engineering Contractors. These are the formal acknowledgements for the purpose of section 6 of the Copyright Act 1956.

Chapter 1

Determination at common law

Introduction

'Determination' of a contract occurs where a valid and enforceable contract is brought to an end prematurely *either* by its becoming impossible of performance by circumstances which were unforeseeable at the time the contract was formed *or* by the actions of one or both parties. This book is not, therefore, concerned with the situation where a contract is by its nature invalid or unenforceable, e.g. by reason of illegality or because it is defective in some way as a legally enforceable agreement between the parties.

It is an interesting feature of many standard forms of construction contract that their express provisions do not include rights to determine the contract itself but merely confer rights to determine the employment of the contractor under it, i.e. to relieve the contractor of his obligation to complete the work which he undertook. The contract itself remains in existence and the forms usually spell out in detail the rights and obligations of the parties where either of them exercises the express power of determination of employment. There is no consistency of terminology in the contract forms prepared by various organisations, e.g. the words 'determine' and 'terminate' are used synonymously.

A contract may be determined before completion at common law or by the exercise of express rights set out in the contract itself. In the latter case, the determination clause often seeks to improve on the common law rights of the parties by giving grounds for determination which would not entitle one party to determine at common law. Most determination clauses also specify the rights and obligations of the parties following the exercise of the power of determination, and leave the common law rights of the parties

1

intact. This is a typical feature of the various standard forms discussed in subsequent chapters.

This point is of some significance since, where the ground of determination is not one which would be treated as repudiatory at common law, it has been held that the party determining is entitled only to such remedy as the contract itself specifically provides: *Thomas Feather & Co. (Bradford) Ltd* v. *Keighley Corporation* (1953). In that case a contract clause provided, somewhat ungrammatically:

> 'Contractor shall not assign or underlet this contract or any part of it or enter into a sub-contract except with the consent of the Corporation. Compliance with these conditions is of the essence of this contract and in the event of non-compliance by the Contractor it shall be lawful for the Corporation to adopt either of following remedies:
>   (i) The Corporation may absolutely determine the contract, or,
>   (ii) The Corporation may call on Contractor in respect of such non-compliance for the sum of £100 by way of liquidated and ascertained damages and not by way of penalty.'

The contractors did sub-contract in breach of this provision and the corporation determined the contract. The work was completed by another contractor and the corporation claimed the extra cost of £21,000 as damages for breach of contract. The High Court held that they were not so entitled. Lord Goddard CJ said that the contract clause conferred a specific right on the corporation

> '. . . that is that they can put an end to the contract once and for all. I would have expected to find, if it was intended that, in those circumstances, the contractor would be liable for damages, that there would have been an express provision put in to that effect. I think that this provision simply gives the Corporation a right to terminate the contract, which they would not otherwise have had, and that it gives them nothing more'.

This chapter deals with determination before completion at common law. Subsequent chapters consider the express determination provisions of the commonly used standard forms of construction contract.

Frustration

Frustration is sometimes referred to as supervening impossibility of performance. The essence of the doctrine is that both parties are excused from further performance of their obligations and neither is liable to the other for any damage resulting. The contract is brought to an end by events which make performance of the contract fundamentally different from that contemplated at the time the contract was made.

In *Davis Contractors Ltd* v. *Fareham Urban District Council* (1956), which is the leading English case on this topic, Lord Radcliffe stated the doctrine in these terms:

> '. . . frustration occurs whenever the law recognises that without default of either party a contractual obligation has become incapable of being performed because the circumstances in which performance is called for would render it a thing radically different from that which was undertaken by the contract. *Non haec in foedera veni.* It was not this that I promised to do. . . . There must be . . . such a change in the significance of the obligation that the thing undertaken would, if performed, be a different thing from that contracted for.'

Davis Contractors Ltd v. *Fareham Urban District Council* itself illustrates the limitations of the doctrine and, as Lord Denning MR put it in the later case of *The Eugenia* (1964), 'it must be more than merely more onerous or more expensive. It must be positively unjust to hold the parties bound.'

In *Davis* the contractors tendered to build seventy-eight houses within a period of eight months. A covering letter with the tender stated that it was 'subject to adequate supplies of material and labour being available as and when required to carry out the work within the time specified'. After further negotiations a formal contract was entered into which did not incorporate the terms of the covering letter. The contract was on a firm price basis. For various reasons – principally lack of skilled labour – the work took twenty-two months to complete. The contractors completed the work and, *inter alia*, contended that owing to the long delay due to the scarcity of labour the contract had been frustrated and that they were entitled to be paid on a *quantum meruit* basis. The claim failed; the contract had not been frustrated. Its performance had merely become more onerous than the parties had contemplated. This is not a ground for relieving a party of his contractual obligations.

> 'The proper test for frustration may be formulated as follows: If the literal words of the contract were to be enforced in the changed circumstances, would this involve a fundamental or radical change from the obligation originally undertaken?' (*Chitty on Contracts*, 25th edition, paragraph 1405.)

In the *Davis* case it is quite clear that the answer to this question was 'no', and construction contracts have rarely been held to be frustrated.

One building case where the doctrine was held to operate is *Metropolitan Water Board* v. *Dick, Kerr & Co. Ltd* (1918). There, in July 1914, the contractors agreed to construct reservoirs near Staines within a period of six years. The contract empowered the engineer to extend the time for completion if the work should be 'unduly delayed or impeded' by any 'difficulties, impediments, obstructions, oppositions . . . whatsoever and howsoever occasioned'. War broke out, and in February 1916 the work was stopped by the Minister of Munitions who ordered the plant and materials to be sold. This prohibition was still in force in November 1917. Notwithstanding the wide power given to the engineer to extend time, the House of Lords held that the interruption was of such a character and duration as vitally and fundamentally to change the conditions of the contract, and that the contractors were entitled to regard the contract as at an end. As Lord Dunedin said, the government prohibition

> '. . . has by its consequences made the contract, if resumed, a work under different conditions from those of the work when interrupted . . . the contract being a measure and value contract, the whole range of prices might be different. It would in my judgment amount, if resumed, to a new contract . . .'

Self-induced frustration cannot be relied on. This is illustrated by *Mertens* v. *Home Freeholds Co. Ltd* (1916), a decision of the Court of Appeal. The facts, in brief, were that in May 1916 the defendants contracted to build a house for the plaintiff. Shortly after commencement it became apparent to the defendants that their price was too low. In July 1916 a government order prohibited building work except under licence. The defendants applied for a licence but deliberately delayed the work so as to ensure that the licence would not be granted. The licence was refused and the plaintiff was thereby prevented from employing others to do the work – as he was entitled to do under the contract – until 1919, when the cost of completion had been considerably increased. It was held that the defendants were not entitled to say that the contract had been frustrated by the refusal of a licence since they had themselves deliberately induced that refusal. The plaintiff was therefore able to recover from them the additional cost of completion.

Lord Sterndale put the point succinctly:

'No man is entitled to take advantage of circumstances as frustration of the contract if he has brought those circumstances about himself.'

The onus of proving that the frustrating event is self-induced lies on the party making this allegation: *Joseph Constantine Steamship Line Ltd* v. *Imperial Smelting Corporation Ltd* (1942).

In general it may be said that the frustrating event must be unforeseeable as well as outside the control of the parties, but difficulties arise where the contract between the parties provides for the *type* of event which occurred. This does not necessarily prevent the contract being discharged by frustration: whether or not it does so depends upon the interpretation of the provision in question. There are numerous illustrations of this, including *Metropolitan Water Board* v. *Dick, Kerr & Co. Ltd* (1918) (discussed above) where it was held that, despite the breadth of the extension of time clause, the contract was nonetheless frustrated. As Lord Justice Asquith remarked in the later case of *Sir Lindsay Parkinson & Co. Ltd* v. *Commissioners of Works and Public Buildings* (1950), 'it was held that the parties who framed that provision did not and could not have contemplated an interruption of so extreme a nature, and the provision was read as impliedly excluding it.'

A recent illustration is the case of *Wong Lai Ying* v. *Chinachem Investment Co. Ltd* (1979), a decision of the Privy Council on appeal from the Court of Appeal of Hong Kong. Contracts for the sale of flats under construction provided that:

'. . . should any unforeseen circumstances beyond the Vendor's control arise whereby the Vendor becomes unable to sell the said undivided share and apartment to the Purchaser as hereinbefore provided, the Vendor shall be at liberty to rescind the agreement forthwith and to refund to the Purchaser all instalments of purchase price paid . . . hereunder without interest or compensation and upon such rescission and . . . repayment . . . this Agreement shall become null and void as if the same had not been entered into and neither party hereto shall have any claim against the other in respect hereof.'

During construction a landslip caused the debris of a thirteen storey block of flats to fall upon the site, completely obliterating the works. Because work was suspended for a period of more than three months the building permit lapsed, and it was not possible to get a new permit until over three years later. The landslip was held to be a frustrating event and, on its true interpretation, the clause quoted could not be read as applying to that event. The contract was accordingly frustrated. Lord Scarman said:

'The clause, coming at the end of a contract, replete with specific provisions and time limits, was plainly intended to confer upon the vendor a remedy of rescission if a dispute arose or it became clear that he could not complete in accordance with the contract, provided he acted "forthwith" to terminate the contract. It does not follow from the provision of a summary remedy avoiding litigation in such circumstances that the parties must have agreed that their contract would continue after an unforeseen natural disaster . . .'

The latest construction case in which frustration was considered is *Wates Ltd* v. *Greater London Council* (1983) where the Court of Appeal considered whether inflation could constitute a frustrating event. The case arose out of a contract for the construction of housing units for the council. The contract was the GLC version of JCT 63 and included a fluctuations provision (clause 31) which, after the contract had run for some time, both parties agreed was not properly compensating Wates for the then (1972) current level of inflation.

The parties therefore entered into a Supplemental Agreement in October 1972 in order to compromise various disputed claims and substitute an alternative fluctuations provision. This was based on the government's 'housing cost yardstick' which had been regularly updated in the years before 1972. The government changed its policy and the index was no longer updated. This caused financial loss to the contractors. The contractors claimed £421,000 based on their interpretation of the Supplemental Agreement and, when the GLC refused to pay, treated the employer's refusal as a wrongful repudiation of the contract and withdrew from site. The GLC contended that this was a repudiation by the contractor.

The Court of Appeal, affirming the trial judge, held that the Supplemental Agreement had not been frustrated. Lord Justice Stephenson summarised the position in this way:

> 'Things may have turned out differently from what the parties contemplated in that inflation increased not at a trot or a canter, but at a gallop. But that difference in degree and tempo was not so radical a difference from the inflation contemplated and provided for so as to frustrate the contract. It could only frustrate the contract if it were coupled with the [government's] failure to keep up with it and provide for it by increasing the [index] or by some other method. And in fact the contract did provide for it . . . though not as effectively as Wates would have liked if they had contemplated it.'

At common law, frustration released both parties from further performance of the contract. It did not affect any legal rights which had already accrued or payments which had been made under the contract terms, the maxim being 'the loss lies where it falls'. One effect of this rule was that where a lump-sum contract was frustrated the contractor could recover nothing in respect of the work which he had done up to the time of discharge because he had not completed all the work: *Appleby* v. *Myers* (1867).

The harshness of the common law is illustrated by *Chandler* v. *Webster* (1904) where, under a contract to hire a room to view the coronation procession of King Edward VII in 1902, the sum of £100 had been paid. A balance of £41 15s. remained to be paid when the contract was frustrated by the cancellation of the procession owing to the king's illness. It was held that the hirer could not recover the £100 and remained liable for the balance, because the agreed payment date fell before the date when the contract was frustrated by the cancellation of the coronation.

This arbitrary rule was overruled by the House of Lords in *Fibrosa Spolka Akyjna* v. *Fairbairn Lawson Combe Barbour Ltd* (1943). In that case the parties contracted in July 1939 for the sale and delivery of machinery to Poland and £1000 was paid in advance on account. Before any of the machinery was delivered Poland was overrun by Germany, and the outbreak of war frustrated the contract. The House of Lords, overruling *Chandler* v. *Webster*, held that the £1000 was repayable since the money had been paid upon a consideration which had wholly failed.

This was only a partial solution to the problem, as was noted by Viscount Simon LC who said:

'While this result obviates the harshness with which the previous view in some instances treated the party who had made a prepayment, it cannot be regarded as dealing fairly between the parties in all cases and must sometimes have the result of leaving the recipient who has to return the money at a grave disadvantage. He may have incurred expenses in connection with the partial carrying out of the contract which are equivalent, or more than equivalent, to the money which he prudently stipulated should be prepaid but which he now must return for reasons which are no fault of his. He may have to repay money, though he has executed almost all of the contractual work, which will be left on his hands. These results follow from the fact that the English law does not undertake to apportion a prepaid sum in such circumstances . . .'

The effect of the *Fibrosa* case was, therefore, that money paid under a contract which was frustrated was repayable, but only if the consideration for the payment had wholly failed. The common law remedy was therefore imperfect because there could be no recovery if the consideration had only partially failed, and no allowance could be made for expenses incurred by the payee. Lords Atkin and Wright shared the Lord Chancellor's views, and the legislature acted speedily by enacting the Law Reform (Frustrated Contracts) Act 1943.

The Law Reform (Frustrated Contracts) Act 1943 is concerned with the consequences of frustration and creates statutory remedies enabling the court to award restitution in respect of benefits conferred by contracts governed by English law which have been discharged by frustration. In Scotland, restitution is permitted at common law: *Cantiare San Rocco SA* v. *Clyde Shipbuilding and Engineering Co.* (1924). The 1943 Act applies to contracts frustrated on or after 1 July 1943.

The Act does not apply to certain types of contract, namely certain charterparties, contracts of insurance or contracts for the carriage of goods by sea, or to certain contracts under the Sale of Goods Act 1979: section 2(5). None of these is germane to this book.

The first case to be decided under the 1943 Act was *BP Exploration Co. (Libya) Ltd* v. *Hunt (No 2)* (1982), which ended up in the House of Lords, although the most helpful judgment in the case is that of Mr Justice Robert Goff, whose decision was upheld by both the Court of Appeal and the House of Lords. Mr Justice Robert Goff's judgment is a most interesting analysis of the Act and this commentary is based on the views which he expressed.

The most important provisions are contained in section 1(2) and (3). Section 1(2) deals with money paid in advance. It not only confirms the *Fibrosa* case but extends it to cases of partial failure of consideration. It also allows a party who has been paid in advance to set off his expenditure in reliance on the contract. In estimating expenses incurred, section 1(4) provides that sums may be included for overhead expenses, and for work or services performed personally. Section 1(2) reads:

> 'All sums paid or payable to any party in pursuance of the contract before the time when the parties were so discharged (in this Act referred to as "the time of discharge") shall, in the case of sums so paid, be recoverable from him as money received by him for the use of the party by whom the sums were paid, and, in the case of sums so payable, cease to be so payable: Provided that, if the party to whom the sums were so paid or payable incurred expenses before the time of discharge in, or for the purpose of, the performance of the contract, the court may, if it considers it just to do so having regard to all the circumstances of the case, allow him to retain or, as the case may be, recover the whole or any part of the sums so paid or payable, not being an amount in excess of the expenses so incurred.'

Section 1(3), in contrast, enables someone who has conferred a valuable benefit (other than money) on the other party before a frustrating event to recover a sum not exceeding the value of the benefit. That sub-section reads:

> 'Where any party to the contract has, by reason of anything done by any other party thereto in, or for the purpose of, the performance of the contract, obtained a valuable benefit (other than a payment of money to which the last foregoing subsection applies) before the time of discharge, there shall be recoverable from him by the said other party such sum (if any), not exceeding the value of the said benefit to the party obtaining it, as the court considers just, having regard to all the circumstances of the case and, in particular, (a) the amount of any expenses incurred before the time of discharge by the benefited party in, or for the purpose of, the performance of the contract, including any sums paid or payable by him to any other party in pursuance of the contract and retained or recoverable by that party under the last foregoing subsection, and (b) the effect, in relation to the said benefit, of the circumstances giving rise to the frustration of the contract.'

The common and fundamental principle underlying both these provisions and the whole Act is to prevent the unjust enrichment of either party in the contract at the expense of the other.

Claims under section 1(2) – money paid in advance
In principle an award under section 1(2) is one simply of repayment of money which has been paid to the defendant in reliance on the contract, subject to an allowance in respect of expenses incurred by the defendant. The court or arbitrator has no discretion, except in the allowance for expenses which must, of course, have been incurred in, or for the purpose of, the performance of the contract.

Claims under section 1(3) – valuable benefit
In order for a claim under section 1(3) to succeed, it must be shown that by reason of something done by the plaintiff, under the contract, the defendant has obtained a valuable benefit (other than payment of money) before the contract was frustrated. The valuable benefit has to be identified and valued, and the value forms the upper limit of the award. The court may then award the

plaintiff an amount (not exceeding the value of the benefit) which it considers just in all the circumstances. The *Hunt* case makes it clear that the benefit is in an appropriate case the end product of the services, and this is so in building contracts. Mr Justice Robert Goff gave a construction industry example:

'Let me take the example of a building contract. Suppose that a contract for work on a building is frustrated by a fire which destroys the building and which, therefore, also destroys a substantial amount of work already done by the plaintiff. Although it might be thought just to award the plaintiff a sum assessed on a *quantum meruit* basis, probably a rateable part of the contract price, in respect of the work he has done, the effect of section 1(3)(b) will be to reduce the award to nil, because of the effect, in relation to the defendant's benefit, of the circumstances giving rise to the frustration of the contract. It is quite plain that, in section 1(3)(b), the word 'benefit' is intended to refer, in the example I have given, to the actual improvement to the building, because that is what will be affected by the frustrating event; the subsection therefore contemplates that, in such a case, the benefit is the end product of the plaintiff's services, not the services themselves. This will not be so in every case, since in some cases the services will have no end product; for example, where the services consist of doing such work as surveying, or transporting goods. In each case it is necessary to ask the question: what benefit has the defendant obtained by reason of the plaintiff's contractual performance? But it must not be forgotten that in section 1(3) the relevance of the value of the benefit is to fix a ceiling to the award. If, for example, in a building contract the building is only partially completed, the value of the partially completed building (i.e. the product of the services) will fix a ceiling for the award; but the stage of the work may be such that the uncompleted building may be worth less than the value of the work and materials that have gone into it, particularly as completion by another builder may cost more than completion by the original builder would have cost. In other cases, however, the actual benefit to the defendant may be considerably more than the appropriate or just sum to be awarded to the plaintiff, in which event the value of the benefit will not in fact determine the quantum of the award.'

There are problems in valuing the benefit under the Act, as the *Hunt* case itself makes clear, and in Mr Justice Robert Goff's view, the plaintiff takes the risk of depreciation or destruction of the building by the frustrating event, e.g. a contractor does work which doubles in value by the date of frustration, and the building is so severely damaged by the fire that the contract is frustrated. The valuation of the residue must be made on the basis of the value at the date of the fire.

In relation to the defendant's benefit, the court must have regard to the effect of the circumstances giving rise to frustration, and so a contractor will not necessarily or even usually get paid for the value of the work he has done, although it seems that he would be so paid if the employer had expressly agreed to insure the work against fire. Where the benefit does not consist of money, the defendant's enrichment will rarely be equal to the plaintiff's expense. In such, the basis measure of recovery in restitution is the reasonable value of the plaintiff's performance: in the case of services, a *quantum meruit* or reasonable remuneration.

It should also be noted that the terms of the contract may have a bearing on the assessment of the just sum. Those terms may serve to indicate the full scope of the work to be done and are therefore relevant to the sum to be awarded in respect of the work. The contract price is always relevant as providing some evidence of what will be a reasonable sum and may in fact provide a limit to the sum awarded.

A final consideration is the effect of section 2(3) of the Act which indicates that the statutory provisions can be overridden by an express term in the contract, e.g. clause 64 of the ICE Conditions of Contract for Civil Engineering Works, 5th edition, which provides for the payments to be made in the event of the contract being frustrated.

Section 2(3) reads:

'Where any contract to which this Act applies contains any provision which, upon the true construction of the contract, is intended to have effect in the event of circumstances arising which operate, or would but for the said provision operate, to frustrate the contract, or is intended to have effect whether such circumstances arise or not, the court shall give effect to the said provision and shall only give effect to the foregoing section of this Act to such extent, if any, as appears to the court to be consistent with the said provision.'

The effect of this provision is quite simple. If the contract contains any term which, on ordinary principles of interpretation, is intended to have effect as specified in section 2(3), the court can only give effect to section 1 of the Act to the extent which is consistent with the contract provision.

To quote Mr Justice Robert Goff again:

'Examples of such provisions may be terms which have the effect of precluding recovery of any award under the Act, or of limiting the amount of any such award, for example, by limiting the award to the contractual consideration or a rateable part thereof. Similarly, the parties may contract on the terms that the plaintiff shall not be paid until the occurrence of an event, and by reason of the frustration of the contract that event does not or cannot occur; then, if on a true construction of the contract the court concludes that the plaintiff has taken the risk of non-payment in the event of such frustration the court should make no award by virtue of section 2(3) of the Act. Such may be the conclusion if the contract contains an express term imposing on the plaintiff an obligation to insure against the consequences of the frustrating event. Another example considered in argument was a loan of money advanced to a businessman on the terms that it was to be repaid out of the profits of his business. Such a term should not automatically preclude an award in the event of frustration, for example, if the businessman is incapacitated the day after the loan is made; but if the business consists, for example, of a ship, which strikes a reef and sinks, then it may be that the court, having regard to the terms of the contract and the risk taken thereunder by the lender, would make no award. But in such cases the court should only refuse to make an award if it is satisfied that the plaintiff has, by the contract, taken the risk of the consequences of the frustrating event. The principle is the same as in those cases where the contract consideration controls the amount or basis of the award under the Act; the court should not act inconsistently with the contractual intention of the parties applicable in the events which have occurred. But, such cases apart, the court is free to make an award which differs from the anticipated, contractual performance of the defendant.'

Taken overall, it may be said that the provisions of the Law Reform (Frustrated Contracts) Act 1943 are not entirely satisfactory as regards construction contracts and a contractor may, in fact, be no better off than at common law and may, in many cases, recover little, if anything.

Repudiation

There is a distinction between repudiation in the narrow sense and repudiation by defective performance. The former is conduct which expressly or implicitly makes it clear that the repudiating party will not perform the contract, while the latter arises where a contracting party's performance is so grossly defective as to go to the root of the contract.

Where the contract is repudiated by one party and the other party accepts the repudiation, the contract is brought to an end and the innocent party is excused from further performance. The position was put simply by Lord Blackburn in *Mersey Steel & Iron Co.* v. *Naylor, Benzon & Co.* (1884):

'Where there is a contract in which there are two parties, each side having to do something, if you see that a failure to prepare one part of it goes to the root of the contract, goes to the foundation of the whole, it is a good defence to say: "I am not going on to perform my part of it when that which is the root of the whole and the substantial consideration for any performance is defeated by your misconduct".'

The essential point is that the wrongful repudiation does not itself discharge the contract. The contract will only be terminated if the other party accepts the repudiation. He may elect not to do so and insist that the other party perform his contractual obligations, although he can still sue for damages in respect of any loss which he sustains as a result of the breach: *Suisse Atlantique Société d'Armement Maritime SA* v. *NV Rotterdamsche Kolen Centrale* (1966).

'Anticipatory repudiation' occurs where one party states or

shows by his conduct that he has no intention of performing a future obligation, and is often termed 'anticipatory breach': *The Mihalis Angelos* (1971). Although he may treat the contract as being terminated immediately, the innocent party need not accept the repudiation but may await the time for performance. The proposition is illustrated by *White & Carter (Councils) Ltd* v. *McGregor* (1961).

In that case the respondent's sales manager, acting within his authority, contracted with the appellants for fixing to litter-bins plaques advertising the respondent's business. On the day that he heard of the contract the respondent sent a letter of cancellation to the appellants, but they refused to accept it. The contract was for a period of 156 weeks and, under its terms, the whole of the contract price became due should any instalment remain unpaid for a period of four weeks. The respondent did not pay the first instalment and the appellants sued to recover the whole price. The House of Lords held that they were so entitled.

Lord Reid said:

'If one party to a contract repudiates it . . . the innocent party has an option. He may accept that repudiation and sue for damages for breach of contract whether or not the time for performance has come; or he may if he chooses disregard or refuse to accept it and then the contract remains in full effect. . . . It is . . . impossible to say that the appellants should be deprived of their right to claim the contract price merely because the benefit to them as against claiming damages and re-letting their advertising space might be small in comparison with the loss to the respondent.'

The important practical point in this striking case is that on facts of that kind the plaintiff was able to go ahead and perform the contract in full rather than having to allow the contract to be terminated and sue for damages. In the context of construction contracts this principle is of considerable importance since it not infrequently happens that one or other party wrongfully repudiates before performance is due. Suppose, for example, that having entered into a contract the contractor realises he has grossly underestimated and advises the employer that he is no longer willing to perform. Such a statement would undoubtedly amount to an anticipatory breach of contract and, if not accepted by the employer, the terms of the contract would continue in full force, including any liquidated damages clause. However, if the employer does not accept the repudiation the guilty party has in effect a time for repentance and may elect to perform. Even if he does not do so he may escape liability if, for example, the contract is frustrated before the time for performance arrives. This is shown by the old case of *Avery* v. *Bowden* (1855) where the defendant chartered the plaintiff's ship at Odessa and undertook to load a cargo within forty-five days. Before the time for performance had elapsed the defendant repeatedly told the plaintiff that he could not provide the cargo. However, the plaintiff elected for the ship to remain at Odessa in the hope that the cargo would be forthcoming. Before the final expiry of the forty-five days the Crimean War broke out, thereby making performance of the contract illegal. The defendant was held to be relieved of his obligation. Had the plaintiff accepted the breach and left the port, he would have been able to recover damages.

Conversely, this rule can operate against the defendant where, as a result of market forces, prices rise between the date of anticipatory breach and the date set for performance. In such circumstances, if the innocent party does not accept the breach but awaits the time for performance, the damages would be assessed at the prices ruling at the date for performance.

The *White & Carter (Councils) Ltd* case raises questions as to whether the contractor is entitled to go ahead and complete the contract where it is wrongfully terminated by the employer. In *London Borough of Hounslow* v. *Twickenham Garden Developments Ltd* (1970) – a case arising out of a contract in JCT 63 terms – the contractors claimed to be entitled to insist upon performing the contract despite the employer's alleged repudiation of it and despite the employer's protests, and a number of examples were discussed in argument and are referred to in the judgment:

'A contract to erect buildings on land is let; a few days later the landowner unexpectedly learns that he can obtain a far more advantageous planning permission for developing the land, and he thereupon repudiates the contract; but the contractor insists on performing it, even though the landowner must then either abandon the more valuable development and accept the far less profitable buildings or else pull those buildings down when they have been completed and then carry out the more fruitful scheme. Another landowner lets a contract to erect an extravagant building which his wealth can afford; before much work has been done his fortune collapses, and he can pay for the building only by using all that is left to him; yet the contractor insists on performing the contract. A third landowner contracts with an artist to paint extensive frescoes in a new building over a period of two years; the landowner then receives a handsome offer for the unadorned building, provided vacant possession is delivered forthwith; yet the artist insists on painting on for the rest of the two years.'

As Mr Justice Megarry pointed out, examples like these suggest that there must be some limit to the *White & Carter* principle, and he noted two important limitations which appeared in Lord Reid's speech. First, the peculiarity of the case was that the appellants could perform the contract without any co-operation from the respondents. This is manifestly not the case under a building contract where the employer's co-operation is essential. Second, 'it may well be' that if a person has no legitimate financial or other interest in performing the contract rather than claiming damages, 'he ought not to be allowed to saddle the other party with an additional burden to himself'.

Mr Justice Megarry was loath to apply the *White & Carter* decision to any category of case which was not fairly within the contemplation of the House of Lords, saying that the case before him was one in which the contractor could not perform without the active co-operation of the employer and the work was being done on the employer's property. In his view – rightly, it is submitted – it is doubtful 'whether the *White* case can have been intended to apply where the contract is being performed by doing acts to the property owned by the party seeking to determine it'.

Repudiation in the narrow sense may be by words or conduct. Any conduct relied on must be unequivocal and must indicate a clear intention not to fulfil the contractual obligations. Thus in *J.M. Hill & Sons Ltd* v. *London Borough of Camden* (1980), in reaction against late payment by a local authority, contractors cut their labour and plant on site and slowed-down. They maintained their presence on site, however, and also their supervisory staff, canteen facilities and insurance arrangements for those employed on the site. The Court of Appeal ruled that this did not amount to repudiation, as contended by the local authority. The contractors did not purport to leave the site and their subsequent conduct indicated that they intended to treat the contract as subsisting.

Various common instances of repudiation by the parties to a construction contract may now be considered.

Repudiation by employer

(a) Failure to give possession of the site

Total failure by the employer to give possession of the site to the contractor will normally constitute repudiation: *Roberts* v. *Bury Commissioners* (1870); *Freeman* v. *Hensler* (1900). Mere interference with the contractor's possession of the site does not, however, necessarily amount to repudiation. Thus, in *Earth & General Contracts Ltd* v. *Manchester Corporation* (1958), the employers gave the contractor three days' notice under a forfeiture clause entitling them to take possession of plant and materials without vitiating the contract upon the contractor's going into voluntary liquidation. Before the three days had expired the employers entered on the site, controlled the movement of the contractor's vehicles and stencilled their name on some of the plant. The High Court held that this conduct did not amount to repudiation by the employer.

Wrongful ejection of the contractor from site by the employer will also amount to repudiation, but mere delay in giving the contractor possession will not generally amount to repudiation. However, if the delay in giving possession is so unreasonable as to indicate an intention not to be bound by the contract, this would constitute a repudiation: *Smart & Co.* v. *Rhodesian Machine Tools Ltd* (1950).

The Australian case of *Carr* v. *J.A. Berriman Pty Ltd* (1953) is very instructive. In the contract the employer undertook to excavate over the site to certain levels and, having done so, to give possession of the levelled site to the contractor at the end of May 1950. He failed to do so and the contractor made several telephone calls over a period of time asking when the site would be available. He received no satisfactory reply. In July 1950 he was told by the architect that the fabrication of steelwork, which formed a part of his contract, was to be done by another firm under arrangements already made by the employer. It was held that the two breaches of contract taken together undoubtedly amounted to repudiation. On the possession point, the High Court of Australia stated that failure to give possession, which might continue for so long and in such circumstances as to show an intention not to carry on with the contract, constituted a breach of contract.

Failure to give possession of the site to the contractor on the due date is undoubtedly a breach of contract. It is an implied term in every building contract that the employer will give possession of the site to the contractor to enable him to complete his obligations by the contractual date: *Freeman & Son* v. *Hensler* (1900). Most standard form contracts have an express term dealing with the giving of possession and in every case the contractor is entitled to damages for breach of such an implied or express term. If there is no contractual provision entitling the architect to grant an extension of time in respect of late possession, the contractor's obligation will then be to complete within a reasonable time once possession is given and any liquidated damages provision will be inoperable.

However, the employer will not be in breach of his obligation to give sufficient possession of the site to the contractor if the contractor is wrongfully excluded from the site by a third person for whom the employer is not responsible in law. This is illustrated by *Porter* v. *Tottenham Urban Council* (1915), a decision of the Court of Appeal, where the contractor was forced to abandon the work because of a threatened injunction from an adjoining owner, who claimed that the site of a temporary roadway was his property. That claim was held to be unfounded, but the contractor's claim for damages against the council in respect of the consequent delay was dismissed. There was no implied warranty by the employer against wrongful interference by third parties with free access to the site. This case may be usefully contrasted with the recent decision of the Court of Appeal in *Rapid Building Group Ltd* v. *Ealing Family Housing Association Ltd* (1985), where the contractor was denied possession of the site because of the presence of squatters, against whom the employer had taken no action. This was held to be a breach of JCT 63, Clause 21(1), which is the clause providing for the employer to give possession of the site to the contractor on the named day.

It is unsafe for a contractor to assume that the employer's failure to give possession on the due date or to give possession of the entire site will necessarily amount to repudiation. *Carr* v. *J.A. Berriman Pty Ltd* (1953) suggests that delay in giving possession alone may not be repudiatory conduct by the employer, whose conduct must be such as to demonstrate clearly an intention not to be bound.

Moreover, although the general rule in ordinary building projects is that the contractor is entitled to exclusive possession of the whole site, the extent and degree of possession depends on the facts and circumstances. For example, if a project is to be built in two blocks and the employer fails to give possession of the entire site, this will amount to no more than a technical breach unless the failure actually prevents the contractor from getting on with the job. The difficulty is compounded by the fact that few, if any, standard form contracts define 'the site' with any degree of precision.

The best statement of the position is to be found in *London Borough of Hounslow* v. *Twickenham Garden Developments Ltd* (1970) where Mr Justice Megarry, as he then was, said of a contract in JCT terms:

'The contract necessarily requires the building owner to give the contractor such possession, occupation or use as is necessary to enable him to perform the contract, but whether in any given case the contractor in law has possession must, I think, depend at least as much on what is done as what the contract provides . . .'

(b) Failure to pay
Unjustified failure to pay an amount due under the contract or the unjustified withholding of interim or progress certificates by the architect or engineer will not, in general, amount to repudiation. The authority for this proposition is the leading case of *Mersey Steel and Iron Co.* v. *Naylor, Benzon & Co.* (1884) which concerned a contract for the sale of steel to be delivered by instalments, the instalments to be separately paid for within three days of receipt of the shipping documents. On erroneous legal advice, the buyers postponed payment and the sellers purported to treat the refusal to pay as a repudiation of the contract. The House of Lords held that payment for a previous delivery was not a condition precedent to the delivery of the next instalment. To establish repudiation the conduct of the guilty part must have been such as to amount to an absolute refusal to perform the contract.

Lord Blackburn discussed the earlier case of *Withers* v. *Reynolds* (1831) where R. agreed to supply W. with straw, to be delivered at a stated rate during a specified time. W. agreed to pay R. 33*s*. per load for each load of straw so delivered on his premises. After several deliveries had been made, W. refused to pay for the last load delivered and insisted on always keeping one payment in arrear. It was held that this conduct amounted to repudiation in that it constituted a persistent refusal to carry out the terms of the contract as agreed.

In *Withers* v. *Reynolds*, W. was in effect saying 'you carry out your side of the bargain, but I will not carry out mine', which amounted to saying 'I will not perform'. In *Mersey Steel and Iron Co.* v. *Naylor, Benzon & Co.*, on the other hand, the buyers had simply suspended payment for what they considered good grounds and evinced a desire to carry on with the contract once the imagined legal problem had been resolved.

Applied to the construction industry, the principle appears to be that if the employer refuses to make an interim payment until the contractor carries out his obligations this will not constitute repudiation, but a stated intention not to pay in any event would clearly do so. Moreover, persistent delay in payment can no doubt amount to repudiation if sufficiently serious but a simple delay of a few days in payment, even if persistently repeated, would probably not amount to repudiation. Under the commonly used standard forms of contract the remedy of the contractor is to sue for payment under the certificate and, if there is a dispute as to payment, the employer may plead a set-off or counterclaim in appropriate circumstances.

Refusal to pay sums due can clearly amount to repudiation, a point illustrated by *Moschi* v. *Lep Air Services Ltd* (1972), the facts of which are not material. The House of Lords there held that a company's failure to pay more than £10,060 out of £24,000 payable in instalments then due was a breach constituting a repudiation of the contract. In the words of Lord Diplock

'. . . the debtor's failures to pay the instalments of the existing debt were in themselves sufficient to deprive the creditor of substantially the whole benefit which it was the intention of the parties that he should obtain from the contract, even if his failures to perform other obligations were left out of account.'

The express terms of the contract may, and usually do, confer a right of determination on the contractor in respect of non-payment against certificates, and such provisions are discussed in subsequent chapters.

Related problems concerning payment are under-certification by the architect or engineer, refusal or failure by him to issue certificates at the proper time or at all and interference by the employer with the issue of certificates. There is no doubt that a building owner who suffers loss as the result of negligent over-certification by his architect is entitled in law to recover that loss from the architect (*Sutcliffe* v. *Thackrah* (1974)) and this principle would clearly apply to a contractor who suffered loss as a result of negligent undercertification: see *Croudace Ltd* v. *London Borough of Lambeth* (1985).

There is a substantial body of case law dealing with the position of certifiers, the starting point being *Hickman & Co.* v. *Roberts* (1913). There the employer instructed the architect not to issue a certificate until the contractor's account for extras was received. The House of Lords held that it was an implied term of the contract that the employer would not interfere with the architect's independent exercise of his duties as certifier and the contractor was entitled to sue for payment without a certificate.

There is also a positive duty on the employer to ensure that the architect or engineer properly performs his duties as certifier. In *Panamena Europa Navigation Co. Ltd* v. *Frederick Leyland & Co. Ltd* (1947), a contract for the repair of a ship provided for payment to be made after the issue by the employer's surveyor of a certificate that the work had been carried out satisfactorily. The surveyor wrongfully refused to issue the certificate until he was supplied with information to which he erroneously contended he was entitled. The House of Lords, affirming the Court of Appeal, held that the repairers were entitled to recover payment without the certificate. In the Court of Appeal – in a judgment which was approved by the House of Lords – Lord Justice Scott set out the legal principles involved:

> 'It is quite clear that it is in the interest of both parties that the certifying person should carry out the function they both intend him to perform, and on ordinary principles of interpretation we must look to the language used by those parties in their contract to ascertain the scope and nature of their function. . . . I think the court ought to imply an undertaking by the owners that in the event of its becoming known to them that their

surveyor was departing from the function which both parties had agreed he was to perform, they would call him to book and tell him what his real function was. . . . In the result, I am of the opinion that they were under a contractual duty to keep their surveyor straight on the scope of what I metaphorically call his "jurisdiction", by which I do not mean that he was in any sense an arbitrator, but only that as an expert entrusted with the duty of impartiality within a certain sphere he had to form his opinion with judicial independence within that sphere.

'It follows from my premises that in failing to inform [the surveyor] that he was going outside and away from the limits of his function, [the defendants] broke their implied undertaking. One result of this was, I think, repudiation, upon which the plaintiffs could have elected to rescind and to claim damages if they so chose, but another result in law was that . . . the plaintiffs were entitled instead to treat the defendants as preventing the performance of the term of the contract in question, and also as waiving it as a condition precedent to the plaintiffs' right to sue . . .'

There is no doubt that these principles apply equally to the issue of certificates by the architect or engineer under a construction contract, as has been held by a Commonwealth court in *Perini Corporation* v. *Commonwealth of Australia* (1969).

(c) Prevention or hindrance
There is 'a positive rule of the law of contract that conduct of either promisor or promisee which can be said to amount to himself "of his own motion" bringing about the impossibility of performance is in itself a breach': Lord Atkin in *Southern Foundries (1926) Ltd* v. *Shirlaw* (1940). In other words, if the employer by his own acts makes performance by the contractor impossible or wrongfully prevents performance this will amount to a repudiation: *William Cory & Son Ltd* v. *City of London Corporation* (1951).

Acts of hindrance or prevention by or on behalf of the employer which render completion impossible will therefore amount to repudiation, the basis being an implied term that neither party will prevent the other from performing the contract. So in *Holland, Hannen & Cubitt (Northern) Ltd* v. *Welsh Health Technical Services Organisation* (1981) it was accepted that the following terms were to be implied in a contract entered into in JCT 63 standard form:

- That the employers and their architects and agents would do all things necessary on their part to enable the contractors to carry out and complete the works expeditiously, economically and in accordance with the contract.
- That the employers and their architects and agents would not in any way hinder or prevent the contractors from so carrying out and completing the works.

Whether the contractor is entitled to treat the contract as repudiated by the employer depends on the nature and degree of the hindrance or prevention. So in *Kingdom* v. *Cox* (1848) failure of the employer's architect to provide drawings within a reasonable time was held to amount to a repudiation since it prevented the contractor from completing the work, the dates for the provision of the information being specified in the contract.

Repudiation by contractor

(a) Abandonment of work
Where the contractor abandons the work or refuses to carry it out, this is a repudiation. For example, in *Marshall* v. *Mackintosh* (1898) there was a contract for the demolition and re-building of an hotel. The contractor wrongfully abandoned the work before completion and the employer was held entitled to exercise a right of re-entry reserved to him under the contract since the contractor's action amounted to a repudiation. Abandonment of the work or refusal to carry on is plainly a breach which goes to the root of the contract: *Hoenig* v. *Isaacs* (1952).

(b) Defective performance
In the case of an ordinary lump sum contract, faulty or defective workmanship or minor omissions by the contractor do not constitute repudiation where the work is substantially completed. In *Hoenig* v. *Isaacs* (1952) a contractor undertook to decorate and furnish the defendant's flat for £750. The terms of payment were 'net cash as the work proceeds, and balance on completion'. The defendant paid a total of £400 by instalments, occupied the flat and used the furniture. He refused to pay the balance, stating that

some of the work done and furniture supplied was defective, although there had been substantial compliance with the contract. The Court of Appeal held that the defendant was liable for the balance of the price, less a deduction based on the cost of making good the defects.

Lord Justice Denning, as he then was, said:

> 'When a contract provides for a specific sum to be paid on completion of specified work, the courts lean against a construction of the contract which would deprive the contractor of any payment at all simply because there are some defects or omissions. . . . It is not every breach . . . which absolves the employer from his promise to pay the price, but only a breach which goes to the root of the contract, such as an abandonment of the work when it is only half done. Unless the breach goes to the root of the matter, the employer cannot resist payment of the price. He must pay it and bring a cross-claim for the defects or omissions or, alternatively, set them up in diminution of the price.'

In *Hoenig* v. *Isaacs* the point was not strictly whether the contractor had repudiated the contract but rather whether he had performed it in such a way that the employer was entitled to refuse to pay, and it may be usefully contrasted with the later decision of the Court of Appeal in *Bolton* v. *Mahadeva* (1971), which emphasises that relevant factors to be taken into account include both the nature of the defects and the proportion between the cost of rectifying them and the contract price. In that case, the plaintiff agreed to install a central heating system in the defendant's house for a lump sum price of £560. The work was done defectively so that the system did not perform effectively. It gave off fumes and failed to heat the house adequately. The cost of putting right the defects was £174. The Court of Appeal held that it was impossible in these circumstances to say that there had been substantial performance, and the installer was held not entitled to recover anything at all.

An accumulation of defects which, taken singly, might well not have amounted to repudiation, may well, taken *en masse*, constitute such a non-performance or repudiation or breach going to the root of the contract as entitles the employer to treat the contract as at an end. This sentence is based on an observation of

Lord Justice Holroyd Pearce, as he then was, in *Yeoman Credit Ltd* v. *Apps* (1961) which was cited with approval by His Honour Judge Stabb QC in *Sutcliffe* v. *Chippendale & Edmondson* (1971), holding that a combination of defective work, delay and other factors, did amount to repudiation.

His Honour said:

> 'I take the view that the whole combination of circumstances that then existed . . . did justify the plaintiff in ordering the contractors off the site. I think that their manifest inability to comply with the completion date requirements, the nature and number of complaints from sub-contractors and [their] own admission that in May and June the quality of work was deteriorating and the number of defects was multiplying, many of which [they] had tried unsuccessfully to have put right, all point to the truth of the plaintiff's expressed view that the contractors had neither the ability, competence or the will by this time to complete the work in the manner required by the contract.'

The circumstances in *Sutcliffe* v. *Chippendale & Edmondson* were, perhaps, somewhat extreme and it was the combination of circumstances which amounted to repudiation. The general principle is that defective work during the currency of the contract, while the contractor is properly on site and before the date for completion, does not generally amount to repudiation unless the defects are so substantial that the contractor manifestly has no hope of rectifying them.

Indeed, in his dissenting speech in *P. and M. Kaye Ltd* v. *Hosier & Dickinson Ltd* (1972) Lord Diplock suggested, in the context of a contract in JCT terms, that

> 'Upon a legalistic analysis it might be argued that the temporary disconformity of any part of the works with the requirements of the contract even though remedied before the end of the agreed construction period constituted a breach of contract for which nominal damages could be recoverable. I do not think that makes business sense. Provided that the contractor puts it right timeously I do not think that the parties intended that any temporary disconformity should of itself amount to a breach of contract by the contractor.'

This is a statement of great weight, but in the later case of *Lintest Builders Ltd* v. *Roberts* (1980) the Court of Appeal expressed no views on it and in practice the matter would only be of importance if the architect or engineer is not empowered to require the remedying of defective work.

(c) Delay in performance
In a construction contract time is not normally 'of the essence' and so, in general, delay on the part of the contractor will not amount to repudiation. Delay will, however, amount to repudiation if it is of such a nature, duration and extent as to show that the contractor intends not to be bound by the contract, because it then goes to the root of the contract. The history of the law is extensively reviewed by the House of Lords in *United Scientific Holdings Ltd* v. *Burnley Borough Council* (1978), which is essential reading for anyone faced with problems in this area.

Even where, as is the usual case, the contract stipulates a period for completion, the stipulation about time will not be regarded as a term going to the root of the contract. The case often quoted in this connection is *Chandler Bros Ltd* v. *Boswell* (1936), a decision of the Court of Appeal, which is principally of importance in connection with the subject of implied terms in building contracts.

One of the points at issue was whether a sub-contractor was in delay or, more precisely, in breach of a provision requiring him 'to proceed with the works with reasonable rapidity'. Lord Justice Greer said that it had been argued that

'. . . there was a slowing down of the work by the sub-contractor . . . as would in itself be enough to justify putting an end to this contract. . . . It is not right for everybody to do with speed that which the contract requires a contractor to do with speed. It is not every small breach of contract which justifies putting an end to the contract at common law. . . . I see nothing in the evidence . . . to show that the [sub-contractor] had acted in such a way as to show an intention to repudiate the contract so as to release the contractor from further performance.'

Where time is of the essence of the contract the contractor's failure to complete on time might well amount to repudiation and termination may take place as soon as the date for completion has passed because then, in effect, the delay has frustrated the venture. Time will be of the essence where the contract states this expressly: see, for example, the form of contract devised by Liverpool Corporation and referred to in *Peak Construction (Liverpool) Ltd* v. *McKinney Foundations Ltd* (1970) where it was succinctly described by Lord Justice Salmon, as he then was, as containing among 'the most one-sided, obscurely and ineptly-drafted clauses in the United Kingdom'. The relevant clause provided that 'time shall be considered as of the essence of the contract on the part of the contractor' and went on to provide for both extensions of time and liquidated damages, thereby neatly negating the effect of the opening phrase.

In certain circumstances, time can be implicitly of the essence. This will not normally be the case in a building contract but it might be so where the building was being erected for a specific purpose, e.g. the construction of a stadium to house the next Olympic Games, or something of that sort.

Even where time is not of the essence of the contract it can be made so by giving notice if completion is not achieved within a reasonable time. This is so whether the contract is one for the sale of goods (*Hartley* v. *Hymans* (1920)), or for work and materials as building contracts are (*Charles Rickards Ltd* v. *Oppenheim* (1950)).

The notice given making time of the essence must be 'reasonable'. In *Stickney* v. *Keeble* (1915) it was made clear that reasonable notice must give sufficient time for the outstanding work to be completed. Lord Parker of Waddington said:

'In considering whether the time so limited is a reasonable time the court will consider all the circumstances of the case. No doubt what remains to be done at the date of the notice is of importance, but is by no means the only relevant fact. The fact that the purchaser has continually been pressing for completion, or has before given similar notices which he has waived, or that it is specially important to him to obtain early completion, are equally relevant facts . . .'

Even where there is substantial delay by the contractor, the wise employer will give formal notice that continued delay will be treated as repudiation. A case in which notice was held to be inadequate is *Felton* v. *Wharrie* (1906) where a demolition contract provided for completion within forty-two days of commencement and for liquidated damages for non-completion. After the contract time expired, the contractor was asked when he could finish and replied that he could not say. Thirteen days after that inquiry the employer, without warning, entered on site and refused to allow the contractor to carry on. It was held that the employer's entry was wrongful and that he had no right to terminate the contract. The position would have been different had he given proper notice or, quite probably on the facts, had the employer stated his intention of treating the delay as a repudiation at the time the work ought to have been completed and not waited thirteen days before acting without warning. If termination is justified then the contract is at an end.

(d) Other breaches of contract

Other breaches of contract by the contractor can amount to repudiation provided the term goes to the root of the contract. This is often a difficult matter to establish and English case law is not very helpful in a construction context. Sub-letting part of the contract in breach of an express contract term has been held not to amount to repudiation: *Thomas Feather & Co. (Bradford) Ltd* v. *Keighley Corporation* (1953). In South Africa it has been held that the contractor's failure to provide a surety or performance bond as required by the contract was breach of a fundamental or essential term going to the root of the contract and constituted repudiation: *Swartz & Son (Pty) Ltd* v. *Wolmatansstad Town Council* (1960).

Termination by agreement

An existing contract may always be brought to an end by a later contract between the parties, but the law is both complex and technical. The safest and simplest way of doing this is to enter into the new contract *under seal*, whether or not the original contract was so made.

As a matter of strict law, it is not necessary to do this where both parties still have obligations to perform under the original contract, which will normally be the case. In such an instance each party agrees to release his contractual rights in consideration of a release by the other party so that each is giving up something of value. This is called 'bilateral discharge', and the new contract will be enforceable even if it is made orally or in writing and not under seal.

Where one party has fulfilled all his obligations under the original contract but the other has not, e.g. where a contractor has carried out all the work but the employer has not paid for it, release will only be effective if executed under seal or if valuable consideration is given for the release. The latter is called 'accord and satisfaction'. In construction contracts problems can arise where, for example, the contractor agrees to accept less than full payment for the work he has done and the work is in no way defective.

The sort of difficulties that can arise are shown by *D. & C. Builders Ltd* v. *Rees* (1966). The plaintiff building contractors carried out work for the defendant for which the defendant did not pay. Being in dire financial straits, the plaintiff was persuaded by the defendant's wife to accept a smaller sum than was due and to give a receipt which was stated to be 'in completion of the account'. It was held, on a preliminary issue, that the plaintiff was entitled to sue for the balance of the money as the alleged discharge was unenforceable since there was arguably no valid consideration and, in the words of Lord Denning MR, 'the debtor's wife held the creditor to ransom'.

His Lordship said:

> 'The creditor is barred from his legal rights only where it would be *inequitable* for him to insist on them. Where there has been a *true accord*, under which the creditor voluntarily agrees to accept a lesser sum in satisfaction, and the debtor *acts on* that accord by paying the lesser sum and the creditor accepts it, then it is inequitable for the creditor afterwards to insist on the balance. But he is not bound unless there has been truly an accord between them.'

Settlement by a lesser sum than that due would, it is suggested, be valid and binding if there was a genuine dispute as to whether the work was defective and therefore worth less than the contract price.

Remedies for breach

Where a contract has been terminated by repudiation which has been accepted the remedy of the injured party is a claim for damages, the other normal remedy for breach of contract, i.e. specific performance, being clearly inappropriate.

Damages are monetary compensation and in the normal case are assessed by the court or arbitrator and are called 'unliquidated damages'. In contrast, 'liquidated damages' are the sum fixed and agreed by the parties in advance as the amount payable in the event of a specified breach of contract – usually, in construction contracts, for the breach of late completion – and they are outside the scope of this book. Liquidated damages are adequately dealt with in the general books on building contracts and at length in our book *Building Contract Claims* (Granada, 1983), chapter 2.

An award of damages is intended to put the injured party in the position he would have been in had the breach not occurred, so far as money can do so. However, this broad principle is limited by what is known as the rule in *Hadley* v. *Baxendale* (1854) as follows:

'Where two parties have made a contract which one of them has broken, the damages which the other party ought to receive in respect of such breach of contract should be, either such as may fairly and reasonably be considered arising naturally, i.e. according to the usual course of things, from such breach of contract itself, or such as may reasonably be supposed to have been in the contemplation of both parties at the time they made the contract, as the probable result of the breach of it.'

This test thus limits the amount of damages recoverable since it excludes damage arising *indirectly* from the breach, even though it might not have been incurred had it not been for the breach, and further limits the type of damage to that which the parties would reasonably have expected to arise from such a breach had they put their minds to it at the time of entering into the contract. Damages falling outside these limits are said to be too remote.

Consequential loss can be recovered under this rule if it was within the contemplation of the parties. For instance, in a case involving an indemnity arising out of a contract for electric wiring it was stated that damages paid to third parties resulting from an accident would be recoverable: *Re Fulham Borough Council & The National Electric Construction Co. Ltd* (1905).

Often the word 'consequential' may not have the meaning which the person using it intended. For example, in *Croudace Construction Ltd* v. *Cawoods Concrete Products Ltd* (1978) an exemption clause in a supply contract provided that the suppliers 'are not under any circumstances to be liable for any consequential loss or damage caused or arising by reason of late supply' and a variety of other defaults. Lord Justice Megaw, in the Court of Appeal, said that the word consequential 'does not cover any loss which directly and naturally results in the ordinary course of events' from the breach of contract.

Procedurally, there are two kinds of damages: general and special. 'General damages' are those which the law will presume to have resulted from the breach and which do not have to be specifically pleaded. 'Special damages', in contrast, are those which the law will not presume to have occurred, e.g. loss of profit, and these must be specifically pleaded and proved as having been incurred.

The subject of damages is a very wide one and for a full discussion reference may be made to *McGregor on Damages* (14th edition) which is the leading textbook on the topic.

Repudiation by employer
Where the employer repudiates the contract and the repudiation is accepted by the contractor, the contract is terminated. In those circumstances, since the contractor has been prevented from performing his contract by default of the employer, he is himself excused from further performance and may recover damages: *Appleby* v. *Myers* (1866); *Mackay* v. *Dick* (1880). The measure of damages will be governed by the rule in *Hadley* v. *Baxendale* (1854), i.e. the value of the work done at contract rates, the loss of profit which would have been earned on the work not done, and associated costs such as payments to suppliers in respect of goods no longer usable. The contractor is, of course, expected to mitigate his loss, e.g. by re-selling or using elsewhere goods supplied but not used, if it is practicable to do so.

The question of loss of profit arose in *Wraight Ltd* v. *P.H. & T. (Holdings) Ltd* (1968) – a case brought under the determination clause in JCT 1963 and corresponding to JCT 80, clause 28, discussed in chapter 2. The point at issue was whether the contractor was entitled to the loss of the profit on the job which he would have earned had the contract been completed. Mr Justice Megaw, as he then was, held that the loss of profit was so recoverable. He said

'. . . [contractors] are, as a matter of law, entitled to recover that which they would have obtained if this contract had been fulfilled in terms of the picture visualised in advance but which they have not obtained . . .'

In some situations it may be to the contractor's disadvantage to sue for damages for breach of contract. The situation is neatly summarised in Hudson's *Building Contracts*, 10th edition, page 601:

'In cases where the work is partly carried out and the contract is repudiated, a contractor should consider his position carefully before deciding to sue for damages for breach of contract, since it has been held that in such a case he may elect not to sue for damages but instead bring an action in *quantum meruit* for the work done by him. In a case where the contractor's rates are highly profitable it is obviously likely to be the best course to sue for loss of profit. If, on the other hand, the contract rates or price are low or unecomomic, it may well be that a reasonable price for the work done will be more advantageous to him, particularly if a substantial amount of work has been done prior to the employer's repudiation'.

A claim on a *quantum meruit* is one in quasi-contract or restitution and is a claim for a reasonable sum. In *Lodder* v. *Slowey* (1904), a decision of the Judicial Committee of the Privy Council, this was held to be an option open to the contractor in such circumstances. *Quantum meruit* means, literally, 'as much as is deserved', which is not a claim for a precise sum. It is a question of fact dependent on the circumstances of each particular case as to what is reasonable remuneration. In our experience, the claim would normally be formulated on the basis of actual cost plus a reasonable margin for overheads and profit on that particular type of work, but the amount would be reduced by such factors as the claimant's own inefficiency, etc. A claim on a *quantum meruit* may be made only where work has been partially completed.

If the employer repudiates the contract before any work has been done at all, the contractor's only remedy is in damages. The correct basis for a claim of this type is the contract price less what would have been the cost of doing the work.

Where work has been partly performed and the contractor elects to sue for damages, he can either claim the expenditure that has been incurred plus the net profit that would have been earned or a proportion of the price according to the amount of work completed together with loss of anticipated profit on the remainder.

If he wishes, the contractor (instead of suing for loss of profits) can elect to claim the expenditure which he has lost in reliance on the contract. This can be very useful where it is unclear whether the contract would in fact be profitable.

The best example is *Anglia Television Ltd* v. *Reed* (1971), a decision of the Court of Appeal, where an actor repudiated his contract with the result that a proposed television play had to be abandoned. The plaintiffs claimed £2,750 wasted expenditure as damages for breach of contract, of which the greater part had been laid out by them before the contract was entered into. The issue was whether both the pre- and post-contractual expenditure could be recoverable and no argument was put forward as to whether, had the production gone ahead, it would have generated sufficient income to cover the outlay. The Court of Appeal allowed the plaintiffs' claim. Lord Denning MR said that in such a case the plaintiff has an option. He can either claim loss of profit or wasted expenditure. He cannot claim both, but if he elects for wasted expenditure 'he is not limited to the expenditure incurred *after* the contract was concluded. He can also claim the expenditure *before* the contract, provided it was such as would reasonably be in the contemplation of the parties as likely to be wasted if the contract was broken'.

This principle – for which there was earlier authority – was applied by Mr Justice Hutchison in the recent case of *CCC Films (London) Ltd* v. *Impact Quadrant Films Ltd* (1984) where it was emphasised that the plaintiff may always frame his claim in the alternative way if he chooses, because 'to hold that there had to be evidence of the impossibility of making profits might in many cases saddle the plaintiff with just the sort of difficulties of proof that this alternative measure is designed to avoid'. However, a claim for wasted expenditure cannot succeed in a case where, even had the contract not been broken by the defendant, the returns earned by the plaintiff's exploitation of the contractual right would not have been sufficient to recoup the expenditure: *C & P Haulage Ltd* v. *Middleton* (1983).

The same principles apply where the repudiation is the employer's responsibility in law, e.g. repudiation by the architect or engineer or prevention caused by directly-employed contractors and so on: *Duncanson* v. *Scottish Investment Co.* (1915).

Repudiation by contractor

Where the contractor's repudiation consists of a failure to complete, the measure of damages is straightforward. It is the difference between the cost of completion and the unpaid balance of the contract price: *Mertens* v. *Home Freeholds Co. Ltd* (1921).

In the case of defective work, the position is less clear. *Prima facie* the measure of damages is the cost of remedying the defects plus loss of use or profit and other relevant direct losses suffered or incurred as a result of the breach.

Formerly, the courts adopted an apparently rigid rule that the cost of remedying the defects must be assessed at the earliest date when the repairs might have been put in hand but the present tendency is for the courts to adopt a more flexible approach. So in *Radford* v. *Defroberville & Lange* (1977) Mr Justice Oliver held that, in the circumstances of the case, the defendant could not 'complain that it is unreasonable for the plaintiff to delay carrying out the work for himself before the damages have been assessed, more particularly where his right to any damages at all is being contested, for he may never recoup the cost'.

In an appropriate case, therefore, the court may in fact assess the costs at the date of the trial: *Bevan Investments* v. *Blackhall & Struthers* (1977). Although this was a New Zealand decision, the English Court of Appeal reached the same conclusion in *Dodd Properties (Kent) Ltd* v. *Canterbury City Council* (1979).

In that case the Court of Appeal laid down that the fundamental principle as to damages was that the measure was that sum of money which would put the injured party in the same position as that in which he would have been if he had not sustained injury and that the general rule was that damages were to be assessed at the date of the breach. That rule is, however, subject to many exceptions and qualifications and in that case, in which there was a material difference between the cost of repair at the date of the wrongful act and the cost when the repairs could, having regard to all the relevant circumstances, first reasonably have been under-taken, the damages were to be assessed by reference to the later date. That decision was applied in *London Congregational Union* v. *Harriss and Harriss* (1985) when, amongst other factors, the successful plaintiffs' financial state was taken into account, and damages were assessed at a later date, and purely economic loss (in the form of lost rental income) was taken into account.

Possession of the site following determination

An important practical question which arises where the contract is determined is whether the contractor is entitled to remain in possession of the site. The problem usually arises where the employer purports to determine the contract, either under its express terms or at common law, and the contractor disputes the validity of the determination and claims to be entitled to remain on site.

In *London Borough of Hounslow* v. *Twickenham Garden Developments Ltd* (1970) Mr Justice Megarry, as he then was, held that, in order to obtain an injunction removing the contractor from the site, it was necessary in these circumstances for the employer to show that he had an undoubted right to determine the contract or the contractor's employment under it. He refused to grant an interim injunction pending decision as to the validity of the purported determination, thus allowing the contractor to remain in possession and effectively holding the employer to ransom by refusing to allow another contractor access to the site to complete the work.

In so far as it purports to lay down any general principle, this decision has been almost universally condemned on both legal and practical grounds, and most of the lengthy judgment proceeded on the basis of the somewhat esoteric rules relating to licences and on the supposed existence of an implied negative term by the employer that he would not revoke the contractor's licence to occupy the site while the contract period was running. Had the employer been able to establish that the determination was valid, the decision would undoubtedly have been different since a valid determination by either party will undoubtedly revoke the contractor's licence to occupy the site.

The better and, we submit, the correct view was taken by the

Supreme Court of New Zealand in *Mayfield Holdings Ltd* v. *Moana Reef Ltd* (1973) where Mr Justice Mahon declined to follow the *Twickenham Garden* case. There, disputes rose between the parties to a building contract and the employer refused to make further payments. In retaliation the contractor slowed down work, and the employer called in new contractors who were denied access by the first contractor. Mr Justice Mahon granted an injunction restraining the contractor from entering, remaining or otherwise trespassing on the site or interfering with the employer's possession of it before trial. The learned judge said:

'The practical exigencies of performance of a building contract must be kept in mind. The purported forfeiture by the owner may be based on alleged departure from the contract specifications. Must the owner be compelled to stand by while his action for breach awaits trial, and watch the building being completed in a manner which may ultimately be decided to have been in breach of the contract? Certainly if the departure from the contract terms were clear and unanswerable I should imagine that nothing in the *Twickenham Garden* case would prevent the issue of an interlocutory injunction dismissing the contractor from the site, subject to correct notices of forfeiture being given, but whenever the supposed breach was a matter of genuine controversy, as it so often is, the *Twickenham Garden* decision would maintain the contractor not only in possession of the site but in continuation of the works on a disputed basis. It is difficult to accept that either the contractor or owner would ever have agreed, at the formulation of their contract, to any express term carrying with it such drastic consequences . . .'

Chapter 2

Determination under the JCT contracts

Introduction

The standard forms of contract produced by the Joint Contracts Tribunal are the most commonly used standard terms in the United Kingdom. At present, the following forms are available:

- Standard Form with Quantities ⎫
- Standard Form without Quantities ⎬ JCT 80
- Standard Form with Approximate Quantities ⎭
- Fixed Fee Form of Prime Cost Contract — FF
- Intermediate Form 1984 — IFC 84
- Standard Form with Contractor's Design 1981 — D & B
- Agreement for Minor Building Works 1980 — MW

All the JCT contracts give both parties an express right of determination on the happening of specified events, not all of which amount to breaches of contract at common law. The determination clauses seek to improve on the common law rights of the parties and go on to specify the rights of the parties after the exercise of the power of determination.

In all these contracts the determination is said to be of the contractor's employment under the contract and not of the contract itself. The contract, therefore, remains in full force in respect of all other matters. The effect of determination is to relieve the contractor of his obligation to perform further work under the contract or to remove his right to do so, depending upon who is exercising the right of determination. Indeed, the determination clauses go on to specify the relative rights and obligations of the parties in the event of determination of employment.

The JCT determination provisions are not particularly well-drafted, and in some cases it may be advisable for the employer or the contractor to rely on his common law rights. None of the JCT forms excludes these common law rights, as is made plain, for example, by the opening phrase of JCT 80, clause 27.1.: 'Without prejudice to any other rights or remedies which the employer may possess . . .'

The effect of this phrase was considered by Judge Stabb QC in *Sutcliffe* v. *Chippendale & Edmondson* (1971). It was contended on behalf of the defendant architects that the employer's right to determine the contractor's employment under the predecessor of clause 27.1 (i.e. JCT 63, clause 25) was limited to the rights specified in that clause. In the alternative, it was argued that the employer's rights were limited to repudiatory acts no less than the examples of default set out in the clause. The judge rejected both arguments and held that the plaintiff was justified in terminating the contract at common law. 'Without prejudice to any other rights or remedies which the employer may possess' has the simple effect of preserving those rights in addition to and alongside the specific rights conferred by the contract.

As will be seen, the determination clauses lay down a somewhat complicated procedure, and if there is some procedural irregularity the position may be saved by the employer (or contractor) relying on his common law rights.

JCT 80 with Quantities

There are four provisions for determination, each of which will be considered in turn. They are:

Clause 22C.2 – Insurance of existing structures and the works by the employer – determination by either party.
Clause 27 – Determination by the employer.
Clause 28 – Determination by the contractor.
Clause 32 – Outbreak of hostilities – determination by either party.

Clause 22C.2 – Insurance of existing structures and the works by the employer – determination by either party
This clause reads as follows:

'*Loss or damage – applicable provisions*

22C.2   If any loss or damage affecting the Works or any part thereof or any unfixed materials or goods referred to in clause 22C.1 is occasioned by any one or more of the Clause 22 Perils then, upon discovering the said loss or damage, the Contractor shall forthwith give notice in writing both to the Architect and to the Employer of the extent, nature and location thereof and

22C.2   .1 the occurrence of such loss or damage shall be disregarded in computing any amounts payable to the Contractor under or by virtue of this Contract:

22C.2 .2 .1 if it is just and equitable so to do the employment of the Contractor under this Contract may within 28 days of the occurrence of such loss or damage be determined at the option of either party by notice by registered post or recorded delivery from either party to the other. Within 7 days of receiving such a notice (but not thereafter) either party may give to the other a written request to concur in the appointment of an Arbitrator under article 5 in order that it may be determined whether such determination will be just and equitable;

.2 .2 upon the giving or receiving by the Employer of such a notice of determination or, where a reference to arbitration is made as aforesaid, upon the Arbitrator upholding the notice of determination, the provisions of clause 28.2 (except clause 28.2.2.6) shall apply.

22C.2   .3 If no notice of determination is served under clause 22C.2.2.1, or, where a reference to arbitration is made as aforesaid, if the Arbitrator decides against the notice of determination, then

.3 .1 the Contractor with due diligence shall reinstate or make good such loss or damage, and proceed with the carrying out and completion of the Works;

22C.2 .3 .2 the Architect may issue instructions requiring the Contractor to remove and dispose of any debris; and

.3 .3 the reinstatement and making good of such loss or damage and (when required) the removal and disposal of debris shall be treated as if they were a Variation required by an instruction of the Architect under clause 13.2.'

Clause 22C will apply only where work is being carried out to an existing structure and in such a case the insurance risk is carried by the employer. The destruction of the subject-matter of the contract would render its continuance nugatory and in any event would amount to frustration at common law: *Taylor* v. *Caldwell* (1863) and chapter 1, pages 3-14. This is a special provision for determination by either party and it should be noted that where clause 22C applies delay caused by fire, etc. is not a ground on which the contractor may determine under clause 28.

The clause only becomes operable:

(1) If any loss or damage caused by the clause 22 perils – which are the normal insurable risks such as fire, lightning, storm, tempest, flood, etc. – affects the whole or part of the works or any unfixed materials and goods intended for incorporation in the works; and,
(2) 'If it is just and equitable' to determine the contractor's employment. This phrase is deplorably vague and the clause lays down no criteria to aid in its interpretation. The best view is that the provision is aimed at the situation where the whole subject-matter of the contract is destroyed or where the amount of remedial work which would be necessary to restore the position is so great that it would be inequitable to compel the contractor to carry it out as a variation under clause 22C.3.

The parties have only twenty-eight days from the *occurrence* of the loss or damage to serve the notice of determination on the other party, who then has only seven days from *receipt* of the notice within which to give to the other party a written request to concur in the appointment of an arbitrator to decide whether the determination would be just and equitable.

The notice of determination is to be served by registered post or recorded delivery, and the legal position is not entirely clear if the notice is served effectively in some other way, e.g. by personal delivery. This point is of importance as regards determination notices generally, since if the use of registered post or recorded delivery is mandatory then failure to use it would invalidate the notice altogether.

In *Goodwin* v. *Fawcett* (1965) it was decided that the words were not mandatory. The judge said that 'only on the strictest construction' of the clause could the view that a notice of determination was not valid be supported if the prescribed method of service were not followed. Instead, he preferred to interpret the contract 'in a commonsense business way as a building contract'. The Court of Appeal adopted a similar approach in *J.M. Hill & Sons Ltd* v. *London Borough of Camden* (1980), and in particular Lord Justice Ormrod said that he was 'much disposed to construe that part of the condition . . . sensibly and regard it as a directory provision only . . .'

A different view has, however, been taken in other jurisdictions:

Eriksson v. *Whalley* (1971) (New South Wales); *Central Provident Fund Board* v. *Ho Bock Kee* (1981) (Republic of Singapore).

As regards termination or forfeiture notices generally, it is desirable that the prescribed method of service be followed although it would appear that, in general, failure to do so will not invalidate the notice.

When notice of determination is given under clause 22C.2 and is accepted or is upheld by an arbitrator, the settlement of the contract up to the date of determination is carried out in accordance with clause 28.2 except that 'any direct loss and/or damage caused to the contractor or to any nominated sub-contractor by the determination' is not recoverable. The provisions of clause 28.2 are discussed on pages 73-5.

Clause 27 – Determination by employer
In the local authority editions clause 27 reads:

'27   **Determination by Employer**

Default by Contractor
27.1   Without prejudice to any other rights or remedies which the Employer may possess, if the Contractor shall make default in any one or more of the following respects, that is to say:
27.1   .1 if without reasonable cause he wholly suspends the carrying out of the Works before completion thereof; or
27.1   .2 if he fails to proceed regularly and diligently with the Works; or
27.1   .3 if he refuses or persistently neglects to comply with a written notice from the Architect/Supervising Officer requiring him to remove defective work or improper materials or goods and by such refusal or neglect the Works are materially affected; or
27.1   .4 if he fails to comply with the provisions of either clause 19 or 19A, then the Architect/Supervising Officer may give to him a notice by registered post or recorded delivery specifying the default. If the Contractor either shall continue such default for 14 days after receipt of such notice or shall at any time thereafter repeat such default (whether previously repeated or not), then the Employer may within 10 days after such continuance or repetition by notice by registered post or recorded delivery forthwith determine the employment of the Contractor under this Contract; provided that such notice shall not be given unreasonably or vexatiously.

Contractor becoming bankrupt etc.
27.2   In the event of the Contractor becoming bankrupt or making a composition or arrangement with his creditors or having a winding up order made or (except for the purposes of amalgamation or

reconstruction) a resolution for voluntary winding up passed or having a provisional liquidator, receiver or manager of his business or undertaking duly appointed, or having possession taken, by or on behalf of the holders of any debentures secured by a floating charge, of any property comprised in or subject to the floating charge, the employment of the Contractor under this Contract shall be forthwith automatically determined but the said employment may be reinstated and continued if the Employer and the Contractor, his trustee in bankruptcy, liquidator, provisional liquidator, receiver or manager as the case may be shall so agree.

Corruption

27.3   The Employer shall be entitled to determine the employment of the Contractor under this or any other contract, if the Contractor shall have offered or given or agreed to give to any person any gift or consideration of any kind as an inducement or reward for doing or forbearing to do or for having done or forborne to do any action in relation to the obtaining or execution of this or any other contract with the Employer, or for showing or forbearing to show favour or disfavour to any person in relation to this or any other contract with the Employer, or if the like acts shall have been done by any person employed by the Contractor or acting on his behalf (whether with or without the knowledge of the Contractor), or if in relation to this or any other contract with the Employer the Contractor or any person employed by him or acting on his behalf shall have committed any offence under the Prevention of Corruption Acts, 1889 to 1916, or shall have given any fee or reward the receipt of which is an offence under sub-section (2) of section 117 of the Local Government Act 1972 or any re-enactment thereof

Determination of employment of Contractor – rights and duties of Employer and Contractor

27.4   In the event of the employment of the Contractor under this Contract being determined under clauses 27.1, 27.2 or 27.3 and so long as it has not been reinstated and continued, the following shall be the respective rights and duties of the Employer and the Contractor;

27.4   .1 the Employer may employ and pay other persons to carry out and complete the Works and he or they may enter upon the Works and use all temporary buildings, plant, tools, equipment, goods and materials intended for, delivered to and placed on or adjacent to the Works, and may purchase all materials and goods necessary for the carrying out and completion of the Works;

27.4   .2 except where the determination occurs by reason of the bankruptcy of the Contractor or of him having a winding up order made or (other than for the purposes of amalgamation or reconstruction) a resolution for voluntary winding up passed, the Contractor shall if so required by the Employer or by the Architect/Supervising Officer on behalf of the Employer within 14 days of the date of determination, assign to the Employer without payment the benefit of any agreement for the supply of materials or goods and/or for the execution of any work for the purposes of this Contract but on the terms that a supplier or sub-contractor shall be entitled to make any reasonable objection to any further assignment thereof by the Employer;

.2 .2 unless the exception to the operation of clause 27.4.2.1 applies the Employer may pay any supplier or sub-contractor for any materials or goods delivered or works executed for the purposes of this Contract (whether before or after the date of determination) in so far as the price thereof has not already been paid by the Contractor. The Employer's rights under clause 27.4.2 are in addition to his obligation or discretion as the case may be to pay Nominated Sub-Contractors as provided in clause 35.13.5 and payments made under clause 27.4.2 may be deducted from any sum due or to become due to the Contractor or shall be recoverable from the Contractor by the Employer as a debt;

27.4 .3 the Contractor shall as and when required in writing by the Architect/Supervising Officer so to do (but not before) remove from the Works any temporary buildings, plant, tools, equipment, goods and materials belonging to or hired by him. If within a reasonable time after any such requirement has been made the Contractor has not complied therewith, then the Employer may (but without being responsible for any loss or damage) remove and sell any such property of the Contractor, holding the proceeds less all costs incurred to the credit of the Contractor;

27.4 .4 the Contractor shall allow or pay to the Employer in the manner hereinafter appearing the amount of any direct loss and/or damage caused to the Employer by the determination. Until after completion of the Works under clause 27.4.1 the Employer shall not be bound by any provision of this Contract to make any further payment to the Contractor, but upon such completion and the verification within a reasonable time of the accounts therefor the Architect/Supervising Officer shall certify the amount of expenses properly incurred by the Employer and the amount of any direct loss and/or damage caused to the Employer by the determination and, if such amounts when added to the monies paid to the Contractor before the date of determination exceed the total amount which would have been payable on due completion in accordance with this Contract, the difference shall be a debt payable to the Employer by the Contractor; and if the said amounts when added to the said monies be less than the said total amount, the difference shall be a debt payable by the Employer to the Contractor.'

The private editions are slightly different. The changes are:

● In clause 27.1.4 the reference to clause 19A (fair wages) is deleted.

● Clause 27.3 is entirely deleted and the reference to it in clause 27.4 is therefore also deleted.

Default by contractor
Clause 27.1 specifies the defaults by the contractor which entitle the employer to determine the contractor's employment under the contract by following the procedure specified in the clause. Of those grounds, three are very difficult to establish in practice and in most cases there is room for dispute as to whether or not the contractor's alleged conduct falls within the provisions.

Suspension of work. The default consists of the contractor 'wholly' suspending the carrying out of the works before completion 'without reasonable cause'. A partial suspension is not sufficient; the operative word is 'wholly', which means 'completely, totally or entirely'. Anything less than total cessation of work is not sufficient but may, of course, constitute failure to proceed regularly and diligently for the purposes of clause 27.1.2. It is possible – though unlikely – that the *de minimis* rule might apply so that the employer might be entitled to rely on this ground for determination if only an insignificant amount of the work were continuing on site.

Suspension does not imply that the contractor must necessarily have left the site but merely that no work is being carried on. There must not only be a suspension but a suspension 'without reasonable cause', and this is where the difficulty for the employer arises. There will always be some cause for the contractor wholly suspending the works; the question of whether the cause is *reasonable* is a difficult one to determine. It is suggested that if the employer is himself in default in a manner which would entitle the contractor to determine his own employment under clause 28 or at common law, this would constitute 'reasonable cause', e.g. the architect's failure to issue necessary instructions or the employer's failure to pay sums properly due under certificates.

Even if the contractor has valid grounds for complaint – which might be held in arbitration to constitute a reasonable cause – he would be well advised not to abandon work entirely since this would plainly be a repudiation entitling the employer to regard the contract itself as being at an end.

Curiously, it has been held that in some circumstances suspension of the work by the contractor does not amount to repudiation at common law but rather to an affirmation of the contract. This was the holding in *F. Treliving & Co. Ltd* v. *Simplex Time Recorder Co. (UK) Ltd* (1981), where a sub-contractor threatened to suspend work unless a disruption claim of his was met. This resulted in the defendants employing another sub-contractor.

Judge Stabb QC expressed the view that 'suspension' as opposed to abandonment of the work, far from constituting repudiation, in fact constituted affirmation of the contract. 'Suspend,' he said, 'eliminates the essential quality for repudiation by refusal to go on and introduces a temporary quality into the stop.' On the facts, the sub-contractors had not shown a clear intention to abandon and refuse further performance of the contract.

Moreover, in this case the defendants had acknowledged the validity of the sub-contractor's claim and made a promise of payment which was not kept. It is clear that the judge considered the sub-contractor's conduct in suspending or threatening to suspend the work to be reasonable, and it is suggested that the same principle would apply to clause 27.1.1 when considering whether there was 'reasonable cause' for suspension. This view is also borne out by *J.M. Hill & Sons Ltd* v. *London Borough of Camden* (1980).

Failure to proceed regularly and diligently. This is the most difficult ground of all for the employer to establish, although it is a breach of the contractor's express obligation (clause 23.1) 'regularly and diligently' to proceed with the works after being given possession of the site. How are regularity and diligence to be measured? Simple failure by the contractor to comply with his own programme – which is not a contract document – is not in itself a breach of contract.

In *Hounslow Borough Council* v. *Twickenham Garden Developments Ltd* (1970) Mr Justice Megarry, as he then was, discussed the meaning of the phrase and said:

> 'These are elusive words on which the dictionaries help little. The words convey a sense of activity, of orderly progress, and of industry and perseverance; but such language provides little help on the question of how much activity, progress and so on is to be expected . . . it may be that there is evidence that could be given, whether of usage among architects, builders and building owners or otherwise, that would be helpful in

construing the words. At present, all that I can say is that I remain somewhat uncertain as to the concept enshrined in these words.'

In *Lintest Builders Ltd* v. *Roberts* (1978) Mr Justice O'Connor, having quoted Mr Justice Megarry's consideration of the phrase 'regularly and diligently', said:

> 'With those sentiments I wholeheartedly agree. The [employer's] submission is that the word "regular" should be construed as to the method by which the work is done and it is submitted by the employers that method involves the proper lay-out and proper execution of the work in due course and that, if the work is improperly done so that it is done with defects, then there is a breach of their duty to do the work in a "regular" manner. "Diligence", it is said, has a time concept and they are to work conscientiously on time.
>
> 'For my part, whatever be the meaning of the phrase . . . it does not seem to me that it is capable of the gloss which the employers seek to put upon it. . . . The mere fact that defects in the course of the work arise, which is absolutely common form in all building contracts, does not mean that there has been a breach of the term "to do the work in a regular fashion". I would not so hold.'

Removing labour and plant from the site might well be evidence of a lack of intention to proceed regularly and diligently: Lord Justice Lawton in *J.M. Hill & Sons Ltd* v. *London Borough of Camden* (1980). All the factors must be taken into account and it seems that whether the contractor is proceeding regularly and diligently is a question of fact, depending on all the circumstances.

If correct, the recent case of *Greater London Council* v. *Cleveland Bridge & Engineering Co. Ltd* (1984) casts doubt on the utility of this ground. Clause 19 of the contract between the parties there provided for the contractors to be discharged if they failed to exercise due diligence or expedition in the performance of the contract. Mr Justice Staughton held that while neglect by the contractors to execute the work in this manner might entitle the employer to discharge them under clause 19, it would not by itself be a breach of contract on the part of the contractors. In the result, the overall deadline had been complied with, and since it was a general principle of building contracts that it was for the contractor to plan and perform his work as desired within the contract period, it could not be said that the contractors had failed to exercise due diligence and expedition.

At the time of writing the case is under appeal, but certainly employers need to exercise caution in relying on the contractor's failure to proceed regularly and diligently with the works as a ground on which to determine employment unless, of course, the contractual completion date has passed or it is patently obvious that it will not be met.

Failure to remove defective work. This ground is not as wide as might appear at first sight. The contractor must either refuse or persistently neglect to comply with an architect's instruction issued under clause 8.4 requiring 'the removal from the site of any work, materials or goods which are not in accordance with this contract'. In *Holland, Hannen & Cubitt (Northern) Ltd* v. *Welsh Health Technical Services Organisation* (1981), His Honour Judge Newey QC drew attention to the curious feature of this form of contract that the architect is given no specific power during the course of the works to instruct that defective work be remedied but only to instruct that it be totally removed from the works. A valid clause 8.4 instruction or notice must have been issued before this ground for determination is invoked *and* there must be either an outright refusal or a persistent neglect to comply with its terms. Persistence suggests that there must have been reminders which have been ignored. A simple failure by the contractor to comply with a written instruction under clause 8.4, without a reminder, could not be said to be persistent.

Furthermore, it is a precondition that 'the works are materially affected', which is a rather vague qualification. It could mean material effect on progress of the works, or that if the works were to be completed with the defect unremedied they would not be fit for their intended purpose, or that if the defective work were unremedied for an extended period it would seriously affect subsequent work, e.g. a defective foundation which would lead to anything erected on it becoming unsafe.

In fact, this is a long-stop provision. The employer has an alternative remedy under clause 4.1.2 to employ others to carry out the instruction. On balance, it is thought that failure to remedy defects which could be easily remedied at any time during progress would not be grounds for determination under this provision or at common law.

A common problem arises where the architect alleges that work is not up to the required standard of appearance, e.g. facing brickwork or fair-faced concrete. Almost inevitably the question arises as to whether the architect's opinion on the matter is reasonable having regard to the specification requirements in the contract. It is suggested that unless the workmanship is so poor as to be manifestly below any standard that might reasonably be required, failure to comply with a clause 8.4 notice issued in consequence would not give rise to a right of determination under this provision.

Assigning or sub-letting without consent. Clause 19 requires the contractor to obtain the employer's written consent to any assignment of the contract and further requires him to obtain the written consent of the architect before sub-letting any portion of the works. The latter consent is not to be 'unreasonably withheld'.

Sub-letting without consent would not be a repudiatory breach at common law (*Thomas Feather & Co. (Bradford) Ltd* v. *Keighley Corporation* (1953)) but would give rise to a claim for nominal damages. It is arguable that the employer is not obliged to pay for sub-contracted work where he has not agreed to sub-contracting. Clause 27.1.4 makes both assignment and sub-letting without consent a ground for determination. It is not clear whether assignment by the contractor of monies due under the contract, e.g. to a factoring house, is within the prohibition, but probably it is: *Helstan Securities Ltd* v. *Hertfordshire County Council* (1978), a decision on a similarly-worded provision in another standard form, although in that case the point was whether the assignee could sue the employer for the contract monies.

Failure to comply with 'fair wages' provision. In the local authority edition, clause 19A requires the contractor to comply with the Fair Wages Resolution of the House of Commons of 14 October 1946. Although that resolution has now been rescinded, observance of it remains a term of this contract and breach is still a ground for determination. It is thought, however, that for the employer to determine the contractor's employment on this ground for a mere casual or inadvertent breach of clause 19A would be held to be unreasonable or vexatious under the proviso to clause 27.1.

Procedure. The determination procedure is based upon two notices both of which should be served by registered post or recorded delivery, although failure to follow the specified method of post would not necessarily invalidate the notice if it could be proved or were admitted that it had been received: *Goodwin* v. *Fawcett* (1965); *J.M. Hill & Sons Ltd* v. *London Borough of Camden* (1980), page 41.

The first notice must specify the default and must be issued by the architect. The object of the notice is to put the contractor on warning and to give him an opportunity of remedying his default, and it is therefore important that the notice is explicit.

In *London Borough of Hounslow* v. *Twickenham Garden Developments Ltd* (1970) Mr Justice Megarry said, when dealing with a notice given under the corresponding clause in JCT 63:

> 'I do not read the condition as requiring the architect, at his peril, to spell out accurately in his notice further and better particulars, as it were, of the particular default in question. All that I think the notice need do is to direct the contractor's mind to what is said to be amiss . . .'

In that case the architect's notice, which was held to be effective, merely said 'I therefore hereby give notice under clause 25(1) of the contract . . . that in my opinion you have failed to proceed regularly and diligently with the works.'

If the contractor denies the default he should immediately inform the architect and also, it is suggested, give notice of arbitration in order to protect his position although, oddly, this is not one of the matters which can be referred to immediate arbitration under Article 5.2.

The contractor has fourteen days from *receipt* of the first notice in which to remedy the default. It is desirable that the precise date of receipt can be ascertained, e.g. by requiring advice of delivery from the post office, although there is a presumption that a letter properly addressed and posted will be received on the next working day – a presumption which may now appear to have little foundation in fact in view of the current deterioration of postal services. The contract uses the words 'continue such default', and whether or not the contractor has done this is a matter of fact. It seems that if the contractor starts to remedy the default within the fourteen days this is sufficient, even though the remedy might not be completed within that time.

The second notice is served by the *employer* and not by the architect and it is the determination notice. Notice served by the architect or by anyone other than the employer himself would be invalid and ineffective. Where the employer is a local authority or other body corporate the notice would be valid if signed by anyone having apparent authority to bind the employer. In general, however, it would be safest if the letter is signed by the senior official of the body concerned, e.g. the chief executive of a local authority or the managing director of a limited liability company. Once again, the use of registered post or recorded delivery is specified.

The effect of this notice is to determine the employment of the contractor under this contract 'forthwith' which, in this context, means 'immediately, at once, without delay or interval' (*Oxford English Dictionary*). The determination notice may be served within ten days of the expiry of the time limit for compliance with the architect's notice. The employer therefore has that period in which to decide whether to take the drastic step of determination.

The foregoing applies in respect of the first default of the kind specified in the architect's notice. Any repetition of the *same* default will entitle the employer to serve notice of determination within ten days from the repetition without need for a further warning notice from the architect.

It is submitted that the repetition need not be of the identical default but may be of a default of the same kind. For instance, if the architect's notice relates to a failure to remove specified defective work and this is complied with, a subsequent failure by the contractor to comply with an instruction to remove other defective work is a repetition of such default within the meaning of the clause.

However, it must be borne in mind that the whole of this clause is subject to the proviso that the employer's notice of determination 'shall not be given unreasonably or vexatiously'. In relation to the same words in clause 28.1 the Court of Appeal has expressed the view that 'unreasonably' in this context would render such a notice invalid in relation to 'something accidental or purely incidental so that the court could see that the [party] was taking advantage of the other side in circumstances in which, from a business point of view, it would be totally unfair and almost smacking of sharp practice':

Lord Justice Ormrod in *J. & M. Hill & Sons Ltd* v. *London Borough of Camden* (1980). 'Vexatiously' means without good grounds merely to cause annoyance or embarrassment or irritation.

Contrary to certain statements made by some of the commentators, it is not thought that an invalid exercise of the power to determine the contractor's employment would necessarily constitute an unlawful repudiation of the contract. In *Woodar Ltd* v. *Wimpey Ltd* (1980), the House of Lords held that a party who purported to rescind a contract under an honest but mistaken belief about the rights conferred by the contract was not to be treated as repudiating it. Lord Wilberforce said:

> 'So far from repudiating the contract, the appellants were relying on it and invoking one of its provisions, to which both parties had given their consent. And unless the invocation of that provision was totally abusive, or lacking in good faith (neither of which is contended for), the fact that it has proved to be wrong in law cannot turn it into a repudiation. . . . It would be a regettable development of the law of contract to hold that a party who *bona fide* relies upon an express stipulation in a contract in order to rescind or terminate a contract should, by that fact alone, be treated as having repudiated his contractual obligations if he turns out to be mistaken as to his rights. Repudiation is a drastic conclusion which should be only held to arise in clear cases of a refusal, in a matter going to the root of the contract, to perform contractual obligations.'

Again, in *Canterbury Pipe Lines Ltd* v. *The Christchurch Drainage Board* (1979), the New Zealand Court of Appeal held that while the employer's exercise of its purported right of determination was invalid, the contractor's conduct also was wrongful in unjustifiably suspending work. The contractor was only therefore able to recover the unpaid value of the contract work, the retention held by the employer and the tender deposit. The contractor was not entitled to *quantum meruit* or loss of profit, which would have been the case had the employer wrongfully repudiated the contract.

Insolvency of contractor
Clause 27.2 provides for the contractor's employment to be

determined 'automatically' on the happening of any of the events specified in the clause. Broadly, they may be said to be insolvency situations, and in effect treat insolvency as a breach of contract justifying determination. At common law insolvency is not a breach at all, but rather a misfortune.

No doubt on practical grounds it is sensible to provide for determination in a true insolvency situation, i.e. bankruptcy in the case of an individual or a partnership and certain types of liquidation, but the operation of this clause is fraught with difficulties.

There appears to be no legal or practical justification for treating the appointment of a receiver by debenture holders as a ground for determination. The position is that normally the receiver is bound by existing contracts and, unlike a trustee in bankruptcy or liquidator, has no statutory or other right to disclaim contracts even if they are unprofitable. The matter was put clearly by Lord Haldane in *Parsons* v. *Sovereign Bank of Canada* (1913), a decision of the Judicial Committee of the Privy Council. His Lordship said:

> 'The company remains in existence, but has lost its title to control its assets and its affairs. . . . In the absence of a liquidation, the *persona* of the . . . company remains legally intact though controlled by the receivers and managers . . . there appears to be no reason for saying that the possession of the undertaking and assets [by the receivers and managers] . . . put an end to these contracts. The company remained in legal existence and so did the contracts until put to an end otherwise.'

Similarly, in *George Barker (Transport) Ltd* v. *Eynon* (1974), where *Parsons* v. *Sovereign Bank of Canada* was applied, a contract was held to have remained in force despite the appointment of a receiver, having been entered into in the ordinary course of business. The receiver's duty, said Lord Justice Edmund Davies,

> '. . . being to carry on the business so as to preserve the goodwill, he must fulfil company trading contracts entered into before his appointment or render it liable in damages if unwarrantably declined. . . . Neither the receiver nor the

debenture holders were in any way relieved by the former's appointment from the obligations which . . . the company had undertaken.'

In our view, therefore, it could be very much in the employer's interests for the contract to continue following the receiver's appointment, whereas through the automatic determination of employment under the clause the receiver is not bound to continue with the contract.

Even where there is a true insolvency situation and a trustee in bankruptcy or liquidator is appointed, the provisions are of doubtful legal validity. If insolvency is used as a pretext for automatic determination, the courts might hold that the employer had repudiated the contract and was himself in breach. Furthermore, the trustee in bankruptcy and liquidator have a statutory right to disclaim any unprofitable contract: Bankruptcy Act 1914, section 54(1)(8); Companies Act 1948, section 323(1). The automatic determination provision may well not be valid as against the trustee in bankruptcy or liquidator even though it is so in the case of the appointment of a receiver: *Re Walker, ex parte Barter* (1884). It follows that it is doubtful how far the provisions of clause 27.4, setting out the rights and duties of the parties after determination, are good against a trustee in bankruptcy or liquidator who disclaims successfully.

It is our view that the employer is unwise to rely on clause 27.2 as printed, and it is only if clause 27.2 applies in an insolvency situation that clause 27.4 can be relied on. In practice it would often be better and to the advantage of both parties to permit the trustee in bankruptcy or liquidator to complete the contract. Clause 27.4 applies after a valid determination of the contractor's employment 'and so long as it has not been reinstated and continued'. This supposes that the contractor can be allowed to resume work if thought desirable. But in the case of insolvency the effect of the clause is obscure. Although the law allows the parties to a contract to arrange for the determination of a party's employment on insolvency, clause 27.4 arguably conflicts with the general principle of insolvency law that in such a case the insolvent person's assets should be fairly distributed amongst all the creditors.

Whatever the position may be, if the employer intends to rely on the clause he is well advised to inform the contractor, his trustee in bankruptcy or liquidator of his reliance on it, even though the clause does not specifically require this, so as to avoid a claim that he has waived his rights under it if – as sometimes happens – the work is permitted to continue.

It is, in general, unwise for the employer to rely on 'automatic determination'. Practically, it is better to rely on clause 27.1. Shortage of cash seldom comes about overnight, and in the normal course of events the defaults specified in clause 27.1 can be *indicia* of a contractor's impending insolvency. Other warning signs include:

● Sudden disappearance of plant or materials from site.
● High management turnover.
● Excuses about late deliveries of materials.
● Complaints by sub-contractors about non-payment.
● A general lack of diligence in carrying out the work.

Two recent cases deal with the consequences of a contractor's liquidation under a contract in JCT 63 terms, the principles of which apply equally to JCT 80. In *Willment Brothers Ltd* v. *North-West Thames Regional Health Authority* (1984) the employers stopped a cheque for £102,424 due under an interim certificate when they learned, on the day after issuing and posting the cheque, that the contractor had appointed a liquidator and ceased work on site. The contractor's liquidator sued only on the cheque, arguing that it was to be treated as cash and the employers could not off-set the amount of their counterclaim arising from the breach or termination of the contract. The Court of Appeal held that the employers were entitled to set-off their counterclaim against the contractor's claim under section 31 of the Bankruptcy Act 1914, which is applied to insolvent companies by section 317 of the Companies Act 1948. That section provides:

'Where there have been mutual credits, mutual debts or other mutual dealings, between a debtor against whom a receiving order shall be made under this Act and any other person proving or claiming to prove a debt under the receiving order, an account shall be taken of what is due from the one party to the other in respect of such mutual dealings, and the sum due from the one party shall be set off against any sum due from the other party, and the balance of the account, and no more, shall be claimed or paid on either side respectively; but a person shall not be entitled under this section to claim the benefit of any set off against the property of a debtor in any case where he had, at the time of giving credit to the debtor, notice of an act of bankruptcy committed by the debtor and available against him.'

The operation of that provision is mandatory and it is not permissible to contract out of it: *National Westminster Bank Ltd* v. *Halesowen Presswork & Assemblies Ltd* (1972). The plaintiffs were an insolvent company and there was a debt due to them from the employers, i.e. the amount due under the certificate. The employers were '. . . a person proving or claiming to prove a debt. . . .' in the winding-up of the insolvent contractors. There had been 'mutual dealings' as evidenced by the working of the building contract. The judgment of the Court of Appeal, given by Lord Justice O'Connor, was on the basis that the contractors accepted the validity of the automatic determination clause, but the point was not argued and the contractors' counsel conceded that they were under a contingent liability to the employer which was provable in winding up.

The second case, *Farley* v. *Housing & Commercial Developments Ltd* (1984), was also concerned with mutual dealings and again arose out of a contract in JCT 63 terms. Mr Justice Neill decided that the rules in section 31 of the Bankruptcy Act 1914, quoted above, mean that the position as between the parties to a building contract must be determined at the date of liquidation. This, amongst other things, precluded a subsequent purported assignment of the contractor's rights against the employer to the exclusion of any claims that the employer might have against the contractor.

Corruption by contractor

Clause 27.3 entitles the employer to determine the contractor's employment 'under this or any other contract' for corrupt practices, which are in any event a criminal offence under the Prevention of Corruption Acts 1889 to 1916 and section 117(2) of the Local Government Act 1972. It should be noted that this right to determine arises even if the contractor has no knowledge of the corrupt act of his agent or employee and the provision is cast in very wide terms. No special procedure is laid down but it is suggested that determination would be immediate on summary notice from the employer.

As noted earlier, this provision does not appear in the private editions of JCT 80 – presumably on policy grounds, since it is not thought that corrupt practices are any more prevalent in the public than in the private sector.

Procedures following determination

Clause 27.4 sets out the rights and duties of the parties following a valid determination of the contractor's employment under the earlier provisions of the clause and 'so long as [the contractor's employment] has not been re-instated and continued'. Despite the decision in *London Borough of Hounslow* v. *Twickenham Garden Developments Ltd* (1980), discussed on pages 36-7, it is the generally-held view that the contractor is bound to give up possession of the site if his employment is determined, even if the ground for determination or its validity is being disputed by the contractor. Interestingly, however, in IFC 84 (discussed at pages 78-87), the consequences of a determination under that provision have been spelled out with greater clarity and it is there stated (clause 7.4) that 'without prejudice to any arbitration or proceedings in which the validity of the determination is in issue' then, on determination, 'the contractor shall give up possession of the site of the works . . .'; and, for the avoidance of doubt, it is highly desirable that clause 27.4 should be similarly amended. It is also potentially defective in other respects.

Whatever the ground for determination, i.e. contractor's default, insolvency or corruption, clause 27.4.1 confers on the employer a right to engage another contractor to complete the works and confers upon the employer and the completion contractor a right to enter on the works. The same provision goes on to confer the right to use 'all temporary buildings, plant, tools, equipment, goods, and materials intended for, delivered to and placed on or adjacent to the works'.

Even though this provision is valid *inter partes*, it can only extend to goods, etc. which belong to the contractor in law. It cannot, therefore, confer rights on the employer in respect of goods which belong to third parties, e.g. because they have been sold to the contractor subject to a retention of title clause, or to plant, etc. which has been hired to him and to which he has no title in law. In such cases, therefore, the provision is defeated by the rights of third parties, as is exemplified by the now well-known case of *Dawber Williamson (Roofing) Ltd* v. *Humberside County Council* (1979).

In that case, a domestic sub-contractor delivered slates to site but was not paid for them by the contractor, although their value had been certified under the main contract and paid to the main contractor by the employer. The main contractor became insolvent and the sub-contractor successfully claimed payment for the slates from the employer when they were used for completion of the building. Title in the slates had not passed to the main contractor under the sub-contract.

In the Scottish case of *Archivent Sales & Developments Ltd* v. *Strathclyde Regional Council* (1984), a different conclusion was reached. Archivent had supplied ventilators to the main contractor under a contract substantially in JCT 63 form. The main contractor fixed the ventilators and was paid for them. He did not pay Archivent and went into liquidation.

The sale to the main contractor incorporated Archivent's terms of sale, one of which sensibly provided that 'until payment of the price in full is received by [us], the property in goods supplied . . . shall not pass to the customer'. Lord Mayfield held that the clause was effective to prevent title passing until payment.

However, the local authority employer successfully pleaded the provisions of section 25(1) of the Sale of Goods Act 1979. This states, in simple terms, that where a purchaser of goods obtains possession of them but then sells them on to a third party who receives them in good faith and without notice of any lien or other adverse right of the original seller, the third party will acquire a good title to the goods. Archivent were therefore unsuccessful in their claim. This reasoning rests on the basis that the nature of the contract between employer and main contractor amounts to a sale of the materials and therefore falls within the Sale of Goods Act 1979. It has been widely assumed in England that the contract is not one of sale of goods but one for work and materials, in which case section 25(1) of the 1979 Act could not apply. This assumption seems to underlie the decision in *Dawber Williamson*.

Clause 27.4.2 is important. It does *not* apply where the contractor's employment has been determined by actual insolvency involving bankruptcy or winding-up, but it applies to all other grounds for determination including the appointment of a receiver or manager. Each of its two paragraphs will be considered separately.

Assignment of supply and sub-contracts. Clause 27.4.2.1 requires the contractor to assign to the employer without payment the benefit of any contract of sale or sub-contract. This is conditioned on him being so requested by the employer *or* the architect within fourteen days of the date of determination. In practice the employer will often wish to make a further assignment of the relevant contracts to the completion contractor, hence the further provision that such further assignment will be subject to a right of reasonable objection by the supplier or sub-contractor concerned, though the reason for the inclusion of this provision is obscure since it seems to be unenforceable by the supplier or sub-contractor who is not a party to this contract.

The general law only allows the assignment of contractual rights; it does not permit the assignment of contractual duties: *Tolhurst* v. *Associated Portland Cement Manufacturers (1900) Ltd* (1902).

The advantage to the employer of clause 27.4.2.1 may be more apparent than real. Clause 19.4 of JCT 80 stipulates that it is to be a condition of any sub-contract with a domestic sub-contractor that his employment is determined immediately upon the determination for any reason of the main contractor's employment. This provision is reflected in clause 31 of BEC/FASS/CASEC Domestic Sub-contract DOM/1. A similar provision also appears in clause 31 of the JCT Standard Form of Nominated Sub-contract NSC/4/4a. It follows that there is little, if any, benefit to be assigned since under those sub-contracts there is no obligation upon the sub-contractor to carry out any further work.

Payments to suppliers or sub-contractors. Clause 27.4.2.2 empowers the employer to pay directly any supplier or sub-contractor for any materials or goods delivered or work done but not already paid for by the contractor. The wording is 'may pay' and not 'must pay', and is in addition to any obligation or discretion to pay nominated sub-contractors direct under other contractual provisions. If the employer does make such payments he has the right to deduct them from any sum due or to become due to the contractor or to recover the amount as a debt, i.e. by legal proceedings.

In practice this is an extremely valuable right in the employer's hands and is certainly a bargaining counter in negotiations to get the work completed. Clearly the employer should have regard to the amount which may be payable to the contractor upon determination, the retention in his hands, etc. As noted earlier, the provision does not apply where the ground for determination is true insolvency since there was considerable doubt whether it would be enforceable against the contractor's trustee in bankruptcy or liquidator: *British Eagle Ltd* v. *Air France* (1975).

Removal of contractor's plant, etc. from site. Clause 27.4.3 requires the contractor to remove from the site 'any temporary buildings, plant, tools, equipment, goods and materials belonging to or hired by him' upon being required in writing to do so by the architect. Since clause 27.4.1 (above) gives the employer a right to use such items for completion of the works, the contractor will presumably only be required to remove them when they are of no further use; but see the comment on page 57 about such items hired-in by the contractor.

The remainder of the sub-clause confers on the employer a power of sale in respect of such items if the contractor does not comply with the architect's written request within 'a reasonable time'. This right is naturally restricted to such items which belong in law to the contractor and does not extend, for instance, to plant hired by him or goods which are subject to hire-purchase agreements. The employer is exempted from any loss or damage to items sold should he exercise this power. The employer is to hold 'the proceeds less all costs incurred to the credit of the contractor'.

Some doubt has been cast on whether in fact an employer exercising this power of sale can pass a good title to a third party. We see no problem in this respect. If the goods, etc. are the property of the contractor in law and are not subject, for example, to a reservation of title in favour of the original seller there appears to be no difficulty since the employer clearly has the contractor's authority to sell them in these circumstances: Sale of Goods Act 1979, section 21.

In an insolvency situation, it is conceivable that the phrase 'holding the proceeds less all costs incurred to the credit of the contractor' might be the subject of argument, in the sense that the contractor's trustee or liquidator might require the employer to account for the proceeds in full: *Re Winter, ex parte Bolland* (1878). However, there is authority for saying that proceeds of such a sale may be used by the employer to set-off against his own debt because the property is in his hands with authority to sell it and convert it into money: *Re Caldicott* (1884). The question of set-off is fully discussed below, pages 61-3.

Settlement of accounts. Financial settlement following employer determination is covered by clause 27.4.4. The employer is relieved of the obligation to make any further payment to the contractor until after completion of the works and settlement of the account. The settlement must take place within a reasonable time of completion. Even where an amount has been certified prior to determination in favour of the contractor but has not been paid – whatever the reason for non-payment – the employer is still not obliged to honour the certificate.

No further certificate for payment to the defaulting contractor will be issued by the architect. Instead, the architect is to 'certify the amount of expenses properly incurred by the employer and the amount of any direct loss and/or damage caused to the employer by the determination'. This must be done within a reasonable time of completion and the employer is entitled to off-set the amount so certified by the architect against the balance to the defaulting contractor for the whole of the contract works on the assumption that he had completed them.

This means that, in addition to a final account being drawn up for the completion contractor, a final account will also have to be drawn up for the whole of the contract works as if the original contractor had completed them, including the effects of all variation instructions, etc. issued after the determination, the amounts of any direct loss and/or expense payable to the original contractor in respect of events before the determination, the notional amounts of all nominated sub-contractors' and suppliers' accounts as if they had continued with the works uninterrupted, etc. From this sum must be deducted amounts already paid to the defaulting contractor. The balance will represent 'the total amount which would have been payable on due completion in accordance with [the] contract'.

A full account must then be drawn up of all the employer's expenses incurred in achieving completion of the contract together with 'the amount of any direct loss and/or damage caused to him by the determination'. There are, therefore, two separate elements to the employer's entitlement as certified by the architect. The *expenses* element, it is submitted, would be the costs of having the work completed; for example, the amount payable to the replacement contractor under the completion contract and the amount of any professional fees incurred in connection with the completion contract which would have not otherwise have been incurred, such as the quantity surveyor's fees for drawing up the completion bills of quantities and possibly for negotiating a completion contract.

'Direct loss and/or damage' means

'. . . what is its usual, ordinary and proper meaning in the law: one has to ask whether any particular matter or items of loss or damage claimed has been caused by the particular matter. . . . If it has been caused by it, then one has to go on to see whether there has been some intervention or some other cause which prevents the loss or damage from being properly described as being the direct consequence of the [matter]': Mr Justice Megaw in *Wraight Ltd* v. *P.H. & T.* (*Holdings*) *Ltd* (1968).

In other words, it is the equivalent of damages at common law.

In the money claims clause of JCT 80, the expression 'direct loss and/or expense' is used to the same effect. We share the view expressed by Donald Keating QC (*Building Contracts*, 4th edition, page 359) that in the context of clause 27 the wording 'direct loss and/or expense' is not used so as 'to keep quite distinct the two elements which go to make up the architect's certificate under [clause 27.4.4] as allowable or payable to the employer subject to the credit in favour of the contractor.'

The direct loss and/or damage certified by the architect will include damages for delay in completion, costs of insuring the works before the completion contract is entered into, salaries of personnel such as clerks of works employed during the same period, costs of securing the site and of any necessary emergency works, and so on.

As regards liquidated damages, there can be little doubt that where the determination is under clause 27.1 the phrase 'without prejudice to any other rights or remedies which the employer may possess' preserves his right to claim liquidated damages for the delay in completion consequent upon the determination. The same phrase does not appear in clause 27.2 and clause 27.3, but it has been suggested that the phrase 'the total amount which would have been payable on due completion in accordance with this contract' in clause 27.4.4 would be the amount payable after deduction of liquidated damages. In any event it is suggested that when the date for completion of the original contract is reached, whether this is the original date for completion in the appendix or any extended date fixed by the architect in relation to delays on the original contract (including any further extensions which would have been due for events occurring after determination had the original contractor completed), the architect must issue his certificate of non-completion under clause 24.1 which is the condition precedent to the employer's right to liquidated damages.

The final settlement therefore comprises the off-setting of the employer's expenses and direct loss and/or damage as certified by the architect against the amount which would have been payable to the contractor had he completed the work. It is unlikely that this will result in any balance being due from the employer to the defaulting contractor, but if there is this is payable as a debt. This is important because, where the original contractor is insolvent, the employer is entitled to rely on statutory mutual dealings provisions which are of considerable practical utility where an employer has more than one contract with the insolvent contractor.

These rules are set out in section 31 of the Bankruptcy Act 1914 and section 317 of the Companies Act 1948. They apply to the case 'where there have been mutual credits, mutual debts or other mutual dealings . . .' In such a case 'an account shall be taken of what is due from one party to the other in respect of such mutual dealings . . .', i.e. the employer may set off an amount payable to a contractor on one contract against the amount payable by the contractor to him on another: see *Re Arthur Sanders Ltd* (1981) where one of the leading liquidators accepted that the employer was entitled to set-off retention held on one contract against a substantial balance payable by the contractor on another. See also *Willment Bros Ltd* v. *North-West Thames Regional Health Authority* (1984) and *Farley* v. *Housing & Commercial Developments Ltd* (1984) discussed on pages 55-6. The significance is, of course, that any amount payable to the employer on the settlement of accounts would simply form an unsecured claim in the insolvency and the employer would in fact be unlikely to obtain any payment at all. It is therefore much in his interests to set-off if it is possible to do so.

The provision entitling the employer to recover his expenses and direct loss and/or damage is of particular importance where the ground for determination is the contractor's insolvency. In the absence of this express provision, which is binding upon a trustee in bankruptcy or liquidator, the employer would not be entitled to recover for these items because insolvency is not a breach of contract.

The following is a summary of the major items to which the employer may be entitled on determination:

Heading	Comment
1 Expenses	
1.1 Amount payable to completion contractor.	As certified by the architect on the completion contract.
1.2 Fees payable in respect of the completion contract.	That is, additional fees which would not otherwise have been payable.
2 Loss and/or damage	
2.1 Costs of securing the site.	The employer must take reasonable steps to secure the site, e.g. employment of watchmen or security cover while the site is unoccupied.
2.2 Costs of any emergency work.	That is, protection of work done or work necessary to ensure the stability of the uncompleted work.
2.3 Costs of remedying any defects in the original work.	This is loss and/or damage because otherwise the remedial work would have been done free of charge by the contractor.
2.4 Cost of insuring the works while unoccupied.	Contractor's insurance will cease on determination. If the employer originally insured, there will no doubt be an additional premium payable.
2.5 Legal costs in connection with the determination and associated professional fees.	Competent legal and professional advice is essential.
2.6 Costs of disposing of contractor's plant, etc.	Less proceeds of sale. Often a credit in favour of contractor.

2.7 Salaries of employer's staff in connection with the contract during period of delay.	See *Tate & Lyle Ltd* v. *GLC* (1982).
2.8 Expenses associated with 2.7.	E.g. accommodation, travel, subsistence, etc.
2.9 Loss of use and occupation.	This would include loss of foreseeable profit if the contract is for a commercial building, E.g. office premises for let.
2.10 Temporary accommodation during period of delay in completion.	E.g. hotel bills, storage and removal costs, etc. in the case of a domestic dwelling.
2.11 Site charges which become employer's responsibility.	E.g. rates.
2.12 Extra payments to directly employed contractors due to delay.	
2.13 Additional interest on capital employed or finance charges.	
2.14 Inflation costs.	If not taken into account in completion contract costs.
2.15 Liquidated damages.	Where claimed, these may be deemed to cover some of the foregoing. There must be no duplication.

Clause 28 – Determination by the contractor
In the private editions clause 28 reads:

'28 **Determination by Contractor**
Acts etc. giving ground for determination of employment by Contractor

28.1 Without prejudice to any other rights and remedies which the Contractor may possess, if

28.1 .1 the Employer does not pay the amount properly due to the Contractor on any certificate (otherwise than as a result of the operation of the VAT Agreement) within 14 days from the issue of that certificate and continues such default for 7 days after receipt by registered post or recorded delivery of a notice from the Contractor stating that notice of determination under clause 28 will be served if payment is not made within 7 days from receipt thereof; or

28.1 .2 the Employer interferes with or obstructs the issue of any certificate due under this Contract; or

28.1 .3 the carrying out of the whole or substantially the whole of the uncompleted Works (other than the execution of work required under clause 17) is suspended for a continuous period of the length named in the Appendix by reason of:

28.1 .3 .1 *force majeure*; or

.3 .2 loss or damage to the Works (unless caused by the negligence of the Contractor, his servants or agents or of any sub-contractor, his servants or agents) occasioned by any one or more of the clause 22 Perils; or

.3 .3 civil commotion; or

.3 .4 Architect's instructions issued under clause 2.3, 13.2 or 23.2 unless caused by reason of some negligence or default of the Contractor; or

.3 .5 the Contractor not having received in due time necessary instructions, drawings, details or levels from the Architect for which he specifically applied in writing provided that such application was made on a date which having regard to the Completion Date was neither unreasonably distant from nor unreasonably close to the date on which it was necessary for him to receive the same; or

.3 .6 delay in the execution of work not forming part of this Contract by the Employer himself or by persons employed or otherwise engaged by the Employer as referred to in clause 29 or the failure to execute such work or delay in the supply by the Employer of materials and goods which the Employer has agreed to provide for the Works or the failure so to supply; or

.3 .7 the opening up for inspection of any work covered up or the testing of any of the work, materials or goods in accordance with clause 8.3 (including making good in consequence of such opening up or testing), unless the inspection or test showed that the work, materials or goods were not in accordance with this Contract;

28.1 .4 the Employer becomes bankrupt or makes a composition or arrangement with his creditors or has a winding-up order made or (except for the purposes of an amalgamation or reconstruction) has a resolution for voluntary winding-up passed or a provisional liquidator, receiver or manager of his business or undertaking is duly appointed, or possession is taken, by or on behalf of the holders of any debentures secured by a floating charge, of any property comprised in or subject to the floating charge;

then the Contractor may thereupon by notice by registered post or recorded delivery to the Employer or Architect forthwith determine the employment of the Contractor under this Contract; provided that such notice shall not be given unreasonably or vexatiously.

Determination of employment by Contractor – rights and duties of Employer and Contractor

28.2 Upon such determination, then without prejudice to the accrued rights or remedies of either party or to any liability of the classes mentioned in clause 20 which may accrue either before the Contractor or any sub-contractors shall have removed his or their temporary buildings, plant, tools, equipment, goods or materials or by reason of his or their so removing the same, the following shall be the respective rights and liabilities of the Contractor and the Employer:

28.2 .1 the Contractor shall with all reasonable dispatch and in such manner and with such precautions as will prevent injury, death or damage of the classes in respect of which before the date of determination he was liable to idemnify the Employer under clause 20 remove from the site all his temporary buildings, plant, tools, equipment, goods and materials and shall give facilities for his sub-contractors to do the same, but subject always to the provisions of clause 28.2.2.4;

28.2 .2 after taking into account amounts previously paid under this Contract the Contractor shall be paid by the Employer:

.2 .1 the total value of work completed at the date of determination, such value to be computed as if it were a valuation in respect of the amounts to be stated as due in an Interim Certificate issued under clause 30.1 but after taking account of any amounts referred to in clauses 28.2.2.3 to .6;

.2 .2 the total value of work begun and executed but not completed at the date of determination, the value being ascertained in accordance with clause 13.5 as if such work were a Variation required by the Architect under clause 13.2 but after taking account of any amounts referred to in clauses 28.2.2.3 to .6;

.2 .3 any sum ascertained in respect of direct loss and/or expense under clauses 26 and 34.3 (whether ascertained before or after the date of determination);

.2 .4 the cost of materials or goods properly ordered for the Works for which the Contractor shall have paid or for which the Contractor is legally bound to pay, and on such payment by the Employer any materials or goods so paid for shall become the property of the Employer;

.2 .5 the reasonable cost of removal under clause 28.2.1;

.2 .6 any direct loss and/or damage caused to the Contractor or to any Nominated Sub-Contractor by the determination.

28.2 .3 The Employer shall inform the Contractor in writing which part or parts of the amount paid or payable under clause 28.2.2 is or are fairly and reasonably attributable to any Nominated Sub-Contractor and shall so inform each Nominated Sub-Contractor in writing.

The local authority editions differ in that clause 28.1.4 is omitted, presumably on the assumption that local authorities do not get into financial difficulties. This assumption may not always be entirely justified in the light of current political events!

Default by employer

Clause 28.1 specifies certain defaults by the employer which entitle the contractor to determine his own employment under the contract by following the procedure specified in the clause. Confusingly, it adds other grounds which are the fault of neither party.

Failure to pay on certificates. Clause 30.1.1.1 states that the contractor is entitled to payment of amounts certified by the architect as due to him within fourteen days of the issue of the certificate. Clause 28.1.1 provides that if payment is not made within that time the contractor may issue a notice stating that he will determine his own employment unless payment is made within seven days of receipt of the notice. The notice must be served by registered post or recorded delivery and it is advisable for the contractor to ask the post office for advice of delivery so that he may know the date of receipt. The valid service of this preliminary notice is a condition precedent to the contractor's right to determine.

The default consists in not paying 'the amount properly due to the contractor on any certificate' in due time. It must be noted that clause 30.1.1.2 gives the employer the right to deduct certain sums from the amount stated as due in the certificate, e.g. liquidated damages if appropriate, payment of premiums where the contractor has failed to insure the works if he is required to do so by the contract, etc. Clause 30.1.1.3 requires the employer to notify the contractor in writing where he has exercised any such right. Consequently the 'amount properly due' is not necessarily the sum stated on the certificate, but that amount less any deductions properly made and duly notified.

This valuable right – which the contractor would not have at common law – emphasises the importance of cash flow under this contract. The contract has a right to be paid on time and it is for the employer so to arrange his financial affairs that payment is made in due time and in strict accordance with the provisions of the contract. Certain local authorities and other large organisations are quite notorious in this respect.

Interference with certificates. Interference with or obstruction of certificates by the employer can be a difficult ground to establish. The important point is that the architect must act independently and the independent exercise of his professional duty must not be interfered with by or on behalf of the employer. Conduct which would fall within this clause, for example, would be where a local authority architect declined to issue a certificate pending the decision of one of the council's committees, or where work is funded by some external agency, not a party to the contract, and that agency's consent is required.

In *R.B. Burden Ltd* v. *Swansea Corporation* (1957) the House of Lords considered the meaning to be attached to this ground of determination under an earlier version of the contract. Lord Tucker said:

'I think, without attempting an exhaustive enumeration of the acts of the employer which can amount to obstruction or interference, that the clause is designed to meet such conduct of the employer as refusing to allow the architect to go on to the site for the purpose of giving his certificate, or directing the architect as to the amount for which he is to give his certificate or as to the decision which he should arrive at on some matter within the sphere of his independent duty. I do not think that negligence or errors or omissions by someone who, at the request, or with the consent, of the architect is appointed to assist him in arriving at the correct figure to insert in his certificate can amount to interference. Interference, to my mind, connotes intermeddling with something which is not one's business, rather than acting negligently in the performance of some duty properly undertaken. Nor do I think that the conduct found against [the quantity surveyor] obstructed the issue of a certificate; it may have resulted in the issue of a certificate for a smaller sum than that which was due, but that is, in my view, a matter for arbitration under clause 27 and not a ground for repudiation under clause 20. I think the use by the learned official referee of the words "the sort of certificate" to which the appellants were entitled shows the difference between the interpretation which he put on these words and that which I have endeavoured to suggest as correct.'

Suspension of the works for a continuous period. This ground in fact comprises seven sub-grounds not all of which are the fault of the employer or his architect, and it would have been better had these sub-grounds been more clearly distinguished. The first three of them are completely outside the control of either party and there is no reason for including them in this clause in light of the consequences which follow.

Before clause 28.1.3 becomes operative, three conditions must be satisfied:

(1) The carrying out of the whole or substantially the whole of the uncompleted works must be suspended. This does not apply to the rectification of defects arising during the defects liability period under clause 17 and so even if such works are suspended for the appropriate period this is not a ground for determination.

(2) The suspension must be for the continuous period specified in the appendix. Usually this period is one month except in relation to loss or damage occasioned by the perils referred to in clause 22, when the period of time is three months. It is essential that these periods are stated in the appendix since they are not otherwise assumed. If periods are not so stated this provision becomes inoperative.

(3) The suspension must be caused by one or more of seven specified events. The first three of these events are outside the control of either party; the next three are defaults by the employer or those for whom he is vicariously responsible in law; and the seventh event is the exercise of a right by the architect on behalf of the employer which may nevertheless cause a suspension of the works. Some comment on each of these events is appropriate.

Force majeure. This is a French law term which is wider in its meaning than the common law term 'act of God' which is an overwhelming superhuman event: *Oakley* v. *Portsmouth & Ryde Steam Packet Co.* (1856). In fact, under the present contract the term *force majeure* has a restricted meaning because many matters such as war, strikes, fire and exceptional weather are expressly dealt with elsewhere in the contract. There appear to be no reported cases dealing with the matter in the context of JCT contracts, and the usually-quoted English authority is *Lebeaupin* v. *Crispin* (1920) where Mr Justice McCardie accepted that:

'This term is used with reference to all circumstances independent of the will of man and which it is not in his power to control. . . . Thus war, inundations and epidemics are cases of *force majeure*; it has even been decided that a strike of workmen constitutes a case of *force majeure*. . . . [But] a *force majeure* clause should be construed in each case with a close attention to the words which precede or follow it and with due regard to the nature and general terms of the contract. The effect of the clause may vary with each [contract].'

In fact, as used in the JCT contracts and other construction contracts the term is of limited effect and decisions on the meaning of the term when used in other types of contract are of little assistance. The case of *Matsoukis* v. *Priestman & Co.* (1915) may be of assistance. It was held there that the general coal strike of 1912 and the breakdown of machinery were within the term but that it did not cover bad weather, football matches or a funeral.

Loss or damage caused by clause 22 perils. These are the insurable risks defined in clause 1.3 as follows:

'fire, lightning, explosion, storm, tempest, flood, bursting or overflowing of water tanks, apparatus or pipes, earthquake, aircraft and other aerial devices or articles dropped therefrom, riot and civil commotion (excluding any loss or damage caused by ionising radiations or contamination by radioactivity from any nuclear fuel or from any nuclear waste from the combustion of nuclear fuel, radioactive toxic explosive or other hazardous properties of any explosive nuclear assembly or nuclear component thereof, pressure waves caused by aircraft or other aerial devices travelling at sonic or supersonic speeds)'

While the occurrence of such loss or damage is a ground for extension of time under clause 25.4.3 irrespective of their cause, their occurrence is only a ground for determination if they are not 'caused by the negligence of the contractor, his servants or agents or of any sub-contractor, his servants or agents', and it is submitted that if caused by the negligence of sub-sub-contractors the exclusion will still apply despite *Manchester City Council* v. *Fram Gerrard Ltd* (1974). In *Petrofina (UK) Ltd* v. *Magnaload Ltd* (1983), Mr Justice Lloyd held that a 'contractor's all risks' policy extended to cover an accident caused by the negligence of sub-sub-contractors, and the *Fram Gerrard* case involved the interpretation of an indemnity clause. Such clauses are always interpreted strictly, and the interpretation of Mr Justice Lloyd is to be preferred in the present context on grounds of commercial convenience and reality.

Civil commotion. This phrase is 'used to describe a situation which is more serious than a riot but not as serious as civil war: *Levy* v. *Assicurazioni Generali* (1940). The essential element is one of turbulence or tumult, though it is not necessary to show that the acts were done at the instigation of an outside organisation': *A Building Contract Dictionary* by Vincent Powell-Smith and David Chappell (1985).

Specified architect's instructions. Three types of instruction are listed:

Clause 2.3 – Discrepancies or divergences between drawings, etc.
Clause 13.2 – Variations or provisional sum expenditure.
Clause 23.2 – Postponement of work.

There is a distinction between 'the works' and 'work'. Under JCT 80 'the works' means either the work contracted for (as in Article 1), or the site, as in clause 8.5. In contrast, 'work' means 'work carried out under the contract' as in clause 13.1.1.1.

Late architect's instructions. The limitations should be noted; the contractor must have made a specific application to the architect in writing at the correct time. For a full discussion of this problem area see the present authors' *Building Contract Claims*, page 57.

Work not forming part of the contract and supply of materials, etc. by employer. Clearly, where the employer has undertaken to have work not forming part of the contract done by himself or by others, or has undertaken to supply materials or goods for the works, and there is a delay, this is the employer's responsibility in law.

Opening-up for inspection or testing. Since this is the exercise of a right specifically given to the architect under clause 8.3 it seems strange that it should be considered grounds for determination. However, in practice it is highly unlikely that a delay for so long as one month would arise from the architect's exercise of this power.

Insolvency of employer. Although not strictly a default, for the purposes of clarity clause 28.1.4 (which appears in the private editions only) is best dealt with here.

Unlike determination on grounds of the contractor's insolvency, the determination is not automatic, but is conditioned on notice served by the contractor at his discretion. In general, our commentary on pages 52-6 applies here also.

Procedure
The procedure for determination is straightforward. It is effected by the contractor serving notice on the employer *or* the architect by registered post or recorded delivery. No particular form of notice is specified but it is suggested that it should be drafted with care and refer specifically to the cause of determination in precise terms. In the case of determination for non-payment (clause 28.1.1) there should be reference to the warning notice. The determination takes effect 'forthwith'.

For comments on the 'not . . . unreasonably or vexatiously' proviso and on service of notices generally, see pages 50-52.

Procedures following determination
The post-determination procedures and rights and duties of the parties are laid down in clause 28.2. The whole clause is said to be 'without prejudice to the accrued rights or remedies of either party' which means that the parties' rights prior to determination remain fully in existence, e.g. the right of the employer to have defective work made good at the contractor's expense. Its operation is also without prejudice 'to any liability of the classes mentioned in clause 20 which may accrue either before the contractor or any sub-contractors shall have removed his or their temporary buildings, [etc.] or by reason of his or their removing the same'. This refers to the contractor's liabilities and indemnity to the employer in respect of personal injury or injury to property arising out of the carrying out of the works.

Subject to this, when the contractor's employment under the contract is validly determined the provisions of clause 28.2 govern the relationship of the parties.

Removal of plant, etc. As discussed previously (see page 57), the contractor's licence to occupy the site comes to an end on determination. Clause 28.2.1 obliges him 'with all reasonable dispatch' to remove from the site all his temporary buildings, plant, tools, equipment, goods and materials and to give all his sub-contractors facilities to do the same. This he must do reasonably and taking all necessary precautions to prevent injury, death or damage to persons or property. This does not, of course, extend to materials which already have become the employer's property through payment or which the employer has a right to purchase: see clause 28.2.2.4 (below).

Payment. The contractor's rights to payment are extensive and are detailed in clause 28.2.2. Briefly, they are as follows:

(1) Total value of work completed at date of determination.
(2) Total value of work begun but not completed at that date, valued as if it were a variation under clause 13.
(3) Any direct loss and/or expense recoverable by the contractor under clauses 26 and 34.3.
(4) Cost of materials or goods properly ordered for the works for which the contractor has paid or is legally bound to pay. On payment, such items becomes the property of the employer.
(5) Reasonable costs of removal of temporary buildings, plant, etc. under clause 28.2.1.
(6) Any direct loss and/or damage caused to the contractor or any nominated sub-contractor by the determination.

The meaning of 'direct loss and/or damage' is discussed on page 62, and the case of *Wraight Ltd* v. *P.H. & T. (Holdings) Ltd* (1968) is particularly relevant since it establishes the contractor's right to recover, *inter alia*, the loss of profit and overhead contribution which he would have received had the contract proceeded to completion.

Both items (5) and (6) would seem extremely unfair to the employer where the determination has arisen because of events which are outside the control of either party, *viz. force majeure*, damage by insurable risks and civil commotion, or even because of the exercise of a right to open up and inspect the works. In our view there is no justification for allowing the contractor to recover what in effect amounts to damages for breach of contract in these circumstances. It seems extraordinary to us that the Joint Contracts Tribunal should have permitted this grossly unfair provision to remain in JCT 80 in face of sustained and authoritative criticism.

In item (6) it is sometimes remarked that there is no express reference to any direct loss and/or damage sustained by domestic sub-contractors as a result of the determination. It is an interesting feature of the BEC/FASS/CASEC Domestic Sub-contract DOM/1

1980, which is designed for use in conjunction with JCT 80, that clause 31 – which provides for the automatic determination of the domestic sub-contractor's employment should the main contractor's employment under the main contract be determined – carefully omits any reference to a domestic sub-contractor's entitlement to direct loss and/or damage arising from the determination. There is thus no obligation upon the contractor to make any payment of this kind to any domestic sub-contractor employed under DOM/1.

Direct loss and/or damage caused to any nominated sub-contractor is expressly included and there is a corresponding provision in the JCT Standard Form of Nominated Sub-contract (NSC/4 or NSC/4a) in clause 31.2.

Contractually the architect has no role to play in settling the amounts due to the contractor, but in practice both he and the quantity surveyor will no doubt be involved. The terms of clause 28.2.3 referring to payments to nominated sub-contractors require the employer himself to inform the contractor and any nominated sub-contractor in writing of the amounts 'fairly and reasonably attributable to any nominated sub-contractor' in the settlement under clause 28.2.2. This does not amount to certification and gives rise to no entitlement to direct payment on the part of nominated sub-contractors in the event of non-payment by the main contractor.

Clause 32 – Outbreak of hostilities
This clause reads as follows:

'32 **Outbreak of hostilities [u]**

Notice of determination of the Contractor's employment
32.1 If during the currency of this Contract there shall be an outbreak of hostilities (whether war is declared or not) in which the United Kingdom shall be involved on a scale involving the general mobilisation of the armed forces of the Crown, then either the Employer or the Contractor may at any time by notice by registered post or recorded delivery to the other, forthwith determine the employment of the Contractor under this Contract:
Provided that such notice shall not be given
32.1 .1 before the expiration of 28 days from the date on which the order is given for general mobilisation as aforesaid, or
32.1 .2 after Practical Completion of the Works unless the Works or any part thereof shall have sustained war damage as defined in clause 33.4.

Protective work etc.

32.2   The Architect may within 14 days after notice under clause 32.1 shall have been given or received by the Employer issue instructions to the Contractor requiring the execution of such protective work as shall be specified therein and/or the continuation of the Works up to points of stoppage to be specified therein, and the Contractor shall comply with such instructions as if the notice of determination had not been given. Provided that if the Contractor shall for reasons beyond his control be prevented from completing the work to which the said instructions relate within 3 months from the date on which the instructions were issued, he may abandon such work.

Payment

32.3   Upon the expiration of 14 days from the date on which a notice of determination shall have been given or received by the Employer under clause 32.1 or where works are required by the Architect under clause 32.2 upon completion or abandonment as the case may be of any such works, the provisions of clause 28.2 (except clause 28.2.2.6) shall apply and the Contractor shall also be paid by the Employer the value of any work executed pursuant to instructions given under clause 32.2, the value being ascertained in accordance with clause 13.5 as if such work were a Variation required by an instruction of the Architect under clause 13.2.

---

[u] The parties hereto in the event of the outbreak of hostilities may at any time by agreement between them make such further or other arrangements as they may think fit to meet the circumstances.'

For this clause to operate there must be an outbreak of hostilities 'involving the general mobilisation of the armed forces of the Crown'. The clause would not, therefore, operate in such cases as the United Kingdom's involvement in the Korean War or the Falklands Islands hostilities neither of which involved 'general mobilisation'.

It entitles either party to determine the employment of the contractor forthwith by notice served on the other by registered post or recorded delivery. There are two provisos:

● The notice cannot be given until twenty-eight days have expired from the date of the general mobilisation order; *or*
● Until practical completion of the works unless they or part of them have sustained war damage as defined in clause 33.4.

Clause 32.2 empowers the architect to instruct the contractor to carry out protective work and/or to continue the works up to a convenient point of stoppage. Such an instruction must be given within fourteen days after the determination notice shall have been given or received by the employer. If for reasons beyond his control, e.g. by reason of his workforce having been called up or materials not being available, the contractor is prevented from completing such works within three months of the date on which the architect's instruction was issued, the contractor is authorised to abandon it.

Payment on determination is governed by clause 28.2 (discussed on pages 74-5), except that the contractor is not entitled to recover any direct loss and/or damage caused by the determination. Any work carried out pursuant to an architect's instruction under clause 32.2 is to be paid for as if it were a variation under clause 13.2.

The provisions of clause 28.2 apply as from the expiry of fourteen days from the date on which a determination notice was given or received by the employer or upon completion or abandonment of any work ordered by the architect under clause 32.2.

The footnote to clause 32 points out that the parties may, if they wish, make an agreement for further or other arrangements.

Other versions of JCT 80

The foregoing commentary has been written around the 1980 edition of the JCT Standard Form with Quantities. The provisions in the Standard Form without Quantities are identical, and those in the Standard Form with Approximate Quantities differ only in that references to clause 13 are changed to clause 14.

In the Fixed Fee Form of Prime Cost Contract 1967 issue, October 1976 revision, the determination clauses are:

Clause 16 (B)(b)(i) – Insurance determination.
Clause 21 – Determination by the employer.
Clause 22 – Determination by the contractor.
Clause 28 – Outbreak of hostilities.

Essentially the provisions are the same as those in JCT 80 with Quantities, except that the terms of payment in clauses 22 and 28 are altered to refer to prime cost rather than to valuation as a variation. Moreover, in clause 21(3)(c) – which corresponds to JCT 80, clause 27.4.3 – the employer is given a right to 'remove and sell any such property of *or so far as belonging* to the contractor', the italicised phrase not appearing in JCT 80. The distinction is of no practical significance.

The Intermediate Form 1984 (IFC 84)

The provisions of IFC 84 are similar but not identical to those of JCT 80, the main difference being that the contractor is not entitled to recover 'direct loss and/or damage' for determination consequent upon *force majeure*, loss or damage to the works caused by the specified perils or by civil commotion.

The provisions for determination, each of which will be considered in turn, are:

Clause 6.3C.2(b) – Insurance of existing structures and the works by the employer – determination by either party.

Clause 7 – Determination. This is sub-divided into determination by the employer (clauses 7.1 to 7.4), determination by contractor (7.5 to 7.7) and determination by employer or contractor (7.8 to 7.9).

Clause 6.3C.2(b) – Insurance of existing structures and the works by the employer – determination by either party

Apart from the clause numbering and clause references, this provision corresponds exactly to clause 22C.2 of JCT 80, and the discussion of that clause on pages 40 to 42 applies equally to clause 6.3C.2(b).

Clause 7.2 to 7.3 – Determination by employer

These clauses read as follows:

'**Determination by Employer**

7.1 Without prejudice to any other rights or remedies which the Employer may possess, if the Contractor shall make default in any one or more of the following respects:

(a) if without reasonable cause he wholly suspends the carrying out of the Works before completion thereof; or

(b) if he fails to proceed regularly and diligently with the Works; or

(c) if he refuses or persistently neglects to comply with a written notice from the Architect/the Supervising Officer requiring him to remove defective work or improper materials or goods and by such refusal or neglect the Works are materially affected; or

(d) if he fails to comply with the provisions of either clause

3.2 (*Sub-contracting*),

3.3 (*Named persons*) or

5.7 (*Fair Wages*);

and if the Contractor shall continue such default for 14 days after receipt of a notice by registered post or recorded delivery specifying the default or shall at any time thereafter repeat such default (whether previously repeated or not), then the Employer may thereupon by notice by registered post or recorded delivery determine the employment of the Contractor under this Contract: provided that such notice shall not be given unreasonably or vexatiously.

Contractor becoming bankrupt etc.

7.2 If the Contractor becomes bankrupt or makes a composition or arrangement with his creditors or has a winding up order made or (except for the purposes of amalgamation or reconstruction) a resolution for voluntary winding up is passed or a provisional liquidator, receiver or manager of his business or undertaking is duly appointed, or possession is taken, by or on behalf of the holders of any debentures secured by a floating charge, of any property comprised in or subject to the floating charge, the employment of the Contractor under this Contract shall be forthwith automatically determined but the said employment may be reinstated and continued if the Employer and the Contractor, his trustee in bankruptcy, liquidator, provisional liquidator, receiver or manager as the case may be shall so agree.

Corruption: determination by Employer

7.3 Where the Employer is a local authority, he shall be entitled to determine the employment of the Contractor under this or any other contract, if the Contractor shall have offered or given or agreed to give to any person any gift or consideration of any kind as an inducement or reward for doing or forbearing to do or for having done or forborne to do any action in relation to the obtaining or execution of this or any other contract with the Employer or for showing or forbearing to show favour or disfavour to any person in relation to this or any other contract with the Employer, or if the like act shall have been done by any person employed by the Contractor or acting on his behalf (whether with or without the knowledge of the Contractor), or if in relation to this or any other contract with the Employer the Contractor or any person employed by him or acting on his behalf shall have committed any offence under the Prevention of Corruption Acts 1889 to 1916, or shall have given any fee or reward the receipt of which is an offence under sub-section (2) of section 117 of the Local Government Act 1972 or any re-enactment thereof.'

Clause 7.1 differs from JCT 80, clause 27.1 in five respects:

(1) Failure by the contractor to comply with the provisions of clause 3.3 relating to 'named persons as subcontractors' is an additional ground for determination.
(2) There is no requirement that the warning notice specifying the default be issued by the architect. As the provision is worded, the notice could be issued either by the architect or the employer or, indeed, by someone else duly authorised to act on the employer's behalf, e.g. a solicitor.
(3) While clause 27.1 or JCT 80 gives the employer a period of ten days after the expiry of the warning notice period, or a subsequent repetition of the default, IFC 84, clause 7.1 requires the employer to issue the notice 'thereupon', i.e., it is suggested, immediately or within a very short time. Failure to do so might well amount to a waiver by the employer of his rights under the clause.
(4) Clause 7.1 does not state that the employment of the contractor shall terminate 'forthwith', but the change in wording appears to have no legal significance since the contractor's employment under the contract is determined on receipt of the notice.
(5) Perhaps unintentionally, only unauthorised sub-letting (as opposed to both assignment and sub-letting under JCT 80) is a ground for invoking the determination procedure.

Clause 7.2 – Contractor's insolvency
Apart from minor drafting changes – which have no legal significance – this is a verbatim repetition of JCT 80, clause 27.2.

Clause 7.3 – Corruption
This clause is an exact parallel of its counterpart in JCT 80, to which readers are referred: see pages 56-7.

Clause 7.4 – Consequences of employer determination
Clause 7.4 provides as follows:

'**Consequences of determination under clause 7.1 – 7.3**

7.4   Without prejudice to any arbitration or proceedings in which the validity of the determination is in issue in the event of the determination of the employment of the Contractor under clause 7.1,

7.2, or 7.3 and so long as that employment has not been reinstated or continued then:

(a) the Contractor shall give up possession of the site of the Works subject to the orderly compliance of the Contractor with any instruction of the Architect/the Supervising Officer under the following paragraph;

(b) as and when so instructed in writing by the Architect/the Supervising Officer the Contractor shall remove from the Works any temporary buildings, plant, tools, equipment, goods and materials belonging to or hired by him, and if within a reasonable time after any such requirement has been made the Contractor has not complied therewith then the Employer may (but without being responsible for any loss or damage) remove and sell any such property of the Contractor, holding the proceeds less all costs to the credit of the Contractor;

(c) the Employer may employ and pay other persons to carry out and complete the Works and he or they may (whether or not the Contractor has complied with the requirement to give up possession of the site of the Works) enter upon the Works and use all temporary buildings, plant, tools, equipment, goods and materials intended for, delivered to and placed on or adjacent to the Works, and may purchase all materials and goods necessary for the carrying out and completion of the Works;

(d) until after completion of the Works the Employer shall not be bound to make any further payment to the Contractor but upon such completion and the verification within a reasonable time of the accounts therefor the following matters shall be set out in an account drawn up by the Employer:

− the amount of expenses and direct loss and/or damage caused to the Employer by the determination including the payments made to other persons to carry out and complete the Works;

− the amount paid to the Contractor before the date of determination;

and if the total of such amounts exceeds or is less than the total amount which would have been payable on due completion in accordance with the Contract, the difference shall be a debt payable by the Contractor to the Employer or by the Employer to the Contractor as the case may be.'

Much of our commentary on clause 27.4 of JCT 80 (see pages 57-64) is equally relevant to this provision, but it is necessary to draw attention to certain significant differences. These are as follows:

(1) All the provisions of this clause are stated to be without prejudice to any arbitration or other proceedings in which the validity of the determination is in issue. This means that even if the contractor is challenging the determination of his employment he must nonetheless comply with the provisions of clause

7.4. It governs the rights and duties of the parties 'so long as [the contractor's] employment has not been reinstated or continued'.

(2) The contractor is bound to give up possession of the site to the employer, his licence to occupy it having been determined. This provision overcomes the difficulties thrown up by *London Borough of Hounslow* v. *Twickenham Garden Developments Ltd* (1970): see pages 36 and 57.

(3) The contractor's obligation to give up possession of the site is subject to his duty to comply with architect's written instructions requiring the removal of temporary buildings, etc. from the site.

(4) The employer's power to engage completion contractors and its associated right of entry is expressed to be exercisable 'whether or not the contractor has complied with the requirement to give up possession of the site . . .'

(5) There is no express requirement, as there is in JCT 80, clause 27.4.2, for the contractor to assign to the employer the benefits of sub-contracts and contracts of sale nor any express right of the employer to pay suppliers and sub-contractors for work already done.

(6) On settlement, there is no requirement for the architect to certify the amount of expenses and loss and/or damage incurred by the employer. Instead the employer is required to draw up a settlement account showing the amount of his expenses and direct loss and/or damage and the amount paid to the contractor before the date of determination. The difference is administrative and the employer's entitlements are identical to the corresponding provisions of clause 27.4.4 of JCT 80: see pages 61-2.

Clause 7.5 – Determination by contractor
This provision is a very sensible re-write of JCT 80, clause 28.1 and provides as follows:

'**Determination by Contractor**

7.5.1 Without prejudice to any other rights and remedies which the Contractor may possess the Contractor may give to the Employer a notice by registered post or recorded delivery specifying a matter referred to in this clause 7.5. If the Employer shall continue to make default in respect of the matter specified for 14 days after receipt of such notice or shall at any time thereafter repeat such default (whether previously repeated or not), then the Contractor may thereupon by notice by registered post or recorded delivery determine the employment of the Contractor under this Contract;

provided that such notice shall not be given unreasonably or vexatiously.

The matters referred to in the preceding paragraph are:

7.5.1   the Employer does not pay an amount properly due to the Contractor under clause

4.2 (*Interim Payments*),

4.3 (*Interim Payment on Practical Completion*)

or

4.6 (*Final certificate*);

7.5.2   the Employer interferes with or obstructs the issue of any certificate due under the Contract;

7.5.3   the carrying out of the whole or substantially the whole of the uncompleted Works (other than the execution of the work required under clause 2.10 (*Defects liability*)) is suspended for a continuous period of one month by reason of:

(a) the Architect's/the Supervising Officer's instructions issued under clauses

1.4 (*Inconsistencies*),

3.6 (*Variation*) or

3.15 (*Postponement*)

unless caused by reason of some negligence or default of the Contractor; or

(b) the Contractor not having received in due time necessary instructions, drawings, details or levels from the Architect/the Supervising Officer for which he specifically applied in writing provided that such application was made on a date which having regard to the Date for Completion or to any extended time fixed under clause 2.3 (*Extension of time*) was neither unreasonably distant from nor unreasonably close to the date on which it was necessary for him to receive the same; or

(c) delay in the execution of work not forming part of this Contract by the Employer himself or by persons employed or otherwise engaged by the Employer as referred to in clause 3.11 or the failure to execute such work or delay in the supply by the Employer of materials and goods which the Employer has agreed to supply for the Works or the failure so to supply; or

(d) failure of the Employer to give in due time ingress to or egress from the site of the Works or any part thereof through or over any land, buildings, way or passage adjoining or connected with the site and in the possession and control of the Employer, in accordance with the Contract Documents after receipt by the Architect/the Supervising Officer of such notice, if any, as the Contractor is required to give such ingress or egress as otherwise agreed between the Architect/the Supervising Officer and the Contractor.'

Note: There is clearly a printing error in this clause as set out in IFC 84 since the words 'or failure of the Employer' should appear before 'to give' in the penultimate line.

Our commentary on clause 28.1 of JCT 80 (pages 67-9) is of relevance to this provision, but attention is drawn to the following significant differences between the two clauses:

(1) The employer is given a period of fourteen days in which to cure his default in each case, in contrast to JCT 80, clause 28.1 where this applies only in the case of failure to pay.
(2) The six specified events are *all* defaults by the employer or by those for whom he is responsible in law.
(3) As regards the four items listed in clause 7.5.3, the period of suspension needed to activate the clause is fixed at one month instead of being at the discretion of the parties.
(4) Suspension of work due to opening up for inspection or testing of work and materials is, quite rightly, not a ground for determination.
(5) A fresh cause of suspension is listed in clause 7.5.3(d) (see below).
(6) The determination notice, as well as the warning notice, is to be served on the employer only.

The other differences between clause 7.5 and the corresponding JCT 80 provision are merely of a drafting nature.

The wording of clause 7.5.3(d) should be noted with great care. There must be a failure by the employer to provide access to or egress from the site of the works across any adjoining or connected 'land, buildings, way or passage' which are in his own 'possession and control'. It does not, therefore, cover failure to obtain a wayleave across an adjoining owner's property or the situation where access to the highway is obstructed or where access to the site is obstructed by pickets, demonstrators or the like for whom the employer is not responsible in law: *L.R.E. Engineering Services Ltd* v. *Otto Simon Carves Ltd* (1981); *Porter* v. *Tottenham UDC* (1915). The failure must also result in the carrying out of the whole or a major part of the work being suspended for a continuous period of one month.

Clause 7.6 – Employer's insolvency
This provision is an exact parallel of JCT, private edition, clause 28.1.4, save only that the clause does not specify upon whom the contractor's notice must be served. We suggest that it should be

served upon the employer and not upon the architect. (See the commentary on pages 72-3.)

Clause 7.7 – Consequences of contractor determination
Clause 7.7 reads as follows:

' **Consequences of determination under clause 7.5 or 7.6**

7.7 Without prejudice to the accrued rights or remedies of either party or to any liability of the classes mentioned in clause 6.1 (*Injury*) which may arise either before the Contractor or any sub-contractors shall have removed his or their temporary buildings, plant, tools, equipment, goods or materials or by reason of his or their so removing the same, upon such determination under clause 7.5 or 7.6:

(a) the Contractor shall with all reasonable dispatch and in such manner and with such precautions as will prevent injury, death or damage of the classes in respect of which before the date of determination he was liable to indemnify the Employer under clause 6.1 remove from the site all his temporary buildings, plant, tools, equipment, goods and materials and shall give facilities to his sub-contractors to do the same;

(b) after taking into account amounts previously paid under this Contract the Contractor shall be paid by the Employer the total value of work at the date of determination, any sum ascertained in respect of direct loss and/or expense under clause 4.11 (*Disturbance of progress*), the cost of materials or goods properly ordered for the Works for which the Contractor shall have paid or for which the Contractor is legally bound to pay (and on such payment any materials and goods so paid for shall become the property of the Employer), the reasonable cost of removal under the preceding paragraph and any direct loss and/or damage caused to the Contractor by the determination.'

It will be noticed that there are verbal differences between this clause and JCT 80, clause 28.2 (discussed on pages 73-5). The differences are more apparent than real, the only one of any substance being that the distinction in method of valuation between work fully completed and work begun but not completed has been removed in IFC 84. There is no reference to loss and/or damage caused to named sub-contractors, but this point is covered by the Sub-contract Conditions NAM/SC, clause 29, so that the named sub-contractor's entitlement, including direct loss and/or damage, will be included in the payment made to the contractor.

Clause 7.8 – Determination by either party
Clause 7.9 – Consequences of such determination
The clauses read as follows:

'Determination by Employer or Contractor

7.8.1   Without prejudice to any other rights or remedies which the Employer or Contractor may possess if the carrying out of the whole or substantially the whole of the uncompleted Works (other than the execution of work required under clause 2.10 (*Defects liability*)) is suspended for a period of three months by reason of:
(a) *force majeure*; or
(b) loss or damage to the Works occasioned by any one or more of the Clause 6.3 Perils; or
(c) civil commotion;
then the Employer or the Contractor may by notice by registered post or recorded delivery to the Contractor or to the Employer forthwith determine the employment of the Contractor under this Contract; provided that such notice shall not be given unreasonably or vexatiously.

7.8.2   The contractor shall not be entitled to give notice under clause 7.8.1 where the loss or damage to the Works occasioned by one or more of the Clause 6.3 Perils was caused by the negligence of the Contractor, his servants or agents, or by any sub-contractor, his servants or agents.

Consequences of determination under clause 7.8

7.9   Upon such determination under clause 7.8 (or upon determination under clause 6.3C.2(c)) the provisions of clause 7.7 shall apply with the exception of the words at the end of clause 7.7 "and any direct loss and/or damage caused to the Contractor by the determination".'

The events covered by clause 7.8 are outside the control of either party and the effect of the clause is to remove the unjustifiable anomaly existing in JCT 80 where, in these circumstances, the contractor is entitled to recover direct loss and/or damage, including loss of profit on uncompleted work.

The significant differences between clause 7.8 and JCT 80, clause 28.1.3 (discussed on pages 69-72) are:

(1) Either the employer or the contractor may determine the contractor's employment by notice to the other. The determination takes effect 'forthwith'.

(2) The period of suspension is fixed at three months in each case. Under JCT 80, clause 28.1.3 the period was left to the

discretion of the parties in an appendix entry but was recommended as being three months in the case of loss or damage caused by insurable perils and one month in every other case.

The consequences of determination under clause 7.8 are the same as those discussed on page 85, save that the contractor has no entitlement to recover direct loss and/or damage resulting from the determination.

Under IFC 84 there is no provision for determination on outbreak of hostilities, and in such an unlikely event the position between the parties would be governed by common law (see chapter 1, pages 3–14) as modified by any statutes or regulations made at the time.

The JCT Form with Contractor's Design

As with JCT 80 there are four provisions for determination, and the clause numbering is identical.

Clause 22C.2.2 – Insurance of existing structures and the works by the employer – determination by either party
This provision is identical with its JCT 80 counterpart and readers are referred to the commentary on pages 39–42.

Clause 27 – Determination by employer
The only differences between this provision and its JCT 80 equivalent are the substitution of references to 'the design or construction of the works' in place of 'the carrying out of the works' in clause 27.1.1 and the insertion of a new sub-clause 27.4.1 which reads as follows:

'For the purposes referred to in clause 5.5 [i.e. the clause which requires the contractor to supply "as built" drawings] the contractor shall provide the employer with two copies of, and the employer may retain, all such drawings or details or descriptions as the contractor has prepared or previously provided and drawings and information relating to the works completed before determination of the contractor's employment.'

JCT 80, clauses 27.4.1 to .4 are renumbered 27.4.2 to .5, and the employer is given the power to employ other persons to complete the design as well as the construction of the works in clause 27.4.2 as renumbered.

While superficially there is no difference of substance between these provisions and the corresponding clauses in JCT 80, in practice the difficulties facing the employer are substantial should he elect to exercise his right to determine the contractor's employment. The real difficulty lies in finding a contractor who will take over and complete the original contractor's design as well as construction with all the liabilities with which, potentially, the substitute contractor might be faced should the original contractor become insolvent or no longer have legal existence.

Clause 28 – Determination by contractor
Clause 28 mirrors clause 28 of JCT in virtually identical terms, with two notable differences:

(1) There is an additional ground for determination, namely the suspension of the work for a continuous period of the length specified in the appendix (and normally one month) by reason of 'delay in receipt of any permission or approval for the purposes of development control requirements necessary for the works to be carried out or proceed, which delay the contractor has taken all practicable steps to avoid or reduce' (clause 28.1.2.8). This has reference to such matters as planning permissions and so on and it should be remarked that additional words in the introductory part of clause 28.1.2 make it clear that the determination provisions therein only apply if the *construction* of the works is suspended and *not* their design.
(2) There is no reference to the employer's insolvency as being a ground for determination. This is clearly an error and will presumably be corrected if and when a new edition of this contract is called for.

Extraordinary though this may seem, the new ground for determination does not carry any entitlement of the contractor to recover direct loss and/or expense caused to him by the determination, although the contractor is still entitled to recover it for other causes of determination which are beyond the control of the employer. The former is the effect of the wording of clause 28.2.6.

Clause 32.1 – Determination on outbreak of hostilities
This is equivalent to the identical clause in JCT 80, as to which see page 75.

The Agreement for Minor Building Works 1980

Clause 7.0 covers determination by both parties and reads as follows:

'Determination

7.1 The Employer may but not unreasonably or vexatiously by notice by registered post or recorded delivery to the Contractor forthwith determine the employment of the Contractor under this Contract if the Contractor shall make default in any one or more of the following respects:

.1 if the Contractor without reasonable cause fails to proceed diligently with the Works or wholly suspends the carrying out of the Works before completion;

.2 if the Contractor becomes bankrupt or makes any composition or arrangement with his creditors or has a winding up order made or (except for the purposes of reconstruction) a resolution for voluntary winding up passed or a receiver or manager of his business or undertaking is duly appointed or possession is taken by or on behalf of any creditor of any property the subject of a charge.

In the event of the Employer determining the employment of the Contractor as aforesaid the Contractor shall immediately give up possession of the site of the Works and the Employer shall not be bound to make any further payment to the Contractor until after completion of the Works. Provided always that the right of determination shall be without prejudice to any other rights or remedies which the Employer may possess.

Determination by Contractor

7.2 The Contractor may but not unreasonably or vexatiously by notice by registered post or recorded delivery to the Employer forthwith determine the employment of the Contractor under this Contract if the Employer shall make default in any one or more of the following respects:

.1 if the Employer fails to make any progress payment due under the provisions of clause 4.2 hereof within 14 days of such payment being due;

.2 if the Employer or any person for whom he is responsible interferes with or obstructs the carrying out of the Works or fails to make the premises available for the Contractor in accordance with clause 2.1 hereof;

.3 if the Employer suspends the carrying out of the Works for a continuous period of at least one month;

.4 if the Employer becomes bankrupt or makes a composition or arrangement with his creditors, or has a winding up order made or a resolution for voluntary winding up passed or a receiver or manager of his business is appointed or possession is taken by or on behalf of any creditor of any property the subject of a charge.

Provided that the employment of the Contractor shall not be determined under clauses 7.2.1, 7.2.2 or 7.2.3 hereof unless the Employer has continued the default for seven days after receipt by registered post or recorded delivery of a notice from the Contractor specifying such default.

In the event of the Contractor determining the Employment of the Contractor as aforesaid the Employer shall pay to the Contractor, after taking into account amounts previously paid, such sum as shall be fair and reasonable for the value of work begun and executed, materials on site and the removal of all temporary buildings, plant, tools and equipment. Provided always that the right of determination shall be without prejudice to any other rights or remedies which the Contractor may possess.'

Clause 7.1 – Determination by the employer

It will be seen that the employer may determine the contractor's employment on two of the same grounds as those set out in JCT 80, clause 27, i.e. if without cause the contractor:

● fails to proceed diligently with the works; *or*
● wholly suspends the carrying out of the works before completion.

Under this clause both defaults must be 'without reasonable cause'. The commentary on pages 45-6 is of equal relevance to this provision. There is no provision for determination for failure to comply with an instruction to remove defective work or materials since the architect is given no specific power in this respect, nor is there any power to determine in respect of unauthorised assignment or sub-letting or for breach of the fair wages provision.

The third ground – contractor's insolvency – does not give rise to automatic determination, but the employer is given the option to determine in that event. Oddly, insolvency is described specifically as a 'default'.

There is no provision for any warning or preliminary notice, but in our view it would be advisable for the employer to warn the contractor of his intention to determine unless the default is corrected. Under clause 7.1 determination follows immediately upon service of the employer's notice by registered post or recorded delivery.

On determination of his employment the contractor must give up possession of the site. If he does not do so within a reasonable time he is, in law, a trespasser.

The employer is not bound to make any further payment to the contractor until the works are completed, which would presumably be by a replacement contractor. The clause contains no further express provision as to what is to happen on determination, other than to preserve the employer's rights and remedies at common law. In fact it may be advantageous for the employer to determine the contract at common law rather than under the express determination provisions if he has grounds for so doing.

In *Thomas Feather & Co. (Bradford) Ltd* v. *Keighley Corporation* (1953), discussed on page 2, it was made clear that where a party is terminating under an express contractual provision he will only be entitled to such further remedy as the contract gives him. Under clause 7.1 the employer's common law rights are preserved, but the employer needs to establish that there is a breach of contract amounting to repudiation by the contractor.

Insolvency is certainly not a breach of contract at common law, and therefore it is submitted that in such a case the employer has no right to recover the additional cost of completion or any other costs or damages incurred.

Failure to proceed diligently with the works may be a technical breach of contract, giving rise to a claim for a nominal damages if accepted by the employer, but it is not in our view a repudiatory breach: see pages 47-8.

The default of wholly suspending the works before completion without reasonable cause is capable of amounting to repudiatory conduct. Then, as Lord Goddard CJ said in *Thomas Feather*:

'If the contractor repudiates a contract, and shows by his conduct that he does not mean to be bound by it, then, of course, the building owner can recover any extra cost to which he may be put by way of damages.'

Effectively therefore, under clause 7.1, if the employer exercises his right of determination this in itself gives him no right to damages whatever, nor has he any other claim against the contractor because the contract is silent. It merely gives him a right to bring the contractor's employment to an end on specified grounds. If he is to recover anything he must proceed by way of an action for breach of contract at common law, when he will be able to recover only such damages as arise directly from the breach itself and not from the actual determination unless he can establish that breach amounts to a repudiation which would in any case have entitled him to bring the contract to an end.

Suppose that the contractor wholly suspends work. This is a breach of contract, but it is not necessarily repudiatory in character unless it can be shown that the contractor has no intention of proceeding with the works at all: see page 46. If the employer therefore exercises his right to determine the contractor's employment on this ground, the contractor may argue successfully that the suspension was only temporary and that he had every intention of proceeding with the work in due course. In that event, at the very best, the employer's entitlement to damages would be in respect of the delay resulting directly from the suspension and would not extend to the additional costs of completion by another contractor.

It is our view that clause 7.1 is gravely defective in a number of important respects:

(1) It confers on the employer no right to direct loss and/or damage arising from the determination.
(2) It gives him no rights over the contractor's plant or materials similar to those conferred by clause 27.4.1 and clause 27.4.3 of JCT 80. It has been suggested that the employer would have a lien over such items, but the weight of authority is against this – Hudson's *Building Contracts*, 10th edition, pages 678 – 679.
(3) It gives the employer no rights in respect of materials or goods delivered to the works but not certified for payment following determination.
(4) In the case of true insolvency the employer's rights as against the trustee in bankruptcy or liquidator are virtually non-existent if determination is made on that ground. In fact his rights to determine at all on that ground are in doubt, for the reasons advanced on pages 53-5.

Clause 7.2 – Determination by the contractor
The contractor is given the right to determine his own employment

should the employer default in any of the following respects:

- If the employer fails to make progress payments in accordance with clause 4.2, i.e. twenty-eight days from the issue of the certificate.
- If the employer or any person for whom he is responsible interferes with or obstructs the carrying out of the works.
- If the employer or any person for whom he is responsible fails to make the premises available to the contractor for carrying out the works.
- If the employer himself suspends the carrying out of the works for a continuous period of one month.

It should be noted that there is no provision that these defaults must be 'without reasonable cause', but in each case the contractor must serve a preliminary notice on the employer by registered post or recorded delivery. The notice must specify the default and the employer has seven days from receipt of the notice in which to cure the default. If he fails to do so, the contractor may forthwith determine his own employment by notice served on the employer by registered post or recorded delivery.

A further ground for determination is the employer's insolvency – also and wrongly described as a default. No preliminary notice is necessary, and determination follows directly on service of notice of determination.

The wording of clause 7.2.1, dealing with late payment, is curious if it is intentional. Under clause 4.2 the employer is to pay the contractor amounts certified by the architect as progress payments within fourteen days of the date of the certificate. Payment is therefore due no later than the expiry of that period. Clause 7.2.1 suggests that the contractor must then wait a further fourteen days, making twenty-eight days in all, before he may issue a warning notice, which gives the employer a further seven days from receipt in which to pay. This seems to us manifestly unjust and contrary to both business practice and common sense.

Interference with or obstruction of the carrying out of the works would be a breach of contract at common law. It is interesting that the nearest equivalent provision in JCT 80, clause 28.1, which is delay in the execution of work not forming part of the contract by the employer or others engaged by him, requires the work actually to be suspended for a specific period before the right to determine arises. The current provision is therefore and justifiably much more stringent.

Failure to make the premises available to the contractor – which is broadly equivalent to failure to give possession of the site under other JCT forms – is here made a specific ground for determination whereas in other cases the contractor must rely on his common law rights, which would entail acceptance of the employer's default as a repudiation.

The reason for the inclusion of the provision entitling the contractor to determine 'if the employer suspends the carrying out of the works for a continuous period of one month' is obscure because the employer has no right to suspend the works. Arguably, the architect might have a right to order suspension under his general powers to issue instructions under clause 2.5. Even if this is accepted, it is suggested that this would not fall within clause 7.2.3 in the absence of any reference to those for whom the employer is responsible. It is suggested that the only way in which the employer could effectively suspend the work would be by physically preventing the contractor from carrying it out, e.g. by refusing access, which would in any case come under clause 7.2.2 and would amount to a repudiatory breach of contract at common law.

There is no other reference to suspension of the works for any other cause such as those which are contained in JCT 80, clause 28.1.3 (see page 70).

The contractor is given a specific right to payment following determination of his own employment of a fair and reasonable sum for work done, materials on site and the costs of removal of temporary buildings, plant, tools and equipment. He is given no specific right to claim direct loss and/or damage although his common law rights and remedies are preserved. His position is therefore the same as that of the employer under clause 7.1, i.e. he must establish that there has been a breach of contract from which he has suffered direct damage in excess of his entitlement to payment under the contract. However, if he is to establish a claim for loss of profit on work not done as a result of the determination he must establish that the employer's default is a repudiatory breach. Not all the defaults listed in clause 7.2 are repudiatory in nature, e.g. failure to pay will not normally be regarded as repudiatory: see pages 68-9.

Chapter 3

Determination under the ACA Form of Building Agreement

Introduction

The second edition of the ACA Form of Building Agreement was published in 1984. There is also a British Property Federation edition of the contract which differs from its parent in a number of respects. The determination provisions in both editions are in identical terms, however, except that in the BPF edition

- references are to the client's representative and not to the architect; and
- since adjudication is not an optional provision in the BPF edition the paragraphs referring to adjudication are not marked for deletion.

In this contract the word 'termination' rather that 'determination' is used, but this is of no significance. As in the JCT forms, the contract itself is not terminated but merely the employment of the contractor under it. The provisions are:

Clause 20 – Termination.
Clause 21 – Termination due to causes outside the control of both parties.
Clause 22 – Consequences of termination.

These clauses read as follows:

'20   **Termination**

Termination by Employer
20.1   Upon the happening of one or more of the following events, namely if the Contractor:

(a) without reasonable cause (and subject always to Clause 21 of this Agreement) substantially suspends the execution of the Works or any Section before the taking-over of the same;

(b) fails or neglects to comply with his obligations under Clauses 9.1 or 9.2 of this Agreement;

(c) without reasonable cause fails to proceed regularly and diligently with the Works or any Section;

(d) refuses or neglects to comply with any instruction which the Architect is empowered by this Agreement to give;

(e) shall otherwise be in breach of this Agreement;

then the Employer may, in addition to any other power enabling him to terminate this Agreement, serve notice (referred to as "the Default Notice") on the Contractor specifying the event and requiring its remedy and if the Contractor fails to remedy the same within * [10] working days of service of the Default Notice or if the Contractor, at any time after service of the Default Notice, commits any further substantially similar breach of this Agreement, the Employer may by further notice (referred to as "the Termination Notice") forthwith terminate the employment of the Contractor:

Provided always that if either party shall refer any dispute or difference under this Clause 20.1 to the Adjudicator within * [10] working days of service of the Default Notice and provided that the Adjudicator shall give his decision in accordance with the provisions of Clause 25.2, then the Employer shall not be entitled to serve the Termination Notice until the Adjudicator shall have given such decision: Provided further that if no reference is made to the Adjudicator before service of the Termination Notice by the Employer, then the Employer's entitlement to terminate the Contractor's employment under this Clause 20.1 shall not be open to challenge in any proceedings between the parties whether by way of arbitration or otherwise.

Delete if no Adjudicator, number must be same as 20.1 above

Termination by the Contractor

20.2 Upon the happening of one or more of the following events, namely if the Employer:

(a) does not pay to the Contractor the amount properly due and payable on any certificate (subject to any deductions which the Employer may be entitled to make);

(b) obstructs the issue of any certificate due under this Agreement;

(c) is otherwise in breach of this Agreement and such breach has prevented the Contractor from carrying out any of his obligations * for a continuous period of [20] working days,

then the Contractor may, in addition to any other power enabling him to terminate this Agreement, serve notice (referred to as "the Default Notice") on the Employer specifying the event and requiring its remedy and if the Employer fails to remedy the same within * [10] working days of service of the Default Notice, the

Contractor may by further notice (referred to as "the Termination Notice") forthwith terminate his employment:

Provided always that if either party shall refer any dispute or difference under this Clause 20.2 to the Adjudicator within * [10] working days of service of the Default Notice and provided that the Adjudicator shall give his decision in accordance with the provisions of Clause 25.2, then the Contractor shall not be entitled to serve the Termination Notice until the Adjudicator shall have given such decision: Provided further that, if no reference is made to the Adjudicator before service of the Termination Notice, then the Contractor's entitlement to terminate his employment under this Clause 20.2 shall not be open to challenge in any proceedings between the parties, whether by way of arbitration or otherwise.

Delete if no Adjudicator, number must be same as 20.2 above

Termination on insolvency

20.3 Either party may terminate the Contractor's employment by notice to the other forthwith if any distress or execution shall be levied upon such other party's property or assets or if such other party shall make or offer to make any arrangement or composition with its creditors or commit an act of bankruptcy or if any petition or receiving order in bankruptcy shall be presented or made against him or (if he is a limited company) any resolution or petition to wind up such company's business (other than for the purpose of a bona fide reconstruction or amalgamation without insolvency) shall be passed or presented or if a receiver of such company's undertaking property or assets or any part of them shall be appointed.

21. **Termination due to causes outside the control of both parties**

Termination due to causes outside the control of both parties

21.1 If the Contractor shall be prevented or delayed from executing the
* Works for a period of [60] consecutive working days or more by:

(a) *force majeure*; or
(b) the occurrence of one or more of the contingencies referred to in Clause 6.4; or
(c) war, hostilities (whether war be declared or not), invasion, act of foreign enemies, rebellion, revolution, insurrection, military or usurped power, civil war, riot, commotion or disorder;

then either party may by notice to the other forthwith terminate the Contractor's employment under this Agreement.

22. **Consequences of termination**

Payment where Employer terminates

22.1 If the Contractor's employment is terminated by the Employer under Clause 20.1 or 20.3, the Employer shall not be bound to make any further payment to the Contractor until the full and final cost of completion of the Works by others has been ascertained but upon such cost being ascertained, the Architect shall certify the amount of any damage, loss and/or expense suffered or incurred by the Employer, and, if such amount when added to the monies paid to the Contractor before the date of termination exceeds the total amount due to the Contractor calculated in accordance with Clause 16.2 up to the date of termination, the difference shall be a debt payable to the Employer by the Contractor.

Payment where Contractor terminates

22.2   If the Contractor's employment is terminated by the Contractor under Clause 20.2 or 20.3, the Architect shall ascertain and certify under Clause 16.2 the total amount properly due to the Contractor up to the date of termination (including, but without limitation, the Contractor's costs of protecting and securing the Works as required by Clause 22.4) and the Employer shall pay such amount to the Contractor within [10] working days of certification of it.

number must be same as 16.3

Payment where termination due to causes outside the control of both parties

22.3   If the Contractor's employment is terminated by either party under Clause 21, the provisions of Clause 22.2 shall apply but neither party shall have any claim against the other for any damage, loss and/or expense arising out of or in connection with such termination.

Possession of Site on termination

22.4   Upon service of a Termination Notice by either party under Clauses 20 or 21 and notwithstanding that the validity of such termination is disputed by the Contractor, the Contractor shall immediately deliver to the Employer possession of the Site and shall properly protect and secure the Works.

Common law rights

22.5   Subject to Clause 22.3, termination of the Contractor's employment by either party shall not prejudice the rights of either party to sue for and recover any damage, loss and/or expense suffered or incurred by him arising out of or in connection with any breach by the other of this Agreement prior to such termination and generally to enforce any of his rights and remedies in relation to anything done prior to such termination.

Drawings

22.6   Upon any termination of the Contractor's employment, the Contractor shall deliver to the Employer all drawings, details, documents and information prepared by or on behalf of the Contractor for the Works and the provisions of clause 3.3 shall apply.

Contractor's sub-contractors and suppliers

22.7   Upon any termination of the Contractor's employment and, if the Employer so requires, the Contractor hereby agrees and consents to the novation to the Employer, without payment, of the Contractor's entire benefit, right and interest in and under any sub-contract between the Contractor and any sub-contractor or supplier and the Contractor agrees, forthwith upon receipt of a written request from the Employer, to do all acts and execute all documents necessary to make such novation effective.'

Note: Numbers of working days shown in boxes may be changed if not appropriate.

Termination by the employer

Termination is conditioned upon the contractor being in default in one or more of five respects. Each ground will be considered in turn.

Suspension
The work or section concerned must be 'substantially' suspended by the contractor before taking-over and the suspension must be without reasonable cause. The dictionaries are of little help in explaining what is meant by 'substantially' but it is clearly not the same as 'wholly' which is the word used in JCT 80. It is not necessary for the work to be totally suspended but the suspension must affect progress to a considerable degree. The reference to clause 21 is to the contractor being delayed from carrying out the works for a period of sixty consecutive working days as a result of matters beyond the control of both parties.

Assignment or sub-letting without consent
Clause 9.1 prohibits assignment of contractual rights and obligations by either party without the consent of the other. The proviso to that clause does, however, permit the contractor to assign his rights to payment to another, e.g. to a factoring house. For discussion, see page 49.

Failure to proceed regularly and diligently with the works
The failure must be without reasonable cause. This ground corresponds to JCT 80, clause 27.1.2, and readers are referred to the discussion on page 49.

As in JCT 80, this default is a breach of an express term of the contract – in this case, clause 11.1.

Refusal or neglect to comply with instructions
There is no requirement that the refusal or neglect should be 'persistent'. Thus an isolated failure would in theory give rise to

the operation of the termination procedure. Such a course is not advised except in an extreme case. The instruction must be one which the architect (or client's representative) 'is empowered by this agreement to give'. A list of the instructions which the architect (or client's representative) is empowered to give is set out in clause 8.1 and could scarcely be in wider terms. This default is a breach by the contractor of the obligation imposed on him by clauses 1.1 and 8.1.

Otherwise in breach of this agreement

This is an extremely comprehensive ground and entitles the employer to invoke the termination procedure for any breach of contract by the contractor, however minor the breach might be. It is not subject to any limitation whatsoever, but in practice should be exercised with discretion.

Termination procedure

Upon the contractor committing one or more of the specified defaults the employer (*not* the architect or client's representative) may – not must – serve a Default Notice in writing on the contractor. The notice must specify the default and require its remedy. Requirements for notices generally are set out in clause 23.1 and are that they shall be in writing, sent by pre-paid first class post or by actual delivery to the contractor's address stated on page 1 of the agreement unless the contract documents specify another address, such as a branch office, for delivery. If posted, the notice is deemed to have been given two working days after the date of posting. If delivered physically, the notice would be effective from the date of actual delivery.

Despite the provisions of clause 23.1, it is strongly advised that the Default Notice should be sent by registered post or recorded delivery and that advice of delivery be obtained. If delivered by hand, a receipt should be obtained from someone having apparent authority to receive the notice on behalf of the contractor.

The contractor has ten working days from the date of service in which to remedy the default. If he fails to do so or, at any time after service, commits 'any further substantially similar breach' the employer may serve a Termination Notice which terminates the contractor's employment 'forthwith'.

The powers in clause 20.1 are in addition to the employer's common law powers in respect of repudiatory breach.

Where adjudication is the method of disputes settlement – as is always the case in the BPF edition – *either party* may refer any dispute or difference under clause 20.1 to the adjudicator for decision, e.g. if the contractor disputes that he is in default as specified in the Default Notice. This must be done within the ten working days allowed for the contractor to remedy the default.

Reference to the adjudicator temporarily suspends the employer's power to serve the Termination Notice until the adjudicator has given his decision, which he must do within a period of five working days of being requested to settle the dispute.

The adjudicator's decision is final and binding on both parties until taking-over of the works: see clause 25.3. This is so even if one or other of the parties exercises his right to refer the matter to arbitration. It follows that if the adjudicator's decision is that the Default Notice is unjustified or invalid then the employer has no right to terminate the contractor's employment under clause 20.1.

The second proviso to clause 20.1 is extremely important. Its effect is that if no reference is made to the adjudicator, the employer's entitlement to terminate the contractor's employment cannot be challenged in any legal or arbitral proceedings. If adjudication is not a term of the contract – and it is optional under the ordinary ACA contract – then there would not be this limitation on the contractor's right to challenge the termination.

Consequences of employer determination
These are spelled out in clause 22.

Payment (clause 22.1)
The employer is not obliged to make any further payment to the contractor 'until the full and final cost of completion of the works by others has been ascertained'. When this has been done, the position regarding settlement appears to be exactly the same as under the corresponding provision under JCT 80: see pages 74-5.

Possession of the site (clause 22.4)
When a termination notice is served the contractor is under a twofold duty:

● He must immediately give up possession of the site even if he is disputing the validity of the termination.

● He must properly protect and secure the works.

Drawings (clause 22.6)
When his employment is terminated the contractor is required to deliver to the employer all drawings, details, documents and information which he has prepared or had prepared for the works. He must preserve their confidentiality: see clause 3.3 of the agreement.

Sub-contractors and suppliers (clause 22.7)
The object of this provision is to ensure that the employer acquires the benefit of any sub-contract or contract of supply into which the contractor has entered for the purposes of the works. This is done by novation, i.e. a tripartite agreement between the contractor, the employer and the sub-contractor or supplier in question whereby the original sub-contract or supply contract is rescinded and a new agreement is substituted between the employer and the sub-contractor or supplier. This can only be done with the agreement of the sub-contractor or supplier and is presumably to be done on terms that there would be a further novation in favour of the completion contractor.

Clause 22.7 requires the contractor to do everything necessary to bring the novation about, without payment to him, upon a written request from the employer.

Common law rights (clause 22.5)
Termination of the contractor's employment by the employer is stated to be without prejudice to the rights of either party to sue and recover any damages, etc. incurred as a result of any breach of the agreement before termination.

The clause also preserves all other rights and remedies of the parties in relation to anything done before the termination.

Termination by the contractor

Clause 20.2 specifies three defaults by the employer which entitle the contractor to invoke the termination procedure.

Failure to pay
The actual default consists in the employer's failure to pay the

amount certified as due by the architect (or client's representative) within ten working days of the certificate. This is subject to any deductions which the employer may be entitled to make.

Obstructing the issue of certificates
As in JCT 80, the reference is to *any* certificate and not merely to certificates for payment.

Otherwise in breach of this agreement
Again, this sweeping-up ground covers any breach of contract, major or minor, but in this case the breach must have prevented the contractor from carrying out *any* of his obligations for a continuous period of twenty working days. This, in effect, seems to require that the work must be at a complete standstill for this period, which effectively confines its operation to major breaches of contract.

Termination procedure
This is exactly the same as in the case of employer determination (see pages 100-101).

Consequences of contractor termination

Payment (clause 22.2)
This straightforward provision requires the architect (or client's representative) to ascertain and certify the amount properly due to the contractor up to the date of termination together with the contractor's costs of protecting and securing the works.

In the BPF edition, where a Schedule of Activities is used, this ascertainment must include the value of activities started but not completed at the time of termination which otherwise would not be payable under the operation of clause 16.2.

The employer must pay the amount certified to the contractor within ten working days of certification.

It is to be noted that, in contrast to the equivalent provision where the employer has terminated, the contractor is given no specific entitlement to recover damages in respect of the determination. We are not certain whether this is by accident or design. The contractor's only entitlement in this respect would arise at common law – see the discussion of the similar position under the JCT Minor Works Agreement, page 94.

Other matters

In all other respects the consequences of termination are the same as when the employer terminates (see pages 101-102).

Termination on insolvency

Clause 20.3 is a common-form provision providing for either party to terminate the employment of the contractor on grounds of the other's insolvency, etc. Termination is not automatic but is brought about 'forthwith' on service of written notice. The provisions of clause 23.1 apply.

Consequences of termination for insolvency

Depending on which party terminates the contractor's employment, the position as regards payment is covered by clause 22.1 or clause 22.2 as appropriate. In all other respects the situation is the same as for termination for any other cause as discussed on pages 101-103.

Termination due to causes outside the control of both parties

Clause 21 provides that either party may terminate the contractor's employment by written notice served on the other where the contractor is prevented or delayed from carrying on with the works for a period of sixty consecutive working days by reason of one or more of three classes of event. The termination follows directly from the service of the notice, and the provisions of clause 23.1 apply to its service. The events are:

● *Force majeure* (see the discussion on pages 70-71).
● Occurrence of insurable risks. These are the risks which are to be insured against under clause 6.4, e.g. fire, flood, tempest, etc. There is no limitation on the power of termination should such damage arise through the contractor's own negligence, in contrast with JCT 80, clause 28.1.3.2, page 70 where, however, the power of determination is conferred on the contractor alone.
● War, etc. This ground is self-explanatory. It is comprehensive and wider than its JCT equivalent.

Consequences of termination

Save in respect of payment, the consequences of determination are the same as where the contractor's employment is terminated by either party for default: see pages 101-102.

Indeed, the payment provisions are identical to those where the contractor determines his own employment under clause 20.2 or clause 20.3 including, it would seem, payment to the contractor for the cost of protecting and securing the works. There is an express exclusion of any claim by either party for 'any damage, loss and/or expense arising out of or in connection with such termination'. This is a curious provision since clause 22.2 gives neither party the right to claim such loss or damage anyway.

Chapter 4

Determination under the Government Conditions of Contract – GC/Works/1

Introduction

The full title of this document is 'General Conditions of Government Contracts for Building and Civil Engineering Works', mercifully abbreviated to Form GC/Works/1. The current edition is the second and was published in September 1977.

Form GC/Works/1 has many unusual features, perhaps because of its provenance. In the field of determination two of these features are the lack of any express term entitling the contractor to determine and the inclusion of a right of the employing authority to determine the contract unilaterally without reason.

The determination clauses are:

Clause 44 – Special powers of determination.
Clause 45 – Determination of contract due to default or failure of contractor.
Clause 46 – Provisions in case of determination of contract.
Clause 55(2) – Determination for corruption.

These clauses will be considered in a more logical order than that used by the draftsman. We refer to 'the employer' in our commentary, whereas the contract refers to 'the authority'.

Determination for contractor's default

Clause 45 reads as follows:

'The Authority may without prejudice to the provisions contained in

Condition 46 and without prejudice to his rights against the Contractor in respect of any delay or inferior workmanship or otherwise, or to any claim for damage in respect of any breaches of the Contract and whether the date for completion has or has not elapsed, by notice absolutely determine the Contract in any of the following cases, additional to those mentioned in Condition 55 hereof:

(a) if the Contractor, having been given by the SO a notice to rectify, reconstruct or replace any defective work or a notice that the work is being performed in an inefficient or otherwise improper manner, shall fail to comply with the requirements of such notice within seven days from the service thereof, or if the Contractor shall delay or suspend the execution of the Works so that either in the judgment of the SO he will be unable to secure the completion of the Works by the date for completion or he has already failed to complete the Works by that date;

(b) (i) if the Contractor, being an individual, or where the Contractor is a firm, any partner in that firm, shall at any time become bankrupt, or shall have a receiving order or administration order made against him or shall make any composition or arrangement with or for the benefit of his creditors, or shall make any conveyance or assignment for the benefit of his creditors, or shall purport to do so, or if in Scotland he shall become insolvent or notour bankrupt, or any application shall be made under any Bankruptcy Act for the time being in force for sequestration of his estate, or a trust deed shall be granted by him for behoof of his creditors; or

(ii) if the Contractor, being a company, shall pass a resolution, or if the Court shall make an order, that the company shall be wound up, or if the Contractor shall make an arrangement with his creditors or if a receiver or manager on behalf of a creditor shall be appointed, or if circumstances shall arise which entitle the Court or a creditor to appoint a receiver or manager or which entitle the Court to make a winding-up order; or

(c) in a case where the Contractor has failed to comply with Condition 56, if the Authority (whose decision on this matter shall be final and conclusive) shall decide that such failure is prejudicial to the interests of the State:

Provided that such determination shall not prejudice or affect any right of action or remedy which shall have accrued or shall accrue thereafter to the Authority.'

Clause 45 sets out in effect four specific defaults by the contractor which entitle the employer to determine the contract absolutely. In common with the other standard forms, it also treats insolvency and related matters as a default giving rise to the right of determination.

The power to determine is stated to be without prejudice to the employer's 'rights against the contractor in respect of any delay or inferior workmanship or otherwise, or to any claim for damage in respect of any breaches of the contract'. This is reinforced by the proviso at the end of the clause which is probably unnecessary. The statement that the right of determination is also 'without prejudice to the provisions contained in condition 46' is meaningless since clause 46 only comes into effect when the contract is determined under this clause.

The power of determination may be exercised by the employer at any time whether or not the date fixed for completion has been passed. Determination is said to be absolute although it would seem to be the intention that clause 46 at least, as well as all the other rights and remedies of the employer under the contract, should remain in existence.

The grounds of determination are now dealt with individually.

Failure to rectify defective work

The superintending officer (SO) is required to give a preliminary notice to the contractor 'to rectify, reconstruct or replace any defective work'. If the contractor fails to comply with the notice within seven days from its service the employer may then issue a determination notice.

Clause 1(6) governs all notices given under the contract. The notice is to be in writing, typescript or printed 'and if sent by registered post or recorded delivery to the last known place of abode or business of the contractor shall be deemed to have been served upon the date when in the ordinary course of post it would have been delivered to him' – i.e. on the next working day following posting, a presumption which in these days may not accord with reality.

Performing the work in an inefficient or otherwise improper manner

This is open to wide interpretation but its purport is obvious. Again, the SO is required to issue a warning notice and the contractor has seven days from service of the notice in which to cure the default before the employer can issue a determination notice.

Delay or suspension of the execution of the works

No warning notice is required. The power to determine is exercisable immediately. The delay or suspension must be such that 'in the judgment of the SO' the contractor will be unable to complete the works by the date fixed for completion *or* the date for completion has already passed (in which event clearly there must have already been delay or suspension). The judgment of the SO is not stated to be final and conclusive and can thus be reviewed on arbitration under clause 61.

It is important to appreciate the breadth of this power. Once the completion date has passed the employer has in effect a discretionary right to determine the contract. The contractor is given no opportunity to improve his performance.

Insolvency

Clause 45(b) is cast in the widest possible terms and as is usual in construction industry standard form contracts extends to grounds which do not amount to insolvency, e.g. the appointment of a receiver or manager. Indeed, in the case of a company the circumstances which can entitle the employer to determine extend beyond even those set out in the JCT forms to the situation where circumstances arise which entitle the court or a creditor to appoint a receiver or manager or which entitle the court to make a winding-up order even if that entitlement is not exercised.

As in the case of similar contract provisions in other standard forms, the validity of the clause is in doubt in the case of true insolvency: see pages 52-6.

Failure to comply with clause 56

Clause 56 deals with the admission of unauthorised persons to the site. Special security considerations apply to most government projects and the security of the State is and must be paramount. Failure by the contractor to comply with the provisions of clause 56 can be a very serious matter and clearly justifies summary determination of the contract. The determination can only take place if the employer decides that the contractor's failure 'is prejudicial to the interests of the State'. The employer's decision on this matter is final and conclusive and is therefore not open to review in arbitration or otherwise.

Determination for corruption

Clause 55 reads as follows:

'**Corrupt gifts and payments of commission**

55 (1) The Contractor shall not

(a) offer or give or agree to give to any person in Her Majesty's service any gift or consideration of any kind as an inducement or reward for doing or forbearing to do or for having done or forborne to do any act in relation to the obtaining or execution of this or any other contract for Her Majesty's service or for showing or forbearing to show favour or disfavour to any person in relation to this or any other contract for Her Majety's service; or

(b) enter into this or any other contract with Her Majesty or any Government Department in connection with which commission has been paid or agreed to be paid by him or on his behalf or to his knowledge, unless before the contract is made particulars of any such commission and of the terms and conditions of any agreement for the payment thereof have been disclosed in writing to the Authority.

(2) Any breach of this Condition by the Contractor or by anyone employed by him or acting on his behalf (whether with or without the knowledge of the Contractor) or the commission of any offence by the Contractor or by anyone employed by him or acting on his behalf under the Prevention of Corruption Acts, 1889 to 1916, in relation to this or any other contract for Her Majesty's service shall entitle the Authority to determine the Contract and/or to recover from the Contractor the amount or value of any such gift, consideration or commission.

(3) Any dispute or difference of opinion arising in respect of either the interpretation or effect of this Condition or of the amount recoverable hereunder by the Authority from the Contractor shall be decided by the Authority, whose decision on that matter shall be final and conclusive.'

This provision is self-explanatory. The power of determination arises in respect of corrupt practices under *any* contract with the Crown and is summary, although clearly some form of notice would be required to effect it. In addition to other consequences of determination, the employer has the right to recover the amount or value of the bribe, etc. 'from the contractor'. Presumably this power would be exercised if it was not possible to recover the ill-gotten gains from the actual recipient, as to which see *Reading* v. *Attorney-General* (1951).

Consequences of determination for default

These are set out in clause 46 as follows:

'**Provisions in case of determination of Contract**

46 (1) If the Authority, in the exercise of the power contained in Conditions 45 or 55, shall determine the Contract, the following provisions shall take effect:

(a) all sums of money that may then be due or accruing due from the Authority to the Contractor shall cease to be due or to accrue due;

(b) the Authority may hire any persons in the employment of the Contractor and with them and/or any other persons provided by the Authority may enter upon and take possession of the Site and of all things (whether or not for incorporation) which are on the Site, and may purchase or do anything requisite for the completion of the Works, or may employ other contractors to complete the same, and the Contractor shall have no claim whatsoever in respect of such action by the Authority;

(c) the Contractor shall (except where determination occurs by reason of any of the circumstances described in Condition 45(b)(i) and (ii)), if required by the Authority, assign to the Authority without further payment, the benefit of any sub-contract or contract for the supply of any things for incorporation which he may have made in connection with the Contract and the Authority shall pay to any such sub-contractor or supplier the price (or the balance thereof remaining unpaid) which the Contractor may have agreed to pay thereunder;

Provided that any part of the price (or balance) so paid which the SO has certified as having been covered by any previous advance shall be forthwith recoverable by the Authority from the Contractor;

(d) notwithstanding that the Authority has not required assignment in accordance with sub-paragraph (c) above the Authority may pay to any nominated sub-contractor or nominated supplier any amount due to him which the SO has certified as having been covered by any previous advance and the amount so paid shall be forthwith recoverable by the Authority from the Contractor; and

(e) the SO shall certify the cost of completion, which shall include –

(i) the cost of any labour or things (whether or not for incorporation) provided to secure completion of the Works, including the making good of any defects and/or faulty work, together with the addition of such percentage to cover superintendence and establishment charges as may be decided by the Authority (whose decision on that matter shall be final and conclusive);

(ii) the cost of work executed by other contractors to secure completion of the Works, including the making good of any defects and/or faulty work; and

(iii) the amount of liquidated damages which may under Condition 29 have become due from the Contractor at the date of determination in respect of any delay in the completion of the Works.

(2) If the cost of completion, after taking into account all credits from any sales of any things (whether or not for incorporation) brought on the Site by the Contractor prior to the date of determination, added to the actual sums paid to the Contractor up to the said date, is less than the sum which would have been payable to the Contractor for due completion, the Contractor shall be paid the difference, but the amount so payable shall not exceed the aggregate of

(i) the value of the work executed up to the date of determination;

(ii) the value of any such things (being things which were for incorporation) as are subsequently incorporated in the Works or otherwise disposed of; and

(iii) the value of any such things (being things which were not for incorporation) which are disposed of;

less the amount already paid under the Contract. Any such things as are unsold or unused when the Works are completed shall be returned to the Contractor.

(3) If the cost of completion, added to the sum actually paid to the Contractor up to the date of completion, exceeds the sum which would have been payable to the Contractor for due completion, the Authority may apply the proceeds of the sale of any things (whether or not for incorporation) which are on the Site in reduction of such excess and any deficit shall be recoverable from the Contractor. If after such excess has been met there remains any residue of the proceeds of the sale of any such things, and/or any such things remain unsold, such residue or (as the case may be) such things unsold shall be paid or returned to the Contractor.'

Clause 46(1) may be summarised as follows:

(1) No further payment is to be made to the contractor except

under the terms of clause 46(2).

(2) The employer is given the power to hire any employee of the contractor for the purposes of completion.

(3) The employer is also empowered to enter upon and take possession of the site and to take possession of everything on it, including the contractor's plant, machinery, etc. However, clearly this power is not effective in respect of plant, etc. which belongs to third parties, and it is possible that, in the case of the bankruptcy of a contractor who is an individual, the provision would be defeated by the operation of the doctrine of reputed ownership: *Re Fox* (1948).

(4) The employer is given the power to do anything necessary for the completion of the works including the employment of completion contractors, purchase of materials, etc. The 'contractor has no claim whatsoever in respect of any such actions taken by the employer.

(5) Except where the determination arises from insolvency, etc. the employer may require the contractor to assign without further payment the benefit of any sub-contract or contract of supply. Where assignment does take place, the employer undertakes to pay any sub-contractor or supplier the price (or unpaid balance) which the contractor has agreed to pay. The proviso to clause 46(1)(c) is important. If any part of the price (or balance) has been certified by the SO as having been covered by a previous advance, the employer may recover it from the contractor forthwith.

(6) Irrespective of whether assignment has taken place, the employer may pay direct to any nominated sub-contractor or supplier any amount due which the SO has certified as having been covered by a previous advance. The amount of any direct payment is forthwith recoverable from the contractor. On the face of it this is operable even in the event of insolvency, but in that event the trustee or liquidator might successfully resist the direct payment: see *British Eagle Ltd* v. *Air France* (1975).

(7) The SO is to certify the cost of completion. This is to include:
● The cost of any labour or things provided to secure completion of the works, including the making good of any defects and/or faulty work, plus a percentage to cover superintendence and establishment charges. This percentage is at the sole discretion of the employer and its decision is expressed as being final and conclusive.

- The cost of work executed by other contractors to secure completion, similarly including the costs of making good.
- Liquidated damages up to the date of determination. Liquidated damages are not therefore recoverable for the time taken by the employer to complete.

There is no contractual provision for the employer to recover direct loss and/or damage and any such claim would have to be brought at common law. For discussion, see page 62.

Payment

After taking into account the proceeds of any sale by the employer under the authority impliedly given by clause 46(3) in respect of plant and unused materials, etc. brought on site prior to determination, the cost of completion as certified by the SO is to be added to the sums paid to the contractor prior to determination. If the total so arrived at is less than the sum which would have been payable to the contractor had he completed, the difference is payable to the contractor by the employer.

However, the amount so payable is not to exceed the aggregate of:

 (i) the value of the work executed up to the date of determination;
 (ii) the value of any materials or goods for incorporation which have been incorporated or otherwise disposed of; and
(iii) the value of any plant, etc. not for incorporation which has been disposed of

less the amount already paid under the contract.

In simple terms, therefore, the contractor gets no more than the value of the work he has done, materials, plant, etc. incorporated in the works or disposed of, less what he has been paid already.

Any items which are unsold or unused when the works are completed are to be paid to the contractor.

Under clause 46(3), if the cost of completion as certified by the SO when added to the sum already paid to the contractor exceeds what would have been payable to the contractor had he completed the work then the employer may sell any plant, materials, etc. remaining after completion and apply the proceeds to reduce the deficit. Any balance remaining is recoverable from the contractor, presumably by legal action. If the proceeds of sale exceed the deficit, the balance is or any unsold items are to be returned to the contractor.

It will be seen that these provisions entail the preparation of a notional final account for the whole of the works including all variations, etc. as if they had been completed by the contractor, as is the case under JCT 80: see page 61.

Special powers of determination

Clause 44 reads as follows:

'Special powers of determination

44 (1) The Authority shall, in addition to any other power enabling him to determine the Contract, have power to determine the Contract at any time by notice to the Contractor, and upon receipt by the Contractor of the notice the Contract shall be determined but without prejudice to the rights of the parties accrued to the date of determination and to the operation of the following provisions of this Condition.

(2) (a) The Authority shall as soon as practicable, and in any case not later than the expiration of three months from the date of such notice or of the period up to the date for completion, whichever is the shorter, give directions (with which the Contractor shall comply with all reasonable despatch) as to all or any of the following matters

   (i) the performance of further work in accordance with the provisions of the Contract;

   (ii) the protection of work executed under the Contract in compliance with directions given under sub-paragraph (i) above;

   (iii) the removal from the Site of all things whether or not they were for incorporation;

   (iv) the removal of any debris or rubbish and the clearing and making good of the Site;

   (v) the termination or transfer of any sub-contracts and contracts (including those for the hire of plant, services and insurance) entered into by the Contractor for the purposes of or in connection with the Contract; or

   (vi) any other matter arising out of the Contract with regard to which the Authority (whose decision on the matter shall be final and conclusive) decides that directions are necessary or expedient.

(b) The Authority may at any time within the period referred to in subparagraph (a) above by notice to the Contractor vary any direction so given or give fresh directions as to all or any of the matters specified in that sub-paragraph.

(3) (a) In the event of the determination of the Contract under this Condition there shall be paid to the Contractor

    (i) the net amount due, ascertained in the same manner as alterations, additions and omissions under the Contract, in respect of work executed in accordance with the Contract up to the date of determination;

    (ii) the net amount due, ascertained in the same manner, in respect of any works or services executed in compliance with directions given by the Authority under paragraph 2(a)(i), (ii), (iii), (except in so far as it relates to things which were for incorporation being things which the Contractor elects to retain), (iv) and (vi) of this Condition;

    (iii) the net amount due on the basis of fair and reasonable prices for any things for incorporation which the Contractor with the consent of the Authority, has elected not to retain as his own property and which at the date of determination

        (a) had been supplied by the Contractor and properly brought on the Site by him and at his expense in connection with and for the purpose of the Contract, but had not been incorporated in the Works; or

        (b) were in course of manufacture by the Contractor in connection with and for the purposes of the Contract and were not lost or damaged by reason of any of the accepted risks; and

    (iv) any sum expended by the Contractor on account of the determination of the Contract in respect of the uncompleted portion of any sub-contract and contracts (including those for the hire of plant, services and insurance) entered into by the Contractor for the purposes of or in connection with the Contract, to the extent to which it is reasonable and proper that the Authority should reimburse that sum; and

    (v) any sum expended by the Contractor in respect of any contract of employment which is expended on account of the determination of the Contract or which, but for this provision, would represent an unavoidable loss by reason of the determination, to the extent to which it is reasonable and proper that the Authority should reimburse that sum.

(b) If the Works or any part thereof or any things to which sub-paragraph (a)(iii)(a) above relates are at the date of determination, or if directions are given in pursuance of paragraph (2)(a) of this Condition at the date for completion of the Works, lost or damaged by reason of any of the accepted risks and such loss or damage was not occasioned by any failure on the part of the Contractor to perform his obligations under Condition 25, the net amount due shall be ascertained as if no loss or damage had occurred.

    (c) There shall be deducted from any sum payable to the Contractor under this paragraph the amount of all payments previously made to the Contractor in respect of the Contract, and the Authority shall have the right to retain any reserves accumulated in his possession at the date of determination until the final settlement of all claims made by the Contractor under this paragraph.

    (d) The Contractor shall for the purposes of this paragraph keep such wage-books, time-sheets, books of account and other documents as are necessary to ascertain the sums payable hereunder and shall at the request of the Authority provide (verified in such manner as he may require) any documents so kept and such other information as he may reasonably require in connection with matters arising out of this Condition.

(4) All things not for incorporation which are brought on the Site at the Contractor's expense shall (whether damaged or not) re-vest in and be removed by him as and when they cease to be required in connection with the directions given by the Authority under paragraphs (2)(a)(i), (ii), (iii), (iv) and (vi) of this Condition. The Authority shall be under no liability to the Contractor in respect of the loss thereof or damage thereto caused by reason of any of the accepted risks.

(5) If upon the determination of the Contract under this Condition the Contractor is of the opinion that he has suffered hardship by reason of the operation of this Condition he may refer the circumstances to the Authority, who, on being satisfied that such hardship exists, or has existed, shall make such allowance, if any, as in his opinion is reasonable, and his decision on that matter shall be final and conclusive.

(6) The Contractor shall, in any substantial sub-contract or contract made by him in connection with or for the purposes of the Contract, take power to determine such sub-contract or contract in the event of the determination of the Contract by the Authority upon terms similar to the terms of this Condition, save that the name of the Contractor shall be substituted for the Authority throughout except in paragraphs (3)(a)(iii), (3)(d) and (5).'

Clause 44 gives the employer a discretionary power to terminate the contract at any time, with or without reason. The clause does not require that the contractor be in default in any respect. There is no limit on the exercise of this power and in effect the employer has the option of terminating the contract under this clause as opposed to doing so under clause 45 or clause 55.

The power is said to be 'in addition to any other power enabling him to determine the contract', i.e. at common law or under the other express provisions for determination. No minimum or other length of notice is specified, but the notice must be in writing: see clause 1(6).

Clearly the unbridled exercise of this power would make nonsense of the contractual situation, and the intention plainly is that it is a reserve power to be used only in the most exceptional circumstances. Its inclusion can only be justified because of the special position of government departments as employers.

The contract is brought to an end when the contractor *receives* the notice, and the determination is said to be 'without prejudice to the rights of the parties accrued to the date of determination' and to the operation of the succeeding sub-clauses: clause 44(1).

Clause 44(2) sets out the employer's powers following determination. These powers may be exercised 'not later than the expiration of three months from the date of [the determination notice] or of the period up to the date for completion, whichever is the shorter'. These words are ambiguous. They can be read as suggesting that the power of determination may not be exercised after the date for completion has been passed, but this would appear to conflict with the words 'at any time' in clause 44(1) which seem to give the employer the unfettered right to determine at any time irrespective of whether the completion date has been passed or not. On the other hand – and we prefer this view – the words can be read as suggesting that if the employer exercises its right of determination under the clause after the date of completion has passed then its powers under sub-clause (2) must be exercised immediately upon determination.

The powers are to direct the contractor as to the following matters:

(1) To perform further work. The words 'in accordance with the provisions of the contract' suggest that the work must be of a kind contemplated by the contract, either as work originally included as contract work or as a kind which could be ordered as a variation.
(2) The protection of such work. It is curious that the wording seems to limit the protection to the work ordered under clause 44(2)(a)(i) and not to work already executed before determination.
(3) The removal from site of all things whether or not for incorporation.
(4) The removal from site of debris and rubbish and clearing and making good the site.

(5) The termination or transfer of related sub-contracts or contracts. Presumably the word 'transfer' means 'assignment'. Unless the sub-contract or contract contains an express term providing for automatic determination consequent upon the termination of the main contract, the contractor may be liable for damages which he would recover under clause 44(3)(a)(iv) below. Furthermore, sub-clause (6) requires the contractor to include in any 'substantial' sub-contract or contract a term similar to this.

(6) Any other matter arising out of the contract. This power is limited to matters arising out of the contract and does not extend to any matters not originally contemplated by it. The employer's decision is stated to be final and conclusive but it is submitted that the conclusiveness and finality relate only to the question of whether the direction is necessary and expedient. The question of whether it relates to a matter arising out of the contract is therefore, we suggest, reviewable in arbitration or litigation.

The effect of clause 44(2)(b) is that at any time during the period specified the employer may vary directions already given or issue fresh ones. This would suggest that if the determination occurs after the date for completion has passed, no variation or fresh direction may be ordered after the original directions have been given.

The contractor is under a duty to comply with all directions given under clause 44(2) with all reasonable despatch.

The important matter of payment is dealt with by clause 44(3) which sets out the contractor's financial entitlement. This comprises:

(1) The net amount due in respect of work executed. This is to be valued in the same way as 'alterations, additions and omissions' under the contract, i.e. by measurement and valuation under the terms of clause 9(1). This clause does not contain any express reference to any entitlement to recover direct expense incurred by the contractor and recoverable by him prior to the date of determination, but it is suggested that such sums must be included.

(2) The net amount due in respect of work executed under clause 44(2)(a). This amount also is to be ascertained in the same

way. There is no express reference to clause 44(2)(b) but again it is suggested that work ordered thereunder must be paid for. The value of things intended for incorporation but which the contractor has elected to retain is excluded.

(3) A fair and reasonable price for things intended for incorporation which the contractor has elected not to retain. The contractor does not have unfettered discretion as to whether or not to retain such items, but may only elect not to retain them with the consent of the employer. Further, to be considered under this provision the things concerned must have been either (a) supplied by the contractor and *properly* brought on to the site by him and at his expense, or (b) be in the course of manufacture by the contractor in connection with and for purposes of the contract. In the latter case their value is to be excluded if they have been lost or damaged by reason of any of the accepted risks as defined in clause 1(2) which sets out the normal insurable risks such as fire, flood, tempest, etc.

(4) Sums expended by the contractor in respect of uncompleted sub-contracts and contracts. Payment in respect of these sums is limited 'to the extent to which it is reasonable and proper [for the employer to] reimburse'. Consequently, the contractor is unable to recover any sums in excess of what it would be reasonable for him to have to pay as compensation to sub-contractors, suppliers and so forth. Regard must also be had to sub-clause (6) regarding terms to be included in 'substantial' sub-contracts and contracts regarding their determination. Failure by the contractor to meet those requirements would, it is submitted, preclude any claim under this head for sums which the contractor may have to pay under such sub-contracts or contracts.

(5) Sums in respect of contracts of employment. This is also limited since it must be 'reasonable and proper' that the employer should reimburse the amount. An example of where such a payment might be claimed would be if, as a result of the determination, the contractor had to terminate the employment of an employee with a fixed term contract such as a site agent, or the contractor's share of any statutory redundancy payment.

Clause 44(3)(b) provides that if any of the works or anything provided for incorporation in the works (other than things in the course of manufacture) are lost or damaged by any of the 'accepted risks' as defined in clause 1(2), their value is to be ascertained and paid to the contractor as if they had not been so lost or damaged. This is conditional upon the loss or damage not having been occasioned by the contractor's failure to comply with clause 25 which requires him to take reasonable precautions against the accepted risks.

Clause 44(3)(c) is in some ways a curious provision. Reasonably enough, it starts off by saying that payments previously made to the contractor are to be deducted from the sums payable under the preceding provisions. However, it then goes on to give the employer the right 'to retain any reserves accumulated in his possession at the date of determination until the final settlement of all claims made by the contractor under this paragraph'.

Commenting on an earlier version of this clause, I.N. Duncan Wallace QC rightly notes that this

'amounts to a provision that, should the contractor have the temerity to make any claim under the clause, sums in the hands of the [employer] and admittedly due on the basis of previous payments can be withheld simply because the contractor is claiming further sums. There seems to be no possible justification for such a provision in any contractual situation, and the policy . . . seems frankly inexplicable' (*Further Building and Engineering Standard Forms*, 1973, page 58).

We agree with and adopt that observation.

Clause 44(3)(d) requires the contractor to keep wage books, etc. to enable the ascertainment of sums payable to him after determination. A similar provision to this must be included in 'substantial' sub-contracts or contracts: clause 44(6).

Clause 44(4) deals with things not for incorporation (e.g. plant, etc.) which are brought on to the site at the contractor's expense. It ties in with the vesting provisions of clause 3 by which ownership of such things is vested in the employer for the purposes of the works. These items 'whether damaged or not' shall 're-vest in and be removed by' the contractor 'as and when they cease to be required in connection with the' directions in respect of further work, etc. issued by the employer under clause 44(2)(a). It should also be noted that the employer is under no liability to the contractor in respect of loss or damage to such items through any of the accepted risks, and they are therefore at the contractor's risk even though possibly being used by others.

Hardship allowance

Clause 44(5) is an unusual provision which in effect enables the employer to make an *ex gratia* payment to the contractor if the latter is able to show that he has suffered 'hardship' as a result of the determination. A dictionary definition suggests that 'hardship' is something causing suffering or privation, which would indicate that this clause can only be invoked in extreme circumstances. An allowance under this clause is entirely discretionary and the employer's decision is 'final and conclusive'.

It is understood that, in practice, on the rare occasions when payments have been made under clause 44(5) they have been on a generous scale and have included something for loss of profit, which seems only right in these circumstances. The allowance is not the equivalent of damages, which are not provided for under clause 44, and would not be claimable at common law because the operation of this clause would not constitute a breach of contract, repudiatory or otherwise.

Substantial sub-contracts, etc.

As already indicated, clause 44(6) requires the contractor to include in any *substantial* sub-contracts or contracts a clause entitling him to determine them in the same way as the employer may determine the main contract under clause 44 and including the same consequences of such determination. Failure to comply with this provision may seriously affect the contractor's entitlements under the preceding provisions.

Chapter 5

Determination under Civil Engineering Contracts

Introduction

The majority of civil engineering works in the UK are carried out under the ICE Conditions of Contract for Works of Civil Engineering Construction, now in its fifth edition, which was published in June 1973. Internationally, such work is carried out under the similar form sponsored by the International Federation of Consulting Engineers and the International Federation of Building and Public Works, commonly known as the FIDIC Form, which is in fact based on the fourth edition of the ICE Conditions of Contract. The current edition of the FIDIC Form was published in 1977.

The determination clause in the ICE Conditions is clause 63 which provides for determination by the employer only. The ICE Conditions also make provision for payment in the event of frustration (clause 64) and for determination of the contract by the employer in the event of the outbreak of war (clause 65). The ICE Form contains no express provision entitling the contractor to terminate for default by the employer so in these circumstances the contractor must rely on his rights at common law.

The FIDIC Conditions in respect of forfeiture are very similar to the ICE provisions, save that the time periods mentioned are extended to twenty-eight instead of fourteen days and fourteen instead of seven days respectively, and there are minor changes of wording which have no particular significance. The FIDIC clause for payment in the event of frustration is identical with the ICE provision, despite a minor change in wording, but there is a clause (clause 65) dealing with what are called 'special risks' which include the outbreak of war in any part of the world.

Forfeiture under the ICE Conditions

Clause 63 reads as follows:

'Forfeiture

63. (1) If the Contractor shall become bankrupt or have a receiving order made against him or shall present his petition in bankruptcy or shall make an arrangement with or assignment in favour of his creditors or shall agree to carry out the Contract under a committee of inspection of his creditors or (being a corporation) shall go into liquidation (other than a voluntary liquidation of the purposes of amalgamation or reconstruction) or if the Contractor shall assign the Contract without the consent in writing of the Employer first obtained or shall have an execution levied on his goods or if the Engineer shall certify in writing to the Employer that in his opinion the Contractor:

(a) has abandoned the Contract; or

(b) without reasonable excuse has failed to commence the Works in accordance with Clause 41 or has suspended the progress of the Works for 14 days after receiving from the Engineer written notice to proceed; or

(c) has failed to remove goods or materials from the Site or to pull down and replace work for 14 days after receiving from the Engineer written notice that the said goods materials or work have been condemned and rejected by the Engineer; or

(d) despite previous warning by the Engineer in writing is failing to proceed with the Works with due diligence or is otherwise persistently or fundamentally in breach of his obligations under the Contract; or

(e) has to the detriment of good workmanship or in defiance of the Engineer's instructions to the contrary sub-let any part of the Contract;

then the Employer may after giving 7 days' notice in writing to the Contractor enter upon the Site and the Works and expel the Contractor therefrom without thereby avoiding the Contract or releasing the Contractor from any of his obligations or liabilities under the Contract or affecting the rights and powers conferred on the Employer or the Engineer by the Contract and may himself complete the Works or may employ any other contractor to complete the Works and the Employer or such other contractor may use for such completion so much of the Constructional Plant Temporary Works goods and materials which have been deemed to become the property of the Employer under Clauses 53 and 54 as he or they may think proper and the Employer may at any time sell any of the said Constructional Plant Temporary Works and unused goods and materials and apply the proceeds of sale in or towards the satisfaction of any sums due or which may become due to him from the Contractor under the Contract.

Assignment to Employer

(2) By the said notice or by further notice in writing within 14 days of the date thereof the Engineer may require the Contractor to assign to the Employer and if so required the Contractor shall forthwith assign to the Employer the benefit of any agreement for the supply of any goods or materials and/or for the execution of any work for the purposes of this Contract which the Contractor may have entered into.

(3) The Engineer shall as soon as may be practicable after any such entry and expulsion by the Employer fix and determine *ex parte* or by or after reference to the parties or after such investigation or enquiries as he may think fit to make or institute and shall certify what amount (if any) had at the time of such entry and expulsion been reasonably earned by or would reasonably accrue to the Contractor in respect of work then actually done by him under the Contract and what was the value of any unused or partially used goods and materials any Constructional Plant and any Temporary Works which have been deemed to become the property of the Employer under Clauses 53 and 54.

(4) If the Employer shall enter and expel the Contractor under this Clause he shall not be liable to pay to the Contractor any money on account of the Contract until the expiration of the Period of Maintenance and thereafter until the costs of completion and maintenance damages for delay in completion (if any) and all other expenses incurred by the Employer have been ascertained and the amount thereof certified by the Engineer. The Contractor shall then be entitled to receive only such sum or sums (if any) as the Engineer may certify would have been due to him upon due completion by him after deducting the said amount. But if such amount shall exceed the sum which would have been payable to the Contractor on due completion by him then the Contractor shall upon demand pay to the Employer the amount of such excess and it shall be deemed a debt due by the Contractor to the Employer and shall be recoverable accordingly.'

Exactly what is contemplated by clause 63 is not at all clear. Clause 63 says that 'the employer may . . . enter upon the site and the works and expel the contractor therefrom without thereby avoiding the contract or releasing the contractor from any of his obligations or liabilities under the contract or affecting the rights and powers conferred on the employer or the engineer by the contract . . .' and the word 'forfeiture' is used. Presumably the intention is that the clause should be treated in the same way as the comparable JCT provisions with their reference to 'determination of the employment of the contractor', and the contract makes its own provision for what is to happen in the event of the employer exercising his rights under the clause.

In *E.R. Dyer Ltd* v. *The Simon Build/Peter Lind Partnership* (1982) – a case on the FCEC conditions of sub-contract – Mr Justice Nolan subjected clause 63 to a careful analysis. In his view

> '. . . the whole purpose of the clause [is] to enable the employer to continue with the completion and maintenance of the work and that by invoking his powers to that end under the clause, the employer assumes duties to the contractor which he remains obliged to perform . . .'

In the learned judge's view, if the employer invokes his clause 63 rights he does not in fact terminate or determine the contract. In the absence of a provision of this type, however, the employer would have no right to expel the contractor from the site and his doing so would be a repudiatory breach of contract, but the whole provision is ineptly drafted and obscure.

Like the building forms of contract, the ICE Conditions treat insolvency, etc. as in effect a breach of contract justifying determination of the contractor's employment, here described as 'forfeiture'. Similarly, assignment without the previous consent in writing of the employer is a ground for determination, as is the fact that the contractor has had an execution levied on his goods. Curiously, there is no mention – as there is under the JCT forms – of possession being taken on behalf of debenture holders of the contractor's property subject to a floating charge, which is a much more likely event.

Determination on grounds of insolvency is not automatic; it is an employer option. Even so, it is uncertain whether determination in this event is effective where the contractor's liquidator or trustee in bankruptcy chooses to exercise his option under insolvency legislation to continue with the contract: see Hudson's *Building and Civil Engineering Contracts*, 10th edition, pages 778-788, and pages 52-7 above.

There are five defaults by the contractor which are stated to be grounds for forfeiture, the engineer's written certificate being a condition precedent to their being relied on by the employer. These defaults may be considered as follows.

Abandonment of the contract
This would in any case be a repudiation of the contract at common law. Some positive act of the contractor is certainly required such as complete withdrawal of all labour and plant from the site.

Failure to commence the works
Clause 41 requires the contractor to commence the works 'on or as soon as is reasonably possible after the date for commencement of the works to be notified by the engineer in writing which date shall be within a reasonable time after the date of acceptance of the tender'. Mere failure to commence on the date for commencement is therefore not a breach since the contractor is given a reasonable time after that date on which to commence. Moreover, the contractor's failure to commence after receipt of notification of the date for commencement must be 'without reasonable excuse'.

Clause 63(1)(b) is ambiguous since there is some doubt as to whether the requirement of written notice from the engineer requiring the contractor to proceed applies to a failure to commence as well as to suspension of progress. An ordinary reading of the clause suggests that the notice requirement only applies to suspension and not to commencement. The contrary view has been taken by I.N. Duncan Wallace in his commentary on the similarly worded provision in the FIDIC Form, where he states:

> 'What is needed here is the original clause 41 order in writing, a further notice under this provision, then a certificate of the engineer, and then an employer's seven days' notice': *The International Civil Engineering Contract*, page 157.

He has taken the same view of the current clause in other commentaries. In view of the ambiguity it would clearly be a wise precaution for the engineer to issue a written notice, although strictly this is unnecessary.

Suspension of progress
Suspension of progress, if persisted in, would be a repudiatory breach at common law. Suspension implies a complete stoppage of work and this ground undoubtedly requires a fourteen day notice in writing from the engineer, followed by his certificate, before the employer can issue his own seven day notice of forfeiture.

Failure to remove goods or materials or replace work
Once again this ground is conditioned on the engineer issuing a written notice condemning the work, etc. under clause 39 which itself gives the employer an alternative remedy of employing someone else to remove the goods or replace the work and recover the cost of so doing from the contractor. On its wording, clause 63(1)(c) would not seem to apply to a failure on the part of the contractor to put right defects during the period of maintenance under clause 49.

Failure to proceed with due diligence
This is a very difficult ground to establish. Simple failure of the contractor to keep up to his own programme does not necessarily indicate lack of diligence and it is suggested that persistent slow progress, which will clearly mean that the contractor cannot possibly complete within the contract period, must be required. The failure to proceed must not be due to the fault of the employer or the engineer. For instance, failure by the employer to pay monies certified as due may justify the contractor in slowing down: see *J.M. Hill & Sons Ltd* v. *London Borough of Camden* (1980). Previous written warning from the engineer is required and it is submitted that the contractor must be given a reasonable period after the warning in which to remedy his default before the engineer is justified in issuing his certificate of default.

Persistent or fundamental breach of obligations
This is a catch-all provision and is not very happily worded. The contractor must be persistently or fundamentally in breach of the contract despite previous written warning from the engineer. 'Persistent' suggests a course of conduct continued over a period of time while 'fundamental' must mean going to the root of the contract and presumably refers to a breach of a condition in the legal sense, i.e. a major term of the contract. Abrahamson suggests (*Engineering Law and the ICE Contracts*, 4th edition, page 279) that the contractor's failure to provide a programme under clause 14 amounts to a fundamental breach, but we suggest that this would only be so in a very extreme case, i.e. if the lack of a programme made the engineer's task of administering the contract impossible, though it has to be admitted that there is no other sanction available to the employer in respect of the contractor's failure to provide a programme.

Sub-letting to the detriment of good workmanship or in defiance of the engineer's instructions

Clause 4 deals with sub-letting which is only permitted with the written consent of the engineer. Strangely, it seems that simple withholding of consent by the engineer is not sufficient to invoke forfeiture but that the engineer must expressly forbid sub-letting unless the sub-letting is to the detriment of good workmanship. It would seem, moreover, that even if the engineer has given his consent to sub-letting, if in the event it proves to be detrimental to good workmanship this ground of forfeiture may be invoked. This would therefore seem to be a very valuable provision from the employer's point of view. No doubt the threat of forfeiture against the contractor would in most cases lead to his exercising any powers of forfeiture which he may have against the defaulting sub-contractor.

Procedure and consequences

Forfeiture is effected by the employer giving seven days' notice in writing to the contractor. That notice must, by the terms of clause 68, be sent by post or left at the contractor's principal place of business or registered office. Although not specifically required, it is suggested that registered or recorded delivery post should be used or a receipt required if the notice is delivered by hand. The wording of the notice demands careful consideration. It should state the employer's intention to enter on the site and expel the contractor. The object of the notice is not to give the contractor an opportunity to remedy his default but simply to give him the opportunity to vacate the site before expulsion, and in effect it operates to terminate the contractor's licence to occupy the site.

Clause 63(1) appears to assume that the employer's notice is necessarily valid, but presumably the contractor could seek to challenge its validity by legal action and might seek an injunction restraining the employer from entering upon the site. The position in this event is obscure: see the discussion on pages 36–7 relating to the position under the JCT determination clauses. Alternatively, the contractor might invoke the arbitration provisions: see clause 66.

Once the employer has exercised his right of re-entry he may either complete the works himself or employ another contractor to do so. The exercise of the right of forfeiture and re-entry is expressly stated not to avoid the contract or release the contractor from his obligations and liabilities under it or affect the rights and powers conferred on the employer or the engineer by the contract itself. It is thought that the right of forfeiture conferred by clause 63 is in addition to, and not in substitution for, the employer's common law right to treat the contract as repudiated, and in an appropriate case the employer might well be advised to rely on his common law rights.

The clause confers on the employer and/or the completion contractor the right to 'use for such completion so much of the constructional plant temporary works goods and materials which have been deemed to have become the property of the employer under clauses 53 and 54 . . .'. Under clause 53(2) 'all plant [which by clause 53(1)(a) means "any constructional plant temporary works and materials for temporary works" but excludes "any vehicles engaged in transporting any labour plant or materials to and from the Site"] goods and materials owned by the contractor or by any company in which the contractor has a controlling interest shall when on the site be deemed to be the property of the employer'. Further, clause 53(3) requires the contractor when hiring plant as so defined to include in the hire agreement a clause enabling the employer to secure the transfer of the hire agreement to himself or a completion contractor. The employer would therefore seem to have the right to use any plant, etc. standing on the site but of course these contract provisions cannot be used to defeat third-party rights if such exist.

The clause goes on to confer on the employer a right of sale in respect of constructional plant, etc, which has been deemed to have become his property under clause 53(2) and of unused goods and materials and to 'apply the proceeds of sale in or towards the satisfaction of any sums due or which may become due to him from the contractor under the contract'. The majority view is that these powers are valid against an insolvent contractor's liquidator or trustee in bankruptcy, but the point does not appear to have been tested.

Clause 63(2) confers a further seemingly important power on the employer by enabling the engineer to require the contractor to assign to the employer the benefit of any agreement for the supply of goods or materials and/or the execution of work. Abrahamson (*Engineering Law and the ICE Contracts*, 4th edition, page 208) makes the very valid point that 'it is not at all certain that the employer is entitled to enforce this provision if the contractor's employment is forfeited for bankruptcy or liquidation'. (For discussion on this difficult area see pages 52-6.) The opening words of clause 63(2) are meaningless. 'The said notice' refers to the forfeiture notice which must be sent by the employer and not the engineer, but it is the latter who must require assignment. The provisions of the sub-clause may be unworkable in practice because assignment would entitle the employer to the benefit of sub-contracts while leaving the contractor responsible for payment. It is, therefore, suggested that a fresh agreement with the sub-contractor should be entered into.

The financial aspects of forfeiture are dealt with in clauses 63(3) and 63(4). The former provides for the engineer to certify the amount reasonably due to the contractor for work done, and for goods, materials, plant and temporary works deemed to have become the employer's property at the date of forfeiture, i.e. at the time of the employer's entry. He is to do this 'as soon as practicable' after the employer's entry and his powers appear to be quite unfettered. He may, but not must, make inquiries. It is not clear why this clause was thought necessary since the value of the work done at the date of forfeiture is in fact irrelevant in light of the payment provisions in clause 63(4). Nonetheless the contract provides for this valuation to be made and it may have some evidential value if the forfeiture is on grounds other than insolvency.

Payment after forfeiture is covered by clause 63(4) which is straightforward. The employer is not bound to make any further payment to the contractor until the period of maintenance expires, although it is suggested that the employer is not entitled to withhold any monies already due to the contractor under clause 60. Payment to the contractor is therefore deferred until the end of the period of maintenance, which is defined in clause 49(1) as 'the period of maintenance named in the appendix to the form of tender calculated from the date of completion of the works or any section or part thereof certified by the engineer in accordance with clause 48'.

Indeed, no payment is due until the costs of completion and maintenance, any damages for delay in completion, and all other expenses incurred by the employer have been ascertained and certified by the engineer. The reference to 'damages for delay in completion' is interesting and on its wording would indicate that not only liquidated damages accrued due at the date of forfeiture are covered, but also liquidated damages until the actual completion date: see *Re Yeadon Waterworks Co. & Wright* (1895).

The contractor is to be paid the value of the contract as it would have been had he completed it, less the employer's costs and expenses as certified by the engineer and, of course, monies previously paid.

Payment in the event of frustration

For a discussion of discharge by frustration, see pages 3-14.

This matter is governed by clause 64, which reads as follows:

> '**Frustration**
>
> *Payment in event of Frustration*
> 64 In the event of the Contract being frustrated whether by war or by any other supervening event which may occur independently of the will of the parties the sum payable by the Employer to the Contractor in respect of the work executed shall be the same as that which would have been payable under Clause 65(5) if the Contract had been determined by the Employer under Clause 65.'

No comment is necessary, since payment is on the same basis as if the contract had been determined on the outbreak of war under clause 65 (see below).

Determination on outbreak of war

In essence, clause 65 provides for what is to happen in the case of an outbreak of war. So far as it is physically possible to do so, the contractor is to continue to execute the works for a period of twenty-eight days. If the works are not completed within that period the employer is entitled to determine the contract, i.e. bring the contract itself to an end, although clauses 65, 66 and 68 are preserved and govern the rights of the parties. Determination is effected by means of written notice to the contractor and is operative 'forthwith'.

The contractor is then to remove his plant, etc. with reasonable dispatch, and clause 65(5) regulates his entitlement to payment. The contractor's entitlement is as follows:

● Payment for work executed before the determination, valued at the contract rates and prices.
● Payment in respect of preliminary items.
● Cost of materials or goods reasonably ordered and for which the contractor has received delivery or was obliged to accept delivery.
● A sum certified by the engineer in respect of expenditure reasonably incurred in anticipation of completing the works.
● Any additional sums payable under clause 65(6)(b), (c) and (d), i.e. cost of repairing war damage if so required, special fluctuations if the price fluctuations clause cannot be operated, and any special costs arising from government statutes, orders, etc.
● Reasonable cost of removal of plant, etc.

Forfeiture under FIDIC Conditions

The provisions of the FIDIC Contract relating to forfeiture, frustration and outbreak of war are not significantly different from their ICE counterparts. Despite its international provenance, the conditions are drafted with English law in mind and consequently the conditions as printed may not be effective under certain foreign jurisdictions.

Readers are referred to *The International Civil Engineering Contract* by I.N. Duncan Wallace for a discussion of the problems involved and to an article by J.E. Goedel in *The International Construction Law Review*, Volume 1, pages 50 – 72, which sets out recommendations for a review of these conditions.

Chapter 6

Determination under sub-contracts

Introduction

A number of specially-drafted sub-contracts are available for use with the various standard forms of main contract considered in previous chapters. The determination provisions naturally parallel those in the corresponding main contract, but each of them (with one exception) contains provision for automatic determination of the sub-contractor's employment if for any reason the main contractor's employment under the main contract is brought to an end.

In this chapter consideration will be given to the determination provisions in the following forms of sub-contract:

- The BEC/FASS/CASEC Domestic Sub-contract (DOM/1) 1980.
- The JCT Nominated Sub-contract (NSC/4/4a) 1980.
- The JCT Sub-contract Conditions for named sub-contractors under the Intermediate Form of Building Contract (NAM/SC) 1984.
- The ACA Form of Sub-contract 1984.
- The FCEC Form of Sub-contract 1984.

At present there is no published set of sub-contract conditions designed for use in conjunction with GC/Works/1, though at the time of writing such a sub-contract form is understood to be in an advanced state of preparation.

Domestic sub-contract DOM/1

There are three provisions for determination, which must each be considered in turn. They are:

Clause 29 – Determination of the employment of the sub-contractor by the contractor.
Clause 30 – Determination of employment under the sub-contract by the sub-contractor.
Clause 31 – Determination of the contractor's employment under the main contract.

Clause 29 – Determination of the employment of the sub-contractor by the contractor

Clause 29 reads as follows:

'29 **Determination of the employment of the Sub-Contractor by the Contractor**

Default by Sub-Contractor

29.1 Without prejudice to any other rights or remedies which the Contractor may possess, if the Sub-Contractor shall make default in any one or more of the following respects:

29.1 .1 if without reasonable cause he wholly suspends the carrying out of the Sub-Contract Works before completion thereof; or

29.1 .2 if without reasonable cause he fails to proceed with the Sub-Contract Works in the manner provided in clause 11.1; or

29.1 .3 if he refuses or persistently neglects after notice in writing from the Contractor to remove defective work or improper materials or goods and by such refusal or neglect the Works are materially affected, or wrongfully fails to rectify defects, shrinkages or other faults in the Sub-Contract Works, which rectification is in accordance with his obligations under the Sub-Contract; or

29.1 .4 if he fails to comply with the provisions of either clause 26 or clause 32;

then the Contractor may issue a notice to the Sub-Contractor by registered post or recorded delivery specifying the default. If the Sub-Contractor shall either continue such default for 10 days after receipt of such notice or shall at any time thereafter repeat such default (whether previously repeated or not) then the Contractor may within 10 days after such continuance or repetition by notice by registered post or recorded delivery forthwith determine the employment of the Sub-Contractor under the Sub-Contract; provided that such notice shall not be given unreasonably or vexatiously.

Sub-Contractor becoming bankrupt etc.

29.2   In the event of the Sub-Contractor becoming bankrupt or making a composition or arrangement with his creditors or having a winding up order made or (other than for the purposes of amalgamation or reconstruction) having a resolution for voluntary winding up passed, or having a provisional liquidator, receiver or manager of his business or undertaking duly appointed, or having possession taken by or on behalf of the holders of any debentures secured by a floating charge, of any property comprised in or subject to the floating charge, then the Contractor may, without prejudice to any other rights or remedies of the Contractor, by written notice, forthwith determine the employment of the Sub-Contractor under the Sub-Contract.

Contractor and Sub-Contractor – rights and duties

29.3   In the event of the employment of the Sub-Contractor under the Sub-Contract being determined under clause 29.1 or 29.2 the following shall be the respective rights and duties of the Contractor and the Sub-Contractor:

29.3   .1 the Contractor or his Sub-Contractor or agent may use all temporary buildings, plant, tools, equipment, goods and materials intended for, delivered to and placed on or adjacent to the Works, and may purchase all materials and goods necessary for the carrying out and completion of the Sub-Contract Works;

29.3   .2 .1 except where the determination occurs by reason of the bankruptcy of the Sub-Contractor or of him having a winding up order made or (other than for the purposes of amalgamation or reconstruction) a resolution for voluntary winding up passed, the Sub-Contractor shall if so required by the Contractor within 14 days of the date of determination, assign to the Contractor without payment the benefit of any agreement for the supply of materials or goods and/or for the execution of any work for the purposes of the Sub-Contract but on the terms that the supplier or sub-sub-contractor shall be entitled to make any reasonable objection to any further assignment thereof to the Contractor;

.2 .2 unless the exception to the operation of clause 29.3.2.1 applies the Contractor may pay any supplier or sub-sub-contractor for any materials or goods delivered or works executed for the purposes of the Sub-Contract (whether before or after the determination) insofar as the price thereof has not already been paid by the Sub-Contractor;

29.3   .3 the Sub-Contractor shall as and when required by a direction of the Contractor so to do (but not before) remove from the Works any temporary buildings, plant, tools, equipment, goods and materials belonging to or hired by him. If within a reasonable time after any such requirement has been made the Sub-Contractor has not complied therewith, then the Contractor may (but without being responsible for any loss or damage) remove and sell any such property of the Sub-Contractor holding the proceeds less all costs incurred to the credit of the Sub-Contractor.

29.4 The Sub-Contractor shall allow or pay to the Contractor in the manner hereinafter appearing the amount of any direct loss and/or damage caused to the Contractor by the determination. Until after completion of the Sub-Contract Works under clause 29.3.1 the Contractor shall not be bound by any provision of the Sub-Contract to make any further payment to the Sub-Contractor. Upon such completion the Sub-Contractor may apply to the Contractor and the Contractor shall pay to the Sub-Contractor the value of any work executed or goods and materials supplied by the Sub-Contractor to the extent that their value has not been included in previous interim payments. The Contractor, when calculating the payment to be made to the Sub-Contractor, may deduct therefrom any cash discount specified in the Appendix, part 7, and, without prejudice to any other rights of the Contractor, the amount of any direct loss and/or damage caused to the Contractor by the determination.'

In fact this clause corresponds closely to JCT 80, clause 27, which is discussed on pages 42-63. The differences between the main contract clause and clause 29 are:

● The words 'contractor' and 'sub-contractor' and 'sub-sub-contractor' are substituted for 'employer' or 'architect' and 'contractor' and 'sub-contractor' respectively.
● In place of 'failure to proceed regularly and diligently with the works' is 'failure to proceed with the sub-contract works in the manner provided in clause 11.1', i.e. 'in accordance with the details in the appendix part 4 and reasonably in accordance with the progress of the [main contract] works'. It would seem easier to establish this ground under DOM/1 than it is to establish 'failure to proceed regularly and diligently' under the main contract.
● There is reference to failure 'to rectify defects, shrinkages or other faults' which does not appear in the main contract.
● The period for continuance of default after the preliminary notice is ten days instead of fourteen days.
● Determination in the event of the sub-contractor's insolvency, etc. is discretionary and not automatic.
● There is no reference to determination for corrupt practices as there is in clause 27.3 in the local authorities edition of JCT 80.
● There is no specific reference to a right in the main contractor to employ others to complete the sub-contract works. This is probably of no significance as the contractor would enjoy that right in any event.

● The provisions for payment are necessarily different in that the architect will not be involved and there is therefore no question of certification. Instead, there is provision for the sub-contractor to apply to the main contractor for final payment (if any) after completion of the sub-contract works.

It should be noted that the question of determination is a matter entirely for the main contractor and the architect has no involvement in the process: *James Longley & Co. Ltd* v. *Borough of Reigate and Banstead* (1982), a decision of the Court of Appeal.

Clause 30 – Determination of employment under the sub-contract by the sub-contractor
Clause 30 reads:

'30   **Determination of employment under the Sub-Contract by the Sub-Contractor**

Acts etc. giving ground for determination of employment by Sub-Contractor

30.1   Without prejudice to any other rights or remedies which the Sub-Contractor may possess if the Contractor shall make default (for which default a remedy under any other provisions of the Sub-Contract would not adequately recompense the Sub-Contractor) in any of the following respects:

30.1   .1 .1 if without reasonable cause he wholly suspends the Works before completion; or

.1 .2 if without reasonable cause he fails to proceed with the Works so that the reasonable progress of the Sub-Contract Works is seriously affected; or

.1 .3 if he fails to make payment in accordance with this Sub-Contract;

then the Sub-Contractor may issue to the Contractor a notice by registered post or recorded delivery specifying the default. If the Contractor shall continue such default for 10 days after receipt of such notice or if the Contractor shall at any time thereafter repeat such default (whether previously repeated or not) the Sub-Contractor may thereupon by notice by registered post or recorded delivery determine the employment of the Sub-Contractor; provided that such notice shall not be given unreasonably or vexatiously.

30.1   .2 Where the Sub-Contractor has suspended the further execution of the Sub-Contract Works under clause 21.6 the Sub-Contractor will not be entitled to issue a notice of determination in respect of any default under clause 30.1 until 10 days after the date of commencement of the suspension.

Determination of employment by Sub-Contractor – rights and duties of Contractor and Sub-Contractor

30.2 Without prejudice to the accrued rights or remedies of either party or to any liability of the classes mentioned in clause 6 which may accrue before the Sub-Contractor shall have removed his temporary buildings plant, tools, equipment, goods or materials or by reason of his so removing the same, the respective rights and duties of the Sub-Contractor and Contractor upon determination under clause 30.1 shall be as follows:

30.2 .1 the Sub-Contractor shall with all reasonable dispatch and in such manner and with such precautions as will prevent injury, death or damage of the classes in respect of which he is liable to indemnify the Contractor under clause 6 remove from the site all his temporary buildings, plant, tools, equipment, goods or materials subject to the provisions of clause 30.2.2.4;

30.2 .2 after taking into account amounts previously paid under the Sub-Contract the Sub-Contractor shall be paid by the Contractor:

.2 .1 the total value of work completed at the date of determination, such value to be ascertained in accordance with clause 21;

.2 .2 the total value of work begun and executed but not completed at the date of determination, such value to be ascertained either under clause 16 as if it were a Valuation of a Variation (where clause 15.1 applies) or under clause 17 (where clause 15.2 applies);

.2 .3 any sum ascertained in respect of direct loss and/or expense under clause 13.1 (whether ascertained before or after the date of determination);

.2 .4 the cost of materials or goods properly ordered for the Sub-Contract Works (but not incorporated therein) for which the Sub-Contractor shall have paid or is legally bound to accept delivery and on such payment by the Contractor any materials or goods so paid for shall become the property of the Contractor;

.2 .5 the reasonable cost of removal under clause 30.2.1;'

The wording of clause 30.1 differs materially from its counterpart (clause 28.1, see page 68) in the main contract. They are natural differences because of the material difference in position and function between the employer under the main contract and the contractor under the sub-contract.

Clause 30.1 specifies three defaults by the main contractor which entitle the sub-contractor to determine his own employment under the sub-contract by following the procedure specified in the clause.

Suspension of work

Apart from a minor difference in wording of no significance, the position is the same as in clause 27.1.1 of JCT 80 and the reader is referred to the commentary on pages 45-9.

Failure to proceed with the main contract works

Clause 30.1.1.2 differs substantially in its effect from the equivalent provision in JCT 80, clause 27.1.2, which entitles the employer to determine the main contractor's employment 'if he fails to proceed regularly and diligently with the works'. Here the ground is if the main contractor's conduct of the works seriously affects the reasonable progress of the sub-contract works, and the main contractor's failure to so proceed must be without reasonable cause.

'Without reasonable cause' is a key phrase and it is our view that there must be some fault on the part of the main contractor himself or on the part of those for whom the main contractor is responsible in law, e.g. other sub-contractors. So, for example, delay to the main contract works caused by another domestic sub-contractor would probably not amount to a 'reasonable cause'; but the position is more complicated in the case of nominated sub-contractors because of the provision entitling the main contractor to an extension of time for delay 'on their part', with the corresponding right of the sub-contractor to an extension under clause 11.10.7 of DOM/1. On the other hand, breaches of contract by the employer, including failure to pay (see *J.M. Hill & Sons Ltd v. London Borough of Camden* (1980)), would seemingly constitute 'reasonable cause'.

This would seem an easier ground to establish than failure to proceed 'regularly and diligently' under the main contract because of the likely existence of a programme agreed between main contractor and sub-contractor, and the details which may be set out in part 4 of the Appendix to the sub-contract relating to commencement and completion of the sub-contract works.

It is to be noted that the interference with progress must be of a nature which differs substantially from that which would give the sub-contractor a right to recovery of direct loss and/or expense under clause 13.1. There the 'regular' progress of the sub-contract works must be 'materially' affected. Here it is 'reasonable' progress which must be 'seriously' affected and this would imply that a substantially greater degree of interference with progress is necessary before the sub-contractor can opt to exercise a right of determination as opposed to recovery of direct loss and/or expense.

Failure to make payment

The default in clause 30.1.1.3 is failure to make payment in accordance with clause 21 under which the first payment is due not later than one month after the date of commencement of the sub-contract works on site or, if so agreed, off site. Interim payments are thereafter due at periods not exceeding one month and all such payments must be made within seventeen days following the date when they become due. The default covers both timing and amount of payment so that a failure to pay an amount calculated in accordance with clause 21 would also be grounds for determination. An alternative remedy available for an unpaid sub-contractor is the right to suspend execution of the sub-contract works under clause 21.6, discussed on pages 182-5. Clause 21 is not a 'pay when paid' clause but entitles the sub-contractor to payment for work done irrespective of whether the main contractor receives payment for that work from the employer.

Because there is no provision in the sub-contract for ascertainment of amounts due by an independent third party such as the architect, it can be very difficult for the sub-contractor to establish failure to pay amounts due to a degree sufficient to entitle him to exercise the right of determination with safety.

Procedure

As with determination of the main contractor's employment by the employer under JCT 80, the determination procedure is based upon two notices both of which should be served by registered post or recorded delivery. Only the second notice is subject to the qualification that it must not be given 'unreasonably or vexatiously'.

The main difference between the procedure under DOM/1 and that under clause 27.1 of JCT 80 is that the main contractor need only continue the default for ten days as opposed to fourteen days following receipt of the preliminary notice. Whereas JCT 80, clause 27.1, requires the employer to serve the determination notice within ten days after the expiry of the initial period, clause 30.1 of DOM/1 requires the service of the determination notice 'thereupon' if he wishes to exercise his right to determine his employment. Since the dictionary definition of 'thereupon' is 'immediately or upon that point', it is suggested that the sub-contractor must act immediately if he is not to be taken to have waived his rights.

For further discussion of notices, etc. see pages 41-2.

Under clause 30.1.2 the sub-contractor who has exercised his right to suspend work for non-payment under clause 21.6 cannot issue the final notice of determination until ten days after the date of commencement of the suspension. Since he must give seven days' notice of his intention to suspend, it would seem that on the expiry of that period he may suspend work and at the same time issue a preliminary notice of default under clause 30.1. He is thus provided with a useful tactical gambit.

Procedures following determination

The procedures following determination in clause 30.2 mirror those of main contract clause 28.2 where the main contractor determines his own employment: see pages 73-6 for discussion.

There is, however, one notable omission and that is that the sub-contractor has no express entitlement to recovery of *direct loss and/or damage* caused by the determination. It is not certain whether this is by design or by oversight but the inclusion of such a right in the equivalent clause in the JCT Nominated Sub-contractor Form NSC/4 suggests the latter, and DOM/1 should be amended accordingly since its omission seriously affects the sub-contractor's rights. The opening reference to the sub-contractor's right of determination being 'without prejudice to any other rights or remedies which the sub-contractor may possess' leaves open the possibility of a common law action for damages – which would include loss of profit and other foreseeable consequential loss – if the ground relied on amounted to a repudiatory breach at common law. Even so, the further reference to *accrued* rights and remedies of either party might well be held to be restrictive of that right and in our view there is no justification whatsoever for the omission of an express right to recover loss and/or damage arising from the determination.

Clause 31 – Determination of the contractor's employment under the main contract

Clause 31 reads as follows:

'31   **Determination of the Contractor's employment under the Main Contract**

If the employment of the Contractor is determined under either clauses 27 or 28 of the Main Contract Conditions, then the employment of the Sub-Contractor under the Sub-Contract shall thereupon also determine and the provisions of clause 30.2 shall thereafter apply.'

Determination of the sub-contractor's employment is automatic if the main contractor's employment under the main contract is determined for any reason, whether by the main contractor himself or by the employer. Since the main contractor is entitled to recover direct loss and/or damage resulting from his own determination of his employment, any additional money which he would have to pay to domestic sub-contractors through the operation of this clause would be recoverable from the employer. It is therefore remarkable that under these provisions the domestic sub-contractor has no equivalent right to recover damages, his sole entitlement being the value of work done or materials or goods ordered and the reasonable cost of removal together with any ascertained direct loss and/or expense arising from other causes.

Since this clause is *not* stated to be without prejudice to any other rights or remedies which the sub-contractor may possess, this would seem to deprive him of any right to damages – which would include loss of profit – whatever the reason for the determination, even if it also amounted to a breach of the express or implied terms of the sub-contract.

Domestic sub-contract DOM/2 for use with the JCT Standard Form of Building Contract with Contractor's Design 1981 has determination provisions which are identical in terms with DOM/1, and accordingly no separate commentary is necessary.

Nominated sub-contract NSC/4 and 4a

The three determination provisions are numbered and headed identically with those in DOM/1. They parallel the equivalent provisions in DOM/1 very closely and our commentary is therefore confined to the differences between the two forms of sub-contract. NSC/4a is identical in its terms to NSC/4 and so all references are to the latter version of the sub-contract.

Clause 29 – Determination of the employment of the sub-contractor by the contractor
Clause 29 reads as follows:

'29 **Determination of the employment of the Sub-Contractor by the Contractor**

Default by Sub-Contractor
29.1 Without prejudice to any other rights or remedies which the

Contractor may possess, if the Sub-Contractor shall make default in any one or more of the following respects that is to say:

29.1 .1 if without reasonable cause he wholly suspends the carrying out of the Sub-Contract Works before completion thereof; or

.2 if without reasonable cause he fails to proceed with the Sub-Contract Works in the manner provided in clause 11.1; or

.3 if he refuses or persistently neglects after notice in writing from the Contractor to remove defective work or improper materials or goods and by such refusal or neglect the Works are materially affected, or wrongfully fails to rectify defects, shrinkages or other faults in the Sub-Contract Works, which rectification is in accordance with his obligations under the Sub-Contract;

.4 if he fails to comply with the provisions of either clause 26 or clause 32;

then the Contractor shall so inform the Architect and send to the Architect any written observation of the Sub-Contractor in regard to the default or defaults of which the Contractor is informing the Architect. If so instructed by the Architect under clause 35.24.4.1 of the Main Contract Conditions the Contractor shall issue a notice to the Sub-Contractor by registered post or recorded delivery specifying the default (and send a copy thereof by registered post or recorded delivery to the Architect). If the Sub-Contractor shall either continue such default for 14 days after receipt of such notice or shall at any time thereafter repeat such default (whether previously repeated or not), then the Contractor may (but subject where relevant to the further instruction of the Architect to which clause 35.24.4.1 of the Main Contract Conditions refers) within 10 days after such continuance or repetition by notice by registered post or recorded delivery forthwith determine the employment of the Sub-Contractor under the Sub-Contract; provided that such notice shall not be given unreasonably or vexatiously.

Sub-Contractor becoming bankrupt etc.

29.2 In the event of the Sub-Contractor becoming bankrupt or making a composition or arrangement with his creditors or having a winding up order made or (other than for the purposes of amalgamation or reconstruction) having a resolution for voluntary winding up passed, or having a provisional liquidator, receiver or manager of his business or undertaking duly appointed, or having possession taken by or on behalf of the holders of any debentures secured by a floating charge, of any property comprised in or subject to the floating charge, the employment of the Sub-Contractor under the Sub-Contract shall forthwith automatically be determined. Such determination shall be without prejudice to any other rights or remedies of the Contractor.

Contractor and Sub-Contractor rights and duties

29.3 In the event of the employment of the Sub-Contractor under the Sub-Contract being determined under clause 29.1 or 29.2 the following shall be the respective rights and duties of the Contractor and the Sub-Contractor:

29.3 .1 when the Employer through the Architect nominates a person to carry out and complete the Sub-Contract Works such person may enter upon the Sub-Contract Works and use all temporary buildings, plant tools, equipment, goods and materials intended for, delivered to and placed on or adjacent to the Works, and may purchase all materials and goods necessary for the carrying out and completion of the Sub-Contract Works;

29.3 .2 .1 except where the determination occurs by reason of the bankruptcy of the Sub-Contractor or of him having a winding up order made or (other than for the purposes of amalgamation or reconstruction) a resolution for voluntary winding up passed, the Sub-Contractor shall if so required by the Employer or by the Architect on behalf of the Employer and with the consent of the Contractor within 14 days of the date of determination, assign to the Contractor without payment the benefit of any agreement for the supply of materials or goods and/or for the execution of any work for the purposes of the Sub-Contract but on the terms that the supplier or sub-sub-contractor shall be entitled to make any reasonable objection to any further assignment thereof to the Contractor;

.2 .2 unless the exception to the operation of clause 29.3.2 applies the Contractor, if so directed by the Architect, shall pay any supplier or sub-sub-contractor for any materials or goods delivered or works executed for the purposes of the Sub-Contract (whether before or after the determination) insofar as the price thereof has not already been paid by the Sub-Contractor;

29.3 .3 the Sub-Contractor shall as and when required by a direction of the Contractor or by an instruction of the Architect so to do (but not before) remove from the Works any temporary buildings, plant, tools, equipment, goods and materials belonging to or hired by him. If within a reasonable time after any such requirement has been made the Sub-Contractor has not complied therewith, then the Contractor may (but without being responsible for any loss or damage) remove and sell any such property of the Sub-Contractor holding the proceeds less all costs incurred to the credit of the Sub-Contractor.

29.4 The Sub-Contractor shall allow or pay to the Contractor in the manner hereinafter appearing the amount of any direct loss and/or damage caused to the Contractor by the determination. Until after completion of the Sub-Contract Works under clause 29.3.1 the Contractor shall not be bound by any provision of the Sub-Contract to make any further payment to the Sub-Contractor. Upon such completion the Sub-Contractor may apply to the Contractor who shall pass such application to the Architect who shall ascertain or instruct the Quantity Surveyor to ascertain the amount of expenses properly incurred by the Employer and the amount of direct loss and/or damage caused to the Employer by the determination; and shall issue an Interim Certificate certifying the value of any work executed or goods and materials supplied by the Sub-Contractor to the extent that their value has not been included in previous Interim Certificates; in paying that Certificate the Employer may deduct the amount of the expenses and direct loss and/or damage of the Employer as aforesaid. The Contractor in discharging his obligation to pay the Sub-Contractor such amount may deduct therefrom a cash discount of 2½ per cent and, without prejudice to any other rights of the Contractor, the amount of any direct loss and/or damage caused to the Contractor by the determination.'

The grounds for determination are identical to those set out in clause 29 of DOM/1: see pages 137-8. However, the procedures for determination in the event of sub-contractor default differ as follows:

● Before issuing a notice of default the main contractor must inform the architect and send to him 'any written observation of the sub-contractor in regard to the default or defaults'. This therefore presupposes that the sub-contractor is given an opportunity to comment, which itself presupposes some kind of warning from the main contractor of his intention to seek an instruction from the architect.

● The main contractor is to issue a notice of default to the sub-contractor only if so instructed by the architect. Any notice of default issued without an architect's instruction will be invalid. However, the architect is required to issue the necessary instruction if he 'is reasonably of the opinion that the sub-contractor has made default' (JCT 80, clauses 35.24.1 and 35.24.4.1). The architect's instruction to the main contractor may state that he must obtain a further instruction before determining the sub-contractor's employment.

● Continuance of the default by the sub-contractor must continue for fourteen days (as opposed to ten days) after receipt of the main contractor's notice.

● If the sub-contractor continues the default for fourteen days after the preliminary notice or subsequently repeats such default the contractor may, within ten days, issue a determination notice to the sub-contractor although if the architect has so instructed he must seek a further architect's instruction before doing so. The main contractor must inform the architect that he has issued the notice of determination and in that event the architect must issue further instructions for the nomination of a completion sub-contractor. However, where the sub-contractor's employment has been determined under clause 29.1.3, i.e. after refusal or neglect to rectify defects, etc., the main contractor is to be given the opportunity to agree the price to be charged by the substituted sub-contractor since he may in some circumstances be liable himself to pay for the rectification work without recovery from the employer: see JCT 80, clause 35.18.1.

In the case of the sub-contractor's insolvency, clause 29.2 provides for automatic determination of his employment – a provision already criticised in relation to the similar provision in JCT 80: see page 53. There is no provision in JCT 80 for the main contractor to inform the architect of the insolvency situation, but it would obviously be sensible for him to do so because the architect is obliged by JCT 80, clause 35.24.5 to nominate a completion sub-contractor. However, the architect may delay any further nomination where a receiver or manager of the nominated sub-contractor's business has been appointed 'if there are reasonable grounds for supposing that the receiver or manager is prepared to continue to carry out or fulfil the relevant sub-contract in a way which will not prejudice the interests of the employer, the contractor or any sub-contractor whether nominated or domestic engaged, or to be engaged, upon or in connection with the works'. This sensible provision could well find a place in any revision of the determination provisions of JCT 80, clause 27.2.

The procedure following determination is similar to that provided for by DOM/1, clause 29.3 save only that the architect may instruct the sub-contractor to remove his temporary buildings, etc. from the site. This is in addition to the main contractor's right so to direct.

Provisions for payment differ in the following respects:

● Any application from the sub-contractor for final payment following completion of the sub-contract works must be passed to the architect by the main contractor. The architect must then ascertain, or instruct the quantity surveyor to ascertain, 'the amount of expenses properly incurred by the employer and the amount of direct loss and/or damage caused to the employer by the determination'.

● The architect must issue an interim certificate under the main contract 'certifying the value of any work executed or goods and materials supplied by the sub-contractor to the extent that their value has not been included in previous interim certificates'.

When paying the main contractor the employer is entitled to deduct the certified amount of his expenses, loss and/or damage. The main contractor must then pay the sub-contractor the amount certified by the architect, less his cash discount and less his own direct loss and/or damage caused by the determination which will, of course, include the amount deducted by the employer. Although there is, oddly enough, no specific provision to this effect it is clear that, in the likely event of the amount deductible by the contractor exceeding the amount payable to the sub-contractor, the contractor would have a right to recover the difference at common law, though this will be an empty remedy in the vast majority of cases.

It is to be noted that the express provisions for involvement of the architect in determination of a nominated sub-contractor's employment did not exist in JCT 63 or the associated nominated sub-contract form. In relation to those forms, the Court of Appeal decided in *James Longley & Co. Ltd* v. *Borough of Reigate & Banstead* (1982) that there was no requirement for the architect to be consulted or to issue any instruction in connection with the determination of the nominated sub-contractor's employment by the main contractor. Even under JCT 63, however, the employer through his architect was still obliged to nominate a completion sub-contractor: see *North West Metropolitan Regional Hospital Board* v. *T.A. Bickerton & Sons Ltd* (1970) and *Percy Bilton Ltd* v. *Greater London Council* (1982). One result of the *Bickerton* decision was that the employer had to pay the main contractor whatever was payable to the completion sub-contractor and also bear all his own consequential loss and expense with no right of recovery such as is now conferred on him by the express terms of JCT 80.

Clause 30 – Determination of employment under the sub-contract by the sub-contractor

The wording of this clause is identical with the similarly-numbered clause in DOM/1 with the following two exceptions:

● The omission of any right of determination for the main contractor's failure to make payment in accordance with the terms of the sub-contract. Under NSC/4, therefore, the nominated sub-contractor's only express contractual remedy for non-payment is to suspend the execution of the works under clause 21.8: see pages 183-5.

● The inclusion of an express right to recover 'any direct loss and/or expense caused to the sub-contractor by the determination', thus enabling him in effect to recover damages for the determination. For discussion on the effect of the inclusion of such an express right see the commentary on JCT 80, clause 28 on pages 74-5, and for the effect of its omission from the equivalent clause in DOM/1 see page 142.

Clause 31 – Determination of the main contractor's employment under the main contract

Clause 31 reads as follows:

'31   **Determination of the Main Contractor's employment under the Main Contract**

Determination of Contractor's employment by Employer for default etc. of the Contractor

31.1   If the employment of the Contractor is determined under clause 27 of the Main Contract Conditions, then the employment of the Sub-Contractor under the Sub-Contract shall thereupon also determine and the provisions of clause 30.2 shall thereafter apply.

Determination of Contractor's employment by Contractor for default etc. of the Employer

31.2   .1 If the employment of the Contractor is determined under clause 28 of the Main Contract Conditions then the employment of the Sub-Contractor under the Sub-Contract shall thereupon also determine. The entitlement of the Sub-Contractor to payment shall be the proportion fairly and reasonably attributable to the Sub-Contract Works of the amounts paid by the Employer under clause 28.2.2.1 to .5 of the Main Contract Conditions inclusive together with any amounts paid in respect of the Sub-Contractor under clause 28.2.2.6 of the Main Contract Conditions provided the Sub-Contractor shall have supplied to the Contractor all evidence reasonably necessary to establish the direct loss and/or damage caused to the Sub-Contractor by the determination as referred to in clause 28.2.2.6 of the Main Contract Conditions.

31.2   .2 Nothing in clause 31.2.1 shall affect the entitlement of the Sub-Contractor to the proper operation of clause 21 in respect of the amount, included in the amount stated as due therein, in respect of the Sub-Contract Works in an Interim Certificate of the Architect whose date of issue was prior to the date of determination of the employment of the Contractor under clause 28 of the Main Contract Conditions.'

It will be seen that if the main contractor's employment is determined by the employer due to the main contractor's default or insolvency, the provisions of this clause correspond to those of clause 31 of DOM/1 save that the nominated sub-contractor is given the express right to recover direct loss and/or expense flowing from the determination of his employment. However, if the main contractor determined his own employment under the main contract because of the employer's default or it is determined automatically because of the employer's insolvency, the position is different.

In that event, the sub-contractor's recovery is to be a fair and reasonable proportion of the amount recoverable by the main contractor under the terms of the main contract plus any direct loss and/or damage caused to the sub-contractor by the determination. The latter is subject to the proviso that the sub-contractor has supplied to the main contractor all the evidence reasonably necessary to establish the amount of the direct loss and/or damage which he has suffered or incurred.

The sub-contractor's right to payment of any amounts certified by the architect as due to him prior to the date of the determination of the main contractor's employment is preserved by clause 31.2.2 irrespective of whether the main contractor has received payment from the employer.

Named sub-contract NAM/SC

The determination provisions of NAM/SC are modelled on those of DOM/1, though the clause numbering differs.

Clause 27 – Determination of the employment of the sub-contractor by the contractor. This corresponds to DOM/1, clause 29.

Clause 28 – Determination of employment under the sub-contract by the sub-contractor. This corresponds to DOM/1, clause 30.

Clause 29 – Determination of the contractor's employment under the main contract. This corresponds to DOM/1, clause 31.

The differences between the two sub-contracts flow from the procedure for naming sub-contractors set out in clause 3.3 of the JCT Intermediate Form of Building Contract (IFC 84) which itself contains complicated provisions setting out what is to happen should the named sub-contractor's employment be determined under clauses 27.1 or 27.2 of NAM/SC, or otherwise: see main contract, clause 3.3.6.

Clause 27 – Determination of sub-contractor's employment by contractor

The following are the principal differences between this clause and clause 29 of DOM/1:

- The provision that the right of determination is 'without prejudice to any other rights or remedies which the contractor may possess' is transferred to a separate sub-clause, clause 27.4, placing it beyond doubt that the saving applies to all the provisions of the clause including the consequences which follow determination.
- There is an express right in the contractor to employ others to carry out and complete the sub-contract works.
- An additional sub-clause, clause 27.3.3, provides as follows:

  'The sub-contractor shall pay to the contractor the amounts which the contractor is to recover under clause 3.3.6(b) of the main contract conditions. The sub-contractor, having notice of the terms of the said main contract conditions, undertakes not to contend whether in proceedings or otherwise that the contractor has suffered no loss or that his obligation to pay the contractor under this clause 27.3.3 should be in any way reduced or extinguished by reason of the application of clauses 3.3.4(a) or (b) or 3.3.5 of the main contract conditions'.

  This unusual provision is inserted in order to give the main contractor the right to recover for the benefit of the employer all additional amounts payable to him by the employer under clauses 3.3.4(a) and (b) and 3.3.5 of the main contract, together with an amount equal to any liquidated damages which would have been payable or allowable by the main contractor to the employer had it not been for the operation of the extension of time provisions in those clauses. The named sub-contractor is therefore expressly prevented from contending that the contractor's right of payment and extension of time under those clauses has resulted in his not suffering a loss under the sub-contract and is therefore not entitled to claim any damages from the sub-contractor.

It has been suggested (Jones and Bergman, *Commentary on the JCT Intermediate Form of Building Contract* (Collins, 1985), page 130) that:

'It might conceivably be argued that clause 27.3.3 . . . represents something akin to a penalty provision in that it requires the payment of a sum of money from the named sub-contractor to the contractor which bears no relationship whatsoever to any actual loss suffered or incurred by the contractor.'

The authors cite the views expressed obiter by Lord Denning and Lord Devlin in *Bridge* v. *Campbell Discount Co. Ltd* (1962) in support of this view. That was a hire-purchase case in which the hirer was required to pay a minimum by reference to the total hire-purchase price, by way of what was euphemistically called 'agreed compensation for depreciation', should the hirer exercise his right to terminate the agreement during the period of hiring or if the agreement were terminated by the finance company for default by the hirer. The amount was held to be a penalty, because the agreement had been terminated by the finance company and different views were expressed as to the position where the contract was terminated by the hirer. However, the House of Lords has recently held (in *Export Credits Guarantee Department* v. *Universal Oil Products Co.* (1983)) that a sum cannot be a penalty unless it is payable on an event which is a breach of contract as between payer and payee. Since the sums payable as a result of the operation of clause 27.3.3 are payable upon events which, apart from insolvency, constitute breaches of the sub-contract, they undoubtedly fall within the scope of the present law relating to penalties. However, a court might well hold that since the sub-contractor is only being required to pay the damage which he has caused by his breach, the arrangement was a reasonable one having regard to the structure of the contractual and sub-contractual arrangements.

There is no clause equivalent to clause 29.3.2 of DOM/1 entitling the contractor to pay suppliers or sub-sub-contractors direct for materials or goods delivered or work executed for the purposes of the sub-contract and the price of which has not been paid by the sub-contractor.

The payment provision is set out in clause 27.3.4 and differs from its DOM/1 equivalent, clause 29.4. Clause 27.3.4 reads as follows:

> '27.3 .4 until after completion of the Sub-Contract Works the Contractor shall not be bound to make any further payment to the Sub-Contractor but upon such completion and the verification within a reasonable time of the accounts therefor the following matters shall be set out in an account drawn up by the Contractor:
>
> .4 .1 the amount of expense and direct loss and/or damage caused to the Contractor by the determination including the payments made to other persons to carry out and complete the Sub-Contract Works to the extent not previously paid under clause 27.3.3,
>
> .4 .2 the amount paid to the Sub-Contractor before the date of determination, grossed up to include any cash discount deducted in accordance with clause 19.3,
>
> and if the total of such amounts exceeds or is less than the total amount which would have been payable on due completion in accordance with the Sub-Contract, the difference shall be a debt payable by the Sub-Contractor to the Contractor or by the Contractor to the Sub-Contractor as the case may be. Where an amount is payable by the Contractor to the Sub-Contractor, it shall be treated as if it were a payment under clause 19.3 for the purposes of deducting a cash discount in accordance with clause 19.3.'

The significant points to note are as follows:

● There is no requirement for the sub-contractor to apply to the main contractor for final payment.
● An account must be drawn up by the contractor showing the amount of the expense and direct loss and/or damage caused by the determination, including payment to others for the completion of the sub-contract works, and the amount paid to the sub-contractor before determination must be grossed-up to include the main contractor's cash discount.
● The difference between the amount shown in that account and the amount which would have been payable to the sub-

contractor had he completed is to be treated as a debt payable by the contractor to the sub-contractor or vice versa. If an amount is payable by the contractor to the sub-contractor it is subject to cash discount.

This very clear provision is much to be preferred to the rather obscure wording of clause 29.4 of DOM/1.

Consequences under main contract IFC 84

Clause 3.3.3 of IFC 84 deals with the situation where the named sub-contractor's employment may have to be determined by the main contractor under clause 27 of NAM/SC.

● The contractor is forbidden to determine the sub-contractor's employment other than under clause 27 and is forbidden to accept repudiation of the sub-contract by the sub-contractor, presumably because of the provisions of IFC 84, clause 3.3.6(b).
● The contractor is to advise the architect 'as soon as is reasonably practicable of any events which are likely to lead to any determination of the employment of the named person howsoever arising'. This is obviously a reasonable requirement so that the architect may be warned of impending problems.
● The contractor is to notify the architect of his determination of the sub-contractor's employment stating the circumstances.
● The architect must then issue an instruction to the main contractor, either naming another sub-contractor to complete the works or instructing the main contractor to make his own arrangements for completion (in which event the contractor may sub-let the work to anyone he pleases) or omitting the outstanding balance of the work (in which case the employer may employ others to do it). Different consequences follow according to which option the architect adopts and to the manner in which the original sub-contractor was named.

Sub-contractor named in main contract documents

(1) If the architect names a replacement sub-contractor, the main contractor is paid in respect of the completion of the works according to the price charged by the substitute sub-contractor, the main contract sum being adjusted accordingly. He is also

entitled to an extension of time but *not* to recovery of any direct loss and/or expense from the employer. He also has no entitlement to payment from the employer for any amount payable to the substitute sub-contractor for making good defects in the original sub-contract work. He must therefore look to the defaulting sub-contractor for recovery of any loss or expense which he suffers and for the cost of remedial work.

(2) If the architect instructs the contractor to make his own arrangements for completion of the work, this is to be valued as if it were a variation under the main contract. In effect this means that the completion work will be valued by the quantity surveyor (unless a sum is agreed with the employer himself) on a fair basis, which may not necessarily accord with the manner in which the main contractor has chosen to complete the work. The main contractor is also entitled to an extension of time and to recovery of direct loss and/or expense from the employer.

(3) Where the architect omits the work, the effect of this omission is also to be valued as a variation under the main contract and the contractor will be entitled to an extension of time and recovery of loss and/or expense from the employer. If the employer does not engage others to complete the work but leaves it uncompleted, it would be unlikely that any extension of time would be due but the contractor would be able to recover loss of profit on the work omitted as appropriate. Should the employer engage others to complete the work he thereby takes the consequences should they then cause further delay and disruption to the works, whereas if a substitute sub-contractor had been named the main contractor would bear that risk. This is, therefore, not an option to be adopted if it can be avoided.

Sub-contractor named against provisional sum
Whichever of the three options is chosen by the architect, his instruction is to be regarded as a further instruction issued against the provisional sum so that it will carry all the consequences of possible extensions of time and recovery of direct loss and/or expense by the contractor from the employer. Moreover, if the architect chooses to omit the outstanding balance of the work the employer is given no express right to employ others to complete it and would have no such right under the general law.

Action against defaulting sub-contractor
Clause 3.3.6(b) provides for the contractor to seek to recover from the defaulting sub-contractor the additional amounts payable to him by the employer as a result of the operation of the preceding clauses. We have already discussed the policy of this clause above. It is to be noted that his obligation to take 'such reasonable action as is necessary' so to recover the amounts in question and he is not required to commence arbitration or other proceedings without an indemnity from the employer in respect of legal costs. Failure by the contractor to comply with this clause at all, i.e. if he makes no effort whatever to recover the amounts in question, means that he must repay the amount to the employer, including any liquidated damages for which he would otherwise have been liable for delay in completion of the main contract works.

Clause 28 – Determination of employment by sub-contractor
This clause is identical, *mutatis mutandis*, with clause 30 of DOM/1, subject to two exceptions:

- The proviso stating that the contractual right of determination is without prejudice to any other rights or remedies of the sub-contractor is transferred to a separate sub-clause 28.4, emphasising that it applies to the whole of the clause including provisions for payment.
- The sub-contractor is given an express right to recover any direct loss and/or damage caused to him by the determination.

If the sub-contractor determines his own employment as the result of the main contractor's default, the architect is required to issue instructions and has the same three options as he has in the event of determination by the contractor under clause 27 of the sub-contract. Clause 3.3.6(a) of the main contract IFC 84 provides that the main contractor will not be entitled to recover any additional cost or to any extension of the contract time resulting from this. Further, in the unlikely event of the architect's instruction following determination resulting in a saving in cost this is to be deducted from the main contract sum.

Clause 29 – Determination of the contractor's employment under the main contract
Clause 29 runs as follows:

'29 **Determination of the Contractor's employment under the Main Contract**

If the employment of the Contractor is determined under clauses 7.1, 7.2, 7.3, 7.5, 7.6 or 7.8 of the Main Contract Conditions, then the employment of the Sub-Contractor under the Sub-Contract shall thereupon also determine and the provisions of clause 28.3 shall thereafter apply, save that upon such a determination under clause 7.8 of the Main Contract Conditions the provisions of clause 28.3.2.6 shall not apply.'

Clause 29 is effectively identical to clause 31 of DOM/1 except that the sub-contractor has, by the reference to clause 28.3, an express right to recover direct loss and/or damage caused to him by the determination *except* where the determination arises under clause 7.8 of IFC 84, i.e. by reason of *force majeure*, loss or damage resulting from the insurable risks, or civil commotion – an exception which is entirely justified.

The ACA Form of Sub-contract

First published in 1982, a second edition of this form was issued in 1984. It is designed for use with the ACA Form of Building Agreement though its use is not mandatory under that form. However, it is the only existing form of sub-contract which is compatible with the ACA main contract.

It contains a single clause dealing with termination of the sub-contractor's employment by either party, namely clause 13 which reads as follows:

'13. **Termination**

Termination by the Contractor

13.1 Upon the happening of one or more of the following events, namely if the Sub-Contractor:
 (a) without reasonable cause substantially suspends the execution of the Sub-Contract Works or any part of them before completion of the same;
 (b) fails or neglects to comply with his obligations under Clause 6 of this Agreement;
 (c) without reasonable cause fails to proceed regularly and diligently with the Sub-Contract Works;
 (d) refuses or neglects to comply with any instruction which the Contractor is empowered by this Sub-Contract to give;
 (e) shall otherwise be in breach of this Sub-Contract;

then the Contractor may, in addition, to any other power enabling him to terminate this Sub-Contract, serve notice on the Sub-Contractor specifying the event and requiring its remedy and if the Sub-Contractor fails to remedy the same within ⟦ 10 ⟧ working days of service of such notice or at any time after the service of such notice commits any further substantially similar breach of this Sub-Contract, the Contractor may by further notice forthwith terminate the employment of the Sub-Contractor.

Termination by the Sub-Contractor

13.2   Upon the happening of one or more of the following events, namely if the Contractor:
   (a) does not pay to the Sub-Contractor any amount properly due and payable under this Sub-Contract (subject to any deductions which the Contractor may be entitled to make);
   (b) is otherwise in breach of this Sub-Contract and such breach has prevented the Sub-Contractor from carrying out his obligations for a continuous period of ⟦ 20 ⟧ working days,
   then the Sub-Contractor may, in addition to any other power enabling him to terminate this Sub-Contract, serve notice on the Contractor specifying the event and requiring its remedy and if the Contractor fails to remedy the same within ⟦ 10 ⟧ working days of service of such notice, the Sub-Contractor may by further notice forthwith terminate his employment.

Termination on insolvency

13.3   Either party may terminate the Sub-Contractor's employment by notice to the other forthwith if any distress or execution shall be levied upon such other party's property or assets or if such other party shall make or offer to make any arrangement or composition with its creditors or commit an act of bankruptcy or if any petition or receiving order in bankruptcy shall be presented or made against him or (if he is a limited company) any resolution or petition to wind up such company's business (other than for the purpose of a bona fide reconstruction or amalgamation without insolvency) shall be passed or presented or if a receiver of such company's undertaking property or assets or any part of them shall be appointed.

Termination of Agreement

13.4   If the Agreement is determined or discharged or if the Contractor's employment under the Agreement is terminated for any reason whatsoever before the Sub-Contractor's obligations have been fully performed under this Sub-Contract, then the Contractor may at any time by written notice to the Sub-Contractor forthwith terminate the Sub-Contractor's employment.

Payment where Contractor terminates

13.5   If the Sub-Contractor's employment is terminated by the Contractor under Clause 13.1 or 13.3, the Contractor shall not be bound to make any further payment to the Sub-Contractor until the full and final cost of completion of the Sub-Contract Works by others has been ascertained but upon such cost being ascertained, the Contractor shall ascertain the amount of any damage, loss and/or expense suffered or incurred by him, and, if such amount when added to the monies paid to the Sub-Contractor before the date of termination exceeds the total value of work properly executed together with any adjustments to the Sub-Contract Sum ascertained in accordance with this Sub-Contract up to the date of termination, the difference shall be a debt payable to the Contractor by the Sub-Contractor.

Payment where Sub-Contractor terminates

13.6 If the Sub-Contractor's employment is terminated by the Sub-Contractor under Clause 13.2 or 13.32 or by the Contractor under Clause 13.4 (save where the Agreement is determined or discharged or the Contractor's employment under the Agreement is terminated by reason of any negligence, omission or default of the Sub-Contractor), the Contractor shall ascertain and pay to the Sub-Contractor the total amount properly due to the Sub-Contractor up to the date of termination.

Common law rights

13.7 Termination of the Sub-Contractor's employment under this Sub-Contract shall not prejudice the rights of either party to sue for and recover any damage, loss and/or expense incurred by him arising out of or in connection with any breach by the other of this Sub-Contract prior to such termination and generally to enforce any of his rights and remedies in relation to anything done prior to such termination.

Drawings

13.8 Upon any determination or discharge of this Sub-Contract or upon any termination of the Sub-Contractor's employment, the Sub-Contractor shall deliver to the Contractor all designs, drawings, details, documents and information prepared by or on behalf of the Sub-Contractor in respect of the Sub-Contract Works and the provisions of Clause 2.4 shall apply.'

Note: The figures in boxes may be altered by agreement between the parties.

Clause 13.1 – Termination of the sub-contractor's employment by the contractor

Clause 13.1 specifies five defaults by the sub-contractor, not all of which are of equal seriousness. They are:

● Substantial suspension of the works.
● Assignment or sub-letting without consent.
● Failure to proceed regularly and diligently with the works.

● Refusal or neglect to comply with instructions.
● Other breaches of the sub-contract.

These mirror the main contract provisions for termination of the contractor's employment by the employer, and readers are referred to the commentary on pages 99-102.

The reference to 'any instruction which the contractor is empowered by this sub-contract to give' refers to clause 5.1 where the contractor is given the same power to issue instructions as the architect possesses under the main contract.

The termination procedure is the same as that under the main contract except, of course, that it is the main contractor who serves the notices upon the sub-contractor. There being no adjudicator appointed under the sub-contract, there is no reference to adjudication. The provisions for payment are also the same, *mutatis mutandis*, save that it is of course the contractor who ascertains the amount of his own damage, loss and/or expense. Further comment is unnecessary.

Clause 13.2 – Termination by the sub-contractor
Again, this reflects the equivalent provision in the main form for termination of his own employment by the contractor save that, naturally, the obstruction of the issue of a certificate is not a ground for termination. The procedures are the same – except for the omission of any reference to adjudication – as are the provisions for payment: see commentary on pages 102-105.

Clause 13.3 – Insolvency of either party
This sub-clause corresponds to main contract clause 20.3: see page 97.

Clause 13.4 – Termination of the main contract or the contractor's employment under it
This clause empowers the main contractor to terminate the sub-contractor's employment forthwith by written notice if the main contract is itself determined or discharged or the contractor's employment under it is determined for any reason. This would, of course, cover the situation where the main contractor's employment is brought to an end due to causes outside the control of either party to the main contract: see pages 104-105. Clause 13.6 provides that payment to the sub-contractor in this event should be

equivalent to that to which he is entitled upon his determination of his own employment except where the determination, discharge or termination is due to the sub-contractor's own negligence, omission or default. Thus where the sub-contractor is at fault the rights of the parties would be determined at common law under clause 13.7.

The FCEC Form of Sub-contract

The latest revision of this form was issued in September 1984. It is designed for use in conjunction with the ICE Conditions of Contract. Just as that form contains no contractual provision entitling the contractor to determine his employment under it, so the sub-contract confers no such right on the sub-contractor whose rights in that respect therefore depend on the common law.

There are two relevant provisions:

Clause 16 – Determination of the main contract.
Clause 17 – Determination for sub-contractor's default.

Clause 16 – Determination of the main contract
Clause 16 reads as follows:

'**Determination of the Main Contract**

16. (1) If the Main Contract is determined for any reason whatsoever before the Sub-Contractor has fully performed his obligations under this Sub-Contract, then the Contractor may at any time thereafter by written notice to the Sub-Contractor forthwith determine the Sub-Contractor's employment under the Sub-Contract and thereupon the Sub-Contractor shall, subject to Clause 11 (Property in Materials), with all reasonable speed remove his men and Constructional Plant from the Site.
(2) Upon such a determination of the Sub-Contractor's employment, the other provisions of this Sub-Contract shall cease to have effect and subject to sub-clause (3) hereof, the Sub-Contractor shall be entitled to be paid the full value, calculated by reference to the Price and to the rates and prices contained in any bill of quantities or schedule forming part of this Sub-Contract, of all work properly done on the Site by the Sub-Contractor and of all materials properly bought and left on the Site by the Sub-Contractor, together with his reasonable costs of removing his Constructional Plant from the Site, but less such sums as the Sub-Contractor has already received on account. Furthermore if at the date

of such determination the Sub-Contractor has properly prepared or fabricated off the Site any goods for subsequent incorporation in the Sub-Contract Works and he shall deliver such goods to the Site or to such other place as the Contractor may reasonably direct, then he shall be paid for such goods as for materials properly brought and left on the Site by him.

Provided always that nothing herein shall affect the rights of either party in respect of any breach of this Sub-Contract committed by the other prior to such determination, nor any right which accrued to the Sub-Contractor prior to such determination to receive any payment which is not in respect or on account of the Price.

(3) If the Main Contract is determined by the Employer in consequence of any breach of this Sub-Contract by the Sub-Contractor, then the provisions of the preceding sub-clause as to payment shall not apply, but the rights of the Contractor and the Sub-Contractor hereunder shall be the same as if the Sub-Contractor had by such breach repudiated this Sub-Contract and the Contractor had by his notice of determination under sub-clause (1) of this clause elected to accept such repudiation.'

No amendment was made to this clause in the 1984 revision and so the decision of Mr Justice Nolan in *E.R. Dyer Ltd* v. *The Simon Build/Peter Lind Partnership* (1982) is of equal application to its interpretation.

In that case Dyer were sub-contractors to Simon Build/Peter Lind who were main contractors under ICE Conditions. The sub-contract incorporated FCEC terms. The engineer under the main contract certified under clause 63(1) of the main contract that the main contractors had failed to proceed diligently with the works and had persistently neglected to carry out their contractual obligations. After due notice, which was given expressly without prejudice to the employer's other rights and remedies, the employer expelled the main contractor from the site. In turn, the main contractors wrote to Dyer:

'The main contract has been determined with effect from 2400 hours today. Therefore pursuant to clause 16 of the sub-contract . . . we determine your employment under the sub-contract with effect from 2400 hours today.'

Subsequent arbitration proceedings between the employer and main contractor were settled and the sub-contractors then commenced arbitration proceedings against the main contractors to recover their loss and expense, including loss of profit. The main contractors contended that the sub-contractors were only entitled to the amounts provided under clause 16 as their employment had been properly determined under the clause. A distinguished arbitrator found in favour of the sub-contractors, holding that the main contractor's expulsion from the site under clause 63 did not determine the main contract. Mr Justice Nolan upheld that decision, taking the view that nothing short of accepting a repudiation would do for the purposes of the sub-contract. The words in clause 16(1) are 'if the main contract is determined for any reason whatsoever' and in their ordinary meaning might well be interpreted as covering both forfeiture under clause 63(1) of the main contract and the repudiation of the main contract by some act of omission on the main contractor's part.

Mr Justice Nolan said:

'It is not suggested that the word "determine" in clause 16 . . . bears any special meaning; and I adopt the language of Lord Wilberforce in *Photo Production Ltd* v. *Securicor Transport Ltd* (1980) in relation to termination, an equivalent word, where he said that it means ". . . no more than that the innocent party or, in some cases, both parties, are excused from further performance". Did the invocation and exercise by the employers of the powers conferred by clause 63 determine or terminate the contract in this way?. . . . [The] initial power conferred upon the employer was to enter and expel the contractor without thereby avoiding or releasing the contractor from any of his obligations or liabilities under the contract or affecting the rights and powers conferred on the employer or the engineer by the contract; and that the concomitant powers of the employer to complete the work and to use or sell construction plant, temporary works and materials are accompanied by continuing duties owed by the employer to the contractor. Similarly, sub-clauses (2) and (3) provide for the entry and expulsion to be followed by a quantification of amounts due to the contractor and for their payment to be made after the expiration of the period of maintenance. I do not see how the invocation by the employer of his rights under clause 63 and his exercise of the continuing powers and acceptance of the continuing duties for which that clause provides can be said to have determined or terminated the contract.'

Thus, clause 16 has no application unless the contract is determined in the sense discussed by Mr Justice Nolan, i.e. where there has been a full determination of the main contract in the full legal sense of that word. However, it should be noted (as was accepted by Mr Justice Nolan) that read as a whole clause 16 shows that, save as expressly provided in sub-clause (3), sub-clauses (1) and (2) are wide enough to cover a unilateral determination of the main contract in the exercise of contractual rights including a determination by the employer under the war clause, clause 65(3) of the ICE Conditions.

Unlike the other standard forms of sub-contract discussed in this chapter, determination of the sub-contractor's employment under clause 16(1) is at the main contractor's discretion, possibly to cover the situation where the main contractor is disputing the validity of the main contract determination. The sub-contractor has not 'fully performed his obligations under this sub-contract' until he has met the requirements of clause 13 as regards maintenance and defects.

Determination is effected by written notice served by the main contractor on the sub-contractor, and it is suggested that the procedure for service of notices under clause 68(1) of the main contract ought to be followed even though not specifically referred to. Thus the notice should be sent by post or left at the sub-contractor's registered office or principal place of business. Desirably, recorded delivery or registered post should be used or a receipt obtained if the notice is delivered by hand. (The notices clause in the sub-contract – clause 10 – does not in fact deal with the procedure for the service of notices.)

Determination is effective on receipt of the notice, and the sub-contractor is then obliged to remove his workforce and constructional plant from site with all reasonable speed. 'Constructional plant' has the meaning assigned to it under the main contract (see clause 1(1)) and therefore excludes 'materials or other things intended to form or forming part of the permanent works'.

The duty to vacate the site is subject to the provisions of clause 11, dealing with property in materials and plant, and which purports to give the employer, by a somewhat circuitous route, property in the sub-contractor's constructional plant, etc. and thereby a right to seize, use and finally sell it: see page 130. If the sub-contractor failed to remove his constructional plant from the site it might be that the employer would be an involuntary bailee of it with the powers of sale conferred by the Torts

(Interference with Goods) Act 1977, sections 12 and 13, though the statutory right of sale is hedged about with restrictions which would make it of doubtful value to the employer.

Clause 16(2) is interesting. It provides that when the sub-contractor's employment is so determined 'the other provisions of this sub-contract shall cease to have effect' and sets out in very clear terms the sub-contractor's entitlement to payment, which does not include any loss or damage caused to him by the determination, e.g. loss of profit on work not done. Clause 16(2) does not apply where the determination of the main contract has resulted from the sub-contractor's breach of the sub-contract.

In other cases the sub-contractor's entitlement is as follows:

- The full value of all work properly done on the site calculated by reference to the sub-contract price and the rates and prices in any bill of quantities, etc.
- The full value of all materials properly '*bought*' and left on the site by him. In view of the later reference to materials properly *brought* on the site, it is possible that the word 'bought' is a printing error. It will be appreciated that there is a significant practical difference.
- His reasonable costs of removing his constructional plant from the site.
- The full value of any goods properly prepared or fabricated off site for subsequent incorporation in the works provided that he has delivered them to the site or to some other place as reasonably directed by the contractor.

From the total of these items, amounts already received by the sub-contractor on account are to be deducted and he then receives the net balance. Entitlement to payment is 'upon determination' of the sub-contractor's employment and does not depend on the contractor receiving payment under the main contract.

The proviso to clause 16(2) is important as it preserves the rights of the parties in respect of breaches of the sub-contract committed by either prior to the determination as well as any entitlement of the sub-contractor to payment which is not in respect of or on account of the price, e.g. claims. Arguably, this proviso could entitle the sub-contractor to claim damages for the determination (including loss of profit) if he could establish that the determination of the main contract resulted from a breach of the sub-contract by the main contractor.

Clause 16(3) sets out the rights of the parties as to payment where the employer has determined the main contract because of a breach of the sub-contract by the sub-contractor. In that case, the situation is governed by common law: see chapter 1, pages 31-6. The very clear provision that the main contractor is entitled to treat such a sub-contract breach as a repudiation, acceptance of which is effected by his notice of determination, is a model which might be followed by other draftsmen.

Clause 17 – Sub-contractor's default
Clause 17 reads as follows:

'Sub-Contractor's Default

17.   (1) If the Sub-Contractor:
   (a) fails to proceed with the Sub-Contract Works with due diligence after being required in writing so to do by the Contractor; or
   (b) fails to execute the Sub-Contract Works or to perform his other obligations in accordance with the Sub-Contract after being required in writing so to do by the Contractor; or
   (c) refuses or neglects to remove defective materials or make good defective work after being directed in writing so to do by the Contractor; or
   (d) commits an act of bankruptcy or enters a deed of arrangement with his creditors or, being a company goes into liquidation, (other than a voluntary liquidation for the purposes of reconstruction), or has a receiver appointed of all or part of its undertaking,

then in any such event and without prejudice to any other rights or remedies, the Contractor may by written notice to the Sub-Contractor forthwith determine the Sub-Contractor's employment under this Sub-Contract and thereupon the Contractor may take possession of all materials, Constructional Plant and other things whatsoever brought on to the Site by the Sub-Contractor and may use them for the purpose of executing, completing and maintaining the Sub-Contract Works and may, if he thinks fit, sell all or any of them and apply the proceeds in or towards the satisfaction of monies otherwise due to him from the Sub-Contractor.

(2) Upon such a determination, the rights and liabilities of the Contractor and the Sub-Contractor shall, subject to the preceding sub-clause, be the same as if the Sub-Contractor had repudiated this Sub-Contract and the Contractor had by his notice of determination under the preceding sub-clause elected to accept such repudiation.

(3) The Contractor may in lieu of giving a notice of determination under this clause take part only of the Sub-Contract Works out of the hands of the Sub-Contractor and may by himself, his servants or agents execute, complete and maintain such part and in such event the Contractor may recover his reasonable costs of so doing from the Sub-Contractor, or deduct such costs from monies otherwise becoming due to the Sub-Contractor.'

Surprisingly, this traditionally-worded clause does not reflect the corresponding provision in the ICE Conditions (clause 63(1)). Clause 17(1) is expressed to be 'without prejudice to any other rights or remedies', thus preserving the contractor's common law rights, and sets out four grounds on which the contractor may exercise his right to determine the sub-contractor's employment. The grounds are:

● Failure to proceed with due diligence after being required to do so by the contractor. The requirement must be in writing.
● Failure to execute the sub-contract works or to perform other obligations in accordance with the sub-contract. Again, this after being required to do so in writing by the contractor.
● Refusal or neglect to remove defective materials or make good defective work after being directed to do so by the contractor in writing.
● Insolvency, etc. This is a limited ground, markedly different in wording from that in the main contract but similarly including events which are not true insolvency situations, presumably as a matter of policy.

Abandonment of the sub-contract work is not given as a ground for determination, presumably since this would undoubtedly amount to repudiation at common law while the other grounds specified in the sub-clause would not necessarily do so: see, for example, *Greater London Council* v. *Cleveland Bridge & Engineering Co. Ltd* (1984), holding that a mere failure to proceed with diligence did not amount to a repudiatory breach.

The determination procedure is once again for the contractor to issue a written notice to the sub-contractor, the effect of which is to determine the sub-contractor's employment 'forthwith'. On determination the contractor may:

● Take possession of all materials, constructional plant and other

things brought on to the site by the sub-contractor.
● Use these items for the purpose of executing, completing and maintaining the sub-contract works.
● Sell all or any of them and apply the sale proceeds in or towards the satisfaction of monies otherwise due to him by the sub-contractor.

Seizure and use of the sub-contractor's property and the right of sale probably would be effective against an insolvent sub-contractor's trustee or liquidator (but see *Ex parte Barter*, *re Walker* (1884)). However, both seizure and right of sale would be ineffective against the true owner of the goods or plant, etc: see page 130.

Clause 17(2) sensibly provides that, subject to clause 17(1) which confers additional powers on the contractor, the rights and liabilities of the parties are to be the same as if the sub-contractor had repudiated the sub-contract at common law and the contractor had accepted the repudiation by his determination notice.

Clause 17(3) gives the contractor an alternative remedy to full determination. It empowers him to take part only of the sub-contract works out of the sub-contractor's hands and to carry it out himself or through others. If he exercises that option, the sub-clause enables him to recover the costs involved from the sub-contractor either by way of legal action or by set-off.

Chapter 7

Suspension

The position at common law

Employer's power of suspension

At common law the employer has no power to direct suspension of the work under a construction contract in the absence of an express term in the contract empowering him to do so. Such a term will not be implied, for as Lord Pearson remarked in *Trollope & Colls Ltd* v. *North-West Metropolitan Regional Hospital Board* (1973):

> 'An unexpressed term can be implied if and only if the court finds that the parties must have intended that term to form part of their contract: it is not enough for the court to find that such a term would have been adopted by the parties as reasonable men if it had been suggested to them: it must have been a term that went without saying, a term *necessary* to give business efficacy to the contract, a term which, though tacit, formed part of the contract which the parties made for themselves.'

The ICE Conditions for Civil Engineering Works and the Government Conditions of Contract GC/Works/1 confer on the engineer or superintending officer an express power to direct a suspension of the work. The consequences in terms of cost and delay depend on the reason for the suspension and under the ICE Conditions, as will be seen, a prolonged suspension will entitle the contractor to treat the contract as repudiated.

Neither the JCT nor ACA standard forms of building contract confer an express power of suspension upon the architect in terms but all of them – except JCT Minor Works 1980 – empower the architect to 'postpone the execution of any work to be executed under' the contract or, under the ACA form, to 'postpone the dates shown on the time schedule for the taking-over of the works', etc. The exercise of this power of postponement can amount to suspension where postponement relates to the whole of the work remaining to be done.

Contractor's power of suspension

The contractor has no power to suspend the execution of the work at common law unless the express terms of the contract confer on him a right to do so. The question usually arises where the contractor suspends work temporarily in retaliation for some alleged breach of contract by the employer – usually failure to pay on time.

There are remarkably few cases on this subject and it is scarcely considered by the standard textbooks. The point was argued before the Court of Appeal in New Zealand in *Canterbury Pipe Lines Ltd* v. *The Christchurch Drainage Board* (1979) the material facts of which, for present purposes, are that the engineer withheld certificates for progress payments and the contractor suspended work temporarily. The court felt unable to hold in the circumstances that the contractor was justified in so suspending work. Mr Justice Cooke, delivering the majority judgment of the court, said:

'This case does not call for a decision on whether New Zealand Law recognises a general right in the contractor to suspend work (as distinct from rescinding) by reason of substantial default by the employer in paying a certified progress payment or a progress payment that has fallen due under a contract not requiring certificates. . . . It seems to us as well to leave that question open. Whatever the answer to it, we are against recognising such a right when the architect or engineer has declined to issue his certificate stipulated for by the contract as a condition precedent to the employer's duty to pay. It would disrupt the scheme of these contracts. It could encourage contractors to take the law into their own hands. They might stop work which in the public interest needs to be done promptly. In such cases, if the contractor cannot or does not wish to rescind and cannot prove impossibility or its equivalent, he will be left with whatever remedies regarding the recovery of progress payments may be available to him under the contract. . . . We do not exclude the view that a case of impossibility or its equivalent *might* be made out by proving that for want of money the contractor could not carry on or could not reasonably be expected to do so.'

This case is unsatisfactory in many respects because it does not really answer the vital question. The foregoing passage shows, however, that the law probably is that there is no right to suspend work temporarily merely because the architect or engineer refuses or fails to issue a certificate for payment required by the contract, the issue of which is a condition precedent to the employer's obligation to make payment, as is the situation under the UK standard forms. The contractor has other remedies in those circumstances. For example, under JCT terms, if the architect wrongfully refuses to issue a certificate the contractor may recover payment without it, the architect's failure to perform his duty under the contract being a breach of contract for which the employer is responsible: *Croudace Ltd* v. *Borough of Lambeth* (1984); *Panamena Europea Navigacion* v. *Frederick Leyland & Co. Ltd* (1947).

In the *Canterbury Pipe Lines Ltd* case the New Zealand court carefully reviewed the authorities on suspension in these circumstances, the starting point in England being the decision of the House of Lords in *Mersey Steel & Iron Co.* v. *Naylor, Benzon & Co.* (1884) which concerned a contract for the sale of steel to be delivered by instalments, each instalment to be separately paid for. The House of Lords held that payment for a previous delivery was not a condition precedent to the right to claim the next delivery.

Having referred to this case, Mr Justice Cooke said:

'Obviously the argument which failed in the *Mersey Steel* case could have been advanced with no less force by a building contractor from whom progress certificates or payments had been wrongly withheld. The *Mersey Steel* decision goes far to explain the apparent absence in English building contract law of any recognition of a common law right to suspend work for wrongful withholding of a progress certificate or payment, as distinct from a right to rescind for a breach going to the root of a contract. . . . Apart from suing for interim payments, or requiring arbitration where that is provided for, the remedy – and apparently the only remedy – which the contractor is recognised as having at common law is rescission if a sufficiently serious breach has occurred. If he chooses not to rescind, his own obligations continue. He is bound to go on with the work.'

This is certainly the current state of the law as regards temporary suspension for non-payment, although some standard contract forms confer such a right on the contractor, e.g. clause 31(iii) and clause 34(iv) of the IMechE/IEE Model Form of General Conditions, 'Model Form A', 1976 edition. However, does the contractor have a right to suspend work in other circumstances in the absence of an express term entitling him to do so?

A total suspension of work in circumstances evincing an intention no longer to be bound by the contract would certainly amount to repudiation of the contract at common law: see chapter 1, page 24. A virtual suspension of work was held by the Court of Appeal not to amount to an unlawful repudiation of a contract in JCT terms in *J.M. Hill & Sons Ltd* v. *London Borough of Camden* (1980), but the contractors did not there actually cease work. The contractors merely took away their labour and some plant and temporary buildings – including the quantity surveyor's hut – but they maintained their supervisory staff and did nothing to encourage their sub-contractors to leave.

The majority of construction contracts are in standard form and the contractor's obligation as to progress will be expressly stated in the contract. Thus in JCT 80, clause 23.1, the contractor's obligation is to proceed 'regularly and diligently' with the works and 'complete the same on or before the completion date', and the obligation is expressed similarly in other forms. A mere temporary cessation or suspension of work is not necessarily or usually a breach of that term and there might, indeed, be circumstances in which it was necessary for the contractor to suspend the work, e.g. during a severe period of frost.

Suspension of work *might* amount to an anticipatory breach, but it would require very strong facts so that the contractor was clearly evincing an intention no longer to be bound by the contract. The suspension would have to amount to abandonment of the works and this might be easier to infer in a contract where time is of the essence, which is not usually the case in building contracts.

The position under standard contracts:
Main contract forms

Employer's power of suspension

The ICE Conditions of Contract
Clause 40 deals with the engineer's power on behalf of the employer to order suspension of the progress of the works. The clause reads as follows:

'**Suspension of Work**

40. (1) The Contractor shall on the written order of the Engineer suspend the progress of the Works or any part thereof for such time or times and in such manner as the Engineer may consider necessary and shall during such suspension properly protect and secure the work so far as is necessary in the opinion of the Engineer. Subject to Clause 52(4) the Contractor shall be paid in accordance with Clause 60 the extra cost (if any) incurred in giving effect to the Engineer's instructions under this Clause except to the extent that such suspension is:
   (a) otherwise provided for in the Contract; or
   (b) necessary by reason of weather conditions or by some default on the part of the Contractor; or
   (c) necessary for the proper execution of the work or for the safety of the Works or any part thereof inasmuch as such necessity does not arise from any act or default of the Engineer or the Employer or from any of the Excepted Risks defined in Clause 20.

The Engineer shall take any delay occasioned by a suspension ordered under this Clause (including that arising from any act or default of the Engineer or the Employer) into account in determining any extension of time to which the Contractor is entitled under Clause 44 except when such suspension is otherwise provided for in the Contract or is necessary by reason of some default on the part of the Contractor.

Suspension lasting more than Three Months
(2) If the progress of the Works or any part thereof is suspended on the written order of the Engineer and if permission to resume work is not given by the Engineer within a period of 3 months from the date of suspension then the Contractor may unless such suspension is otherwise provided for in the Contract or continues to be necessary by reason of some default on the part of the Contractor serve a written notice on the Engineer requiring permission within 28 days from the receipt of such notice to proceed with the Works or that part thereof in regard to which progress is suspended. If within the said 28 days the Engineer does not grant such permission the Contractor by a further written

notice so served may (but is not bound to) elect to treat the suspension where it affects part only of the Works as an omission of such part under Clause 51 or where it affects the whole Work as an abandonment of the Contract by the Employer.'

Clause 40(1) confers upon the engineer a general and seemingly unfettered power to order suspension of the whole or part of the works 'for such time or times and in such manner as [he] may consider necessary'. Abrahamson in *Engineering Law and the ICE Contracts*, 4th edition, page 131, suggests that the engineer's power is probably limited to 'a suspension necessary for engineering reasons connected with the construction of the works'. The wording of clause 40(1) does not, in our view, support that interpretation and the engineer may order a suspension for any reason whatever. Indeed, a good reason for him so to order may be the employer's financial circumstances. In practice, of course, an engineer is likely to use this power with caution because of the potentially disastrous situation for the employer which could arise under sub-clause (2). Conversely, the engineer is not bound to exercise his power even where continuance of the work is impracticable, whether or not to do so being a matter within his discretion.

On receipt of the engineer's written order to suspend progress the contractor is bound properly to protect and secure the work so far as the engineer considers this necessary. The contractor is entitled to any extra cost which he incurs in giving effect to the engineer's order, except in five cases where the suspension is:

● Otherwise provided for in the contract.
● Necessary by reason of weather conditions.
● Necessary because of some default on the contractor's part.
● Necessary for the proper execution of the work.
● Necessary for the safety of the works or any part thereof.

In the last two cases, however, the contractor is entitled to payment if the necessity for the suspension arises from any act or default of the engineer or the employer or through any of the 'excepted risks' which are defined in clause 20(3). Indeed, the use of the phrase 'except to the extent that' makes it plain that where only part of a suspension is due to one or more of the causes listed the contractor is entitled to a proportion of the extra cost.

'Cost' is defined in clause 1(5) as being deemed 'to include overhead costs whether on or off the site', and thus the contractor is not entitled to recover loss of profits. The contract gives no assistance as to how overheads are to be calculated but in practice a percentage allowance is usually agreed between contractor and engineer, although this is not strictly speaking correct. The reference to clause 60 is to the method of dealing with interim and final payments under which monthly statements, which would include any cost to be recovered under this clause (which will be subject to retention), are submitted by the contractor to the engineer for agreement and certification and a final account is to be submitted by the contractor to the engineer at the conclusion of the contract for agreement and certification.

The reference to clause 52(4) is important since the sub-clause lays down the procedure for claiming extra payment under this and other clauses. The contractor is to give notice to the engineer in writing of his intention to claim additional payment 'as soon as reasonably possible after the happening of the events giving rise to the claim' and must keep 'such contemporary records as may reasonably be necessary to support any claim he may subsequently wish to make'. The engineer may also, on receipt of the notice, instruct the contractor to keep 'such contemporary records or further contemporary records as the case may be as are reasonable and may be material to the claim of which notice has been given and the contractor shall keep such records'. The contractor is to permit the engineer to inspect the records and to supply him with copies if he requires them.

After the contractor's notice, he is required as soon as is reasonable in all the circumstances to send an interim account to the engineer with full and detailed particulars of the amount claimed and the grounds of the claim and to send further accounts to the engineer at 'such intervals as the engineer may reasonably require'. Failure to comply with these provisions does not disentitle the contractor to payment altogether, but he will only be entitled to payment 'to the extent that the engineer has not been prevented from or substantially prejudiced by such failure in investigating the said claim'. With respect to the timing of the notice, i.e. 'as soon as reasonably possible', it is suggested that the wide interpretation given by the Court of Appeal to the similar phrase 'as soon thereafter as is practicable' in *Tersons Ltd* v. *Stevenage Development Corporation* (1963) would apply. In that case notices given in December and February in respect of variation instructions issued in the previous July and August were held to be in time in all the circumstances. However, this should not be relied on since the circumstances were rather special in that case, and the contractor should invoke the machinery sooner rather than later.

Clause 40(2) covers the situation where the suspension lasts for more than three months. In that event the contractor is entitled to issue a written notice to the engineer requiring permission to proceed within twenty-eight days from receipt of the notice. If permission is not granted within that time the contractor may but is not obliged to:

● Treat the suspension as an omission where the suspension relates to only part of the works. This will then constitute a variation of the works under clause 51 giving the contractor certain entitlements such as an adjustment of the rates for the remaining works so as to compensate for the omission.
● Treat the suspension as an abandonment of the contract where the suspension affects the whole works. This provision is less than clear, but it is suggested that its effect is to enable the contractor to treat the deemed abandonment as a repudiation by the employer entitling him to damages accordingly. In other words, the contractor may elect to treat the contract as at an end and sue for damages which will, of course, include loss of profit: see *Wraight Ltd* v. *P.H. & T. (Holdings) Ltd* (1968).

These rights, are, however, excluded where the suspension:

● Is otherwise provided for in the contract; or
● Continues to be necessary because of some default on the contractor's part. This wording emphasises that it is insufficient that the original suspension was necessary because of default by the contractor. It is its continuance only which is relevant.

Because of the terms of clause 40(2), the engineer will be wise to withdraw any suspension order within three months if it is at all possible to do so, if only to prevent the contractor from claiming that the continued suspension is tantamount to a repudiatory breach of the contract by the employer. Certainly if the initial suspension was due to the contractor's default, but a continued suspension becomes necessary for other reasons, the original suspension order should be terminated and a new order issued on the new ground.

The Government Conditions of Contract GC/Works/1

Clause 7(1)(g) gives the superintending officer (SO) a general power to order 'the suspension of the execution of the works or any part thereof'. In addition, clause 23 gives him power to order suspension of the work to avoid risk of damage from frost, inclement weather or other like causes.

Clause 23 reads as follows:

> '*Suspension for frost, etc.*
> 23   If the SO shall be of the opinion that the execution of the Works or any part thereof should be suspended to avoid risk of damage from frost, inclement weather or other like causes, then, without prejudice to the responsibility of the Contractor to make good defective and or damaged work, the SO shall have power to instruct the Contractor to suspend the execution of the Works or any part thereof and the Contractor shall not resume work so suspended until permitted to do so by the SO. The Contractor shall not be entitled to any increase in the Contract Sum under Conditions 9(2) or 53(1) in respect of any expense incurred in consequence of any such instruction unless he can show that he has complied with all the requirements of the Specification relating to the avoidance of damage due to frost, inclement weather or other like causes.'

The SO's power to order suspension under clause 7(1)(g) is totally unfettered although its exercise may be challenged in arbitration under clause 61. Any extra cost involved as a result of suspension for any reason will be recoverable under clause 9(2) which deals with expense generally arising from SO's instructions and under clause 53 which deals with prolongation and disruption expenses except where the suspension is caused by the contractor's default. This also applies to a suspension ordered under clause 23 except that the exclusion is strengthened in that it is up to the contractor to show, if he requires payment, that he has complied with all the contract requirements for the avoidance of damage by frost, etc.

In clause 23 the phrase 'other like causes' must be interpreted *ejusdem generis* with frost and inclement weather, i.e. the like causes must be of a similar nature. Further to the exceptions mentioned, the contractor's entitlement to payment under either clause 9(2) or clause 53(1) (which very largely overlap in their effect) is limited to 'any expense beyond that otherwise provided for in or reasonably contemplated by the contract' which must have a restrictive effect.

As to the claims procedure, see the present authors' *Building Contract Claims*, chapter 8.

The JCT Forms of Contract

The JCT Standard Form of Building Contract (JCT 80) and Intermediate Form of Building Contract (IFC 84) both give the architect power to 'issue instructions in regard to the postponement of any work to be executed under the provisions of this contract': JCT 80, clause 23.2; IFC 84, clause 3.15. The JCT Standard Form of Building Contract with Contractor's Design, clause 23.2 gives the employer a like power in respect of both design and construction work. The JCT Minor Works Form 1980, clause 3.5 gives the architect a general power to issue instructions to the contractor: 'the architect may issue written instructions which the contractor shall forthwith carry out'. This probably extends to a power to postpone or suspend work. The contrary is, however, arguable in view of the lack of any express right in the contractor to payment, although extension of time would be due under clause 2.2. Indeed, clause 7.2.3 gives the contractor a right forthwith to determine his own employment 'if the employer suspends the carrying out of the works for a continuous period of at least one month'. This would seem to imply a right of suspension which the employer may exercise through the architect.

The power to postpone work is effectively a power of suspension if the postponement relates to the whole of the work remaining to be done, and there is no doubt that the power of postponement extends to the whole of the works to be carried out under the contract as well as to any part of the works.

All the JCT forms which contain a power to postpone work also give the contractor a right to recover any direct loss and/or expense resulting from the inevitable material effect upon regular progress as well as an entitlement to an appropriate extension of the contract time. The present authors have discussed the claims procedures under JCT 80 in *Building Contract Claims*, chapters 2, 4 and 5, to which readers are referred. So far as the Intermediate Form is concerned, the contractor's entitlement to an extension of time arises under clause 2.4.5 and to reimbursement of loss and expense under clause 4.11 and clause 4.12.5. The loss and expense provisions in IFC 84 are similar to those in JCT 80, as are those for extensions of time with some modifications in the notification procedures: see Jones and Bergman, *A Commentary on the JCT Intermediate Form of Building Contract* (Collins, 1985), chapters 4 and 7. The provisions and procedures under the JCT Form 'with contractor's design' (clauses 25 and 26) are identical to those in JCT 80 save that the employer (or the employer's agent) takes the place of the architect, and there is no specific provision for anyone to 'ascertain' the direct loss and/or expense, although in practice this will be done by the employer's agent or the quantity surveyor, if appointed.

Postponement of work which results in the carrying out of the whole, or substantially the whole, of the uncompleted works (other than the rectification of defects during the defects liability period) being suspended for a continuous specified period entitles the contractor to determine his own employment under the contract, as discussed in chapter 2, pages 69-80 and 86-7, and to make various financial claims against the employer.

Interestingly, in *M. Harrison & Co. (Leeds) Ltd* v. *Leeds City Council* (1980) it was held (under JCT 63 terms, which in this respect were identically phrased) that an architect's instruction omitting a PC sum for structural steelwork and authorising the contractor to place an order with a nominated sub-contractor, and which required the contractor to reprogramme part of his work so as to accommodate the sub-contractor's programme, amounted to a postponement of the work.

The possible dangers for architects are also shown by the case of *Holland Hannen & Cubitt (Northern) Ltd* v. *Welsh Health Technical Services Organisation* (1981), where His Honour Judge Newey QC held that an architect's instruction to the contractor ordering him not to carry out finishing work until defective windows installed by nominated sub-contractors had been put right amounted to an order for postponement.

The ACA Form of Building Agreement
Clause 8.1(f) gives the architect the authority to issue instructions 'on any matter connected with the works'. This probably extends to a power to postpone or suspend work, in which case the contractor would be entitled to an extension of time under clause 11.5 and to payment under clause 17.1. The contract does not make provision for the contractor to terminate his employment

merely because work is suspended. Clause 21 gives him a right of termination if work is prevented or delayed for a period of sixty consecutive working days – although that period can be altered by agreement between the parties when the contract is made – if this is due to *force majeure*, etc.: see pages 104-105. Consequently, if the architect does order suspension of the works under clause 8.1(f) and the suspension lasts for an unreasonable period, the contractor is left with his common law rights where the suspension in fact amounts to repudiation. We suggest that an unreasonable period might well be of the order of sixty consecutive working days, although everything will depend on the circumstances.

Clause 11.8 gives the architect effective power to postpone the date for completion of the works in whole or in part and reads as follows:

11.8 '*Acceleration and postponement*
 The Architect may at any time, but not unreasonably, issue an instruction to the Contractor to bring forward or postpone the dates shown on the Time Schedule for the taking-over of the Works, any Section or any part of the Works and the Contractor shall immediately take such measures as are necessary to comply with such instruction and the provisions of Clause 11.3 shall apply to the adjusted date. The Architect shall ascertain and certify a fair and reasonable adjustment (if appropriate) to the Contract Sum in respect of compliance by the Contractor with such instruction and any damage, loss and/or expense suffered or incurred by the Contractor arising out of or in connection with it: Provided that if prior to giving any such instruction the Architect requires the Contractor to give an estimate of the adjustment to the Contract Sum, the provisions of Clause 17 (other than the provisions relating to extensions of time therein contained) shall apply as if an instruction given under this Clause 11.8 were included in Clause 17.1.'

The architect's power to issue a postponement instruction may be exercised at any time but it must not be exercised 'unreasonably'. It would, perhaps, be considered unreasonable if the instruction were issued the day before the date shown in the time schedule for taking-over, though even here the contractor's right to financial reimbursement might be considered an adequate safeguard.

The power is one to postpone completion of work and not its commencement. It can therefore be argued that the architect has no power actually to postpone any operation of the contractor under this clause which is essentially a provision for postponing the date of taking-over. Some degree of suspension might well be implied if it would be reasonable for the contractor to postpone commencement of the work in question in view of the postponed completion date.

On receipt of a clause 11.8 instruction the contractor must immediately take the necessary measures to comply. The contractual consequences of a clause 11.8 instruction are:

● The provisions of clause 11.3 as to damages for delay to completion apply from the adjusted date.
● The contractor must submit to the architect a revised time schedule within ten working days of the date of the instruction: clause 11.9.
● The architect is to ascertain and certify a fair and reasonable adjustment to the contract sum. It should be noted that, before issuing the instruction, the architect may require the contractor to give an estimate of the financial adjustment required by him.

Contractor's power of suspension

None of the standard main contract forms considered gives the contractor a right to suspend work in any circumstances and no such right can be implied: see the discussion on the common law position on pages 170-73.

However, all these forms of contract – with the exception of JCT Minor Works 1980 – place an obligation upon the contractor to take measures to preserve any objects of archaeological or related interest found during the construction operations and in the case of the JCT forms and GC/Works/1 an immediate obligation to cease work in the area of the find if this is necessary.

The clauses in question are:

JCT 80 – clause 34.
JCT with Contractor's Design – clause 34.
ACA – clause 14.
GC/Works/1 – clause 20(2).
ICE – clause 32.

All these provisions require the contractor to seek instructions from the architect, employer or engineer and entitle him to appropriate extensions of time and reimbursement of cost.

Sub-contract forms

Contractor's power of suspension

All the standard sub-contract forms discussed give the main contractor the same powers to issue instructions to the sub-contractor – though generally referred to as 'directions' – as the architect or engineer has under the main contract in relation to the contractor. Consequently, if the main contract works are suspended or postponed, the contractor may and probably will give a like direction to the sub-contractors. In general the sub-contractor will have corresponding rights to reimbursement of loss and/or expense and extension of time to those the main contractor has under the main contract. However – and this is an important point – in no case does the sub-contractor have a right of determination in the case of such suspension independent of determination under the main contract. It is true that in some cases (discussed in chapter 6) the sub-contractor has a right to determine his own employment if the works are suspended by the main contractor 'without reasonable cause'; but it is clear that a suspension of the main contract works by the architect or engineer would be a reasonable cause for suspension and that therefore the sub-contractor would have no rights of determination under his sub-contract.

Sub-contractor's power of suspension

Only the JCT related forms of sub-contract confer on the sub-contractor an express right to suspend work, and this only in the event of the contractor failing to pay amounts due. The terms of each of the three provisions are similar but as they differ in detail must be considered separately.

Domestic sub-contract DOM/1

The relevant provision is in clause 21.6 which reads as follows:

> 'Without prejudice to any other rights and remedies which the Sub-Contractor may possess, if the Contractor shall fail to make any payment to the Sub-Contractor as herein provided and such failure shall continue for seven days after the Sub-Contractor shall have given the Contractor written notice of the same, then the Sub-Contractor may suspend the further execution of the Sub-Contract Works until such payment shall have been made and such suspension as aforesaid shall not be deemed a failure on the part of the Sub-Contractor to proceed with the Sub-Contract Works in accordance with the provisions of this Sub-Contract.'

As the sub-clause is stated to be 'without prejudice to [the sub-contractor's] other rights and remedies', the power of suspension conferred by it does not affect his power to determine his own employment in the event of non-payment under clause 30.1.1.3, discussed on page 141. Equally, it preserves any common law right to treat the sub-contract as having been repudiated: see pages 20-23. However, clause 30.1.2 prevents the sub-contractor from issuing a notice of determination of his employment until ten days after the date of commencement of suspension of work under this provision if he has invoked it.

If the sub-contractor exercises his right of suspension he may claim an extension of sub-contract time under clause 11.13 and direct loss and/or expense under clause 13.1.

Presumably, the sub-contractor will not be able to avail himself of his right to suspend work if the non-payment is due to the contractor having exercised the right of set-off conferred by clause 23 and in particular if the contractor has issued the notice of intention to set-off required by that clause, although this present sub-clause is not expressly stated to be 'subject to clause 23'. In that event, the sub-contractor's remedy is to challenge the set-off and to invoke the adjudicator procedure under clause 24.

The procedure under clause 21.6 is for the sub-contractor to serve written notice on the contractor of the latter's failure to make payment in accordance with the terms of the sub-contract. If the contractor then fails to pay within seven days of the receipt of deemed receipt of the notice, the sub-contractor may immediately suspend the work and continue the suspension until the payment is made. It is suggested that the sub-contractor's notice should be sent by registered post or recorded delivery with advice of receipt.

The position under DOM/2 1981 is identical.

Nominated sub-contract NSC/4 and 4a
Clause 21.8 gives the sub-contractor a right to suspend work for non-payment couched in the following terms:

> 'Right of Sub-Contractor to suspend execution of Sub-Contract Works*
> 21.8 .1 If:
> > .1 .1 subject to clause 23 the Contractor shall fail to discharge his obligation to make any payment to the Sub-Contractor as hereinbefore provided; and
> > .1 .2 the Employer has
> > > either for any reason not operated the provisions of clause

35.13.5 of the Main Contract Conditions,

or has operated those provisions but for any reason has not paid the Sub-Contractor direct the whole amount which the Contractor has failed to discharge,

within 35 days from the date of issue of the Interim Certificate in respect of which the Contractor has so failed to make proper discharge of his obligation in regard to payment of the Sub-Contractor,

then provided the Sub-Contractor shall have given 14 days' notice in writing to the Contractor and the Employer of his intention to suspend the further execution of the Sub-Contract Works, the Sub-Contractor may (but without prejudice to any other right or remedy) suspend the further execution of the Sub-Contract Works until such discharge or until such direct payment is made whichever first occurs.

21.8   .2 Such period of suspension shall not be deemed a delay for which the Sub-Contractor is liable under the Sub-Contract. The Contractor shall be liable to the Sub-Contractor for any loss, damage or expense caused to the Sub-Contractor by any suspension of the Sub-Contract Works under the provisions of clause 21.8.1. The right of the Sub-Contractor under clause 21.8.1 shall not be exercised unreasonably or vexatiously.'

The effect of clause 21.8 is very similar to that of DOM/1, clause 21.6 but the detail differs. In particular, clause 21.8.1.2 defers the sub-contractor's right to issue a notice of intention to suspend work until the employer has had an opportunity to exercise his right (or, where he has entered into the Employer/Sub-contractor Agreement NSC/2 or 2a, his obligation) to make direct payment to the sub-contractor. The period of notice is also extended from seven days to fourteen and the notice must be issued to the employer (*not* the architect) as well as to the contractor. The contractor's right of set-off under clause 23 is expressly referred to in clause 21.8.1.1 and this provision is absolutely clear. It is easier for a nominated sub-contractor to operate this clause than it is for a domestic sub-contractor to operate clause 26.1 of DOM/1 since the contractor's failure is absolutely established if he does not pay the amount certified as due by the architect under the main contract and has not issued a notice of intention to set-off under clause 23. Under DOM/1, of course, since there is no provision for independent certification of the amount of payment, the sub-contractor would have to establish that the amount paid to him by the contractor was not in accordance with the sub-contract – which might be easier said than done. Against this, however, whilst clause 21.8.2

states specifically that the nominated sub-contractor's right to serve notice must not be exercised 'unreasonably or vexatiously' the same phrase does not appear in DOM/1, clause 21.6.

Clause 21.8.2 emphasises that the period of suspension is not deemed to be a delay for which the sub-contractor is responsible. It very sensibly and directly states that the main contractor is liable to the sub-contractor for any loss, damage or expense caused by the suspension which is independent of his right to recover loss and/or expense for disturbance of regular progress of the works under clause 13.2 and is not subject to the requirement of further notice under that clause.

As already mentioned above (page 183), clause 30 does not give the sub-contractor a right to determine his own employment in the event of non-payment by the contractor, and his sole remedy is therefore the right of suspension under the present clause. Otherwise his rights and remedies in the event of suspension of work are the same as those of a domestic sub-contractor under DOM/1.

Named sub-contract NAM/SC
Clause 19.6 provides as follows:

> 'Without prejudice to any other rights and remedies which the Sub-Contractor may possess, if the Contractor shall fail to discharge his obligation to make any payment to the Sub-Contractor as herein provided and such failure shall continue for seven days after the Sub-Contractor shall have given the Contractor with a copy to the Architect/the Supervising Officer written notice of his intention to suspend the further execution of the Sub-Contract Works then the Sub-Contractor may suspend the further execution of the Sub-Contract Works until such discharge occurs. Such suspension shall not be deemed a failure on the part of the Sub-Contractor to proceed with the Sub-Contract Works in accordance with the provisions of this Sub-Contract.'

Apart from minor drafting changes the only significant difference between this clause and clause 21.6 of DOM/1 is the requirement to send a copy of the notice of intended suspension to the architect. This is purely for the architect's information and he has no obligation to take any action on it under the main contract. The rights and remedies of the sub-contractor are identical to those conferred on a domestic sub-contractor by the provisions of DOM/1: see page 183.

Table of Cases

Note

The following abbreviations of Reports are used:

AC
App Cas $\}$ – Law Reports Appeal Cases Series

All ER – All England Law Reports

BLR – Building Law Reports

KB – Law Reports Kings Bench Series

LT – Law Times Reports

Table of Statutes

Index